AF518438

Census—2001 and Human Development in India

Census–2001 and Human Development in India

Edited By

Prof. G. Ramachandrudu
Dr. M. Prasada Rao

SERIALS PUBLICATIONS
New Delhi

First Published–2004

ISBN: 81-86771-45-X

Published by

Head Office : **SERIALS PUBLICATIONS**
4, B.S.S. Hall, Khyber Pass Market,
Civil Lines, Delhi–110054 (India)
Phone: 23245225
Fax: 91-11-23272135
e-mail: serials@satyam.net.in

Branch Office : *4830/24, Prahlad Street, Ansari Road,*
Darya Ganj, New Delhi-110002 (India)

Printed at :

PRINTED IN INDIA

Introduction

India's Population Census 2001 is the first in this millennium, and sixth after independence and fourteenth in the series of decennial Census starting from 1872. The provisional census results of 2001 give information on the growth rate of population, changes in the sex ratio particularly the child sex ratio, literacy, urbanization, occupational structure of workers and slum demography.

India's population is tripled during the past 50 years (1951-2001) from 361 million to 1027 million, an increase of 666 million. The net increase in India's population in the last 10 years (1991-2001) was 181 million as compared to 163 million in the previous decade (1981-1991). The increase in India's population during, 1991-2001 is more than Brazil's population, the fifth largest country in the World with 170 million population. The decadal population growth rate has marginally declined from 23.9 per cent during 1981-91 to 21.4 per cent during 1991-2001.

Although the growth rate for the country as a whole declined, considerable variations exists among the States of India, Kerala recorded the lowest annual growth rate of 0.9 per cent Nagaland, recorded the highest population growth rate of 4.9 per cent. During 1991-2001, the BIMARU state (Bihar, Madhya Pradesh, Rajasthan and Uttar Pradesh) which constitute 41 per cent of India's population experienced growth rates, well above the All India average. The child sex ratio (0-6 years) has declined steeply (more than 50 points) in the four states of Punjab, Haryana, Himachal Pradesh and Gujarat. Prof. Ashish Bose called these states as DEMARU states 'D' stands for Daughters, 'E' stands for Elimination and 'MARU' stand for killing. The volume examines critically the implications of these trends across the states/districts in India and Andhra Pradesh.

The volume focuses on Andhra Pradesh demography. It is reported that there is a steep decline of 40 per cent in the decadal population growth rate from 24.52 per cent during 1981-91 to 13.86 per cent in 1991-2001. Another interesting revelation of the census is that urbanizations is stagnant in the state (27 per cent) and the percentage of slum population is 99 per cent in Chirala town in Prakasam district. These demographic issues are critical for policy makers who naturally look to the researchers in solving problems relating to the human poverty which has a direct bearing on the population growth in the country.

The volume consists of four sections. The first section is on population Census 2001, the second section deals with educational status, the third section contains health and environment and the fourth section is on Human poverty.

Section-I: India's Population Census 2001

The major issues assessed in the first section are declining sex ratios including that of juvenile sex ratios, demographic transition, changes in occupational structure, migration, and urbanization. K.S. James observed that there is an eleven point decline in juvenile sex ratio (in the age group 0-6) from 975 in 1991 to 964 in 2001 in A.P. He explains that there could be four reasons for the decline in sex ratio, viz., sex differentials in mortality, migration, undercount and changes in sex ratio at birth. He calls for more intensive studies in specific historical and cultural contests. K. Narasimhulu in his two papers on population explosion and urbanization trends in India observes that the growth of population has a direct effect on the standard of living of the people. He suggested a number of measures to control population growth. However, he contended that for the success of family planning programme, social awareness is the most important aspect. He expresses concern over the low and stagnant urbanization on one hand and growth of slums and slums population on the other. He emphasizes that more stress should be given to shift agricultural labour to non farm occupations in the rural areas themselves. M. Prasada Rao analyses that the percentage of rural labour engaged in non-farm employment is 18 in AP in 1990-91, and it is increasing marginally over a period of time. He analyses the data on occupational structure at the district level in A.P. He observed that in 12 out of 22 districts, there is a decline in the Rural Non-Farm Employment (RNFE) during 1981-91. He opines that urbanization might have absorbed some of those organized RNFE activities. P. Ramachandran and P. Ramesh have examined the factors in fertility transition in A.P. They observed that in 15 years (1991-96) there is a 38 per cent decline in TFR in AP as against 28 per cent in All India. This has happened despite lower Human Development Index (HDI) (41), Gender Health Index (50) Reproduction Health Index (40) compared with All India. He applied the techniques of Life Table Analysis of Birth Intervals and Proportional Hazard Analysis to the NFHS- II Data (1998-1999) for A.P. The Life Table analysis suggests that the median birth intervals were short for second birth than the third birth among all the regions of A.P. The proportional hazard analysis clearly shows that differentials by regions persist even after controlling for other socio-economic and demographic variables.

N. Sudhakra Rao in his paper highlighted the variations of Women's Status in India. Starting with declining sex ratio from 946 in 1951 to 933 in 2001, he ascertained that health status of women is very low and female infanticide and foeticide are increasing. Son preference and undercount of women in Indian census are the possible reasons for declining sex ratio in India, though he has not provided any evidence to them.

B. Kusuma Kumari and V. Gandhi Babu have analyzed the provisional results of 2001 census. They have highlighted inter regional variations in population growth, literacy and sex ratio in A.P. All the Telangana and Rayalaseema districts (except Hyderabad) have higher decadal growth rate than the State average. In their regression analysis, they found that for every one per cent increase in adult literacy rate, life expectancy at birth increased by 0.17 years (nearly 61 days) and for every one per cent increase in literacy rate causes a decline in infant mortality rate by 1.24 per cent.

Ch. Appa Rao, G. Ramachandrudu and N. Subba Rao have examined the migration trends that caused low population growth in the district of Srikakulam. Using, primary data, they found that there is a possible under count of population in 2001 Census because of seasonal migration in Srikakulam district. They observed that many rural youth are attracted to the city life and they often shuttle between the cities and villages.

B. Ratna Kumari and A.B. Santha Rajyam expressed that gender position may not be changed unless gender relations are altered. Causes for the declining sex ratio, they say that the people believe that girls are liabilities and boys assets. They suggested that young girls must be given training in modern skills and 50 per cent reservation of jobs in both public and private companies.

Radhapushpavathi and D.V.V.S. Verma have highlighted the rapid changes in the occupational structure in growing coastal AP town of Tanuku in West Godavari district. The proportion of labour force working in secondary and tertiary sectors has increased from 67 per cent in 1981 to 72 per cent in 2001. This is because of rapid growth of service sector like Banking, Finance, Trade, Commerce, Transport and Communication.

Ch. Subrahmanyan and B. Ch. Krishna Murthy have discussed the application of Demographic Transition model for developed and developing countries. The pace of demographic transition was rapid in developed countries because of the fact that they got rid off the surplus population of early stages of modernization and the resultant unemployment by international migration. This could not be done in the developing countries because of the fact that the millions of unskilled labour live in perpetual poverty, ill health and illiteracy.

M. Bhavani Shankar Rao has analyzed primary data on living conditions of the construction workers of Visakhapatnam city. He observed that their living conditions are highly deplorable with insufficient earnings, poor housing, ill health and without basic amenities like water and sanitation.

Section 2: Education

K.S. Prasad and K.M. Babu have noted with satisfaction that improvement in this literacy rates for males and females in India is impressive during 1991-2001. They found that the female literacy rate is significantly explaining the variation in life expectancy which is an improvement indicator of health sector.

M.S. Rao and D. Rambabu have analyzed primary data on inter tribe variation in literacy levels in Srikakulam district. The adult female literacy rate is as low as 6 per cent while that of males it is 36 per cent. The authors pointed out that education will improve their rational understanding of social and economic values.

K.S. Murthy and K.V.J. Rao also have analysed primary data on dropout in primary education among Tribals in Viziangaram district. The study concludes that the reasons for dropout of tribal students are location of the school lack of facilities at the School, teacher absenteeism, lack of hostel facilities, assistance to parents, need to look after the young siblings and the need to collect forest produce.

D.P. Rao has examined the trends in the growth of primary education in East Godavari district of A.P. during

1988-89. He observed that the rate of enrollment in the age groups (6-11) and (11-13) has been stable during the study period. The number of children per school has delivered because of the increase in the number of schools in the private sector.

T.N. Devi and K. Subhasini have analyzed the gender disparity in literacy rates in Vizag district of A.P. They found that there are larger gender disparities in rural than urban areas. They suggested that the share of public spending towards gender specific programmes should be increased to allow the women to avail the basic human rights to education and employment.

K.P. Rao has examined the literacy scenario in West Godavari district of A.P. He observed that the special literacy drive in the name of Akshara Mahila Programme involving NGOs have succeeded in improving the levels of literacy in the district. Dealing with the same area. L. Krishna Veni also observed that the special literacy drive in the district have improved literacy rates in the district. She suggested a number of measures to sustain the trend.

D.P. Naidu dealt with the special problem in achieving literacy among tribals since the people are absolutely poor, superstitious and having poor living conditions. He suggested a number of measures suitable to the topology of tribal region, society and economy for improving the educational status among tribals.

Section 3: Health and Environment

P. Satya Sekahar analyzing the Reproductive and Child Health (RCH) survey data concluded that the overall picture in AP indicate that women marry at early age, have desired fertility with short birth intervals (within 24 months) and adopt female sterilization in early age of 24 years. Over 45 per cent of female population in A.P. are in the reproductive age group and is expected to increase in the next few decades due to population momentum. He explains that the sharp decline in TFR was not backed by a comparable decline either in IMR, MMR, or a rise in female literacy and age at marriage.

G. Ramachandrudu, G. Kamalamma and G. Vinaya Kumar have analyzed secondary as well as survey data on the health status of A.P. They observed that the State Government has undertaken Health Sector Reforms around mid 1980's. The number of primary Health Centres, sub-centres and other specialized hospitals initials has been doubled with the assistance of ADB and AP Referral Health System Project. The study clearly brings out that the preference of people is more towards private medical care than that of public. There is an urgent need to reform the public health care institutions so that they can cater to the needs of the poor, otherwise there will be inequalities in health care and the worst sufferers are the poor.

K. Ranigopal in her empirical analysis of the secondary data concluded that the goal of sustainable improvement in the quality of life of the people can be achieved only through the spread of literacy which is a prominent non-health care determinant of health status.

M. Sudha and C. Ratnam have studied the structural changes in the Indian Industrial Sector in terms of pollution intensity and its effects on some life supply system. The study concluded that Indian industry is dominated by the most pollution intensive and load generating (Red) industries during the period from 1973-74 to 1993-94. The structural changes that are taking place in the Indian Industry are in favour of the most pollution intensive industries.

Ramachandrudu, G. and N. Appa Rao do served that big city slum dwellers have a higher quality of life as measured big literacy, poverty and morbidity in their comparative Visakhapatnam and Kakivada towns in A.P. in 1988 his may be due to the implementation of ODA assisted VSIP during 1988-91.

P. Subba Rao analyzed the household survey data of the slum dweller of Vizianagaram town of A.P. He concluded that the urban slum dwellers are effected particularly by environment factors such as poor housing, low quality of sanitation, water pollution, unhealthy occupation and over crowding. These conditions are resulting in communicable and non-communicable diseases.

Section 4: Human Poverty

S. Mahendra Dev observed that even though income poverty in around 25 per cent, human poverty is still high at 40-50 per cent. The structural reform policies of the government are affecting the poor, who are clustering towards big cities. Migration seems to have benefited the source areas while the migrants in the destination are being exploited. He suggested several strategies to take care of the vulnerable groups such as old age population, child labour, widows and socially disadvantaged groups. He concluded that since economic growth is not correlated with some of the human development indicators, direct public action is very much needed in some cases.

S. Subrahmanyam has examined various concepts of measuring poverty. He observed that primary and absolute poverty concepts are more relevant than secondary and relative poverty concepts for a developing country like India. He concluded after analyzing the long period data that incidences of poverty remained around 50 per cent till the end of sixties and then declined rapidly till the end of eighties. In nineties the results indicate that economic reforms have a positive impact on poverty.

K.C. Reddy, U.N. Murthy and M. Sarojini have analyzed the cross section data of Indian States on Education, Child Mortality and Infant morality in 1980s and 1990s. They found that there are huge variations in some of these human development indicates and they are significantly correlated with tax effort index and real per capita educational expenditure.

S. Galab and M.G. Reddy have used the survey data as a part of the District Poverty Initiative Project (DPIP) in selected districts of Andhra Pradesh. They concluded that poverty is more concentrated among SCs and STs, from landless and marginal farmers and female headed households. Incidence of child labour is ranging from 6 per cent in Adilabad to 12 per cent in Anantapur. Child Labour is more among girls than boys in Srikakulam district. They suggested that poverty can be alleviated by improving the asset base of households. Possession of land alone may not tackle the problem of poverty unless land productivity is enhanced through providing access to irrigation.

P. Leela has analyzed the utility of the UNDP's indicator of Gender Empowerment Measures (GEM) and observed that the State budget allocations to these programmes are very meager. She pointed out that inspite of tall claims of economic progress in the state of A.P., it ranks 26 in All India with Female literacy rate of 33 per cent and a male literacy rate of 55 per cent.

B.D. Prasad and S. Haranath have examined to what extent micro credit through Self Help Group (SHG) can help in poverty alleviation in AP. They found that AP alone has about half of the SHGs existing in the country with 3.3 lakhs of women SHGs covering 45.8 lakh several poor women with savings deposits of Rs. 551.4 crores. Unless some NGO helps and guides SHG, it will not be able to succeed.

R. Ramakrishna studied the pattern of employment, income and poverty among agricultural labour (N= 375) in five mandals of Visakhapatnam district. He found that poverty is as higher as 47 per cent in the sample households.

Usha Devi analyzed a macro view of human poverty and found that there is an adverse impact of economic reforms process on the poor and rural people. She suggested that social safety net measures, the state should provide free and compulsory elementary education, access to health care, provide employment and livelihood security and pave the way for sustainable social development.

N. Bhaskara Reddy studied the role of migrated non-local farmers vis-à-vis locals in developing agriculture in Vizianagaram district. Productivity is found to be more for non-local farms because of their innovative and mechanized agricultural practices. He found that the infant mortality rate in the district is about 99 showing a very poor health status while the state average is 68 per 1000 live births. With the investments in agriculture by the migrant non-local farmers migration from the district is arrested to some extent.

This volume gives a comprehensive idea of the implication of the recent census (2001) on different aspect of Human Development and Human Poverty. This book will be very useful to researchers pursuing their studies in social and economic development.

Prof. G. Ramachandrudu
Dr. M. Prasada Rao

Foreword

Achievement of minimum standard of living for all within a reasonable period has been the implicit or explicit objective of development policy in India since the country became independent. This was sought to be achieved by attaining higher growth; by raising purchasing power of the poor through the endowment of land and non-land assets and by generating employment opportunities. Market forces and generic growth strategies are being supplemented by poverty alleviation programmes targeted to the poor.

Poverty reduction has been achieved in most parts of India through a long period of sustained economic growth. In some parts, demographic transition has helped to reduce poverty levels. Even after sustained economic growth over the decades and direct interventions from the policy makers, poverty even in income terms, remains unacceptably large. "About 300 million of Indians" (200 million in rural areas and 100 million in urban areas) remained below the poverty line in 1999-00. What is most disquieting is that the incidence of child-labour is high in India and the estimated number varies between 17.5 and 44.0 million. Equally worrisome feature of labour market is that there are more than 10 million inter-state distress rural migrant workers. Low wage rates, coupled with under-employment are the root causes of inter-state distress migration of farm workers, mainly from dry-land areas.

It is now widely recognized that income poverty reduction is relatively easy to achieve compared to the elimination of multiple deprivation. The volume edited by G. Ramachandrudu and M. Prasada Rao contains papers which address the issues pertaining to the magnitude of deprivation. The volume provides insights into the processes underlying multiple deprivations including gender gaps. The papers have extensively utilized the recent Census as well as National Family Health Survey (NFHS) data. Both the sources provide details about education, housing, ownership of assets; access to health care, safe drinking water, toilet facility, malnutrition and so on.

In order to understanding the process underlying the human poverty, one cannot rely only on Census and NFHS data. In depth field studies provide better insights. This has been taken care of. Some of the papers included in the book are based on quantitative and qualitative data obtained from sample surveys.

A large number of papers have analyzed the demographic transition in Andhra Pradesh. It is a paradox that the state experienced steep decline in fertility despite comparatively higher illiteracy. It is also a surprise that while the sex ratio has improved, it has deteriorated in the children under 6 years. The papers have attempted to resolve the puzzle. This decline in fertility and increase in expectation will increase the proportion of elderly who will be more vulnerable to socio-economic hardship. This problem of graying people are little researched until now. Fortunately, one paper included in the volume has analyzed the sufferings of elderly in the rural and urban areas of one district in Andhra Pradesh. The book highlights the problems of urban deprivation.

Overall, the book contains interesting collection of articles discussion about various aspects of human poverty and I am sure, this book will make a good addition to the existing literature I recommend this book to scholars and policy makers interested in understanding the complexities of human poverty.

Prof. R. Radhakrishnan
Director,
Indira Gandhi Institute
of Development Research
Gen. A.K. Vidya Marg,
Goregaon (EAST),
Mumbai-400 065
and
Former Vice-Chancellor,
Andhra University
Visakapatnam

List of Contributors

Dr. K.S. James, Centre for Economic and Social Studies, Hyderabad.

Prof. K. Narasimhulu, Department of Economics, S.V. University, Tirupathi.

Dr. M. Prasada Rao, Associate Professor of Economics, Andhra University.

Prof. P. Ramachandran & P. Ramesh, Department of Population Studies, S.V. University, Tirupathi.

Prof. N. Sudhakara Rao, Professor of Economics, Nagarjuna University.

Dr. B. Kusuma Kumari, Reader in Economics, St. Joseph's College for Women, Visakhapatnam.

Prof. V. Gandhi Babu, Professor of Economics, Andhra University, Visakhapatnam.

Dr. Ch. Appa Rao, Prof. G. Ramachandrudu & Dr. N. Subba Rao, School of Economics, Andhra University, Visakhapatnam- 530003.

Dr. B. Ratna Kumari, Presently working as faculty member, Centre for Women's Studies, Andhra University, Visakhapatnam.

Mrs. A. B. Santha Rajyam, Presently working as FIP scholar, Department of Economics, Andhra University, Visakhapatnam.

Smt. K. Radha Pushpavathi, Lecturer in Economics, SKSDM College, Tanuku.

D.V.V.S. Varma, General Secretary, Loksatta, A.P. State.

Dr. Ch. Subramanyam, B. Ch. Krishna Murty, Associate Professors in Economics, School of Distance Education, Andhra University.

Dr. M. Bhavani Shankar Rao, Associate Professor, Department of Economics, A.U. Dr. B.R. Ambedkar, P.G. Center, Etcherla.

K. Madhu Babu, Research Scholar Department of Economics, Andhra University, Visakhapatnam.

K. Siva Prasad, Professor of Economics, Andhra University, Visakhapatnam.

Prof. M. Sundara Rao, Head of the Department of Economics, P.G. Center, Etcherla.

Prof. D. Rambabu, Head, Department of Commerce and Management Studies in AU. Dr. B.R. Ambedkar PG. Centre, Etcherla-532402, Srikakulam District, (AP.).

Prof. K. Sreerama Murthy, Professor of Economics, Department of Economics, Andhra University, Visakhapatnam.

Mr. K.V. Jagannadha Rao, Lecturer in Economics, A.P. Residential Junior College, Thatipudi, Vizianagaram District.

Dr. D. Pulla Rao, Department of Applied Economics, Andhra University, Visakhapatnam.

Prof. T. Nirmala Devi, Professor, Centre for SAARC Studies, Andhra University, Visakhapatnam.

K. Subhashini, Research Scholar, Department of Economics, Andhra University, Visakhapatnam.

Dr. K. Parameswara Rao, Associate Professor in Economics School of Distance Education, Andhra University, Visakhapatnam.

Dr. L. Krishna Veni, Head & Associate Professor, Post-Graduate, Department of Economics, Sir C.R.R. College, Eluru-534007 A.P.

D. Parinaidu, M.A., M.Ed., PGDMVWO, Executive Trustee JATTU. Parvathipuram, Vizianagaram District.

Dr. P. Satya Sekhar, Indian Institute of Health and Family Welfare, Vengalrao Nagar, Hyderabad.

Prof G. Ramachandrudu, Professor Economics Andhra University, Visakhapatnam.

Dr. N. Appa Rao, Associate Professor, JNTU College of Engineering, Kakinada, Andhra Pradesh.

Dr. G. Vinay Kumar, Professor and Head, Department of Economics, Andhra University, Visakhapatnam.

Dr. (Mrs.) G. Kamalamma, Research Associate, School of Economics.

Prof. K. Rani Gopal, Professor in Economics Department of Economics, Andhra University, Visakhapatnam.

Dr. M. Sudha, Faculty, ICFAI, University, Visakhapatnam.

Prof, C. Ratnam, Director, Agro Economic Research Centre, Visakhapatnam.

Dr. Subba Rao Pappala, School of Economics, Andhra University.

Prof. S. Mahendra Dev, Director, Centre for Economic and Social Studies, Hyderabad.

Prof. S. Subrahmanyam, Centre for Economic and Social Studies, Hyderabad.

Prof. K.C. Reddy, Professor, Department of Economics, Andhra University, Visakhapatnam, Andhra Pradesh.

Dr. U.N. Moorthy, Associate Professor, Department of Economics, Andhra University, Visakhapatnam, Andhra Pradesh.

Dr. M. Sarojini, Research Associate, Department of Economics, Andhra University, Visakhapatnam, Andhra Pradesh.

Prof. S. Galab, Professor, Centre for Economic and Social Studies, Hyderabad.

Dr. M. Gopinath Reddy, Reader, Centre for Economic and Social Studies, Hyderabad.

Prof. P. Leela, Department of Applied Economics, Andhra University, Visakhapatnam.

Dr. B. Devi Prasad and Dr. S. Haranath, Department of Social Work, Andhra University, Visakhapatnam.

Ramakrishna Rayavarapu, Associate Professor, Department of Cooperation and Applied Economics, Andhra University, Visakhapatnam-530003.

Dr. (Mrs.) P. Usha Devi, Assistant Professor, I.A.S.E., A.U., Visakhapatnam.

Dr. N. Bhaskara Reddy, Associate Professor, Department of Cooperation and Applied Economics, Andhra University, Visakhapatnam-530003.

Contents

1

A Note on the Sex Ratio from 2001 Census Results in Andhra Pradesh

K.S. James

Introduction

Sex ratio is a useful indicator to understand women's health and position in any society. India has distinction along with China and a few other south Asian countries having a deficit of females for a long period. This is largely interpreted as the symptom of low status of women and discrimination of females existing in the country. Unusually high mortality Indian women faced relative to males until recently confirmed this fact. The female mortality registered significantly high rates than males at the younger ages, through it reverted recently. Andhra Pradesh is also not an exception to this pattern. Interestingly, however, there had been an upward trend in the sex ratio[1] of the population in the state according to 2001 census, the first increase after independence. This paper primarily looks at the sex ratio computed from the Census 2001 and portrays its emerging trend and its implication for Andhra Pradesh.

Overall Sex Ratio

It is perplexing to explain the secular decline in sex ratio defined as number of females per 1000 males in the state

1. Sex ratio, in this paper, is defined as females per 1000 males.

between 1951 and 1991. The sex ratio of Andhra Pradesh since independence is presented in Figure 1. To a great satisfaction, for the first time since independence, an increase in the sex ratio of the population is recorded in 2001 census. Four reasons are often mooted to as plausible reasons for such a secular decline in sex ratio. (1) Differential Mortality between males and females, (2) differential undercount of females than males, (3) drop in the female birth leading to adverse sex ratio at birth and (4) large scale surplus emigration of females over males. Visaria (1961) in his path breaking work considered all plausible explanations and conclusively argued that the declining sex ratio is the result of unusually high female mortality relative to males. Although female mortality situation has been improving over a Census increased the doubt about such argument. Going by the argument, it suggests deterioration in quality of Census taking over the period. The post enumeration surveys assessing the extent of undercount in different Census did not give any indication of increasing levels of undercount of females.

Figure 1: Sex Ratio in Andhra Pradesh, 1951-2001

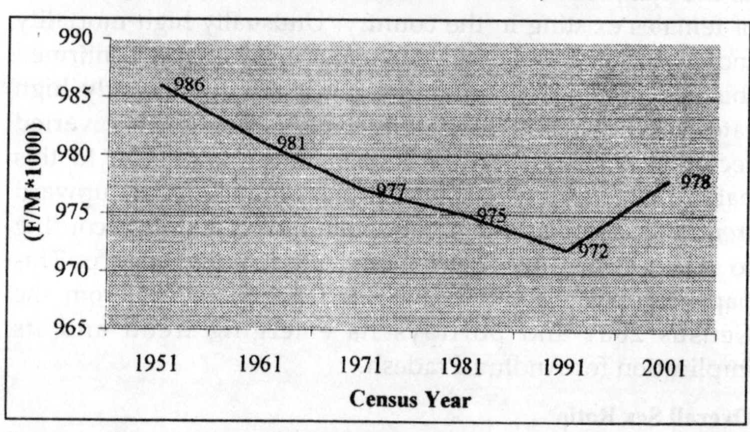

Source: Census of India (2001) *Andhra Pradesh, Provisional Population Totals,* Paper 1 of 2001Series, 29.

Table 1 presents the district level sex ratio of the population in Andhra Pradesh in 1991 and 2001 Census. Most of the districts in the state recorded an increase in the sex ratio. Unexpectedly, however, some districts in the South Coastal Andhra, one of the developed regions of the State, portrays a decline in sex ratio. These districts are East Godavari, West Godavari and Krishna. Other than these three districts, Mahabubnagar also recorded a decline in sex ratio. Nizamabad although recorded a one point decline, its overall sex ratio is favourable to females both in 1991 and 2001 census years.

Table 1: Sex Ratio of Total Population by Districts, Andhra Pradesh, 1991-2001

District	*1991*	*2001*	*2001-1991*
Adilabad	980	989	9
Nizamabad	1017	1016	–1
Karimnagar	986	1000	14
Medak	970	976	6
Hyderabad	933	945	12
Rangareddy	941	941	0
Mahabubnagar	973	970	–3
Nalgonda	962	967	5
Warangal	962	973	11
Khammam	961	975	14
Srikakulam	1012	1013	1
Vizianagaram	1000	1004	4
Visakhapatnam	975	991	16
East Godavari	998	992	–6
West Godavari	994	992	–2
Krishna	969	961	–8
Guntur	970	984	14
Prakasam	970	971	1
Nellore	980	983	3
Cuddapah	955	975	20
Kurnool	953	965	12
Anantpur	946	957	11
Chittoor	966	983	17
Andhra Pradesh	972	978	6

Source: Computed from Census of India (2001) Andhra Pradesh, Provisional Population Totals, Paper 1 of 2001 Series, 29.

District level sex ratio needs to be interpreted cautiously as no control is made for sex specific migration across districts.

It is possible that the decline in the sex ratio in South Coastal Andhra is the result of large-scale in-migration of males from other districts.

The increase in overall sex ratio in Andhra Pradesh could be seen as the result of improvement in mortality among females compared to males in different age groups. The advantage of females in old age mortality had been well established and neither all India nor Andhra Pradesh is an exception to it. However, in recent years there is a consistent decline in adult mortality among females. This could be because of the sharp reduction in fertility rate and consequent reduction in maternal mortality in the State. However, male adult mortality has recorded stagnancy in recent years (James 1996; Krishnaji and James 2002). Thus, at present, male adult mortality as far higher relative to females.

Table 2 presents life expectancy at birth by gender for different years in Andhra Pradesh. It is clear that life expectancy of females is higher than males in all the periods since the 1970. It clearly indicates mortality advantage of females in Andhra Pradesh compared males. Hence, an overall improvement in the sex ratio of the Andhra Pradesh population is not of a surprise.

Table 2: Life Expectancy at Birth by Gender, Andhra Pradesh

Period	*Male*	*Female*	*Difference (F-M)*
1970-75	48.4	49.3	0.9
1976-80	52.2	54.2	2.0
1981-85	57.2	59.8	2.6
1986-90	58.2	60.4	2.2
1991-95	60.3	62.8	2.5
1992-96	60.8	63.0	2.2

Source: Sample Registration System (1999) *Compendium of India's Fertility and Mortality Indicators, 1971-1997*, Registrar General of India, New Delhi.

Juvenile (0-6 age group) Sex Ratio

To a great surprise and dismay, however, a decline in sex ratio is observed in the age group 0-6 between 1991 and

2001 in the state. The decline is to the tune of 11 points from 975 in 1991 to 964 in 2001. Considering census years 1981-2001, the decline amount to around 28 points. The all India pattern also portrays nearly the same picture as far as juvenile sex ratio is concerned (Premi 2001). The 0-6 age group sex ratio for 1991 and 2001 census years is presented in Table 3.

Table 3: Sex Ratio of Child Population (0-6) by Districts, Andhra Pradesh, 1991 & 2001

District	*1991*	*2001*	*2001-1991*
Adilabad	986	964	-22
Nizamabad	979	966	-14
Karimnagar	981	977	-3
Medak	981	964	-17
Hyderabad	963	950	-13
Rangareddy	972	970	-2
Mahabubnagar	981	957	-24
Nalgonda	981	962	-19
Warangal	977	955	-22
Khammam	981	968	-12
Srikakulam	986	976	-11
Vizianagaram	996	981	-15
Visakhapatnam	985	973	-12
East Godavari	994	978	-16
West Godavari	984	977	-7
Krishna	964	959	-5
Guntur	970	955	-14
Prakasam	969	966	-4
Nellore	937	955	19
Cuddapah	968	952	-16
Kurnool	955	944	-11
Anantpur	962	963	1
Chittoor	970	959	-10
Andhra Pradesh	975	964	-11

Source: Same as in Table 1.

The decline is observed in almost all the districts except Nellore and Anantapur. The sharpest decline is observed in the districts of Mahabubnagar, Adilabad and Warangal.

Interestingly, Mahabubnagar and Adilabad are some of the poorest districts in the state. As the decline is observed in almost all the districts covering all regions, it does not likely to follow any particular economic or social pattering.

Of the four plausible reasons for a change in sex ratio (differential mortality, differential undercount, change in sex ratio at birth and sex-specific migration), differential infant and child mortality is often considered as the main reasons for decline in sex ratio at younger ages. However, such explanations do not hold good for Andhra Pradesh, as female advantage is clearly evident both at infancy and childhood. Table 4 presents infant mortality rate by gender for Andhra Pradesh. In a number years, higher instance of female mortality is reported in the state. Therefore, the argument of higher female mortality leading to worsening 0-6 sex ratio can be easily rejected.

Table 4: Infant Mortality by Gender, Andhra Pradesh

Period	*Male*	*Female*	*Difference (F-M)*
1980	102	82	20
1986	83	80	3
1992	73	68	5
1982-92	78	69	9
1988-89 to 1998-99	73	69	4

Source: Sample Registration System, Various years. The last two rows are from National Family Health Surveys (1995-2000) Andhra Pradesh, IIPS, Mumbai.

The second is the possibility of female undercount particularly at younger ages. However, as already pointed out the post enumeration survey conducted in the country has revealed no significant difference in the undercount of males and females in 1991 census. There is no reason to suspect that such undercount has occurred in 2001 census specifically in 0-6 age group.

Thirdly, sex-specific migration leading to decline in sex ratio is quite unlikely in the age group 0-6. In the childhood the migration is always family dependent and in case the family migrate to other districts or states, both male and female children move together.

Hence, there is reason to suspect the possibility of deliberate change in the sex ratio at birth through some means. Although instances of female foeticide taking advantage of modern technology in sex determination is often reported by various press, it was never conceived to be of such magnitude to alter sex ratio of the population. That is why the decline in juvenile sex ratio during 1991-2000 came as a shock to many. At the same time, studies have already pointed out the possibility of increased gender bias in the course of fertility transition in India (Das Gupta and Bhat 1995; Sudha and Rajan 1999)

We have also looked at the juvenile sex ratio for rural and urban areas and presented in Table 5. It is thought that sex determination tests, if widely practised, should be concentrated more in urban areas where such facilities are easily available and should reflect in the decline in urban sex ratio more than rural. The data, however, shows no such indication. Both in rural and urban areas experienced decline in juvenile sex ratio without much exception.

Table 5: Sex Ratio of Juvenile population (0-6 age group) by place of residence in the districts of Andhra Pradesh, 1991-2001

District	*1991*		*2001*		*2001-1991*	
	Rural	*Urban*	*Rural*	*Urban*	*Rural*	*Urban*
Srikakulam	988	976	976	975	-12	-1
Vizianagaram	999	977	986	956	-13	-21
Visakhapatnam	994	969	978	963	-16	-6
East Godavari	991	1003	974	993	-17	-10
West Godavari	989	959	976	981	-13	22
Krishna	968	956	968	942	0	-14
Guntur	970	969	953	961	-17	-8
Prakasam	969	969	967	959	-2	-10

Table Contd.

Table 5: Contd...

Nellore	971	828	955	955	-16	127
Chittoor	972	959	963	946	-9	-13
Cuddapah	969	963	949	952	-20	-11
Anantapur	960	971	961	971	1	0
Kurnool	952	967	941	956	-11	-11
Mahabubnagar	983	958	957	959	-26	1
Rangareddy	980	962	994	945	14	-17
Hyderabad		963		950	0	-13
Medak	982	974	965	956	-17	-18
Nizamabad	984	960	965	972	-19	12
Adilabad	991	969	968	951	-23	-18
Karimnagar	991	944	982	957	-9	13
Warangal	982	953	954	960	-28	7
Khammam	982	974	968	971	-14	-3
Nalgonda	982	977	960	981	-22	4
Andhra Pradesh	979	962	965	958	-14	-4

Source: Same as in Table 1.

Mandal Level Juvenile (0-6) sex ratio

The examination of district level data could not conclusively establish the reasons for decline in juvenile sex ratio in Andhra Pradesh. Hence an attempt is also made to locate areas, which recorded very low juvenile sex ratio. With the Mandal level data available from the Census, those Mandals with very low juvenile sex ratio (less than 925) is considered for the analysis. Nearly 10 per cent of the Mandals in Andhra Pradesh had juvenile sex ratio less than 925. The percentage of Mandals with juvenile sex ratio less then 925 in each of the districts of the state is presented in Table 6.

The result showed that in Guntur and Cuddapah over 20 per cent of the Mandals have juvenile sex ratio less than 925 followed by Vishakhapatnam, Anantapur and Warangal. These districts covered all the three traditional regions of the state (Coastal Andhra. Rayalaseema and Telangana) and are not associated with low or high development. Even those districts with only a few Mandals having low juvenile sex ratio viz., East Godavari, Khammam and Medak, also had

Table 6: Percentage of Mandals with Juvenile Sex Ratio less than 925

District	*Percentage of Mandals*
Adilabad	5.8
Nizamabad	5.6
Karimnagar	0
Medak	4.4
Hyderabad	–
Rangareddy	16.2
Mahabubnagar	14.1
Nalgonda	10.2
Warangal	15.7
Khammam	4.3
Srikakulam	0
Vizianagaram	0
Visakhapatnam	18.6
East Godavari	3.4
West Godavari	6.5
Krishna	6.0
Guntur	21.1
Prakasam	7.1
Nellore	10.9
Cuddapah	21.6
Kurnool	11.1
Anantpur	17.5
Chittoor	12.1

Source: Same as In Table 1.

nothing common to take note of. These facts are re-affirmed in Table 7, with shows the relationship between Mandal with juvenile sex ratio and literacy levels.

It is clear that there is no association between these two variables. Mandals with low and high literacy levels experience low sex ratio signifying lack of relationship. Hence low juvenile sex ratio needs to be understood in the specific historical and cultural contexts than mere development indicators.

However, with the provisional figures at hand, it is too early to predict conclusively on the causes of declining

Table 7: Percentage of Mandals with juvenile sex ratio and female literacy level

	Juvenile Sex Ratio				
Literacy level	*<925*	*925-950*	*950-975*	*975-1000*	*>1000*
0-20	5.41	2.33	2.5	1.83	4.94
20-40	53.15	55.81	50.72	57.51	64.20
40-60	36.04	34.88	40.06	34.80	25.31
60-80	5.41	6.98	6.63	5.86	5.56
No of Mandals	111	215	347	273	162

juvenile sex ratio and particularly the role of female foeticide in augmenting such decline. However, it is also not advisable at this juncture to out rightly dismiss such a possibility. This necessitates more careful study especially in those areas experiencing very low juvenile sex ratio.

Conclusion

The 2001 census has revealed some interesting features of sex ratio in Andhra Pradesh. For the first time since independence, the state registered an improvement of six points in sex ratio from 972 females per 1000 males in 1991 to 978 females in 2001, which is a matter of some satisfaction. This improvement has taken place in most districts in the state. At the same time, a matter of deep concern is the decline in sex ratio of population in the age group 0-6 (juvenile). There is eleven-point decline in juvenile sex ratio from 975 in 1991 to 964 in 2001. Considering 20 years between census years 1981 and 2001, there is nearly 28-point decline in the juvenile sex ratio in the state. This decline is observed in most of the districts in Andhra Pradesh.

Of the four reasons mooted for the decline in sex ratio, viz., sex differentials in mortality, migration, undercount and change in sex ratio at birth, the improvement in the overall sex ratio can be explained by the fact that female death rates have become lower and survival chances of females are more than males in most of the ages. This is particularly true in the adult ages where male mortality is not only far higher than females but tended to stagnate.

However, for the 0-6 age group, there is no reason to believe a worsening mortality for females. The data available from Sample Registration System and National Family Health Survey presents higher levels of infant and child mortality among males compared to females. The other reason often suggested is the relative undercount of females. The undercount of females in the 0-4 and 5-9 age groups has not been very different from males in the earlier two censuses. It is, therefore, unlikely that such phenomena occurred in the 2001 census count. Sex selective migration is unlikely in the younger age groups as both male and female children move together with parents. Hence, one would suspect increasing incidence of female foeticide in the state through the use of available modern techniques. The available data are examined with different angles, looking at rural-urban differentials in juvenile sex ratio and also by considering Mandals with very low sex ratio (less than 925). No relationship is observed between juvenile sex ratio and development indicators. Hence, it is too early to jump into any specific conclusions on the causes of falling juvenile sex ratio although we cannot foreclose entirely the possibility of foeticide. This calls for more intensive studies in specific historical and cultural contexts.

References

Das Gupta, Monica and P.N. Mari Bhat (1995) *Intensified Gender Bias in India: A consequent of fertility decline,* Working Paper No. 95.03, Harvard Center for Population and Development Studies, Cambridge, MA.

Dyson, T. (1988) 'Excess Female Mortality in India: Uncertain evidence of a narrowing differential, in K. Srinivasan and S. Mukerji (eds) *Dynamics of Population and Family Welfare 1987,* New Delhi: Himalayan Publishing Company.

James, K.S. (1996) *Adult Mortality in Andhra Pradesh: Levels, Trends and Determinants,* Working Paper No. 32, Centre for Economic and Social Studies, Hyderabad.

Krishnaji, N. and K.S. James (2002) "Gender Differentials in Adult Mortality in India—With Notes on Rural-Urban Contrasts" *Economic and Political Weekly,* (forthcoming).

Premi, M.K. (2001) The missing Girl Child, *Economic and Political Weekly,* May 26, P:1875-1880.

Rajan, S. I., U.S. Mishra and K. Navaneetham (1991) 'Decline in Sex Ratio: An Alternative Explanation Revisited', *Economic and Political Weekly,* (Dec 21): P:2963-2964.

Rajan, S. I., U.S. Mishra and K. Navaneetham (1992) 'Decline in sex Ratio: An Alternative Explanation Revisited', *Economic and Political Weekly,* (Nov 14), P:2505-2508.

Raju, S. and M.K. Premi (1992) 'Decline in Sex Ratio: Alternative Explanation Re-examined', *Economic and Political Weekly,* (April 25), P:911-912.

Srinivasan, K. (1994) Sex Ratio: What they hide and what they reveal, *Economic and Political Weekly,* December, 17-24, P: 3233-3234.

Sudha, S. and S.I. Rajan. 1999. Female Demographic Disadvantage in India 1981-1991, Sex Selective Abortions and Female Infanticide, *Development and Change,* 30 (3) 585-618.

Visaria, Pravin (1961) *The Sex Ratio of the Population of India,* Census of India, 1961, Monograph no. 10, New Delhi: Registrar General of India.

2

Urbanisation Trends in India

Prof. K. Narasimhulu

Introduction

Urbanization refers to the population of a nation living in urban areas. It may be considered as a very comprehensive process. Urbanization as a process reveals itself through temporal, spatial and sectorical changes in the demographic, social economic, technological and environmental aspects of life in a given society.

A demographic analysis of urbanization in India shows that though the level of urbanization in terms of the proportion of urban population (27.78 per cent according to 2001 Census) is low, the urban population in absolute terms is enormous (285.36 millions as per 2001 Census) which exceed the total population of the developed countries of the world.

Urban Areas:

In the 2001 Census of India, two types of towns were identified:

(*a*) Statutory Towns: All places with a municipality, corporation contonment board of notified town area committee etc., so declared by a state law

(*b*) Census Towns: Place which satisfy the following criteria:

(*i*) A minimum population of 5,000

(ii) Atleast 75% of male working population engaged on non-agricultural pursuits and;

(iii) A density of population atleast 400 persons per square kilo meter.

(c) Urban Agglomeration (UA): It is a continuos urban spread consisting of a town and its adjoining urban outgrowths (OGs) that may have come up near a statutory town or city but within the revenue limits of a village or villages contiguous to the town or city. For Census of India, 2001 it was decided that the core town and the total population of all the constituents should not be less than 20,000.

Table 1: Percentage of Urban Population in India and the States

Sl. No.	*India/State*	*Urban Population (in millions) 2001*	*Percentage of Urban Population to Total Population (U/T) 2001*	*Percentage of Urban Population to Total Population (U/T) 1991*
1	Maharashtra	41.01	42.39	38.73
2	Gujrat	18.89	37.35	34.40
3	Tamil Nadu	27.24	43.85	34.20
4	Karnataka	17.91	33.98	30.91
5	Punjab	8.24	33.95	29.72
6	West Bengal	22.48	28.03	27.89
7	Andhra Pradesh	20.50	27.14	26.84
8	Kerala	8.26	25.96	26.44
9	Haryana	6.11	29.00	24.79
10	Jammu & Kashmir	2.50	24.88	23.83
11	Madhya Pradesh	16.10	26.66	23.21
12	Rajasthan	13.20	23.38	22.88
13	Uttar Pradesh	34.51	20.78	19.89
14	Orissa	5.49	14.97	13.47
15	Bihar	8.67	10.47	13.17
16	Assam	3.38	12.72	22.08
	India	285.3	27.78	25.72

Source: Compiled from Census of India 2001, provisional population Totals.

From Table 1, we can analyse that except for Bihar, Assam and Kerala, the percentage of Urban Population to total population has increased in all the above states for the decade 1999-2001.

Kerala, Jammu & Kashmir, Madhya Pradesh, Rajasthan, Uttar Pradesh, Orissa, Bihar and Assam are having urban population less than the national average, Maharashtra, Gujrat, Tamil Nadu, Karnataka, Punjab, West Bengal, Andhra Pradesh and Haryana are having the urban population per cent more than the national average. Among these states, Tamil Nadu's per cent of urban to total population increases by 9 points. Assam's per cent has declined by 9 points.

In the 2001 Census, Delhi occupies the first place with 93.01 per cent living in urban. Among the states, Goa occupies first with 49.79 per cent urban population followed by Mizoram, Tamil Nadu and Andhra Pradesh, Sikkim, Tripura and Himachal Pradesh occupies last three places with less than 12 per cent.

Table 2: India's Urbanization Trend

Census Year	*Total Population (in millions)*	*Urban Population (in millions)*	*Decennial Growth rate of Urban Population (per cent)*	*Percentage of the urbans to Total Population*	*Annual Exponential growth rate*
1901	238.10	25.85		10.8	
1911	252.09	25.94	0.35	10.3	0.03
1921	252.32	28.09	8.27	11.2	0.79
1931	278.98	33.46	19.12	12.0	1.75
1941	318.66	44.15	31.97	13.9	2.77
1951	361.09	62.44	41.42	17.6	3.47
1961	439.24	78.74	26.41	18.0	2.34
1971	548.16	109.09	38.23	19.9	3.21
1981	685.18	159.73	46.14	23.3	3.83
1991	844.33	217.18	36.19	25.7	3.09
2001*	1027.02	285.3	31.40	27.78	2.71

***Source:** Census of India 2001, Provisional Population Totals.

The Table 2 shows the urbanization Trends in India from 1901 to 2001. It increased steadily upto 1951 and declined in 1961. As compared to the decade 1971-81, the decennial growth rate of 1981-1991 declined by 10 points.

In the decade 1991-2001, the growth of urban population is 31-40, and it again declined by 5 points than the earlier decade. The growth rate has been declined since 1981. The reason for this slowing down of growth rate is due to slowness in economic development. The overall economic development during 1981-91 did not commensurate with the changing upward trend in population growth.

Growth of Million Plus Cities

Table 3: One Million plus urban agglomerations and Cities Their population and Growth Rate

Rank in 2001	*Urban Agglomeration/City*	*Population (in millions)*		*Decennial Growth Rates*	
		2001	*1991*	*2001*	*1991*
1	Greater Mumbai UA	16.36	12.56	30.2	37.1
2	Kolkata UA	13.21	10.86	21.6	18.1
3	Chennai UA	12.79	8.37	52.7	46.2
4	Chennai UA	6.42	5.36	19.8	25.0
5	Bangalore UA	5.68	4.27	38.4	40.6
6	Hyderabad UA	5.53	4.10	29.4	67.0
7	Ahmedabad UA	4.51	3.27	37.8	28.7
8	Pune UA	3.75	2.44	53.6	45.0
9	Surat UA	2.81	1.51	85.3	66.0
10	Kanpur UA	2.69	2.10	27.9	28.3
11	Jaipur M. Crop	2.37	1.51	53.4	49.2
12	Lucknow UA	2.26	1.66	35.8	65.7
13	Nagpur UA	2.12	1.65	28.1	35.9
14	Patna UA	1.70	1.09	55.4	19.6
15	Indore UA	1.63	1.10	48.4	33.1
16	Vadodara UA	1.49	1.11	33.5	20.5
17	Bhopal UA	1.45	1.06	27.3	23.4
18	Combatore UA	1.44	1.13	37.8	66.7
19	Ludhiane M. Crop	1.39	1.01	37.8	66.7
20	Kochi UA	1.35	1.13	19.4	40.3
21	Visakhapatnam UA	1.32	1.04	26.6	73.9
22	Agra UA	1.32	0.90	42.6	—
23	Varanasi UA	1.21	1.01	18.9	27.7
24	Madurai UA	1.19	1.09	9.2	20.5

Table Contd.

Table 3: Contd...

25	Meerut* UA	1.16	0.83	40	—
26	Nashik* UA	1.15	0.72	59.1	—
27	Jabalpur	1.11	0.76	46.5	—
28	Jamshedpur* UA	1.10	0.83	32.0	—
29	Asansol* UA	1.09	0.76	42.7	—
30	Dhanbad* UA	1.06	0.81	30.1	—
31	Faridabad* M.Corp	1.05	0.61	71.9	—
32	Allhabad* UA	1.04	0.84	24.7	—
33	Amritsar* UA	1.01	0.70	42.5	—
34	Vijayawada* UA	1.01	0.83	20.5	—
35	Rajkot* UA	1.00	0.85	17.7	—

Source: Census of India 2001, Provisional Population Totals
UA stands for Agglomentions
M.Corp stands for Municipal Corporation
*these UAs/Cities have newly joined in the list of million plus UAs/ Cities

The provisional population totals for 2001 Census for India by rural-urban areas indicate that there are 35 cities and Urban agglomentions (UAs) or metropolitan cities. The 34 metropolitan cities are located in 13 states excluding capital territory Delhi. This combined population account for 107.8 millions people, comprising 9.5 per cent of the total population. This is 37 millions more than 1991 Census. The major share was due to the newly added cities. A total of 12 cities were added in 2001 census. The new cities are Agra, Meerut, Nashik, Jabalpur, Jameshedpur, Asansol, Dhanbad, Faridabad, Allahabad, Amritser, Vijayawada, Rajkot.

The Bombay UA remains to be the biggest from 1981. At the State level Uttar Pradesh has the largest number of (six) cities (Kanpur, Lucknow, Agra, Varanasi, Meerut, Allahabad), and account for 12 per cent of total plus UA population. Gujrat and Maharashtra has four cities each. Andhra Pradesh, Bihar, Tamil Nadu and Madhya Pradesh has three UAs/Cities each. West Bengal and Punjab has two each and Haryana, Kerala, Rajasthan, Karnataka have one city with million plus population as per 2001 Census.

An analysis of 2001 and 1991 Census decennial growth rates 23 million plus cities of 1991 Census shows that Greater Mumbai, Chennai, Bangalore, Hyderabad, Kanpur, Lucknow, Nagpur, Bhopal, Ludhiana, Kochi, Vadodara and Madurai recorded a negative growth rate and among them Hyderabad, Bhopal Ludhiana, Kochi have declined by more than 20 points.

The highest growth rate was recorded for Surat (85.3%) and lowest for Madurai (9.2%) Kolkata, Delhi, Ahmedabad, Pune, Surat, Jaipur, Patna, Indore, Vadodara, Coimbatore recorded positive rate of growth. Surat, patna, Indore the growht rate improved by 15 points.

Causes of Urbanization

1. **Migration:** The most important factor that affects urbanization is rural-urban migration. Bogue and Zachariah remarked of rural-urban migration by for the major component of urbanization and as the chief mechanism by which all the worlds great urbanisation trends have been accomplished.

   (i) Industriliasation: Migrants from rural areas migrate to urban areas in search of employment in industrial centres of urban areas. Besides Industries, urban areas possess some significant things e.g transport centres, administarative offices, advanced educational health services. Big cities in India keep on evolving and suffering from population explosion from rural areas.

   (ii) Employment: Most of the studies have established that people with higher eduatioanl attainments in the rural areas tend to migrate to the city in research of better job opportunities. As unemployment grows in cosmopolitan cities men with educational qualifications migrate to other areas. Hence, among the urban migrates the uneducated labourers for outnumber those with educational qualifications

became the uneudcated labourers early get employment as labourers.

(iii) Marriage: The number of females who migrate to the Urban areas because of marriage is nearly 40-50% of the total female migrates. So, the marital status also plays an important role in migration to urban areas.

(iv) Business: People migrate to urban areas in search of high business in order to make huge money and wealth for themselves. For example, most of the Marvaries of rural Rajasthan have migrated to cosmopolitan cities like Mumbai, Hyderabad and Calcutta for business purpose.

(v) Sequential Migration: Some people migrate to urban areas because the head of the family or the main worker moves to the urban areas due to promotion or in search of employment.

2. **The rate of natural increase:** Even the natural growth rate in urban areas is lower than that of in the rural areas, it is also an affecting factor in the growth of urbanization.

Consequences of Urbanization

1. Housing Problem: Due to increasing urbanization, providing houses to all the people have become a serious prolblem. Rents are high in the urban areas and even middle class families live in slums.
2. Slums: Another serious consequence of urbanization is the mushroom growth slums in cities and towns. City attracts migrates from surrounding rural and semi-urban areas, who develop slum colonies in the city. These slums are above of poverty and diseases.
3. Unemployment: People in the areas migrate to urban areas in anticipation of better jobs as they are pushed out from rural areas by the pressure on land on account

of growing population. These people are unskilled and without any adequate source of livelihood and add to the heavy existing unemployed people in the city.

4. Social Problems: The co-existance of rich life and dirty slums in all medium and major cities of India has led to a sort discontentment among the urban poor. Poverty, unemployment and lack of access to amenties has led to their involvement into the anti-social activities.

5. Environmental Pollution: Urban Industrialisation lead to the pollution of water, air, noise and land. There is lot of congestion and unhealthy conditions due to slums. Water Pollution leads to the outbreak of epidemics. High traffic on roads in urban areas leads to lot of noise and air pollution.

Conclusion

We can conclude from the above discussion that even though the percentage of urbanisation is low i.e., 27.78% per cent when compared with other developed countries, it is high in terms of population number as it posses a problem for the urban management of the government. We can observe high per cent growth in some million-plus cities which is alarming and deterimental to the economic development and provision of infrastructural facilities.

Large inter-state differential in urbanisation shows that the level of urbanisation has been partial and not showed by all the states uniformly. Some states lag in the process of urbanisation. Therefore there is need for stepping up developmental efforts and diversifying the utilisation of manpower from the agricultural to non-agricultural sector in order to remove regional imbalances.

3

Population Explosion in India

Prof. K. Narasimhulu

World population which stood at two billion at the end of World War II, has crossed six billion mark on October 12, per year, as reported by the United Nations population division, which is the principal agency doing research on population trends. At the present rate of growth at 1.33 per cent or about 79 million annually, world population is projected at 8.9 billion by 2050. If increase go at the present rate for only a thousand years, there would be no standing room for the human race on this earth. However, a whimsical suggestion states that interplanetary travel might be possible by that time, that might reduce earth's population pressure. But seen practically merely moving people on the earth itself is very costly. It is beyond imagination if interplanetary movement would be feasible. Assuming that an individual could be moved to another planet for a ridiculously low cost of one million dollars, it could take 79,000 billion U.S. dollars to get rid of earth's current increase of one year- a sum exceeding the earth's total income.

Population Explosion in India

It is pertinent to mention here that almost the entire increase in population has taken place in the least developed and poorest countries, resulting "demographic train wreck". A study by the World watch Institute warns India which will overtake China as the world's most populous nation in a few years. By 2050, it is expected to have, 1,529 million as against China's 1,478 milion. No denying the present trend of population growth in India is alarming. Its population on October 12, 2000 has crossed one billion, which stood at 35 crore at the time of Independence.

The study by World-watch predicts disaster "for Indian and calamity" starting at Pakistan with its 1998 population of 142 million exploding to 345 million by 2050.

Over one half of the World population is concentrated in Asia. Imagine India alone counts for adding one Australia to its population every year, that is 16 million more mouths to feed while, China is adding only 12 million annually. At the present rate of population growth, life for most Indians would be unbearable-medical facilities would be impossible to provide; expenses on education, housing etc., would be exorbitant; technical and professional education would become the exclusive prerogative of the elite; and scarcity of food would plunge three-fifths of the nation below poverty line.

The availability of arable land in India will be reduced to less than one tenth of a hectare while in Pakistan arable land by 2050 will be reduced to 0.03 of a hectare per head and the three countries—Japan, South Korea and Taiwan-where green land has shrunk to 0.03 hectares per head, import some 70 per cent of their grains needs.

As for water, says World-watch, the withdrawal are now double the rate of aquifer recharge. As a result, "Water tables are falling by one to three meters per year over much of the country. Over pumping today means water supply cutbacks tomorrow, a serious matter where half of the grain harvest comes from irrigated land". The International Water Management Institute Brown estimates that aquifer depletion and the resulting cut backs in irrigation water could drop India's grain harvest by one-fourth. The study says in a country where 53 per cent of all children are malnourished and underweight, a shrinking harvest could increase hunger-related deaths, adding to the six million world-wide who die each year from hunger and malnutrition. India, World watch notes, has achieved impressive gains in its harvest but there have been largely canceled by population growth, living most of its people living close to the margin. Brown sees one-third of humanity-with several other developing countries keeping company with India and Pakistan-sliding into a "demographic dark hole".

On the number of people concerned the growth of population has a direct effect on the standard of living of the people. That is why, despite our spectacular progress in the agricultural and industrial sectors since Independence, our per capital income has not risen appreciably. The appalling over crowding of our cities has brought out a virtual breakdown of transportation, electricity and other services. It has also led to the increase in the rate of crime and conflict in urban and semi urban areas.

The most deplorable is the fact that no political party in India has addressed itself to this biggest danger lurking close to us. Not even during the recent elections, and leader has cared to dwell upon the perils of this challenge. This is perhaps because of the negative impact the coercive 'nasbandi' operations undertaken during the emergency days of the seventies, had on the Congress party. What we have to bear in mind is that not coercion but persuasion through education is the most desirable method for population control. The attitude of ignoring the problem by our political leaders is not going to make this problem disappear.

Causes of Population Growth

We may identify the following important causes for population explosion in India:

1. **Widening gap between birth and death rates:** the average annual birth rate in India has declined from 41.2 per thousand during 1961-71 to 31.2 per thousand during 1981-01. However, in 2001, the birth rate showed

a further decline to 28.5 per thousand. Similarly, the death rate has also shown a decline from 19.2 per thousand 1981-91 decade. And, in 2001 the death rate was 8.2 per thousand. It shows that against birth rate of 30.5 per thousand, the death rate was merely 80.2 per thousand in 2001, and, according to the preliminary estimates of 2001 Census, the birth rate is projected to decline to 27.5 and the death rate to 8.5 during 1991-2001 period. It is this widening gap between birth and death rate that has increased our population rapidly.

It is indeed shocking that in this very age of family planning, one out of every five Indian women in the reproductive age group of 15-45 years is pregnant at any time.

2. **Low age of women at marriage:** In spite of the fact that the minimum marriageable age has been fixed by law, child marriage still continues to be practiced in India. The fertility rate in the age group of 15-18 or 18-21 girls is very much on the higher side than that of girls in the age groups 21-24 and 24-27. The present marriageable age for a girl should be raised above 21 if not 24 if the birth rate is to be controlled.

3. **High illiteracy:** Family planning has a direct link with female education. As per 2001 census, the male literacy percentage in India is 68 per cent against female literacy percentage of 54 per cent.The overall literacy percentage is 65 per cent even after half a century of independence.

We must bear in mind that education makes a person liberal, broadminded, open to new ideas, and rational. If both husband and wife are educated, they can easily and logically of plan their family. But, if either of them or both of them are illiterate, they would be more orthodox, illogical and religious—minded. This is evident from the fact that Kerala which has the lowest birth rate of 22.4 per thousand in India while Rajasthan's appallingly low female literacy rate of 20.48 per cent gives rise to the third highest birth rate of 36.40 per cent in he country.

4. **Religious attitude towards family planning:** The religiously orthodox and conservative people are against the rise of family planning measures. There are women who disfavour family planning measures. The plea that they cannot go against the wishes of God. There are some women who argue that the purpose of a women's life is to bear children.

5. **Poor Primary Health Care:** we have a poor primary health care and deplorable levels of public hygiene. The average age in India is not yet 60 whereas in the developed countries it is into the late 70s. Even Sri Lanka is ahead of us. Many lives are lost as a result of pregnancies and unsafe abortions.

6. **Poverty:** Primary among a large section of Indian population is also responsible for high birth rate. Many families in India produce children not because they are ignorant but because they need them as means of sustenance. If the concerned families stop the children from working, their family sustenance will be affected.

7. **Lack of responsibility in joint family system:** In spite of the fact that nuclius family system has emerged in India as well, a large section of the rural population still lives in a joint family. It is in these joint families that the young married couples go on uninterruptedly with their job of producing child after child.

8. **Lack of recreational facilities:** The fact that the poor have a large army of children's is due also to lack of recreational facilities for the, they cannot afford to go clubs or avail of other recreational facilities, the only source of recreation for them is to indulge in sex and, this leads in multiplication of children. The easiest, cheapest and most efficient method to check libidinal maternities is male sterilization which is the most despised and dreaded technique of birth control in India.

9. **Lack of information and wrong information about family planning measures:** In the distant rural areas, there is lack of information about family planning measure. If at all the Government agencies do reach them, due to widespread illiteracy and ignorance they refuse to adopt such measures. They hold that such measures lead to unhealthy results upon the persons concerned.

Measures to Control Population Growth

The continuing population explosion in our country is one of the biggest causes of worry for the Government of India. It is the biggest challenge facing the Government and the nation although the common man is not yet aware of the dark days ahead.

So, a search is going on for the measure that may be adopted for achieving control over population growth. The following are some of the measures:

1. **Division into Zones and Regions:** A study conducted in February 1990 by two population experts of the Operation Research Group at Baroda has shown how the ineffective of family planning measures can be turned into success. On the basis of fertility pattern, they have divided the country's 350 districts into 16 zones and four regions.

They have identified districts and zones which reflect the positive impact of family planning on the fertility rate, the areas where; fertility rates have remained low despite hardly land family planning efforts, and those regions which are the hard core areas where the maximum, effort is needed. The areas of high fertility are Arunachal Pradesh, Bihar, Haryana, Madhya Pradesh, Uttar Pradesh and Rajasthan. These areas need greater attention. This region wise approach can go a long way in correcting the lacunae in the implementation of the family planning program.

2. **Proper Education:** In the distant rural areas and the poor living in urban areas, there is lack of information about family planning measures. The illiterated land ignorant masses hold that family planning measures lead to unhealthy results upon the persons concerned. As such, they need to be properly educated as to the impact of those measures. The misinformation land misconceived must be dispelled.

3. **Search for New Contraceptives:** The search for a new, inexpensive easy to use, and harmless contraceptive has not met with dramatic success so far. Though pills have come to be accepted in a big way, it is necessary that Indian herbs and also homeopathic remedies be thoroughly investigated for this purpose. Some of the tribals in Andaman and Nicobar Islands have an extremely low rate of fertility. An investigation into their health status land dietary habits may perhaps provide some clue.

4. **Banning Early Marriage:** There is a direct relationship between age, of marriage, attitude towards family planning measures and the rate of fertility. The higher the age, the lower the rate of fertility Girls between 15-18 or also between 18-21 are more fertile than between 21-24. So, if early marriage is banned effectively land marriagble age raised to 21, population can be effectively checked.

Moreover, the family planning measures are usually not popular with the young persons. They detest them on emotional land irrigational grounds. Rationality is the boon of maturity. So, encouragement should be given to late marriages.

5. **Provisions of Recreation Facilities:** It is lack of recreation facilities for the poor that makes them overindulge in sex. So, emphasis should be laid on providing better land more recreation facilities in villages and for the poor in urban areas.

6. Ineligibility for Public Offices: The problem of population control is the most vital to tackle immediately if we want to survive. For this, we have to take drastic measures. It is seen that certain politicians who go on preaching others on the necessity and importance of family planning, have a different standards for themselves. It may appear incredible but a fact that a plitician who makes headline in newspapers in India is the father of eight children. Similarly, there are various other persons holding different public offices, who go on producing children without limit. It is time that a law should be enacted that a person having more than two children should be debarred from holding public office.

Conclusion

The population policy of our Government should aim at controlling the unregulated human growth of numerical strength. For this, family planning needs to be salvaged from the morass into which it has drifted. A variety of measures will have to be introduced to put family planning campaign back on its feet. Emphasis should, however, lie on persuasion. Legal measures are a necessity but more important is the social awareness. We must also check the phenomenon of "children producing children". That is producing children in little age.

4

Inter-District Variations in Rural Farm and Non-Farm Employment in Andhra Pradesh

Dr. M. Prasada Rao

Introduction

This paper seeks to identify the inter-district variations in the shares and growth of Rural farm and Non-Farm Employment (RNFE)[2] in Andhra Pradesh (AP). The focus is on farm and non-farm main workers i.e. workers who had worked for the major part of the year (183 days or more), and whose principal work was in RNFE.[3] We will consider the changes between 1981 and 1991 and 2001. We can identify broadly two categories of RNFE: traditional and modern. In rural communities traditional non-farm activities (such as blacksmithy, carpentry, pottery, weaving, washing, toddy

2. Rural areas are defined as rural in the decennial Census of India as meeting three criteria: that the population is below 5,000; that these areas have a population density of less than 400 persons per square kilometer; and that less than 75 per cent of the male working population should be engaged in non-agricultural pursuits. The definition for rural non-farm employment in the 1991 Census is those workers who have been "engaged in some economic activity during the year preceding enumeration and who are neither cultivators or agricultural labourers but are 'other workers' (non-farm workers)".
3. Marginal workers:" are those who had worked for less than six months (183 days) in the year (Census of India, 1991p. 5.)

tapping, barbering, cobbling, shepherd rearing and cotton cording) continue even though today some are declining. These activities may be grouped under seven headings: crafts, processing of crops, non-factory textiles, traditional forms of transportation and trade/commerce, personal services, repair and construction in homes and fields. The second category consists of modern manufacturing and processing, including sugar and textile factories, oil and grain mills, small factories producing engineering goods, shoes, paper, furniture, soap, matches and small scale quarries. A newly emerging third category consists of rural white-collar workers: public services, health and extension services, credit and marketing agencies, and public works construction (service sector).

For our study we define as a RNFE any household with at least one member in a primary occupation in categories 1V-1X of workers in the 1991 Census. The focus of our analysis bears on the importance of non-farm relative to agricultural employment. We have used the percentage of RNFE to the total employment variable and we have experimented with other structural differences (such as gender) between 1981-91. Also by contrast, we have analysed RNFE in a disaggregated manner using all IV to IX categories (divisions) of RNFE for 1981, 1991 and partly for 2001. The objectives of the paper are; to explain (1) the level of RNFE across districts and (2) the growth of the share of RNFE between 1981-91. As a preliminary step, means, standard deviations and coefficients of variations (CV) were computed for all the variables. The rest of this paper describes inter-district variations in shares, structure (by gender, by industry), and trends between 1981, 1991 and 2001 for farm and non-farm employment.

Trends in the Composition and shares of Rural farm and non-farm employment in A.P. districts-A comparison between 1981, 1991 and 2001:

Why do districts vary in farm and RNFS characteristics and growth? In order to provide some insight into this question, we first consider rural AP as a whole, and then the differences between districts. Rural employment data are considered in this section. The data presented relate to the degree of labour absorption in the farm and RNFS which is measured as the ratio of main workers in the RNFS to main workers in the rural areas. This is computed using Census data, as NSS data is lacking district-wise information.

Only about 18 per cent of total main workers are generally involved with non-farm activities. There are moreover few differences between the share of those involved with the non-farm sector in India and those involved with this sector in AP. Total main workers in the RNFS reached 23 million in 1991. At this time the RNFS share was 17.1 per cent and slightly higher than the 16.8 per cent calculated for 1981 (Table 1). There were 3.9 million workers in the RNFS, 75 per cent were males, compared with 76.3 per cent in 1981. Among all main workers, 61.4 per cent were males compared with 65.4 per cent in 1981. The female employment share in the labour force is higher in the farm sector than in the non-farm sector. Whilst changes occurred with the increasing rate of female labour, the RNFS still appears male-dominated, 39 per cent of all total main workers were females and 25 per cent of those involved with the RNFS were females. In terms of the composition of RNFE for 1991, other services accounted for the highest share followed by trade, household industry and non-household industry. Rising trends could be seen in all sub sectors except for HHI for totals for males but not for females. The analysis of RNFE when deconstructed at the sub-sector level shows that the share of the construction sector is particularly low in total, for both males as well as females.

From Table 1. one can see that the proportion of males involved with the RNFS has slightly increased. The reverse holds for females. Comparisons of growth rates of the workforce by industry groups show that the total agricultural workforce in AP grew at around 2 per cent per annum while the rate of growth for non-farm employment was around 2.2 per cent per annum. For farming, the growth rate of females

Table 1: Growth rate of rural employment in AP (1981 and 1991 Census data)

Category	*Rural (1981)*	*Rural (1991)*	*Per cent Annual Growth Rate*	*Rural (1981) Males*	*Rural (1991) Males*	*Per cent Annual Growth Rate*	*Rural (1981) Females*	*Rural (1991) Females*	*Per cent Annual Growth*
I to IX Total Main Workers	18832869 (100.0)	23026505 (100.0)	2.0	12326971 (100.0)	14145823 (100.0)	1.4	6505898 (100.0)	8880682 (100.0)	3.2
				Agriculture					
(I) Cultivators	7229577 (38.4)	7703384 (33.5)	0.6	5556880 (45.1)	5528638 (39.1)	-0.05	1672697 (25.7)	2174746 (24.5)	2.6
(II) Agri-labourers	7912322 (42.0)	10940275 (47.5)	3.3	3877712 (31.5)	5280400 (37.3)	3.1	4034610 (62.0)	5659875 (63.73)	3.4
(III) Agrl. Allied	515588 (2.7)	435471 (1.9)	-1.7	468345 (3.8)	376359 (2.66)	-2.2	47243 (0.7)	59112 (0.7)	2.3
(I to III) Total Farm workers	15657487 (83.1)	19079130 (82.9)	2.0	9902937 (80.4)	11185397 (79.1)	1.2	5754550 (88.4)	7893733 (88.9)	3.2

Table 1: Contd.

	Rural non-farm								
(IV) Mining	55028 (0.3)	153253 (0.7)	10.8	4904 (0.4)	119162 (0.8)	10.5	11125 (0.2)	34091 (0.4)	11.8
(Va) Household Mfg.	845866 (4.5)	742685 (3.2)	-1.3	556885 (4.5)	395536 (2.8)	-3.4	288981 (4.4)	347149 (3.9)	1.9
(Vb) Non-household Mfg.	526637 (2.8)	690240 (3.0)	2.7	421560 (3.4)	538409 (3.8)	2.5	105077 (1.6)	151831 (1.7)	3.7
(VI) Construction	155805 (0.8)	178854 (0.8)	1.4	136650 (1.1)	158331 (1.1)	1.5	19155 (0.3)	20523 (0.2)	0.7
(VII) Trade	589284 (3.1)	765788 (3.3)	2.7	472822 (3.8)	620850 (4.4)	2.8	116462 (1.8)	144938 (1.6)	2.2
(VIII) Transport	167276 (0.9)	236079 (1.0)	3.5	164870 (1.3)	232460 (1.6)	3.5	2406 (0.04)	3619 (0.04)	4.2
(IX) Other Services	835483 (4.4)	1180476 (5.1)	3.5	627344 (5.1)	895678 (6.3)	3.6	208139 (3.2)	284798 (3.2)	3.2
(IV to IX) Total RNFS Workers	3175379 (16.8)	3947375 (17.1)	2.2	2424035 (19.9)	2960426 (20.8)	2.0	798588 (11.6)	986945 (11.1)	2.1

Notes: RMW: Rural main Workers; Brackets Indicate the percentage share of total main workers.

Sources: Census of India 1981, series-1 India, General Economic Tables, (Tables B.1 to B.5) pp. 242-245.
Census of India 1991, Andhra Pradesh, Population Totals, Sectors-2.

(3.2 per cent) was higher than that of males (1.2 per cent). In the non-farm sector an opposite trend can be marginally noted. The highest (per annum) rural employment growth-rate (between 1981 and 1991) was among agricultural labourers (3.3 per cent). The growth rate of cultivators was the lowest (0.6 per cent). All the sectors apart from agriculture and household manufacturing showed positive growth. Employment in the agricultural allied category declined. The data shows that agriculture and allied categories to the RNFS. The significant growth of agricultural labourers is also a pointer to agricultural distress in the State.

Table 1 indicates that between 1981-1991 in AP there was an increase in mining and quarrying (category IV). This could be due to the liberalization policies applied to cement production and the removal of subsidies to the granite industry. Storage and warehousing also increased from 1981 to 1991. This could be due to the increase in public construction of *godowns* for food grains and essential commodities in all marketing centres, and the encouragement by the authorities to private entrepreneurs to construct warehouses. The number of persons employed in the electricity, gas and water sectors decreased over the 10 year period. This could be due to the change in the billing system by the Electricity Department: the introduction of the slab system led to a considerable decrease in the number of bill collectors. Another reason for this decrease could lie with the introduction of machines in power projects.

Turning to employment trends by gender, the proportion of rural male main workers in agriculture declined. For females there was a marginal increase in the share. Regarding males in the RNFS, there is a continuous increase in mining and quarrying, manufacturing, trade and services, construction and transport. The largest increase for males is in transport, followed by services, trade and construction. For females it is to be seen in manufacturing, transport and services. A striking feature of this Table is that overall female employment outgrew the male employment. This feature was relatively pronounced in most RNFE sectors; indeed in 'allied' and household industry, female employment rose and male employment fell.

From the above discussion it would seem that the level and growth between 1981 and 1991 of rural employment in AP varies across different categories. The differences between males and females also requires explanation. At this stage, the overall conclusion regarding the employment changes in rural AP is that the share of non-farm employment increased very marginally and less than all-India, both for the total and for males. This was mainly due to the increase in the tertiary sector (trade, transport, and construction). The share of non-farm employment for females has marginally declined due to the decline in household industry.

The industrial distribution of the workforce for males for the state as a whole shows that services was the major sector in terms of its share for total and for males in RNFS. For females, household industry had the highest share in RNFS.

It can be seen from the Table 2 there is an increasing disparity across the AP districts in 1981 compared with 1991 (CV has increase from 0.17 to 0.19). When we look at the pattern for males there is more uniformity in the recent period in terms of the proportion in RNFE. This time the change is quite pronounced. The CV for males has gone down from 0.14 to 0.09 and for females has increased from 0.35 to 0.5. The pattern of RNFE is much more diverse across the AP districts than for males. It appears that there seems more spread in RNFE for females. The gender dimension of RNFE has become more pronounced during the decade.

Differences that can be further seen between the districts show that there has been substantial variation across districts in the shares of non-farm employment in total employment. Differences in the proportionate changes on RNFE shares are summarised in Table 6.

Table 2: Proportion of rural non-farm employment to total workers per district in Andhra Pradesh, 1981-1991

District	%RNFE 1981 Total (1)	%RNFE 1991 Total (2)	Pattern of Change in percentage points Total (3) = (2)-(1)	%RNFE 1981 Males (4)	% RNFE 1991 Males (5)	Pattern of Change in percentage points Males (6) = (5)-(4)	% RNFE 1981 Females (7)	%RNFE 1991 Females (8)	Pattern of Change in percentage points Females (9) = (8)-(7)
Nizamabad	23.66	26.53 [1]	2.87	21.54	22.43 [8]	0.89	26.47	30.76 [1]	4.29
Karimnagar	20.74	23.82 [2]	3.09	22.98	25.89 [2]	2.91	17.4	20.68 [2]	3.28
East Godavari	20.45	20.62 [3]	0.17	22.42	23.54 [5]	1.12	14.33	14.91 [4]	0.58
Adilabad	16.37	20.48 [4]	4.11	18.41	23.86 [4]	5.45	12.79	17.11 [3]	4.32
West Godavari	17.63	19.44 [5]	1.81	20.31	24.69 [3]	4.38	11.56	13.04 [5]	1.48
Nalgonda	16.64	18.98 [6]	2.34	19.18	22.34 [9]	3.16	11.79	10.44 [9]	-1.35
Ranga Reddy	22.5	18.73 [7]	-3.77	28.63	27.81 [1]	-0.82	12.26	9.31 [12]	-2.95
Vizianagaram	16.28	17.94 [8]	1.66	20.12	23.01 [6]	2.89	8.93	10.02 [11]	1.09
Nellore	16.12	17.12 [9]	1	18.84	22.23 [11]	3.39	10.65	10.62 [8]	-0.03
Srikakulam	16.65	16.98 [10]	0.33	19.53	21.2 [17]	1.67	11.31	10.88 [7]	-0.43
Visakhaptnam	19.2	16.76 [11]	-2.44	21.97	21.17 [18]	-0.8	13.07	10.42 [10]	-2.65

Table 2: Contd.

Cuddapah	17.95	16.59 [12]	-1.36	20.61	21.45 [13]	0.84	12.06	9.13 [13]	-2.93
Medak	15.71	16.37 [13]	0.66	18.18	21.42 [15]	3.24	10.51	11.77 [6]	1.26
Krishna	16.89	16.26 [14]	-0.63	19.55	22.26 [10]	2.71	11.08	9.03 [14]	-2.05
Chittor	13.97	15.78 [15]	1.81	16.89	21.44 [14]	4.55	7.52	7.93 [15]	0.41
Warangal	16.2	15.59 [16]	-0.61	19.39	21.51 [12]	2.12	10.3	7.83 [16]	-2.47
Khammam	15.21	15.33 [17]	0.12	18.5	20.87 [19]	2.37	8.68	6.43 [22]	-2.25
Guntur	15.09	14.41 [18]	-0.68	18.5	22.51 [7]	4.01	8.93	7.03 [19]	-3.32
Prakasam	16.26	13.93 [19]	-2.33	19.84	21.22 [16]	1.38	10.06	6.74 [21]	-3.32
Kurnool	14.84	13.8 [20]	-1.04	18.66	20.41 [20]	1.75	8.84	7.59 [18]	-1.25
Ananthapur	12.09	13.22 [21]	1.13	15.06	18.51 [22]	3.45	6.62	6.87 [20]	0.25
Mahabubnagar	13.77	12.76 [22]	-1.01	16.64	18.85 [21]	2.21	9.2	7.69 [17]	-1.51
Mean (AP)	17.0	17.3	0.3	19.8	22.2	1.2	11.6	11.2	-0.4
SD	2.8	3.4		2.7	2.1		4.1	5.6	
CV	0.17	0.19		0.14	0.09		0.35	0.5	

Notes: Figures in [] indicate the ranks CV: Coefficient of Variation is (SD/Mean) and SD = standard deviation. Per cent RNFE Percentage of main workers in RNFS to total main workers in rural areas. Per cent change in RNFS between 1981-91.

Sources: Census of India 1991 India Series-1, Provisional Population Totals: Workers and Their Distribution Paper-3 of 1991, pp. 443-448.

Census of India 1991 Andhra Pradesh Series-2, Paper-1 of 1991 Supplement Provisional Population Totals.

For rural AP as a whole there is a small increase in the share in RNFS during 1981-91 (Table 2). Even for males, there is a rise of 2.14 percentage points. Thus there are some trends of variations in rural de-industrialisation.

The central point is that during the period from 1980-81 to 1990-91 in the districts where the RNFS decreased, the per capita value of agricultural output is highly compared with the districts in which the RNFS has increased. This suggests distress diversification overall. One possible inference is that in the districts where RNFS decreased, agriculture was booming and successfully attracted workers out of the RNFS. This made them shift and become less poor, which could be encouraging.

Farm, RNFE shares and growth by district are shown in Tables 3, 4 and 5. Activities absorb varying proportions of workers across districts, and the annual change in the proportions involved in each sector points to a diversification of the rural economy during the decade. The expansion of sub-sectors of activities has resulted in wider opportunities in RNFE for both males and females. Yet, some districts seems to have performed better than others. In terms of growth rates, 12 of the 22 districts displayed increases for total share as well as for male RNFE share.

In the analysis of rural employment for total (males and females combined) employed population at the sectoral level, one can observe important changes in the growth rates between 1981 and 1991 for AP and India. Perhaps most striking is the difference for household industry. The proportion of those employed in this sector has grown by -3.27 per cent per year in AP compared with 0.44 per cent for India. Other sectors which have absorbed employment more rapidly in AP than in India are agricultural labour (roughly twice the rate of India) and by decreasing order mining and quarrying and transport. The other sectors have grown either more slowly in AP than in India or declined more rapidly.

Table 3: District-wise total share and growth rates in rural employment (farm and non-farm) activities (1981 and 1991

		Cultivators		*Agrl. Labour*		*Agrl. Allied Activities*		*HH Industry*		*Non-HH Industry*		*Mining & Quarrying*		*Construction*		*Trade*		*Transport*		*Services*	
District	*Growth of MW*	*%91*	*GR*	*%91*	*GR*	*%91*	*GR*	*%91*	*GR*	*%91*	*GR*	*%91*	*GR*	*%91*	*GR*	*%91*	*GR*	*%91*	*GR*	*%91*	*GR*
Srikakulam	1.69	35.19	-0.59	43.59	3.79	4.24	3.06	3.65	-1.04	1.50	-1.44	0.24	25.81	0.43	1.15	4.18	2.28	0.89	4.17	6.09	4.39
Vizianagaram	1.96	42.74	0.71	37.08	3.14	2.25	2.04	3.39	0.52	2.39	-1.06	0.30	6.55	0.52	4.66	4.29	3.39	1.05	4.82	6.00	6.04
Visakhapatnam	1.72	50.15	1.33	30.79	3.60	2.30	-1.13	3.13	-0.62	1.94	-3.88	0.45	8.12	0.70	-1.78	3.61	0.78	1.40	-1.51	5.53	3.35
East Godavari	1.52	17.81	-2.04	59.23	3.30	2.34	-4.54	3.30	-1.72	2.85	-1.05	0.13	15.48	0.49	0.30	5.05	1.39	1.26	1.54	7.54	5.29
West Godavari	2.11	17.30	-1.51	61.38	3.15	1.87	0.90	2.08	-2.15	3.20	1.86	0.20	27.39	0.52	1.61	4.58	4.31	1.44	4.34	7.42	4.73
Krishna	2.11	20.49	-0.34	61.05	3.25	2.20	1.37	2.04	-1.75	2.98	2.41	0.38	27.84	0.66	-0.07	3.65	3.12	1.74	2.26	4.81	1.49
Guntur	2.18	25.01	0.02	59.08	3.46	1.50	0.49	0.92	-7.37	2.67	-0.26	0.59	12.29	0.75	3.89	3.49	3.66	1.20	4.39	4.79	3.13
Prakasam	2.01	29.23	0.40	54.57	3.59	2.26	0.33	1.56	-5.95	2.26	-0.47	0.30	9.73	0.94	0.33	2.98	1.40	0.91	1.33	4.98	3.18
Nellore	1.51	25.01	-0.73	54.62	2.55	3.24	1.51	2.47	-3.13	2.14	1.77	0.43	5.26	1.15	1.96	3.71	5.40	1.26	3.45	5.96	3.13
Chittor	1.75	43.16	0.49	38.86	2.84	2.20	1.75	2.26	-1.41	2.54	0.74	0.47	23.68	0.75	0.59	3.34	4.64	1.21	5.92	5.21	4.96
Cuddapah	1.03	35.24	0.53	46.30	1.78	1.88	0.26	2.67	-4.22	2.12	-1.64	0.59	0.08	0.96	-0.23	3.22	1.86	1.14	3.22	5.89	2.67
Anantapur	2.16	41.61	1.12	43.34	3.12	1.83	-0.36	2.19	-0.89	1.88	2.76	0.17	8.10	0.95	6.91	2.68	2.58	0.71	4.49	4.64	4.98
Kurnool	2.27	29.30	1.74	56.03	2.83	0.86	-1.38	1.65	-2.47	1.47	-1.24	2.01	5.99	0.73	2.97	2.61	1.02	0.73	2.29	4.60	2.93

Table Contd.

Table 3: Contd.

Mahbubnagar	2.68	41.80	1.41	43.59	4.66	1.86	-1.75	1.77	-6.47	3.00	7.76	0.34	13.71	0.81	4.98	2.68	2.44	0.27	5.78	3.44	2.90
Ranga Reddy	1.38	38.32	1.07	40.52	3.23	2.43	-3.83	1.29	-10.83	4.45	1.13	1.68	19.19	1.28	-0.16	3.80	0.59	1.44	1.79	4.79	-0.85
Medak	2.53	43.41	1.41	38.82	4.10	1.42	-4.27	2.85	-3.1	5.08	8.67	0.54	43.53	0.60	4.04	2.76	3.26	0.66	3.73	3.88	2.62
Nizambad	1.88	37.96	0.50	34.09	3.05	1.42	-3.30	13.39	3.32	3.82	1.05	0.21	12.50	0.74	2.22	3.22	2.53	0.66	4.90	4.49	4.19
Adilabad	1.87	39.17	1.16	39.14	1.77	1.20	-3.73	5.11	1.76	3.70	5.24	3.42	8.63	0.55	2.48	2.43	2.91	0.53	5.79	4.74	4.59
Karimnagar	2.13	35.06	1.35	39.73	2.62	1.38	-6.96	7.05	0.32	6.30	9.90	1.22	9.19	0.87	-0.82	2.46	2.82	0.67	6.52	5.26	3.19
Warangal	2.52	36.55	1.60	46.83	4.05	1.03	-8.86	3.07	-3.32	3.63	8.42	0.46	33.51	0.87	2.16	2.28	1.91	0.81	2.53	4.47	2.55
Khammam	2.47	30.85	0.82	53.56	3.94	1.26	-2.35	1.87	-2.65	2.28	3.23	1.61	11.03	0.73	-5.73	2.67	3.06	1.83	4.99	4.34	2.32
Nalgonda	2.46	34.45	0.84	45.27	3.88	1.29	-7.29	5.49	1.71	3.50	7.28	0.33	46.96	1.24	2.93	3.34	3.39	1.20	9.33	3.88	3.10
AP	0.32	33.45	-1.37	47.51	1.24	1.89	-3.65	3.22	-3.27	3.00	0.69	0.67	3.61	0.78	-0.62	3.33	0.62	1.02	1.37	5.13	1.48
India	0.30	48.15	-0.56	32.17	0.67	1.96	-1.88	0.47	0.44	2.20	-3.28	3.60	0.49	1.04	0.19	3.26	1.57	1.23	1.12	5.92	2.27
Mean	2	34.08	0.51	46.7	3.26	1.92	-1.73	3.32	-2.34	3.03	2.33	0.73	17.03	0.78	1.56	3.32	2.67	1.02	3.91	5.13	3.4
SD	0.42	8.84	1.01	9.25	0.71	0.77	3.28	2.68	3.25	1.18	3.92	0.8	12.56	0.23	2.67	0.75	1.24	0.33	2.24	1.04	1.48
CV	0.21	0.26	1.97	0.2	0.22	0.4	-1.9	0.81	-1.39	0.39	1.69	1.1	0.74	0.3	1.71	0.22	0.47	0.32	0.57	0.2	0.43

Notes: MW = Main workers men+women. %: Percentage of all Rural main workers in 1991. GR: Average Annual Percentage Growth Rates of the proportion between 1981 and 1991.

CV: Coefficient of Variation (= Standard Deviation/Mean); SD = standard deviation.

Sources: Census of India (1991) Series -1, final population total paper 2 of 1992 p. 155.

Census of India 1991 India Series-1, Provisional Population Totals: Workers and their Distribution, paper 3 of 1991 pp. 443-448.

Table 4: District-wise male share and growth rates in rural employment (farm and non farm) activities between 1981 and 1991

District	Growth of MW	Cultivators		Agrl. Labour		Agrl. Allied Activities		HH Industry		Non-HH Industry		Mining & Quarrying		Construction		Trade		Transport		Services	
		%91	GR	%91	GR	%91	GR	%91	GR	%91	GR	91	GR	%91	GR	%91	GR	%91	GR	%91	GR
Srikakulam	1.18	38.14	-1.00	35.26	3.61	5.84	2.19	3.56	-2.24	2.06	-0.91	0.27	21.95	0.66	1.15	5.05	2.19	1.42	4.25	7.74	4.40
Vizianagaram	1.33	44.78	0.00	29.18	2.64	3.25	1.81	3.77	-0.76	3.50	-1.01	0.34	7.07	0.78	5.03	5.23	3.64	1.66	4.69	7.50	5.67
Visakhapatnam	0.95	50.62	0.19	25.79	3.83	3.23	-1.11	3.20	-1.38	2.54	-4.19	0.52	7.92	0.95	-1.28	4.13	1.29	2.16	-1.48	6.87	3.31
East Godavari	1.42	21.18	-2.15	53.27	3.92	3.00	-4.57	3.02	-2.79	3.41	-0.80	0.13	13.59	0.62	-0.07	5.83	1.31	1.66	1.57	7.89	5.59
West Godavari	1.82	23.50	-1.49	51.58	3.42	2.41	0.29	1.82	-4.02	4.06	1.88	0.21	22.79	0.74	1.45	5.66	3.99	2.10	4.26	7.92	4.80
Krishna	1.37	28.31	-0.83	48.26	2.77	3.03	1.06	2.12	-2.86	4.20	2.66	0.41	26.11	0.96	0.73	4.56	3.18	2.70	2.25	5.43	1.75
Guntur	1.42	32.15	-0.75	46.29	3.14	2.05	-0.39	0.98	-9.04	3.85	0.73	0.68	12.99	1.22	3.97	4.69	3.54	2.00	4.38	6.07	3.48
Prakasam	1.27	35.87	-0.37	41.91	3.32	3.23	0.04	1.77	-7.10	3.16	0.88	0.32	10.55	1.50	1.03	4.14	1.69	1.52	1.32	6.58	3.66
Nellore	1.02	31.93	-1.07	42.81	2.34	4.41	1.48	2.62	-4.14	2.86	1.90	0.40	4.14	1.73	2.65	4.26	5.38	1.94	3.39	7.04	3.19
Chittor	1.21	46.50	-0.23	31.29	2.70	2.27	0.55	2.50	-2.18	3.43	0.60	0.59	22.97	1.04	1.30	4.08	4.40	1.83	5.94	6.47	5.04
Cuddapah	0.78	42.49	0.18	35.07	1.79	2.21	-0.71	2.78	-4.31	2.82	-1.22	0.70	1.09	1.31	-0.69	4.03	2.45	1.68	3.25	6.91	2.99
Ananatapur	1.75	48.53	0.69	31.79	3.12	2.64	-0.21	2.55	-1.31	2.61	2.58	0.23	10.15	1.33	6.47	3.50	3.00	1.12	4.58	5.72	4.66

Table Contd.

Table 4: Contd.

Kurnool	1.84	37.05	1.08	43.52	2.79	1.21	-2.10	1.80	-3.33	2.10	-0.85	2.30	6.59	1.14	2.66	3.70	1.38	1.24	2.27	5.93	2.97
Mahbubnagar	1.83	50.76	0.73	29.61	4.70	2.98	-2.04	1.79	-7.94	3.49	7.17	0.45	13.90	1.21	4.46	3.85	2.44	1.26	5.79	4.59	3.12
Ranga Reddy	0.75	42.98	0.64	28.28	3.31	3.43	-4.60	1.49	-11.44	6.33	1.50	1.87	20.03	1.84	-0.32	5.31	0.74	2.39	1.76	6.07	-1.33
Medak	1.55	48.98	0.41	29.13	4.09	2.20	-4.95	2.26	-6.44	5.57	7.51	0.62	39.28	0.85	2.65	4.13	3.16	1.12	3.58	5.13	2.53
Nizamabad	1.25	44.42	0.01	30.20	3.51	2.55	-3.36	4.40	-0.67	3.99	0.44	0.24	11.14	1.11	1.32	5.55	2.65	1.23	4.95	6.31	3.64
Adilabad	1.22	45.34	0.55	29.98	1.25	1.90	-3.97	2.92	-1.89	2.86	1.02	5.58	8.52	0.76	1.67	3.60	3.01	0.88	5.79	6.18	4.71
Karimnagar	1.31	41.00	0.74	30.27	2.06	2.34	-7.07	4.49	-3.88	7.14	8.94	1.85	7.86	1.35	-0.44	3.75	3.37	1.20	6.50	6.60	3.12
Warrangal	1.33	44.15	0.50	33.09	3.10	1.60	-9.23	3.64	-4.37	5.42	9.34	0.61	33.19	1.28	2.52	3.20	2.09	1.36	2.47	5.64	2.58
Khammam	1.75	39.17	0.17	40.01	3.75	1.64	-3.45	2.31	2.99	3.35	3.44	2.39	10.71	1.04	-4.67	3.47	2.89	1.31	5.02	5.31	2.65
Nalgonda	1.48	42.29	-0.01	31.17	2.91	1.77	-7.79	6.43	10.10	5.13	7.70	0.40	43.11	1.62	2.55	4.27	4.02	1.99	9.33	4.93	3.82
A.P	-0.35	39.08	-1.42	37.33	1.73	2.66	-3.50	2.80	4.68	3.81	1.09	0.84	9.15	1.12	0.09	4.39	1.37	1.64	2.04	6.33	2.04
India	-0.14	51.40	-0.70	26.35	0.94	2.08	-1.94	1.96	-3.74	4.03	0.54	0.53	0.79	1.30	1.06	3.99	2.01	1.62	1.54	6.74	2.43
Mean	1.36	40.01	-0.09	36.26	3.06	2.69	-2.19	2.83	-3.82	3.81	2.24	0.96	16.18	1.14	1.55	4.36	2.81	1.63	3.90	6.31	3.47
SD	0.32	8.32	0.82	8.23	0.82	1.02	3.22	1.22	2.99	1.35	3.68	1.24	11.29	0.34	2.38	0.77	1.14	0.47	2.24	0.95	1.49
CV	0.23	0.21	-9.00	0.23	0.27	0.38	-1.47	0.43	0.78	0.35	1.64	1.29	0.70	0.30	1.54	0.18	0.41	0.29	0.57	0.15	0.43

Notes and **Sources:** As previously.

Table 5: District-wise female share and growth rates in rural employment (farm and non-farm) activities between 1981 and 1991

		Cultivators		Agrl. Labour		Agrl. Allied Activities		HH Industry		Non-HH Industry		Mining & Quarrying		Construction		Trade		Transport		Services	
District	Growth of MW	%91	GR	%91	GR	%91	GR	%91	GR	%91	GR	91	GR	%91	GR	%91	GR	%91	GR	%91	GR
Srikakulam	2.57	30.44	0.31	57.02	3.96	1.65	10.52	3.79	1.14	0.60	-3.91	0.19	50.71	0.07	1.07	2.77	2.56	0.03	-0.81	3.43	4.34
Vizianagaram	3.09	39.44	2.17	49.91	3.63	0.63	4.23	2.74	4.23	0.58	-1.45	0.23	5.40	0.11	1.18	2.75	2.65	0.05	15.64	3.56	7.46
Visakhapatnam	3.25	49.3	3.83	39.62	3.35	0.65	-1.30	3.01	1.01	0.88	-2.10	0.33	8.76	0.25	-4.48	2.71	-0.45	0.05	-3.37	3.19	3.52
East Godavari	1.82	7.90	-1.10	76.79	2.15	0.40	-3.88	4.12	1.14	1.20	-2.89	0.15	22.90	0.12	9.71	2.75	1.87	0.06	-0.88	6.51	4.31
West Godavari	2.72	4.36	-1.72	81.85	2.81	0.75	6.60	2.62	1.53	1.41	1.75	0.19	0.00	0.05	8.92	2.33	6.17	0.07	11.94	6.37	4.56
Krishna	3.56	6.80	4.29	83.44	3.76	0.74	4.05	1.90	0.96	0.85	0.54	0.33	32.87	0.14	-6.45	2.04	2.86	0.06	3.35	3.71	0.85
Guntur	3.40	14.61	3.02	77.67	3.73	0.69	3.72	0.84	-3.43	0.95	-4.57	0.46	19.16	0.07	2.18	1.74	4.15	0.04	5.56	2.93	2.13
Prakasam	3.19	19.74	2.78	72.66	3.81	0.87	2.04	1.26	-3.01	0.98	4.93	0.28	8.53	0.14	-6.43	1.34	0.21	0.04	1.87	2.70	1.69
Nellore	2.45	12.92	0.93	75.25	2.76	1.22	1.70	2.21	-0.57	0.89	1.04	0.48	7.20	0.14	-6.49	2.76	5.43	0.07	7.84	4.07	2.95
Chittor	2.86	36.89	2.45	53.10	3.00	2.06	4.87	1.81	0.93	0.87	1.87	0.23	22.96	0.19	-4.60	1.95	5.66	0.04	4.51	2.84	4.60

Table Contd.

Table 5: Contd.

Cuddapah	1.56	20.42	2.14	69.25	1.78	1.21	5.15	2.43	-3.99	0.69	-4.54	0.37	-3.01	0.25	7.25	1.54	-0.75	0.05	1.28	3.80	1.57
Ananthapur	2.87	30.17	2.36	62.47	3.13	0.49	-1.57	1.58	0.33	0.68	4.01	0.08	2.09	0.32	10.55	1.33	0.98	0.03	-0.33	2.85	6.13
Kurnool	2.93	18.39	3.92	73.65	2.86	0.37	3.03	1.44	-0.73	0.59	-3.01	1.61	4.89	0.13	7.83	1.07	-0.55	0.02	3.38	2.73	2.81
Mahbubnagar	3.93	30.15	3.11	61.77	4.64	0.40	1.61	1.73	-3.99	2.35	9.01	0.19	13.15	0.29	8.49	1.16	2.44	0.03	5.32	1.94	2.25
Ranga Reddy	2.37	31.65	1.96	58.05	3.17	1.00	1.37	0.99	-9.35	1.75	0.59	1.40	17.30	0.48	0.79	1.65	-0.05	0.09	3.35	2.95	0.72
Medak	4.08	35.76	3.67	52.13	4.10	0.34	6.46	3.65	1.21	4.40	11.08	0.42	62.67	0.25	16.35	0.86	3.91	0.03	17.19	2.16	2.91
Nizamabad	2.66	30.58	1.37	38.54	2.65	0.13	-1.84	23.68	4.45	3.62	1.88	0.18	15.09	0.31	7.13	0.56	1.27	0.01	0.77	2.40	6.09
Adilabad	2.93	29.99	2.73	52.75	2.24	0.16	2.10	8.36	4.43	4.97	11.40	0.22	14.38	0.24	7.46	0.69	2.17	0.02	6.29	2.61	4.18
Karimnagar	3.26	27.76	2.56	51.37	3.05	0.19	-5.21	10.18	3.81	5.26	11.76	0.45	21.71	0.28	-2.77	0.86	0.33	0.03	7.18	3.62	3.36
Warangal	4.48	25.95	4.87	65.97	4.78	0.24	-4.40	2.27	-0.40	1.12	3.80	0.26	34.63	0.30	0.22	1.00	0.45	0.03	7.58	2.85	2.46
Khammam	3.79	17.33	3.73	75.59	4.12	0.64	4.69	1.16	-1.41	0.55	1.40	0.34	15.58	0.22	-11.13	1.35	3.80	0.04	3.54	2.77	1.37
Nalgonda	4.12	22.81	3.71	66.17	4.62	0.58	-4.58	4.09	3.29	1.09	4.78	0.23	71.49	0.69	4.36	1.97	1.61	0.04	9.04	2.33	1.15
AP	1.47	24.55	-0.46	63.23	0.19	0.67	-0.85	4.44	-1.26	1.71	0.54	0.38	8.38	0.23	-2.29	1.63	-0.93	0.04	0.00	3.21	0.03
India	1.54	38.58	0.44	48.83	-0.31	2.14	1.47	2.90	-2.64	2.30	0.87	0.28	-0.69	0.27	-7.04	1.08	-0.27	0.08	-3.13	3.53	2.02
Mean	3.09	24.70	2.41	63.41	3.55	0.70	1.79	3.90	-0.07	1.65	1.65	0.39	20.38	0.23	2.32	1.69	2.12	0.04	5.01	3.29	3.25
SD	0.73	11.35	1.65	13.06	0.83	0.49	4.15	4.97	3.34	1.49	5.28	0.38	19.58	0.15	7.07	0.74	2.07	0.02	5.19	1.16	1.82
CV	0.24	0.46	0.69	0.21	0.25	0.70	2.32	1.27	46.58	0.90	3.19	0.96	0.96	0.64	3.04	0.44	0.97	0.45	1.04	0.35	0.56

Services and in particular trade (both are tertiary activities) have grown more slowly. The proportion involved in construction has declined over the period in AP whilst it has increased in India (-0.62 per cent compared to 0.19 per cent). In terms of decline, the proportion involved with agricultural allied activities has declined relatively substantially (a 3.65 per cent annual fall in AP compared with a 1.88 per cent fall for India). The shift away from cultivators has been more pronounced in AP. For non-HH industry the decrease occurred in AP and India by an almost similar magnitude. One can thus say that relatively, the involvement with the tertiary sector is different in AP than when compared with India. Moreover in terms of shares, one can say that cultivators and agricultural allied activities have experienced relatively more important declines in AP, compared with India, within these categories. Another sector whose performance would have been outstanding and distinct is the HHI.

The district-wise share and growth rates of rural employment (farm and non-farm) between 1981 and 1991 are also presented in the following tables. The difference in shares of males only among the districts grew between 1981 and 1991. The biggest group of workers in 1991 was agricultural laborers but the sector which expanded most was mining and quarrying. As we have already seen, most sectors have expanded in AP during the decade with the exception of agricultural and allied activities and the HH industry. The districts in which agricultural and allied activities have declined the most are Warangal, Nalgonda, Karimnagar and East Godavari. These districts have not faced a decline of similar magnitude in HH industry. The biggest decline in this sector, albeit from a small base, was in Range Reddy.

For total RNFE, the largest variation in share across districts is for the HH industry (CV = 0.81) in 1991. Differences across districts can also be observed in growth rates for the agricultural and allied sector (a difference of 11 per cent points change between Warangal and Srikakulam). The most pronounced uniformity (i.e. lowest sub-sector CV among districts) in terms of growth rate between 1981-91 is for agricultural labour. The proportion of workers involved as agricultural labourers has increased by a similar proportion across the districts. Besides the district-wide increase of the numbers of workers as agricultural labourers and mining and quarrying, trade has grown throughout AP, with the exception of Visakhapatnam for transport and Ranga Reddy for the service sector, since they are some of the most urbanised districts.

District wise male share and growth rates in rural employment (farm and non-farm) activities between 1981 and 1991, are presented in Table 3, shows that mining and quarrying have most widely differing figures for both shares across districts in 1991 (CV = 1.29).

For males rural (farm and non-farm) breakdown, some changes are worth noting. The proportion of males involved with the HH industry has in fact declined for AP and India, although more for AP (-4.68 per cent per year compared with -3.74 per cent for India). On the other hand a shift might have occurred towards the non-HH industry sector where the signs are the opposite of those of the HHI (non-HHI for males increased by 1.09 per cent for AP and 0.54 per cent for India). Another sector which has expanded towards male employment between 1981 and 1991 has been mining and quarrying. The proportion of the shift in AP has been very pronounced for males compared with India (9.15 per cent compared to 0.79 per cent). On the other hand, the performance of agricultural allied activities for males is similar to that observed for totals, suggesting that what has happened to this sector has had relatively little effect for females (in fact confirmed by looking at Table 5). For the tertiary sector, the proportion of males has increased in AP but by less than India, with the exception of transport which has absorbed males increasing more rapidly in AP than in India. There thus appears to be some relatively important sectoral gender differences over the period which are specific to AP for HH industry (a female sector) and transport and mining and quarrying (a male sector).

Unlike for males, the number of female main workers has increased during 1981-91 for both AP and India, although by slightly less in AP. Similarly to males, the shares of female cultivators and in agricultural and allied activities have resulted in a decrease in AP. Also similarly to males, the growth rate in agricultural labour is positive for females in AP. Yet the extent of all of these changes is much less pronounced for females than for males. This is contrasted with the pattern of positive growth in India for females for cultivators and agricultural allied activities. Contrasts with that is of the males in India, where it has been negative. The share of agricultural labour increased for males in India but decreased for females. The increase for males and females in the agricultural labour sector does not outweigh the decline in the other agricultural sectors. It is thus likely that employment has been found elsewhere.

Mining and quarrying is the sector with the highest growth for females in AP and in fact it is the only sector that would have absorbed females significantly. In AP, the tertiary sector such as trade, transport and services has declined or remain almost stagnant for females. The only naticeable sector of marginal experience has been non-HHI (which experienced 0.54 per cent annual income). Household industry and construction have declined by over 1 per cent per year in AP. The observation for AP contrasts somewhat with the overall India pattern as mining and quarrying decline and services increase.

In terms of the sector to decline for females, AP has performed better than India for HHI, construction and transport. In terms of the expanding sectors AP has done worse than India for non-HHI and services. Finally it remains that in 1991 there were relatively few differences in the share between AP and India for construction, trade, transport and services. For mining and quarrying AP had 1.35 times the proportion of India but for the non-HHI it had only ¾ of the proportion that India had. The key sector for female employment would appear to have been HHI in which 4.44 per cent of females RNFE were concentrated. This was 1.5 times higher than in India in 1991. Within agricultural activities females are predominately engaged as agricultural labour (1.3 times India's proportions).

There is a positive growth rate for agricultural labour in districts. The majority of districts experienced negative growth rates in agricultural and allied activities.

Table 6 separates the AP districts according to the extent of the changes between 1981 and 1991 in the proportion of RNFE to total workers. These changes are also summarised for all workers (male plus female). Whilst there is a broad similarity in the changes in RNFS proportions for the total as well as for males and females, there are some exceptions for female and male workers. Twelve districts show positive growth in the share of RNFS in total workers ranging from a minimum of 0.18 per cent to 4.15 per cent. Similarly there were ten districts showing declines ranging from 0.38 per cent to 3.56 per cent. The largest falls for the total occurred in the districts of Ranga Reddy and Visakhapatnam. On the other hand Adilabad, in contrast experienced a big rise. The majority of the districts have experienced small changes (rise or decline); a smaller number of districts exhibited a medium rise or fall: Ranga Reddy, Visakhapatnam and Adilabad districts for total and for females, although when females are considered, the district of Nizamabad needs to be added.

The grouping shows a heavy decline for the two districts of Ranga Reddy of Visakhapatnam. A location effect, namely nearness to an urban industrial growth centre, might have caused this. On the other hand, Adilabad has distinct agro-climatic endowments. The district also has a large forest area

Table 6: District breakdown by changes in the proportion of RNFE to total workers, AP, 1981-1991

Big falls in RNFS	*Big rise in RNFS*	*Medium fall in RNFS*	*Medium rise in*	*Small changes*
(> 2.44 percentage points)	(> 2.44 percentage points)	1 to 2.44 percentage points)		(↑↓ <1 percentage points)
		For total RNFS workers		
Ranga Reddy Visakhapatnam	Adilabad Nizamabad Karimnagar	Prakasam Cuddapah Mahbubnagar Anantapur Kurnool	Chittor West-Godavari Vizianagaram Nalgonda	Srikakulam Nellore Krishna Medak Warangal East-Godavari Guntur Khammam
		For male workers		
	Adilabad Medak Krishna Karimnagar Guntur Nalgonda Vizianagaram Nellore Anantapur Chittor West-Godavari		Prakasam Srikakulam Warangal Khammam Kurnool Mahbubnag East-Godavari	Ranga Reddy Cuddapah Nizambad Visakhapatnam
		For female workers		
Prakasam Warangal Ranga Reddy Cuddapah Visakhapatnam	Adilabad Karimnagar Nizamabad	Khammam Mahbubnagar Krishna Kurnool Nalgonda Guntur	Vizianagaram Medak West-Godavari	Anantapur Chittor Nellore Srikakulam East-Godavari

Source: Based on Table 2.

(over 7 lakh hectares farming 43.6 per cent of the total geographical area) which is an important source of income to the state. The forest also provides building materials for some industries and is a major supplier of firewood. The bamboo forests are located in industrial complexes in Sirpur

Kagaj Nagar and provide employment to the household industry outside the farm sector. The Sirpur paper mills, the silk factories, the Bellampally chemical and fertiliser factory and the cement factory in Mancherial, are important large scale industries in the state. The district is rich is resources (particularly forests and minerals) as well as possessing a vast potential for agriculture along with the potential for the development of related industries. All those conditions worked favourably towards the growth of the RNFS in the rural Adilabad district[4]. For total RNFE the CV suggests that there are increasing disparities across the state, whereas for males the CV shows that disparities are being reduced and a more uniform/homogeneous pattern is appearing. On the other hand for females there is a marked increase in dispersion.

Table 7 shows district-wise shares in rural farm and non-farm traditional and modern, there is a little difference between AP and India; the proportion of males in rural farm employment and that of females is a little bit lower in AP compared with India (79.07 per cent) compared with 79.83 per cent and 88.89 per cent and 89.55 per cent respectively.

For total, the ratio for 1991 is reversed but again is small (82.85 per cent in AP compared to 82.28 per cent in India) differences are more pronounced in relation to the performance of the predominantly traditional and modern sectors. The biggest change happened for the modern sector where the

4. Deccan Chronicle Survey on Wednesday the 19th April 2000 revealed that the villages in Mahabubnagar districts employ youth who are migrating to urban areas for work. Drought relief is also provided by the AP state government. There is hardly any agricultural work going on the villages, except in a few pockets where groundnut are being harvested. Vast stretches of dried-up fields lie fallow everywhere. As a result of lack of adequate and continuous power supply whatever crop was required in certain areas is almost lost. The voltage is too low to draw water from deep bore wells and cannot water the crop. It is difficult to strike water in the bore well even at 200 feet. Severe drought cause the younger people to move away from Mahabubnagar.

Table 7: District-wise shares and growth rates (GR) in rural employment (farm and non-farm traditional and modern) activities (1981 and 1991)

District	*Cultiva. Agrl. Labour Agrl. Allied (total for 1991) %*	*1981 to 1991 GR (% per year)*	*Tradi-tion (total 1991 (%)*	*1981 to 1991 GR (% per year)*	*Mod-ern 1991 (total)*	*1981 to 1991 GR (% per year)*	*Cultiva. Agri. labour Agri. Allied (males for 1991) %*	*1981 to 1991 GR (% per year)*	*Tradi-tional 1991 (male)*	*1981 to 1991 GR (% per year)*	*Mod-ern 1991 (male)*	*1981 to 1991 GR (% per year)*	*Cultiva. Agri. Allied 1991 (female)*	*1981 to 1991 GR (% per year)*	*Tradi-tional 1991 (female)*	*1981 to 1991 GR (% per year)*	*Mod-ern 1991 (female)*	*GR*
Srikakulam	83.02	-0.04	9.74	0.28	7.24	0.08	79.24	-0.15	11.74	0.95	9.46	0.67	89.11	0.05	7.22	-0.04	3.66	-1.03
Vizianagaram	82.07	-0.20	9.39	1.69	8.55	0.25	77.21	-0.34	11.5	1.84	11.51	0.88	89.98	-0.12	6.3	2.74	3.72	-1.02
Visakhaptnam	83.24	0.30	8.66	-0.01	8.1	-2.59	79.64	0.20	10.87	1.37	10.3	-1.90	89.59	0.30	6.2	-0.99	4.22	-3.81
East Godavari	79.38	-0.02	10.84	1.01	9.78	-0.85	77.45	-0.02	11.89	1.86	11.65	-0.73	85.09	-0.07	10.63	1.11	4.28	-1.16
West Godavari	80.55	-0.22	9.5	0.61	9.94	1.35	77.49	-0.28	11.92	2.59	12.77	1.43	86.96	-0.17	8.99	0.83	4.05	2.13
Krishna	83.74	0.07	6.85	-1.67	9.41	0.70	79.6	-0.10	9.43	1.07	12.83	1.49	90.98	0.23	5.61	-2.57	3.42	-1.05
Guntur	85.59	0.08	5.71	-1.78	8.7	0.52	80.49	-0.12	10.07	2.48	12.44	1.59	92.97	0.21	3.77	-2.73	3.26	-1.93
Prakasam	86.06	0.27	6.54	-1.96	7.39	-1.14	81.01	0.10	10.58	1.18	10.64	0.20	93.27	0.37	3.96	-3.16	2.78	-4.91
Nellore	82.87	-0.12	8.43	-0.70	8.69	2.07	79.15	-0.25	11.04	0.87	11.19	2.53	89.39	0.004	6.28	-0.87	4.34	1.34
Chittor	84.22	-0.21	7.47	0.77	8.31	1.66	80.06	-0.37	10.47	2.75	10.97	2.10	92.05	-0.05	4.65	0.13	3.28	1.13

Table Contd.

Table 7: Contd.

Cuddapah	83.42	0.17	8.56	-1.10	8.03	-0.44	79.77	0.05	10.91	0.65	10.54	0.15	90.88	0.33	6.23	-2.55	2.9	-3.14
Anantapur	86.78	-0.13	6.83	0.51	6.39	1.33	82.96	-0.23	9.72	2.26	8.79	1.89	93.13	-0.03	4.43	0.73	2.44	-0.24
Kurnool	86.19	0.12	6.25	-1.10	7.55	-0.40	81.78	0.05	9.93	1.76	10.48	0.15	92.41	0.14	4.17	-1.46	3.42	-1.58
Mahbubnagar	87.25	0.12	5.21	-4.03	7.55	2.48	83.35	-0.002	8.59	-0.42	10.26	2.94	92.32	0.17	3.67	-4.95	4.02	2.63
Ranga Reddy	81.27	0.48	6.08	-5.43	12.65	0.64	74.69	0.45	10.07	-2.45	17.74	1.21	90.7	0.33	3.94	-5.34	5.37	-0.13
Medak	83.65	-0.11	6.73	-2.72	9.64	3.49	80.31	-0.19	9.13	-0.70	12.29	3.89	88.23	-0.14	5.81	-2.19	5.96	6.22
Nizamabad	73.47	-0.38	17.88	1.62	8.65	0.25	77.17	-0.17	10.31	-0.02	12.12	0.78	69.25	-0.60	26.08	1.88	4.68	-0.29
Adilabad	79.51	-0.50	9.85	1.11	10.63	3.48	77.22	-0.55	10.18	1.94	13.68	3.17	82.9	-0.51	10.97	1.41	6.14	6.57
Karimnagar	76.17	-0.40	12.31	-0.68	11.52	4.30	73.61	-0.45	10.6	-2.12	15.29	4.50	79.32	-0.40	13.8	0.42	6.88	5.16
Warangal	84.41	0.08	7.54	-2.76	8.05	2.61	78.84	-0.22	9.64	-1.74	11.87	4.16	92.16	0.27	5.12	-3.26	2.71	-1.56
Khammam	85.67	0.10	6.21	-1.91	9.12	1.73	80.82	-0.08	9.31	0.82	11.56	1.54	93.56	0.24	3.93	-3.20	2.5	-2.56
Nalgonda	81.01	-0.28	9.37	-0.19	9.61	3.09	75.23	-0.71	8.93	-1.70	13.41	4.57	89.56	0.15	6.42	-1.61	4.02	-0.53
AP	82.85	-0.04	8.35	-0.66	8.8	-1.32	79.07	-0.16	9.13	-0.03	11.80	1.62	88.89	0.05	7.12	-0.70	3.99	0.25
India	82.28	-0.14	9.6	2.10	8.12	1.03	79.83	-0.23	8.70	0.63	11.47	1.24	89.55	0.05	6.43	-0.38	4.02	-0.41

Notes and **Sources:** An in the previous Table.

increase has been in excess of 1 per cent per year over the period; AP has done better than India for males (1.62 per cent compared to 1.24 per cent). In contrast, the situation for females in the modern sector remained stable and even declined in India. The modern sector accounted for about 11.5 per cent for males compared with about 4 per cent for females. The performance in the traditional sector has not been very good for either males of females in AP. Both witnessed declines although the extent of the change has been more pronounced for females. The traditional sector accounted for 9 per cent of employment for males and about 7 per cent for females in AP standing slightly above the India average, which is in fact caused by a very pronounced dispersion for females.

Table 7 represents shares and growth rates of the traditional and modern RNFS. In relation to agriculture-related employment (cultivators, agricultural labour and agricultural allied activities), there are some differences across gender. In total, Mahabubnagar has the largest portion of workers involved in agriculture whilst Karimnagar has the lowest. For males also, these two extreme districts represents the same highest and lowest figures. For females, Karimnagar is again low whilst Khammam has the highest share of female workers in agriculture. Karimnagar thus has the highest proportion of workers for both sexes involved with non-farm activities. This district is also of high agricultural and infrastructural development and is part of a newly irrigated district.

In relation to changes in the proportion of main workers involved with the agricultural sector, a decline has occurred in more than half of the districts (in 12 for total, in 17 for males) with the exception of females. The average annual declines, where they have happened are, however, relatively small (0.5 per cent in Karimnagar for totals, 0.55 per cent for males and females in Adilabad). Again, Adilabad is the district which has witnessed the fastest increase in RNFE for both sexes.

Turning to the traditional and modern breakdown of district non-farm employment, recalling here that we have taken a somewhat arbitrary decision in the separation of the 2 sectors, males dominate both sector. We have equated predominantly traditional RNFE with HHI and other services and predominantly modern RNFE with mining and quarrying, non-HHI, construction, trade and transport. AP out performs India for share of total labour force in modern RNFE. The same pattern occurs for males. In contrast, in AP a smaller share of total workers is involved with traditional non-farm activities than in all-India, but the pattern is reversed for males, (9.1 per cent in AP compared to 8.7 per cent for India). For totals, Nizamabad has the greatest proportion of non-farm workers involved with the traditional sector, while Ranga Reddy has the highest proportion of non-farm workers in the modern sector. The fact that 26.08 per cent of females are involved in Nizamabad in the traditional sector helps to explain the high total share of traditional overall in that district. The district with the highest share of female workers in the modern sector is Karimnagar, (6.9 per cent) although the figure is far behind that of males (15.3) per cent).

The average annual changes in modern sector RNFE have been important for both males and females (4.5 per cent and 5.2 per cent respectively per year over the decade). AP is the State where the rate of total modern RNFE growth has been the highest. The most pronounced increase in the modern sector for females has been Medak (almost twice the increase of males). Acute declines have occurred for females in the modern sector in Visakhapatnam and for males in Ranga Reddy. There are important differences between males and females in their employment in the modern sector. As many as 15 districts have witnessed a decline in the number of females involved in the modern sector and in 11 districts there have been declines in both the modern and traditional sectors simultaneously. We see later that the female RNFE is linked to an increase in female agricultural employment. The pattern is more consistent

Table 8: Changes in RNFS employment, in urban growth, in poverty and per capita value of agricultural output across as districts between 1981 and 1991

Districts	*% RNFE 1981*	*% RNFE 1991*	*Pattern of Change (Percentage points)*	*% of urban Population 1981*	*% of urban Population 1991*	*Difference of urban Population (percentage points)*	*Decadal Growth rate of urban Population*	*% of persons below poverty line 1977-78*	*% of persons below poverty line 1987-88*	*Difference (percention points)*	*Per capita value of Agricultural Output 1987-88*	*Per capita value of Agricultural 1991(1981) constant prices)*	*Difference (rupes)*
RNFS decrease													
Ranga Reddy	22.51	18.95	-3.56	24.29	47.12	22.83	209.19	74.03	32.25	41.78	614.81	817.24	202.43
Visakhapatnam	19.21	16.72	-2.49	31.28	39.76	8.48	61.70	70.28	35.32	34.96	742.14	828.95	86.81
Prakasam	16.25	14.09	-2.16	14.99	16.45	1.46	29.66	58.56	44.14	14.42	1168.7	1238.95	70.24
Cuddapah	17.96	16.52	-1.44	19.40	24.00	4.6	45.11	54.21	24.20	30.01	697.40	1108.92	411.52
Kurnool	14.8	14.06	-0.77	24.49	25.85	1.36	30.12	74.42	38.74	35.68	1026.45	1350.15	323.7
Warangal	16.25	15.69	-0.56	17.24	19.40	2.16	37.66	76.12	56.57	19.55	661.15	888.01	226.86
Khammam	15.22	14.68	-0.54	16.98	20.19	3.21	50.44	42.12	34.97	7.15	739.37	1133.53	394.16
Guntur	15.09	14.63	-0.46	27.53	28.93	1.4	25.51	45.72	37.73	7.99	1398.75	1891.83	493.08
Krishna	16.88	16.46	-0.42	32.54	35.83	3.29	33.45	46.95	27.68	19.27	1412.12	1483.26	71.14
Mahabubnagar	13.76	13.38	-0.38	10.93	11.11	0.18	27.79	73.14	80.08	-6.94	708.52	825.82	117.3
Average	16.80	15.52	-1.28	21.97	26.86	4.83	55.06	66.56	41.17	20.39	916.94	1156.67	239.72

Table Contd.

Table 8: Contd.

RNFS increase													
Adilabad	16.3	20.5	4.15	19.32	23.14	3.82	51.80	82.15	49.14	33.01	586.41	605.33	18.89
Karimnagar	20.73	24.04	3.31	15.79	20.59	4.8	62.19	82.55	59.43	23.12	739.37	1133.53	394.16
Nizamabad	23.68	26.79	3.11	19.21	20.27	1.06	27.93	51.89	38.75	13.14	1040.88	1012.45	-28.43
Nalgonda	16.65	91.11	2.46	11.38	11.87	0.49	30.26	30.29	9.34	30.05	600.44	1733.49	1133.05
West Godavari	17.64	19.5	1.86	20.77	20.83	0.04	22.78	54.35	11.29	43.06	1701.61	1321.35	-380.26
Vizianagaram	16.3	18.11	1.81	15.94	17.20	1.26	25.90	-	51.52	-	742.14	828.95	86.81
Chittor	13.97	15.65	1.68	16.88	19.82	2.94	39.62	63.59	51.14	12.45	802.17	1103.44	301.27
Medak	15.4	16.76	1.36	11.97	14.50	2.33	51.49	77.54	41.39	36.15	658.92	726.26	67.34
Anantapur	12.1	13.28	1.18	20.81	23.51	2.7	40.81	77.84	74.51	3.33	866.76	1126.58	259.82
Nellore	16.12	17.32	1.20	20.76	23.81	6.05	35.95	60.66	60.05	0.61	873.66	1201.77	328.11
East Godavari	20.43	20.67	0.24	22.21	83.85	1.64	31.77	56.75	16.50	40.25	1114.09	1014.38	-99.71
Srikakulam	16.66	16.84	0.18	10.89	12.51	1.62	35.70	77.33	59.36	17.97	646.48	712.96	66.48
Average	17.17	19.05	1.88	17.16	19.33	2.17	38.02	66.81	43.54	21.10	864.41	1043.32	178.91
AP	16.8	17.1	0.3	23.32	26.84	3.52	42.69	63.54	40.78	22.76	N.A	N.A	N.A

Notes: Per cent RNFS means Percentage of main workers in rural non-farm sector to total main workers in rural areas.-'Pattern of change' means percentage change in RNFS between 1981-1991.

Sources: Census of India 1991, Andhra Pradesh, Population Totals, Series-2, pp. 10, 66-73-Sudhakar Reddy (1991) 'Poverty and Agricultural growth in Rural Andhra Pradesh Inter District Analysis', CESS, Hyderabad.

in the traditional sector where the decline in RNFE has been important for males, females and total.

Table 8 separates the districts into 2 categories; those that have experienced an increase in the RNFS from those that have experienced a decrease. We are looking for some characteristics that can be easily identified to account for the RNFS performance. Neither the affluence nor the poverty of a district appears to be associated at the bivariate level with the share of non-farm employment within rural areas (through an examination of scatter plots and correlation matrices which is not reported in the paper). As a first step towards multivariate analysis we plotted the RNFE share against irrigation as a proxy for agricultural development and poverty as well as urbanisation.

The highest percentage decline in RNFE is seen in those districts in which urban population has grown very fast, namely Visakhapatnam and Ranga Reddy. This may be due to the fact that there has been rural migration to urban areas as a result of a decline in traditional industries, or maybe it is a means of accessing urban employment. It was observed in the scatter plot of RNFE and growth of urbanisation that the slackening of the rate of growth of non-farm is mainly due to the slackening of urbanisation. The coefficient of variation of female RNFE across districts increased considerably between 1981-1991. Certain transformations have taken place in districts that seem to have facilitated the establishment of agro-based industries which were labour and female-intensive (for example cashew kernel processing, tabacco processing, and fruit juice manufacturing industries). However these were mostly confined to districts already leading in RNFS share.

There has been relatively little change between 1981 and 1991 in the agricultural sector in AP and India. The share for males has declined and has been little compensated by the small increase for females, generally the total annual decline is in the order of 0.04 per cent for AP and 0.14 per cent for India. However, a point worth nothing is that the average annual decline for males for AP is about a third of that observed for India.

Table 8 enables a rough separation of characteristics specific to the two groups of AP districts regarding their RNFS performance. Focusing on those districts where RNFS has reversed one sees that there are clear trends on average by higher urban population over the decade and by very fast growth in the urban population between 1981 and 1991. Whereas the two groups of districts started in 1977-78 with a similar percentage of people below the poverty line, the districts in which the RNFS has decreased have performed better in reducing their poverty. Some districts have had an excellent performance (such as Ranga Reddy and Kurnool) nevertheless the districts that belong to the 'RNFS increase' group have also done very well so that the pattern is not systematic. As for per capita value of agricultural output, the figure has increased in real terms for both groups, but it has increased by much more for the 'RNFS decrease group'. In particular no district in this group has experienced a decline (compared with 3 districts in the other group).

Finally as expected those districts where the RNFS has declined we have seen the proportions of those involved in RNFE fall by 1.28 percentage points over the period 1981-91. The caveat existing with the data presented in the Table which prevents one from drawing clear inferences is that fluctuations might have occurred during the decades considered.

In total the modern and traditional sectors had similar shares in AP (between 8 and 9 per cent in 1991), a breakdown hardly distinct from that of India (9.6 per cent and 8.12 per cent for modern and traditional) nevertheless there seems to be greater dispersion across districts for the traditional sector when compared with the modern sector.

Provisional Results of 2001 Census

Farm and non-farm shares (not disaggregated data especially other workers) by districts with the available data

Table 9: District-wise total shares in rural employment farm and non-farm activities (Main and marginal) as cultivators, Agricultural laborers, workers in household industry and other workers with percentage to total workers 2001

District	Cultivators			Agricultural laborers			Household Industry			Other workers		
	Totals	Male	Females	Totals	Males	Females	Totals	Males	Females	Total	Males	Females
Srikakulam	23.8	26.9	19.5	49.2	38.9	63.3	4.0	3.3	4.9	23.0	30.9	12.3
Vizianagaram	31.8	34.5	28.6	44.3	34.1	56.6	3.4	3.4	3.4	14.7	20.5	28.0
Visakhapatnam	37.9	38.4	37.2	36.5	30.2	45.7	3.2	2.8	3.8	22.4	28.6	13.3
North coastal	31.1	32.3	28.4	43.3	30.4	55.2	3.5	3.2	4.0	20.0	26.7	17.9
East Godavari	13.5	16.5	5.8	60.1	55.1	73.1	4.0	2.9	6.7	22.4	25.5	14.4
West Godavari	14.3	19.4	4.0	63.5	55.3	79.6	2.7	2.0	3.9	19.3	23.3	12.5
Krishna	14.7	20.0	5.8	60.3	48.3	80.1	2.2	2.0	2.6	22.8	29.7	11.5
Guntur	22.1	27.0	15.7	58.7	47.6	73.2	1.8	1.6	2.0	17.4	23.8	9.1
Prakasam	27.4	31.9	21.5	47.8	36.9	61.8	2.3	2.0	2.7	22.5	29.2	14.0
Nellore	20.8	26.0	12.6	52.0	41.0	69.5	3.7	3.3	4.4	23.5	29.7	13.5
South coastal	18.8	23.5	10.9	57.1	47.4	72.9	2.8	2.3	3.8	21.3	26.9	12.5
Chittor	35.5	37.7	32.3	41.4	34.1	52.0	3.2	2.7	3.8	19.9	25.5	11.9
Cuddapah	28.8	33.5	21.3	45.5	34.8	62.1	3.9	3.3	4.8	21.8	28.4	11.8

Table Contd.

Table 9: Contd.

Anantapur	36.0	41.8	28.3	44.0	32.9	58.5	3.8	3.9	3.8	16.2	21.4	9.4
Kurnool	26.3	31.3	20.3	50.3	41.4	67.2	2.5	2.3	2.7	18.2	25.0	9.8
Rayalaseema	31.7	36.1	25.6	46.0	35.8	60.0	3.4	3.1	3.8	19.0	25.0	10.7
Mahabubnagar	32.5	39.4	24.6	45.1	31.1	61.3	3.7	3.1	4.3	18.7	26.4	9.8
Ranga Reddy	34.1	36.1	31.3	35.0	23.3	54.4	2.2	2.0	2.4	28.7	38.6	14.9
Medak	33.5	38.7	26.9	40.4	30.8	52.5	4.2	2.6	6.2	21.9	27.9	14.4
Nizamabad	31.0	37.6	23.9	32.8	30.0	35.9	14.5	4.2	25.9	21.7	28.2	14.3
Adilabad	36.8	43.1	29.3	35.9	28.0	45.5	8.8	2.9	15.8	18.5	26.0	9.4
Karimnagar	29.2	34.0	23.0	38.0	30.3	46.7	11.9	5.2	19.5	20.9	30.5	10.1
Warangal	33.7	39.1	27.3	43.8	30.1	60.1	4.0	3.9	4.2	18.5	26.9	8.4
Khammam	26.1	31.3	19.2	55.3	43.3	70.8	1.9	1.9	2.0	16.7	23.5	8.0
Nalgonda	27.9	33.7	20.7	45.3	30.3	63.6	4.3	4.3	4.3	22.5	31.7	11.4
Telangana	31.61	37	25.13	41.3	30.8	54.2	6.2	3.34	9.4	20.9	28.86	11.90
AP	27.6	31.8	21.9	47.5	37.9	60.7	4.3	3.0	6.0	20.6	27.3	11.4
Mean	28.08	32.6	21.78	46.7	36.7	60.5	4.4	2.98	6.10	20.6	27.33	12.37
SD	7.33	7.33	8.78	8.9	8.7	11.6	3.22	0.93	6.15	3.11	3.95	4.09
CV	0.26	0.23	0.40	0.2	0.2	0.2	0.74	0.31	1.01	0.15	0.14	0.33

Notes: CV: Coefficient of Variation (=standard Deviation/Mean); SD = standard Deviation.

Source: Census of India 2001 series 29 A.P, Provisional Population Table paper - 3 of 2001 Distribution of workers and non-workers. Publication Director of Census operations A.P.

are presented in Table 9. The biggest group of workers in 2001 was agriculture labour. The largest variation in shares across districts is observed in respect of female workers in household industry (CV= 1.01). There appears to be some important differences in this period gender wise. In relation to agriculture related employment (cultivators and agricultural labour), there are some differences across the districts and across gender.

Visakhapatnam has the highest share of cultivators while East Godavari district has the lowest. Among total cultivators (both males and females taken together), the lowest is 13.5 per cent in the East Godavari district and highest 37.9 per cent in Visakhapatnam district. For males, Adilabad represents highest and the same East Godavari the lowest. For females, also Visakhapatnam has the highest share whilst west Godavari the lowest share.

East Godavari, West Godavari and Krishna district to have high agriculture and infrastructural development and are irrigated districts. In the case of cultivators, CV is low for totals and males when compared with females. It indicators that for cultivators inter district disparities are higher in respect of females.

In the case of agricultural labour, the opposite is true. When compared with females, inter district disparities are higher in the case of males (CV for males = 0.24 and for females = 0.19) High female agricultural labour in West Godavari and East Godavari indicates agricultural development is associated with higher shares of females in agricultural labour. Most of the developed districts like E.G, W.G and Krishna showed very high shares of female agricultural labours 73.1 per cent, 79.6 per cent and 80.1 per cent respectively. While poorest districts like Nizamabad have 35.9 per cent female agricultural labour to cultivators. The ratio of total agricultural labour to total cultivators in E.G is slightly less than 5 (4.5) in totals.

In the case of females, this ratio is 12.6 per cent. Similarly in Krishna district, female agricultural labourers constitute

80.1 per cent, which is 13.8 times cultivators among females. If we look at these ratios in the poorer districts such as Mahaboobnagar the ratio is 1.39 (for all), for males 0.79 and for females it is 2.49. It shows the predominate of agricultural labour as a group in the total workforce and more so among the female workforce.

Among agricultural labourers the average per cent of female workers is 60.48 (higher than for males 36.7 per cent) but the CV for female agricultural labour are 19 per cent compared to that of males which is 24 per cent.

For the State as a whole, this figure is 1.72 for totals, and 2.77 for females. Coming to the CV, there doesn't seem to be much variation across districts. For total cultivators, the CV is 26 per cent, while it is much higher for female cultivators 40 per cent. For agricultural laborers, the CV is 19 per cent for totals and for females and 24 per cent for males.

In household industry, the variation is the highest There are inter district variations in household industry both for males and females and with other workers. For household industry, the variation is low, but higher for females than for males.

There are more of agricultural labour than cultivators in A.P and there are inter district variations in both cultivators, agricultural labour, household industry and other workers. The state of A.P is known for its green revolution and most dynamic agricultural sector which has a long history of successful farming community. Such a modernized agricultural sector appears to have marginalized the small farmers by pushing them out of cultivation and into agricultural labour. The important reason seems to be that the cultivation is no more a profitable importance in A.P, by displacing the poorer sections particularly the small and marginal farmers.

Sumary and Conclusions

The percentage of rural labour force in AP in 1990-91 engaged in RNFE as their prime occupation was 18. As such,

RNFE plays a crucial role in providing additional employment and in generating additional income to rural people, particularly to the poor and to those with little land. RNFE encompasses a wide variety of activities, although services, trade and manufacturing predominate.

The main conclusions of this paper is that the share of RNFE was lower in the 1980s in AP than in India. Moreover, the share of RNFE grew more slowly in the 1980s in AP than elsewhere in India despite slower improvement in output (and in labour absorption) in agriculture.

The analysis of the share of RNFE in total employment (farm + non-farm) reveals that the share of RNFE in AP increased marginally between 1981 and 1991. While employment in the manufacturing sector has increased sharply, employment in household industry witnessed a decline. However, considerable differences are seen across districts, both in RNFE structure and trend.

Twelve out of 22 districts experienced a decline in the shares of RNFE in total employment between the two periods. In the period and for these districts, the proportion of people below the poverty line has also decreased: the falling rural non-farm share may be due to the facts that (1) urbanisation has possibly absorbed some of those engaged in RNFS (more than in the other 10 districts) activities and (2) the per capita value of agricultural output and employment has also increased faster 1981-1991, the share of the RNFS in the total rural workforce has increased faster for male than for female employment. The analysis of the changes in RNFE omits possible effects of urban non-farm employment on the rural workforce.

Trends in RNFE and its Composition in AP and India (1981 and 1991)

There has been an increasing trend in the shares of RNFE in AP and India. However, the RNFE share has been less, and slower growing in the 1980s in AP than elsewhere in

India, despite slower improvement in output (and in labour absorption) in agriculture. So AP is a good place to examine the causes of high-or low-RNFE growth.

There has been an increasing trend in the shares of RNFE in AP and India. However, the RNFE share has been less, and slower growing in the 1980s in AP than elsewhere in India, despite slower improvement in output (and in labour absorption) in agriculture. So AP is a good place to examine the causes of high-or low-RNFE growth.

Census data confirm the rise in RNFE both at the national and state levels, and the predominance of males in RNFE, in 1981 and 1991 both in India and AP. AP, unlike all-India has a rising percentage of agricultural labourers in the rural workforce. With development, poverty is getting concentrated among the agricultural labour households in several districts of AP.

The size of the RNFE viz., the percentage of total main workers engaged in the non-farm sector, in AP was at 16.8% and 17.1% in 1981 and 1991 respectively compared with all-India's 17.7% in 1991. AP's share is not far below all-India's, but AP's share is falling while that of India is growing. There is considerable inter-district variation in the industrial non-farm workers in rural areas was relatively high in Nizamabad and low in Mahabubnagar districts. The share has either declined or increased very little in the districts of Srikakulam, East Godavari. In the remaining parts of the state the increase was moderate. In 1981, the Ranga Reddy district had the highest (22.5%) while Ananthapur has the lowest (12. 1%) figure. In 1991, the Nizamabad district had the highest (26.8%) while Ananthapur had lowest size (13.3%). The inter-district coefficient of variation of RNFE share, in 1981-91 increased marginally. The districts which obtained top ten ranks in 1981 more or less obtained the same ranks in 1991.

The pattern of change in the size of RNFE would not necessarily appear encouraging in terms of economic development; in 12 of 22 districts there was a decrease in the proportion of RNFE between the two periods. However, across the time span and for most of these districts, the proportion of people below the poverty line has decreased, urbanisation has possibly absorbed some of those engaged in RNFS activities, and the per capita value of agricultural output has also increased. One potential cause for concern was the district of Mahabubnagar where there has been an increase in the percentage of persons below the poverty line.

Bibliography

Census of India 1981, series-1 India, General Economic Tables, (Tables B.1 to B.5) pp. 242-245.

Census of India 1991, Andhra Pradesh, Population Totals, Series-2.

Census of India 1991 Series-1, final population total paper2 of 1992 p.155.

Census of India 1991 India Series-1, Provisional Population Totals: Workers and their Distribution, Paper-3 of 1991 pp. 443-448.

Census of India 1991 Andhra Pradesh Series-2, Paper-1 of 1991 Supplement Provisional Population Totals.

Census of India 1991, Andhra Pradesh, Population Totals, Series-2, pp. 10, 66-73.

Sudhakar Reddy (1991) 'Poverty and Agricultural Growth in Rural Andhra Pradesh Inter District Analysis', CESS, Hyderabad

Census of India 1991 Andhra Pradesh Series-2, Paper-1 of 1991 Supplement Provisional Population Totals.

Census of India 2001 series 29 A.P, Provisional Population Table paper— of 2001 Distribution of workers and non-workers. Publication Director of Census operations A.P.

5

Fertility Transition in Andhra Pradesh, Evidence from NFHS-2 Data: An Application of Life Table and Proportional Hazards Approach

P. Ramachandran & P. Ramesh

The state of Andhra Pradesh has attracted the attention of Population Scientists and Policy makers for three main reasons. First, among the southern states of India, Andhra Pradesh has experienced fertility transition after Kerala and Tamil Nadu during the recent years. Second, there is fairly rapid decline in fertility of Andhra Pradesh in the recent past and the factors have not been copiously identified. Third, Andhra Pradesh is the first state to formulate a State Population Policy. The commitment of the Government is indicated by the release of the policy document in 1998 to find solutions to population problems of the State.

The Total Fertility Rate (TFR) has declined significantly from 4.0 in 1981 to 2.5 in 1996, a 38 per cent decline in fifteen years as against 28 per cent decline in India. Though the fertility has declined, the circumstances under which it declined in Andhra Pradesh are quite different from those of Kerala and Tamil Nadu. In spite of having low Human Development Index (41), Gender Health Index (50),

Reproductive Health Index (44) compared with all India (Population Foundation of India, 1998) and the other Southern states, the fertility in A.P has declined. The reasons for low fertility in Kerala were low infant mortality rate, very high literacy and status of women, which are not true of Andhra Pradesh (Zachariah. 1984; Bhat and Irudayarajan. 1990). In terms of social development, Andhra Pradesh is rated lower than the other Southern States. Female literacy and mean age at marriage are low in A.P compared to most other states but much lower than in Kerala and Tamil Nadu. The per capita income in the state is also lower than the National average. In India, there are a good number of states that are socially and economically better of than Andhra Pradesh but have higher fertility. The lessons learnt for the experiences of A.P would be relevant to other Indian states with high fertility than those from Kerala's Tamil Nadu's experience.

Few researchers have studied the Andhra Pradesh's scene, in order to identify the causes of the fertility transition (Balasubramanian, 1999; Srinivasan. 1999; Rayappa, 1994; Ramachandran, 1992; Ramachandrudu, 1992 among others). Though the average level of fertility in the state is low and nearing to the level of replacement, there are notable differentials over time and space. Many studies indicate that the effects of socio-economic and cultural factors on fertility vary from one region to another. Moreover, the existence of substantial variations in the fertility behaviour, across socio-economic categories—place of residence, level of education and occupation—is a pervasive finding of social demography (Freechen and Blanc, 1992; Rodriguez and Aravena, 1991; Cleland, 1985; Singhand Casterline. 1985; United Nations. 1987). Till late 1970s fertility was high in A.P but not as high as in India. The coastal Andhra Pradesh has extremely low fertility; below or near replacement level and Telengana has moderately high fertility. There is a need to see whether the levels and differentials across the regions of the state are due to variations in developmental conditions or to such other factors as cultural, geographic and historical in nature. This necessitates to examine the levels and to analyze differentials in fertility in the regions of Andhra Pradesh by utilizing the recent second round of National Family Health Survey data.

Trends in Population Growth

As per the Census of A.P, there was nearly fourfold increase in the size of population during 1901 (19.1 million) and 2001 (75.7 million), an increase of 56.6 million in the last century and nearly four-fifths of this increase (44.6 millions) was during the second half of the 20th century. The increase in Andhra Pradesh's population was so much conspicuous during the 1981-91 period with the addition of 13 million that could be compared to the increase of 12 million in the first half of the 20th century. The overall growth of population during 1901-2001 was 296 per cent compared to the National growth of 331 per cent.

Trends in Crude Birth Rate

The Crude Birth Rate of Andhra Pradesh has shown a sign of consistent decline from 43 during the decade 1941-51 to 40 during 1951-61 and further down to 35 during the subsequent decade 1961-71. The CBR in Andhra Pradesh has been lower than that of India during the above period (Ramachandrudu and Subramanyam. 1994) The Birth rate in Andhra Pradesh has been on the steady decline since mid-1970s. However, it was rather slow in the 1970s and early 1980s but since mid-1980s, there has been acceleration in the pace of decline. The birth rate in the state has declined from the level of about 35.4 per 1000 population in 1970 to 22.3 in 1998.

Trends in Total Fertility Rate (TFR)

In Andhra Pradesh the Total Fertility Rate (TFR) has declined significantly during the late 1980s and early 1990s. The TFR of Andhra Pradesh is found less than the National level through out the 20th century. Fertility in A.P seems to have remained more or less stable during the period 1961-71. At around a TFR of 5.5 per woman. The pace of decline in fertility hastened with an estimated TFR of 4.7 in 1971, and the decline continued further down to 4.4 in 1976. Further, it decreased to 3.7 in 1986 and to as low as 2.5 in 1996. The percentage of annual decline during the period of 1971-96 was 1.84 for the state as against 1.45 for India. The comparison of TFRs for the period 1976-86 and 1986-96 shows that the rate of decline is higher in the recent decade (3.19 per cent per year) compared to 1.47 during 1976-86 (Table 1). On an average, women in Andhra Pradesh now give birth to only 2.5 children as compared to about 5 children in early 1970s.

Table 1: Trends In Total Fertility Rate, 1971-96, Andhra Pradesh.

Year	*Rural*	*Urban*	*Total*
Total Fertility Rate			
1971	4.83	4.19	4.72
1976	4.56	3.53	4.37
1981	4.10	3.06	3.88
1986	3.90	3.17	3.73
1991	3.08	2.50	2.95
1996	2.70	2.10	2.54
Per cent Annual Decline In TFR			
1971-76	-5.60	-15.76	-7.43
1976-81	-10.03	-13.17	-11.13
1981-86	-4.87	3.58	-3.87
1986-91	-20.88	-21.13	-20.88
1991-96	-12.36	-16.14	-13.85
1971-96	-1.76	1.99	1.84
1986-96	3.08	3.38	3.19

Note: The estimates of TFR refer to the Average of 3 years (i.e., for 1971, it is 1970-72 and like).

The NFHS-1 estimated a CBR of 24.3 and TFR of 2.59 during 1989-92 for Andhra Pradesh as against the national level CBR of 28.7 and a TFR of 3.4 for the same period (PRC, Visakhapatnam Sc IIPS, 1995). It shows that fertility in the state was lower than that of national fertility. The NFHS-2 estimated a TFR of 2.25 for Andhra Pradesh and 2.85 for India during 1996-98. If the recent trend continued, the state is expected to have achieved the replacement level of fertility by the year 1999 (Srinivasan. 1999).

The pace of fertility decline is not uniform across the districts of State. The districts in the Coastal region have experienced a faster pace of fertility transition as compared to the districts in the other two regions. The lowest TFR is observed in the Coastal region (2.12), followed by Rayalaseema (2.75) and Telengana (2.89) region (Ramachandran. 2000).

Three Phases of Fertility Decline

Closer look at the data reveals that the process of fertility decline in A.P can be divided in to the following three states as shown in Table 2 Fertility was almost stagnant during 1971-78; slow decline during 1978-87 and faster decline thereafter. However, these three stages cannot be observed uniformly by residence. In the first stage the decline CBR and TFR wire negligible in rural areas, but there was decline in urban areas. In the second stage, rural areas experienced faster fertility decline but it was marginal in urban areas. In the third stage, both areas have experienced faster decline in fertility. This pattern of fertility decline is perhaps unique in A.P, which requires further investigation.

Table 2: Three phases of fertility transition in Andhra Pradesh

Stage	*Period*	*Crude Birth Rate*			*Total Fertility Rate*		
		Rural	*Urban*	*Total*	*Rural*	*Urban*	*Total*
	1971	35.8	33.8	35.4	4.8	3.8	4.6
1970-78 Stagnant	1978	34.7	28.6	33.6	4.6	3.3	4.4
1978-87 slow	1987	30.9	28.2	30.3	3.8	3.1	3.6
1987-96 Faster Decline	1996	23.5	20.6	22.8	2.7	2.1	2.5

Source: India. Registrar General, Sample Registration System Bulletins, various years.

The determinants of the probability of having subsequent births in Andhra Pradesh for women living in three regions are explored in this paper using the life table and proportional hazards methodology. This will elucidate how the factors influencing parents' demand for children change for one both order to another.

The Data and Methodology

The data used in this paper were collected in the second survey of the National Family health Survey (NFHS-2), 1998-1999. It covered a sample of 3872 households and 4032 ever-married women of age group 15-49. Respondents were also asked a battery of questions about their demographic, socioeconomic and decision making circumstances. The data are thought to be of good in quality and the details of the study design as well as sampling frame are given in the national and state NFHS reports (IIPS, Mumbai and ORC Macro, 1999. NFHS-2: A.P).

Previous research has identified a number of socioeconomic factors that seem to have a bearing on child spacing (U.N., 1993; Nair, 1996). India, only a few studies have examined child spacing patterns, parhaps because of non-availability of appropriate data on complete birth histories. Fortunately, the NFHS-2 obtained complete birth histories from the eligible women with a fairly large sample size. As a result, it is possible to study the child-spacing patterns in detail. This section focuses on the measurement of transitions in the region differentials of family building process with the help of both interval analysis. Two summary measures, mean birth intervals (measuring the tempo of fertility) and the proportions of mothers had a birth by different both orders in different time periods (indicating the quantum of fertility) were calculated based on the life table approach, which takes into account both closed and open birth intervals. Finally, the technique of proportional hazards has been used, which is an extension of the table technique, in order to see the relative effect of Region of women on the risk of subsequent births, controlling for socioeconomic and demographic variables.

The analysis of birth interval data for example. Provides information on the progression from one parity to another as well as the timing of this transition (Ryder, 1980; Srinivasan.

Table 3: Estimates of CBR and TFR by region, Andhra Pradesh

Region/State	*Estimates of CBR*			*Estimates of TFR*		
	1974-80 (1977)	*1984-90 (1987)*	*1996*	*1974-80 (1977)*	*1984-90 (1987)*	*1996*
Coastal Andhra	31.7	26.6	20.6	4.04	2.97	2.12
Rayalaseema	34.5	28.5	23.9	4.58	3.32	2.75
Telangana	35.3	30.1	24.7	4.69	3.58	2.89
State	33.6	28.3	22.8	4.38	3.27	2.54

Source: Balasubrahmanian K. (1999)

1980; Roderiguez and Hobcraft 1980; Hobcraft and Mc Donald, 1984; Yadava et al.. 1992). It is recognized that an analysis of closed birth intervals, though useful to examine the tempo of child bearing. Does not reveal the termination effect. Open birth intervals are useful in this context (Srinivasan, 1980) and life table analysis combines information from both closed and open intervals (Rodriguez and Hobcraft, 1980; Hobcraft and MC Donald. 1984). Here. a closed birth interval of length 'n' is equivalent to the occurrence of the event (the next birth) at time 'f since the previous birth, and is a complete observation. An open interval of length's' is equivalent to the non-occurrence of the next birth at least until time 'f, and indicators form these compared. But constructing life tables for the regions, controlled for other variables, becomes difficult since the number of births in various sub-classes becomes small. Instead, the proportional hazards approach (Cox regression) can be used to estimate the net effect of a factor on the risk of occurrence of an event, controlled for the effects of other variables (Cox. 1972). Hence, a proportional hazards analysis has been employed here to estimate the region effect on the risk for the next birth when controlling for the effects of other socioeconomic variables.

An investigation of period effect will provide some evidence of the demand trend for subsequent births over a period of years. Period effects will help to investigate the evidence of the recent fertility decline an Andhra Pradesh. In order to see the temporal changes over time, the analysis has been carried out for intervals beginning in four quinquennial periods: 1975-79, 1980-84, 1985-89 and 1990-94. Such analysis provides a clear understanding of the trends in the differentials of relative risk of subsequent births by regions. Intervals beginning in the five-year period just before survey i.e., after 1995 are not considered, since truncation bias seriously affects these. Intervals of width 0. Caused due to twin births, are considered as single births. The analysis has been restricted to currently married women and thus, the intervals and risks examined are strictly for women in the married state.

This analysis has been carried out for the second, third and the fourth birth intervals. The number of births of order five and higher is too small in some regions to permit an analysis. Besides, the NFHS-2 data does not allow an examination of the first birth interval, i.e., the interval between marriage and first birth, since progression from woman's marriage to first birth requires accurate information. It was found that in 19 per cent of cases, the date of first birth was within seven months of marriage. This indicates that there is substantial proportion of pre-marital conceptions or that the dates of marriage are not correctly reported. In either case, it is not appropriate to analyze the first birth interval. Hence, the analysis has been carried out only for the second, third and the fourth birth intervals (Ramesh, 2001).

Life Table Analysis of Birth Intervals

As discussed in the Methodology, Life tables using closed and open birth intervals, have been constructed for the second, third, and fourth Intervals from NFHS-2 data for the three regions of A. P boy birth cohorts. Table 4, provides information on median birth interval, i.e. the date by which half of the women had the next birth; and the proportion who had the next birth within 60 months.

Life table analysis of birth intervals clearly indicates that the median second birth interval fluctuated marginally over 1975-79 to 1990-94. The differences in the median second both

Table 4: Life Table Analysis of Birth Intervals by Region 1974-94: NFHS-2 Andhra Pradesh, 1998-99

Region and Period	*Number of Ceases*			*Median Birth Interval (Tempo Aspect)*			*Proportion attaining birth within 60 months (Quantum aspect)*		
	Second	*Third*	*Fourth*	*Second*	*Third*	*Fourth*	*Second*	*Third*	*Fourth*
COASTAL ANDHRA									
1975-79	195	168	106	32.13	33.67	35.50	0.851	0.768	0.689
1980-84	231	215	147	28.64	33.92	52.50	0.879	0.702	0.531
1985-89	259	212	173	29.29	37.50	120	0.849	0.618	0.393
1990-94	301	276	138	30.85	69.77	107.00	0.846	0.478	0.254
RAYALASEEMA									
1975-79	66	47	39	29.00	27.75	30.50	0.924	0.872	0.949
1980-84	88	81	58	27.67	32.10	35.00	0.852	0.778	0.621
1985-89	113	93	77	28.94	27.25	36.63	0.867	0.785	0.675
1990-94	108	116	61	30.67	80.22	59.44	0.869	0.470	0.511
TELANGANA									
1975-79	156	141	108	31.00	30.12	33.50	0.904	0.837	0.750
1980.84	206	182	126	28.20	33.71	36.00	0.888	0.797	0.683
1985-89	231	200	182	29.70	28.00	37.50	.0862	0.825	0.615
1990-94	287	251	183	31.72	37.13	54.68	0.848	0.683	0.522
TOTAL									
1975-79	417	356	253	31.05	31.00	33.63	0.883	0.809	0.755
1980-84	525	478	331	28.37	33.43	40.83	0.878	0.751	0.604
1985-89	603	505	432	29.30	30.79	48.50	0.857	0.731	0.537
1990-94	696	643	382	31.21	49.36	*	0.851	0.557	0.491

Source: Computed from NFHS-2 data file of Andhra Pradesh

Note: For currently married women of age 15-49 only Twins are considered as single births

* Median can not be computed; since the proportion completing the intervals does not reach 0.5.

interval between the regions are very small. The median among Coastal Andhra Women has been longer than the Rayalaseema women in all the four time periods. The difference in the timing of birth between Coastal Andhra and Telengana women is more noticeable and it is larger at third and fourth births. The median fourth birth interval among women of Rayalaseema and Telengana regions has been shorter than Coastal Andhra Women in all the periods clearly showing a greater tendency to have higher order births.

The Telengana women progress to higher order births faster than women of Coastal Andhra and Rayalaseema region, after the second birth. The Coastal Andhra Women have longer intervals after second and higher order births. This implies that Coastal Andhra women will delay their higher order births. On the whole, the tendency to go for a second birth is almost universal among the three regions. It is only after second birth that, the proportion having the next birth within 5 years has declined faster in Rayalaseema from 0.87 to 0.47 as compared to Telengana from 0.83 to 0.68. However, higher proportion of Telengana women go to higher order births than the women in Coastal Andhra and Rayalaseema.

Childlessness is very low. Further, most women in all the regions also go for second birth and this has been observed throughout the periods. The proportion of women progressing to the second birth by the end of 60 and 120 months has declined only marginally over time. However, a sizeable proportion of SC/ST women do have second birth within five years of the first. This proportion has declined substantially over time for the second to third birth among the women of Rayalaseema (from 0.87 to 0.47) and moderately for women of Coastal Andhra (0.77 to 0.48). However, most of Telengana women continue to go for the third child within 60 months.

The proportion of women going from third to fourth has declined from 0.75 to 0.42 in the periods beginning 1975-79 to 1990-94. However, the proportion of women going from third to fourth declined from 0.69 to 0.25 during the same period in Coastal Andhra. Even in the period beginning during 1990-94. More than half of Telengana and Rayalaseoma women are going from third to fourth birth.

In sum, the Life table analysis clearly suggests that the median birth intervals were short for second birth than the third birth among all the regions. Overall. The differentials by regions are conspicuous in the propensity to go for the second and third births. Further, these differentials have widened over time, especially for the progressions to the second and third births. It has been observed that the proportion of women proceeding to higher parities, especially after the second falls across the regions and over time and regional differentials in birth interval at higher order births have widened.

Multivariate Analysis of Birth Intervals Proportional Hazard Analysis

It is possible that the differentials by regions observed in the preceding analysis of birth intervals may, in part be attributable to the socioeconomic characteristics In other to estimate the region effect net of other important socioeconomic variables, the proportional hazard model, which combines the features of life table and regression, are adopted. This technique makes it possible to calculate the risk of having a subsequent birth for a particular group, relative to that for a reference group, while controlling for the effects of the pertinent variables. The risk of a subsequent birth is lower for women in a category with a negative coefficient and higher for those in a category with a positive coefficient relative to those in the reference category. The socioeconomic and demographic variables used as controls are: education of the woman (it is well known from the demographic literature that education has a strong influence on fertility), place of residence (rural or urban residence also may have an effect on fertility), sex of the previous child (given the high preference for a son, the tendency to go for an additional child may depend on the sex of the last child bom); infant survival (death of an infant can influence further childbearing due to biological and replacement effects); age of the woman at the birth of the previous child (it is known that as the age of the woman increases the tempo of child bearing becomes slower and the probability of terminating childbearing rises, both due to biological and social reasons). Work status of woman (working women would have greater exposure in the various matters of the life and would have influence on fertility), standard of living index (proxy for household income) and region. These variables are used in a categorized form and for each factor, a category has been specified as 'reference'. The Cox regression estimates (bata values) for the other categories are shown in Table 6; exp (beta) gives the risk of the next birth for the category relative to the risk for the reference category. The analysis has been carried out for three birth intervals; the second, third and fourth, and for four birth cohorts, (for the intervals beginning in quinquennial periods) 1975-79, 1980-84, 1985-89 and 1990-94.

Second Birth Interval

The results of the Cox regression for the second birth interval shows that the risk of the second birth across the four time periods. The Caste and religion effect, residence, work status, sex of the first child and regions does not seem to influence the chances of having the second birth and are not significant when other socioeconomic and demographic variables are controlled (Table 5). Among the other variables included in the model, the risk of having second birth was significantly higher for high standard of living (as compared to low standard of living) women in 1975-79 and 1985-89 periods; and for women of living (as compared to low standard of living) women in 1975-79 and 1985-89 periods; and for women of age at first birth below 20 (as compared to 20-24 age groups) for the same time periods. The risk was significantly lower for women of ages above 25 (as compared to 20-24 age groups) for intervals during 1985-89 and 1990-94. In all the four time periods, the hazards model showed

Table 5: Estimated regression coefficients and relative risks from cox proporitonal hazards model second birth (1975-94). NFHS-2, Andhra Pradesh, D 1998-1999

Explanatory variables	*Intervals Beginning During*			
	1975-79	*1980-84*	*1985-89*	*1990-94*
REGIONS				
Coastal Andhra	0.0	0.0	0.0	0.0
Rayalaseema	0.2671 1.306	-0.0086 0.991	0.0326 1.033	-0.0287 0.972
Telangana	0.1805 1.198	-0.0263 0.974	-0.0124 0.988	-0.0373 0.972
AGE OF THE RESPONDENTS AT FIRST BIRTH				
20-24 (Ref)	0.0	0.0	0.0	0.0
Below 20	0.1176 1.125	0.1436 1.154	0.4464 1.563***	0.2277 1.256*
25+	-0.2007 0.808	-0.4624 0.630	-0.6588 0.518**	-0.5580 0.572*
INFANT DEATH (FIRST CHILD)				
Survival (Ref)	0.0	0.0	0.0	0.0
Death	0.5226 1.686***	0.3265 1.386**	0.3777 1.459**	0.5112 1.667
SEX OF THE FIRST CHILD				
Male	0.0	0.0	0.0	0.0 0.0
Females	0.1003 1.106	0.1453 1.156	0.0040 1.004	0.0413 1.042
RESIDENCE				
Rural (Ref)	0.0	0.0	0.0	0.0
Urban	-0.142 0868	-0.0642 0.938	0.0062 1.006	-0.0466 0.954

Table 5: Contd.

CASTE AND RELIGION				
OC's (Ref)	0.0	0.0	0.0	0.0
SC/STs	-0.0416 0.959	-0.1135 0.893	0.0198 1.020	0.1159 1.123
OBCs	0.0054 1.005	0.075 1.078	-0.0612 0.941	-0.1052 0.900
Muslims	0.3187 1.375	0.3631 1.438	-0.0090 0.991	0.2756 1.317
Christian	0.0916 1.096	0.1365 1.146	0.0967 1.102	-0.0669 0.935
EDUCATION				
Illiterate (Ref)	0.0	0.0	0.0	0.0
Literate <Middle	0.1469 1.158	0.568 1.058	0.277 1.028	0.1387 1.149
Middle School & Above	0.0354 1.036	-0.0136 0.987	-0.0711 0.931	0.1025 1.108
WORK STATUS				
Non-working (Ref)	0.0	0.0	0.0	0.0
Working	0.023 1.023	0.0792 1.082	-0.0493 0.952	-0.1265 0.881
STANDARD OF LIVING INDEX				
Low (Ref)	0.0	0.0	0.0	0.0
Medium	0.2085 1.232	0.0891 1.093	0.654 1.068	0.1625 1.177
High	0.4567 1.579*	0.019 1.019	0.3942 1.483**	0.1893 1.208
Chi-square value	30.74	22.363	43.62	47.4996
Number of Intervals	416	522	601	691

***p<0.01; **p<0.01; *<0.1

Source: Computed from NFHS-2 data files of Andhra Pradesh

Note: For currently married women of age 15-49 Twins are considered as single births.

that if the first child died. Then the risk of the second birth is much higher than for a woman who had not experienced a child death, which agrees with the earlier findings (Singh et. Al.. 1993; Rajaram et al.. 1994; Khan and Raeside. 1998).

Third Birth Interval

The effects of different categories of variables on the risk of third birth are shown in Table 6. It indicates that risk of having the third birth was higher for women of Rayalaseema (1985-89) and Telengana regions in all the periods except 1980-84 as compared to Coastal Andhra. The relative risk for the third birth is significantly higher for the above periods for Telengana women (1.32 to 1.62), as compared to the women of Coastal Andhra. Further, the chances of having the third birth were higher for SC/STs and OBCs than OCs. And further, the differences between SC/ST- and OBC increased between 1980-84 and 1990-94 i.e.. the relative risk for the third birth is significantly higher for the periods 1980-84 and 1990-94 for SC/ST (1.70 & 2.13). and OBC (1.75 & 1.88) than OCs. The chances of having the third birth were higher for Muslims than OCs in all the four periods. The chances of having the third birth were higher for Christians than 'Other' category only during 1990-94. As expected, women with higher education (1985-89 and 1990-94) and higher age of the mother at the second birth (1985-89). have lower risk of having the third birth. Death of the second child increases the chances for third birth. The risk of having the third birth is higher for ages (at second birth) below 20 (as compared to 20-24 age groups) for intervals beginning during 1975-79 and 1990-94. The sex of the previous child does not show any significance on the risk of the third birth. Among the other variables included in the model, residence, work status, and standard of living do not show any significant effects on the risk of third birth.

Fourth Birth Interval

The risk of having the fourth birth was higher for regions in all the periods for Rayalaseema (except in 1980-84) and

Table 6: Estimated regression coefficients and relative risks from cox proporitonal hazards model third birth (1975-94). NFHS-2, Andhra Pradesh, D 1998-1999

Explanatory variables	*Intervals Beginning During*			
	1975-79	*1980-84*	*1985-89*	*1990-94*
		REGIONS		
Coastal Andhra	0.0	0.0	0.0	0.0
Rayalaseema	0.2036 1.226	0.1075 1.114	'0.43621.547**	0.0692 0.933
Telangana	0.2751 1.317**	0.0607 1.063	0.04337 1.543***	0.4793 1.615***
		AGE OF THE RESPONDENTS AT SECOND BIRTH		
20-24 (Ref)	0.0	0.0	0.0	0.0
Below 20	0.2791 1.322**	0.1699 1.185	0.1139 1.121	0.3016 1.352**
25+	0.0273 1.028	-0.7000 0.497***	-0.4515 0.637*	-0.2536 0.776
		INFANT DEATH (SECOND CHILD)		
Survival (Ref)	0.0	0.0	0.0	0.0
Death	0.3833 1.467**	0.4142 1.513**	0.8582 2.359***	0.4430 1.557**
		SEX OF THE SECOND CHILD		
Male	0.0	0.0	0.0	0.0 0.0
Females	0.0916 1.096	0.1079 1.114	-0.0449 0.956	0.1567 1.170
		RESIDENCE		
Rural (Ref)	0.0	0.0	0.0	0.0
Urban	0.2079 1.231	0.09229 1.109	0.840 1.088	0.0824 1.086

Table Contd.

Table 6: Contd.

		CASTE AND RELIGION		
OC's (Ref)	0.0	0.0	0.0	0.0
SC/STs	0.1482 1.160	0.5315 1.702**	0.1891 1.208	0.7571 2.132***
OBCs	0.0466 1.048	0.5626 1.755***	0.1391 1.141	0.6333 1.884***
Muslims	0.5434 1.722**	0.7979 2.221***	0.3962 1.4986*	0.6605 1.936**
Christian	-0.0026 0.997	0.4350 1.545	0.0030 1.003	0.5923 1.808**
		EDUCATION		
Illiterate (Ref)	0.0	0.0	0.0	0.0
Literate <Middle	-0.0080 0.992	-0.1181 0.889	-0.3644 0.695**	-0.1606 0.852
Middle School & Above	-0.1172 0.889	-0.2604 0.771	-0.3546 0.702	-0.4185 0.658**
		WORK STATUS		
Non-working (Ref)	0.0	0.0	0.0	0.0
Working	0.1338 1.143	0.0441 1.045	0.2099 1.234	-0.1318 0.877
		STANDARD OF LIVING INDEX		
Low (Ref)	0.0	0.0	0.0	0.0
Medium	-0.1097 0.896	0.1717 1.187	-0.623 0.940	-0.2024 0.817
High	-0.0581 0.944	0.0270 1.027	-0.0359 0.965	-0.3446 0.709
Chi-square value	30.195	62.853	86.471	119.911
Number of Intervals	353	476	503	642

***p<0.01; **p<0.01; *<0.1

Source: Computed from NFHS-2 data files of Andhra Pradesh

Note: For currently married women of age 15-49 Twins are considered as single births.

Telengana (except in 1975-79) as compared to Coastal Andhra. Rayalaseema and Telengana region women have a much greater chance than Coastal Andhra women of having a birth after the third, even after controlling the socioeconomic and demographic factors. Moreover, the coefficients has increased over time indicating that the relative risk has increased in the recent periods.

Among the other variables. Caste and religion effect on the risk of the fourth birth is significant in all the periods for SC/STs (except in 1975-79 period) and Muslims. SC/ST and Muslim women have a much greater chance than 'other' category women of having a birth after the third, even after controlling the socioeconomic and demographic factors. Moreover, the coefficient for SC/STs and Muslims has increased over time indicating that the relative risk has increased in the recent periods. For interval beginning during 1990-94, OBCS and Christians have higher risk of having the fourth birth than the 'other' category. Again, as education and standard of living increases, the chances of having the fourth birth decrease. Among the other variables included in the model, women from medium stratum of society have shown relatively lower risk during 1985-89 and 1990-94 periods and higher stratum women during 1975-79, than the women from lower stratum. Sex of the previous child shows significant effect in all periods except in the recent period (1990-94), that is, the relative risk of having the fourth birth is higher if the third birth was a female, than if it was a male. This indicates the effect of son preference, even at fourth birth. For all the cohorts the risk of having the fourth birth is higher in case of the death of the third child. Residence and work status do not show any significant effects on the risk of fourth birth.

It was observed earlier from the life table indicators that relatively higher proportion of Rayalaseema and Telengana women had an additional birth after the second and third births, as compared to Coastal Andhra women. The proportional hazards analysis further shows that this disparity

Table 7: Estimated regression coefficients and relative risks from cox proporitonal hazards model fourth birth (1975-94). NFHS-2, Andhra Pradesh, D 1998-1999

Explanatory variables	*Intervals Beginning During*			
	1975-79	*1980-84*	*1985-89*	*1990-94*
		REGIONS		
Coastal Andhra	0.0	0.0	0.0	0.0
Rayalaseema	0.4901 1.633	0.1666 1.181	0.5386 1.714**	0.8946 2.446***
Telangana	0.14470 1.158	0.4361 1.547**	0.6794 1.973***	0.8277 2.288***
		AGE OF THE RESPONDENTS AT THIRD BIRTH		
20-24 (Ref)	0.0	0.0	0.0	0.0
Below 20	0.1050 1.111	0.1223 1.130	0.3034 1.355*	0.1403 1.151
25+	-0.0995 0.905	-0.2974 0.743	-0.2096 0.811	-0.0901 0.914
		INFANT DEATH (THIRD CHILD)		
Survival (Ref)	0.0	0.0	0.0	0.0
Death	0.6270 1.872**	0.5460 1.726**	0.3081 1.361	0.5469 1.728**
		SEX OF THE THIRD CHILD		
Male	0.0	0.0	0.0	0.0 0.0
Females	0.02636 1.302*	0.4101 1.507**	0.3169 1.373** 0.1539 1.166	
		RESIDENCE		
Rural (Ref)	0.0	0.0	0.0	0.0
Urban	0.1041 1.110	0.2887 1.335	-0.2238 0.800	-0.1213 0.886

Table 7: Contd.

		CASTE AND RELIGION		
OC's (Ref)	0.0	0.0	0.0	0.0
SC/STs	0.0666 1.069	0.5573 1.746*	0.5219 1.685*	0.9294 2.533**
OBCs	-0.0156 0.985	0.2942 1.342	0.2320 1.261	0.6346 1.886*
Muslims	0.6392 1.895**	0.5790 1.784*	1.1441 3.140***	1.6078 4.992***
Christian	-0.1923 0.825	0.5340 1.706	-0.1841 0.832	1.9213 6.830***
		EDUCATION		
Illiterate (Ref)	0.0	0.0	0.0	0.0
Literate <Middle	-0.2915 0.747	-0.0255 0.975	1.000	-0.7157 0.489**
Middle School & Above	0.2520 1.287	-0.0109 0.989	-0.1432 0.867	-0.3183 0.727
		WORK STATUS		
Non-working (Ref)	0.0	0.0	0.0	0.0
Working	-0.0714 0.931	-0.0476 0.954	0.0201 1.020	-0.676 0.935
		STANDARD OF LIVING INDEX		
Low (Ref)	0.0	0.0	0.0	0.0
Medium	-0.1986 0.820	-0.0485 0.953	-0.2580 0.773*	-0.3577 0.699**
High	-0.5090 0.601*	-0.4088 0.664	-0.2942 0.745	-0.3025 0.739
Chi-square value	35.173	43.237	83.553	76.435
Number of Intervals	250	331	430	380

***p<0.01; **p<0.01; *<0.1

Source: Computed from NFHS-2 data files of Andhra Pradesh

Note: For currently married women of age 15-49 Twins are considered as single births.

persists even when other socioeconomic and demographic variables are controlled. Moreover the relative risk for Rayalaseema and Telengana women has increased over years during the period 1975-94.

Conclusions

The analysis of spacing between births based on the fertility histories of women in Andhra Pradesh shows that closed birth intervals do not differ systematically across the regions over the time periods studied. However, the life table indicators based on both closed and open birth intervals vary substantially between Telengana and Rayalaseema-Coastal Andhra after the second birth. The proportion of women of Telengana and Rayalaseema who have the third and subsequent births is higher than in Coastal Andhra and though it has fallen over the years, the gap has. In fact, widened. The proportional hazard analysis clearly shows that differentials by regions persist even after controlling for the other socioeconomic and demographic variables. The fact that the closed birth intervals do not differ much across regions after the second birth and the chances of occurrence of the next birth do. indicate that termination of childbearing rather than spacing has played a major role.

Regional differences do not show a large effect at lower order births. This highlights the fact that the most of the women in A.P, regardless of their region tend to go for the second birth. The tendency to stop childbearing after third birth has gradually filtered down among women of Coastal Andhra, thus widening the differentials in progression at higher orders between coastal Andhra and Telengana-Rayalaseema. To narrow the gap between the regions in fertility and to complete transition efforts should be made in Rayalaseema and Telengana regions by implementing RCH programmes effectively. Further, education of women is not having any influence on fertility in Andhra Pradesh as observed in other countries.

Acknowledgments

The discussions on analytical techniques used in this paper with Prof. P.M.Kulkami, are gratefully acknowledged

References

Balasubramanian, 1999, Pace of Fertility Decline and prospects for Population Stabilization in Andhra Pradesh. *Demography India.* 28 (1), pp. 23-46.

Balasubramanian, K,, and P. Satya Sekhar, 1998, Population (Chapter 3). *In: Andhra Pradesh at 50 (A Data Based Analysis).* Data News Features, Hyderabad.

Bhat, P.N.M,, 1996, Contours of Fertility Decline in India: A District Level Study Based on the 1991 Census. *In:* K. Srinivasan (eds.), *Population Policy and Reproductive Health,* Hindusthan Publishing Corporation, New Delhi.

Bhat, P.N.M and S. Irudayarajan, 1990, Demographic Transition in Kerala Revisited. *Economic and Political Weekly* 25: 1957-1980.

Cleland, J., 1985, Marital Fertility Decline in developing countries; Theories and the evidence, In: J. Cleland and J. Hobcraft, *Reproductive Change in Developing Countries,* Oxford University Press, Oxford.

Freedman. R., and A.K. Blanc. 1992, Fertility Transition: An update, *International Family Planning Perspectives,* 18: 44-50, 72.

Fox, J.(1984), *Linear Statistical models and Related Methods.* New York: John Willy and sons Publications.

Hobcraft, John and John Me Donald (1984) "Birth Intervals". WFS, Comparative Studies, No. 28. Voorburg, Netherlands: International Statistical Institute.

International Institute for Population Sciences (UPS) and ORC Macro, 2000, *National Family Health Survey (NFHS-2), India, 1999-99: Andhra Pradesh,* UPS, Mumbai.

Irudayarajan, S and P. Mohanachandran, 1999, Infant and child Mortality Estimates—Part 1. *Economic and Political Weekly,* 33-19): 1. May 9; pp. 120-40

Kendall, M.G. (1975). *Muitivariate Analysis.* London: Charles Griffin & Company Ltd

Khan, H.T. Abdullah, and Robert Raeside (1998). The determinants of first and subsequent births in urban and rural areas of Bangladesh. *Asia-Pacific Population Journal,* Vol. 13, No. 2, pp. 39-72.

Lee, Elisa T (1993) Function of Survival Time In *Readings in Population Research Methodology. Advance Basic Tools,* George W. Rumsey (eds.,), United Nations Fund, Vol. 6, pp. 21-41.

Little, RJ., Linear Models for WFS Data. Voorburg, Netherlands, International Statistical institute, 1980 June. World Fertility Survey Technical Bulletin No. 9/Tech. 1282P.

Little, RJ., Statistical models for World Fertility Survey data. Voorburg, Netherlands, International Statistical Institute, 1980. 48 p. World Fertility Survey, World Fertility Survey Conference, London, July 7-11, 1980, Methodoicgy Session No 4.

Ni Bhrochain, Maire (1987). Period Parity Progression Rations and Birth Intervals in England and Wales, 1941-1971: a synthetic life table analysis. *Population Studies,* Vol. 41, pp. 103-125.

Population Foundation of India, 1998, Human *Development and* Reared *indices,* B-3B, Qutub Institutional Area, New Delhi.

PRC, Andhra University and IIPS, Bombay, 1995, *National Family Health Survey. Andhra Pradesh, 1992.* International Institute for Population Sciences, Bombay.

Ramachandran, P., P. Ramesh, and S Jareena, 2000, *South India Fertility Transition: Andhra Pradesh Component,* Department of Population Studies, Sri Venkateswara University, Tirupati. (Mimeo).

Ramachandran P., D. Usha Rani and M. Sahadeva Reddy, 1992, Population Growth in Andhra Pradesh: Implications for Population Education' *In: K. Mahadevan et al. (eds.), Health Education for Quality of Life,* B.R. Publishing Corporation, Delhi.

Ramachandrudu, G, M.L. Rao, M.R. Reddy, K VR. Subramanyam, and M Sudhakar Babu, 1992, *Andhra Pradesh Population Scenario.* Population Research Centre, Visakhapatnam (Mimeo).

Ramachndrudu, G. and K.V.R. Subramanyam, 1994, *Andhra Pradesh Population scenario- A Preliminary / Analysis of the 1991 Census,* Twelfth Annual conference, Andhra Pradesh Economic Association, February 1994.

Registrar General, India *Sample Registration System Bulletin (various years).* Office of the Register General, New Delhi.

Rodriguez, Z., and J.N. Hobcrafl, (1980). *Illustrative Analysis.': Life Table Analysis of Birth interval in Colombia.* Scientific Reports, Voorburg, Netherlands: International Statistical Institute.

Srinivasan, K. (1980). *Birth Interval Analysis in Fertility Surveys* WFS, Scientific Reports, No. 7, London: World Fertility Survey.

Srinivasan, K, 1995, *Regulating Reproduction in India's Population: efforts, results and recommendations,* Sage Publications, New Delhi.

Srinivasan, K., 1999, The Indian Mode of Fertility Transition, Editors Desk, *Demography India. 28(I), Jan-June 1999.pp. v-vi.*

6

Indian Women in Transition

Prof. N. Sudhakara Rao

Introduction

One of the key issues that have attained special attention in India in recent times is a women in development. Women's Population, which is presently 496 million in 2001, constitutes roughly 50 per cent of India's population. Women are subjected to various forms of discrimination from centuries together. Though, in nature there is no discrimination between sexes there are less number of females as compared to males in India. India is an exceptional country where males out number the females. Physically and biologically there are differences between men and women human and domestic work anatomy and physiology is different between the two sexes. Women play paramount importance in the perpetuation of human species. Child bearing, Child rearing, women generally look after House maintenance. Similarly performing outside works earning money for livelihood of the family members safe guard and the social and economic interest of the family members is main role attached to men in our society. In the recent times the women's role has increased and at present she is deeply involved not only the biological role of bearing and rearing children but also participating in economic activities other than the domestic works. She is put to hardship because of the dual role played by her in the society. Thus the roles of sexes differ boring on physical, biological and sociological and economic phenomenon. Perfect equality does not exist in the World in any dimension of social, economic and political life's of people perfect equality does not exist even in a country like China. In a country like U.S.A, where women has full freedom and liberty perfect equality does not exist. Hardly 30% of women participate in political activities and 40% in economic activities. The women's role in decision-making is also limited. With some imperfections equality exists in the society. There is an optimum/desired level per equality, which will lead to peace; prosperity and development the optimum may very over space and time (generally limited to 30%).

The Constitution of India provides equal rights to all men and women in the country. But women are not able to enjoy equal status on par with men since economic power (income and assets) and political power is mostly vested with men rather than women. The place of rural women in socio economic and political spheres is more depressed than that of urban counter part in our country. There is a change in the position of women during the last century especially during the second off of the century and more especially during last decade. Women are empowered with social, economic, legal powers. Thus, at present women is in transition in India. We shall examine how women's transition is taking place among the women in India.

The Position of Women in Primitive Society

In the primitive Hindu Society women enjoyed high status. The full-bloomed period of Indian women hood can be historically witnessed during rig vedic period. The Epic period of Ramayana and Mahabaratha to had a respectable place for women. In the Puranas and Ethihathas, women enjoyed high status. Lord Vishnu kept his wife on his chest where as Lord Siva allotted half off his body to his wife. Lord Sive kept Ganga on his head. But after that gradual down fall and degradation started during the period of Smrities. The most obscure and hazy picture was witnessed during medieval ages right from 8th Century A.D. to 19th Century. Women were subjected to all sorts of ill-treatment such as tyranny, oppression, atrocity, exploitation, the customs of sati, Deva dasi, dowry, child marriages, hypergamas marriages, polygamy and restrictions on widows re-marriages effecting dignity and decency of Indian womanhood. Women do not have either social freedom or economic power. Assets are accumulated among men leading to concentration of economic power in the hands of men. Women are looked after as an agent of child bearing and rearing. Men used to pay Kanya Sulkam and purchase women. Women are looked after as symbol of beauty, They are not allowed to divorce and re-marry.

Thus, Indian Women suffered a lot before the beginning of the 20th Century and discriminated socially, economically and politically. However, the situation has changed slowly and women in India after Independence are freer as compared to women in historical and medieval periods.

The Position of Women During Pre-Independence Period

There is some change in the position of women in the beginning of 20th Century. The efforts made by the social reformers as such as Raja ram Mohan Roy, Gurujada Appa Rao a number of social evils such as abolition of Kanya Sulkam, widow remarriages, Taboos on education of women etc., were eliminated to larger extent. The child marriage restrain Act was passed as early as 1929 (Sarada Act). However, the women's literacy could not progress very much. In the year 1901, as 0.69% of the women were literate by 1951 the literacy level increased to 8.9%. It is believed that as compared to India's Independence Movement the question of low status of women in India is considered to be insignificant. Thus there is little change in the status of women during the pre-independence period. Social changes are a slow process and legislative measures adopted will give results only with a time lag.

The Position of Women During Post Independence Period

After Independence, the Government of India has taken several measures to hoist the status of women. The different plans, programmes and policies have laid emphasis on women empowerment and raising the economic, educational, health and political participation of women to match that of men. The Committee of the status of women was appointed as early as 1976. The draft National Policy on empowerment of women was envisaged equal flow benefits in physical and financial terms to women. A national Commission for women was appointed. The Constitution of India guarantees certain rights and privileges to women as fundamental rights and directive principles. It confers on man and women equal rights and opportunity and political economic and social spheres. The constitution imposes a fundamental duty on every citizen to give up all practices derogatory to the prestige of Women. The various measures undertaken by Indian Government. Served a lot to remove the inequalities existing in Indian society. Article 15 of the Constitution prohibits and discrimination on grounds of sex. The Directive Principles of State Policy also state that the state shall direct this policy towards ensuring adequate means of livelihood for women and ensuring equal pay for equal work for both men and women. The safe guard women rights and prevent their exploitation the Government has enacted a number of women specific and women related acts such as Child Marriage Restraint Act of 1951, the Special Marriage Act of 1954 (Amended 1984), The Hindu Succession Act of 1956, the Superstition of Immoral Traffic in Women and Girls Act 1956 (later amended in 1976 and 1986), the Dowry Prohibition Act of 1961, the Maternity Benefit Act of 1966 (Amended 1976), Medical Termination of Pregnancy Act of 1971, the Equal Remuneration Act of 1976 (Amended 1984), the Indian Evidence Act 1983, Family court Act 1984, Indecent Representation of women prohibition Act 1987, Indian Marriage Act 1995 (Amended 1996), the new bill 2001 for protecting women against violence etc. In the 6th Five Year Plan emphasis was laid on raising the employment status of women. The 7th Plan emphasized the need for Human Resource Development in Women. The 8th Plan aims at enabling women to function as equal partners and implement social legislation for women effectively. The 9th Plan has identified improvement of women as on objective.

A part from that International environment is so conductive in increasing the status of women in India the four World Conferences (Mexico 1975, Copen Hagen 1980, Nairobi 1985, Beijing 1995) (the World summit for children 1990, the International Year of Women 1975), the International Conference on Nutrition 1992, the International Conference on Population and Development 1994 gave ample support for Women development Programmes in India. Several legislative measures were undertaken to improve the dignity of women. Measures were undertaken with regard to education, health, abortion, prostitution, infanticide, age of marriage, dowry, divorce, rape, sexual harassment, women's working condition, childlabour, equal pay for equal work, wage remuneration, participation of women in political scenario etc.,

Gender Inequality

Inequalities exist in Indian society in different dimensions. One such dimension in gender inequality. Nature has maintained equality in sexes. Full the countries there are equal number of men and women. Biologically women are much stronger than men, but there are less number of women in India as compared to men. The declining sex ratio is attributed to many cultural, social and economic factors. There were 792 women in India in 1901 and this declined to over time. Gender inequality is measured in Sex ratio 946 in 1951, 941 in 1961, 930 in 1971, 934 in 1981, 927 in 1991 and 933 in 2001. The overall declining manifastation of continuing gender inequality and its accentuations are clearly observed in Indian Scenario.

Women and Health

Health status of women is very low in India as compared to many developing countries. Indian women are characterized by ill-health mal nutrition undernourishment, lack of proper prenatal and antenatal care. They are more anemic and prone to diseases. Maternal Mortality Reproduction often becomes a determinate of the status of women in our society. Maternal Mortality reference to deaths due to pregnancy related causes. The World Bank in its recent report pointed out that maternal mortality is very high in India about 25% maternal deaths to take place in India. There is an excess of maternal mortality and morbidity resulting from physical assaults such as rape, burning, and beating. The high incidence of maternal mortality is associated with unwanted and unplanned pregnancies, mal nutrition, lack of medical checkup, lack of knowledge about health care, poverty, illiteracy, ignorance, low age of marriage, early childhood, greater frequency of births, less spacing, high parity, lack of prenatal and antenatal care, home deliveries, traditional methods of cutting the umbilical card etc. Thus, high incidence of maternal mortality is one of the main reasons for gender inequality in India. It is observed that the maternal mortality is very high the beginning of the 20th Century. It was estimated to be more than 1000 per one-lakh deliveries. It has declined to 437 by 1994. Improvement in Medical and Scientific Technology, include health care, improvement in literacy and educational standards, change in traditions and customs, and let to decline in maternal mortality in India. The maternal mortality is hardly 3-4 in advanced countries. As compared the rate is very high in India. There is every need for further reduction in maternal mortality in India.

Abortion

Abortion is one of the main reasons for gender inequality in India. Abortion is as old as mankind. Killing the child at conception level is called abortion. Abortion may be spontaneous are induced. The incidence of abortion is very high in India. The Preponderance of illegal unscientific and traditional methods of abortion especially in rural India caused a lot of damage to women's health in general, reproductive health in particular. If abortion takes place in

Literacy rates by residence and sex-state, District, Mandal-2001 Literacy rate

	Total			Rural			Urban		
	Persons	Males	Females	Persons	Males	Females	Persons	males	Females
Andhra Pradesh	61.11	70.85	51.17	55.33	66.13	44.36	76.39	83.21	69.34
Adilabad	53.51	65.56	41.38	46.74	59.66	33.88	71.70	81.10	61.95
Nizamabad	53.51	66.27	40.57	48.90	62.68	35.60	72.91	81.91	63.66
Karimnagar	56.00	67.86	44.19	51.23	63.59	38.99	75.36	84.91	65.59
Medak	53.24	65.50	40.68	48.98	61.85	35.91	77.97	87.50	68.95
Hyderabad	79.04	84.11	73.67	-	-	-	79.04	84.11	73.67
Ranga Reddy	66.31	75.02	57.03	53.67	65.75	40.99	77.01	82.74	70.82
Mahbubnagar	45.53	57.87	32.83	41.72	54.45	28.66	76.69	85.56	67.39
Nalgonda	57.84	70.19	45.07	54.08	67.04	40.72	81.89	90.09	73.23
Warangal	58.41	70.01	46.54	52.88	65.03	40.43	80.95	90.24	71.42
Khammam	57.72	67.04	48.16	52.52	62.31	42.48	78.20	85.69	70.55
Srikakulam	55.94	67.90	44.19	53.60	65.86	41.56	74.50	84.07	65.08
Vizianagaram	51.82	63.00	40.73	46.86	58.57	35.21	73.36	82.45	64.47
Vishakapatnam	59.45	68.48	49.99	47.73	58.72	36.78	76.60	83.46	69.59
East Godavari	65.49	69.97	61.00	62.52	66.85	58.15	75.11	80.08	70.16
West Godavari	73.95	78.43	69.45	72.48	76.91	67.99	79.87	84.64	75.21
Krishna	69.91	74.57	65.05	65.56	71.34	59.64	79.00	81.15	76.68
Guntur	62.80	71.32	54.17	58.84	67.88	49.67	72.88	80.14	65.59
Prakasam	57.86	69.78	46.60	54.93	67.44	42.03	73.75	82.52	64.82
Nellore	65.90	74.45	57.24	62.13	71.62	52.53	78.58	83.96	73.12
Cuddapah	64.02	76.98	50.76	61.14	75.02	46.94	73.41	83.43	63.21
Kurnool	54.43	67.36	41.07	50.83	64.72	36.50	66.48	76.22	56.41
Anantapur	56.69	68.94	43.87	52.04	65.13	38.31	70.23	80.10	59.99
Chittoor	67.46	78.29	56.48	63.67	75.36	51.85	80.94	88.62	73.04

Percentage decadal growth, Percentage of child population in the age-group 0-6 by residence and percentage of Urban population to total population state and District 2001

State/District	*Total Rural Urban*	*Population*	*Percentage decaded growth 1991-2001*	*Percentage of child population in the age group 0-6 population*			*Percentage of urban population*
		Persons		*Persons*	*Male*	*Female*	
Andhra Pradesh	Total	75727541	+13.86	12.77	12.87	12.68	27.08
Adilabad	Total	2479347	+19.06	14.47	14.66	14.28	26.47
Nizamabad	Total	2342803	+14.98	13.79	14.15	13.44	18.04
Karimnagar	Total	3477079	+14.47	12.72	12.87	12.57	19.53
Medak	Total	2662296	+17.29	14.50	14.59	14.40	14.45
Hyderabad	Total	3686460	+17.18	11.99	11.96	12.02	100.00
Rangareddy	Total	3506670	+37.41	13.29	13.09	13.49	52.27
Mahabubnagar	Total	3506876	+13.97	15.05	15.15	14.95	10.59
Nalgonda	Total	3238449	+13.55	13.56	13.60	13.50	13.26
Warangal	Total	3231174	+14.63	13.49	13.62	13.36	19.21
Khammam	Total	2565412	+15.78	13.15	13.19	13.11	19.80
Srikakulam	Total	2528491	+8.93	12.66	12.90	12.43	11.00
Vizaianagarm	Total	2245103	+6.36	12.54	12.69	12.40	18.36
Visakhapatnam	Total	3789823	+15.36	12.06	12.17	11.95	39.89
East Godavari	Total	4872622	+7.30	11.85	11.94	11.76	23.33
West Godavari	Total	3796144	+7.92	11.51	11.60	11.42	19.69
Krishna	Total	4218416	+14.05	11.51	11.52	11.49	32.37
Guntur	Total	4405521	+7.27	11.55	11.73	11.38	27.95
Prakasam	Total	3054941	+10.72	12.18	12.21	12.14	15.28
Nellore	Total	2659661	+11.18	11.78	11.95	11.61	22.70
Cuddapah	Total	2573481	+13.48	12.55	12.69	12.40	23.00
Kurnool	Total	3512266	+18.14	14.78	14.93	14.61	22.57
Ananthapur	Total	3639304	+14.31	12.62	12.58	12.66	25.28
Chittoor	Total	3735202	+14.54	12.34	12.49	12.18	21.69

Table showing the total population, Slum population, percentage of Slum population literacy rate and sex ratio of Town and Slum in respect of Urban Agglomerations-Andhra Pradesh-2001

Name of the Urban Agglome Ration	Persons			Literacy rate			Sex ratio	
	Total Population (U.A.)	Slum population	% of Slum population	Urban agglomeration	Slum	Slum Slum	Urban agglom eration	Slum
Adilabad	128196	63913	49.86	73.87	72.46	61.85	976	980
Mancheriyal	118047	49077	41.57	72.41	69.66	60.83	955	978
Ramagundam	236623	94868	40.09	71.59	66.59	57.10	958	952
Karimnagar	215782	34252	15.87	85.02	79.56	70.79	953	965
Hyderabad	5533640	1170424	21.15	78.51	71.5	63.96	938	942
Mahbubnagar	139483	51481	36.91	84.06	77.77	68.22	951	961
Surypet	95029	54069	56.90	81.81	77.62	67.63	931	900
Nalgonda	111745	14296	12.79	88.28	84.95	76.82	959	979
Miryalguda	90670	38245	42.18	79.01	69.47	58.35	955	943
Warangal	577190	230190	39.88	81.11	74.98	63.78	972	982
Kothagudem	105265	74087	70.38	77.58	77.32	69.39	1010	1019
Khammam	196763	64062	32.56	81.83	76.12	67.90	963	972
Srikakulam	117066	48632	41.54	81.09	73.30	64.33	997	1024
Vizianagarm	195462	67525	34.55	75.99	68.35	59.38	1020	1023
Vishakapatnam	1329472	171211	12.88	77.10	72.08	63.32	972	971

Table Contd..

Rajamundry	408341	112003	27.43	76.18	74.58	69.26	986	1003
Kakinada	368672	58369	15.83	75.49	70.59	65.87	1008	1024
Eluru	215343	104716	48.63	78.83	73.58	67.63	1051	1033
Tanuku	71172	25261	35.49	84.10	76.74	72.32	1011	1057
Bheemavaram	141975	45762	32.23	81.72	73.55	68.62	974	1020
Palacole	75753	18970	25.04	83.06	75.70	70.01	1008	1033
Vijayawada	1011152	263973	26.11	79.71	70.59	64.26	904	977
Narasaraopet	97011	58008	59.80	72.56	71.02	62.68	983	979
Chirala	166877	84482	50.63	69.97	68.25	58.86	1004	999
Ongole	152945	3485	2.28	79.39	58.54	51.24	964	999
Kavali	84286	12621	14.97	77.51	61.28	53.35	933	966
Nellore	404922	156346	38.61	79.63	72.38	65.46	982	1000
Gudur	74550	21360	28.65	76.16	74.19	67.10	1006	1001
Cuddapah	260899	33994	13.03	76.96	69.52	61.37	972	968
Kurnool	320619	120387	37.55	68.85	66.11	57.73	966	971
Adoni	161125	22132	13.74	60.86	61.28	51.18	975	990
Nandyal	156216	55648	35.62	72.46	65.20	53.75	974	968
Anantapur	243359	67545	27.76	76.34	65.96	55.44	963	973
Tirupati	302678	75528	24.95	82.75	75.51	65.87	955	970
Madanapalle	107262	22625	21.09	76.45	70.68	60.76	968	952

Sex ratio of population and sex ratio of child population in the age-group 0-6 State, District 2001

State/District	*Sex ratio of total population*			*Sex ratio of child population in the age-group 0-6*		
	Total	*Rural*	*Urban*	*Total*	*Rural*	*Urban*
Andhra Pradesh	978	983	965	964	965	958
Adilabad	989	999	964	964	968	951
Nizamabad	1016	1026	973	966	965	972
Karimnagar	1000	1006	975	977	982	957
Medak	976	981	948	964	965	956
Hyderabad	945	-	945	950	-	950
Ranga Reddy	941	989	926	970	994	945
Mahbubnagar	970	972	954	957	957	959
Nalgonda	927	969	951	962	960	981
Warangal	973	973	973	955	954	980
Khammam	975	974	977	968	968	971
Srikakulam	1013	1013	1011	976	976	975
Vizianagaram	1004	1002	1016	981	986	956
Vishakhapatnam	991	1000	976	973	978	963
East Godavari	992	990	1001	978	974	993
West Godavari	992	985	1019	977	976	981
Krishna	961	976	929	959	968	942
Guntur	984	981	992	955	953	961
Prakasam	971	969	981	966	967	959
Nellore	983	984	980	955	955	955
Cuddapah	975	973	980	952	949	962
Kurnool	965	965	966	944	941	956
Anantapur	957	955	965	963	961	971
Chttoor	983	987	971	959	963	946

proper time and place, it is as safe as maternity. But repeated abortions are dangerous and associated with high mortality and morbidity. Japan experience shows that Pre-mature birth, prevalence of sterility is very high among women under went multiple abortions. The Govt of India passed Medical Termination of Pregnancy Act as early as 1971 with a view to liberalize women from traditional suppression are allowing her to have a free choice of her conception. Abortion is allowed on social, economic and health grounds. Perhaps, the increased incidence of abortion may be one of the causes for increased gender inequality in India.

Literacy rates by residence and sex-State, District-2001

State/District	*Literacy rate*					
	Total		*Rural*		*Urban*	
	Males	*Females*	*Males*	*Females*	*Males*	*Females*
Andhra Pradesh	70.85	51.17	66.13	44.36	83.21	69.34
Adilabad	65.56	41.38	59.66	33.88	81.10	61.95
Nizamabad	66.27	40.57	62.68	35.60	81.91	63.66
Karimnagar	67.86	44.19	63.59	38.99	84.91	65.59
Medak	65.52	40.68	61.85	35.91	86.50	68.95
Hyderabad	84.11	73.67	-	-	84.11	73.67
Range Reddy	75.02	57.03	65.75	40.99	82.74	70.82
Mahbubnagar	57.87	32.83	54.45	28.66	85.56	67.39
Nalgonda	70.19	45.07	67.04	40.72	90.09	73.23
Warangal	70.01	46.54	65.03	40.43	90.24	71.42
Khammam	67.04	48.16	62.31	42.48	85.69	70.55
Srikakulam	67.90	44.19	65.86	48.56	84.07	65.08
Vizianagaram	63.00	40.73	58.57	35.21	82.45	64.47
Vishakhapatnam	68.84	49.99	58.72	36.78	83.46	69.59
East Godavari	69.97	61.00	66.85	58.15	80.08	70.16
West Godavari	78.43	69.45	76.91	67.99	84.64	75.21
Krishna	74.57	65.05	78.34	59.64	81.15	76.68
Guntur	71.32	54.17	67.88	49.67	80.14	65.59
Prakasam	69.78	45.60	67.44	42.03	82.53	64.82
Nellore	74.45	57.24	71.62	52.53	83.96	73.12
Cuddapah	76.98	50.76	75.02	46.94	83.43	63.21
Kurnool	67.36	41.07	64.72	36.50	76.22	56.41
Anantapur	68.94	43.87	65.13	38.31	80.10	59.99
Chittoor	78.29	56.48	75.36	51.85	88.62	73.04

Foeticide and Infanticide

The decline in sex ratio at birth is due to practice of female foeticide (identifying the sex of the foetus and going for abortion) and infanticide i.e., killing an infant because it is a female. Foeticide is a recent development and female infanticide has got large history in India and in many human societies across space and time. Foeticide is more in the urban areas and infanticide is more in the rural areas. Foeticide and infanticide are identified as some of the reasons for gender inequality in the country.

Population, Percentage Decadal Growth 1991-2001, Sex Ratio, Literacy by Sex-Uas, Cites and Towns By Size Class in the State of Andhra Pradesh-2001

Size-class and Name of UA/ City/Town	*Population*	*Percentage Decadal Growth 1991-2001*	*Sex Ratio*	*Literacy rate*		
				Persons	*Males*	*Females*
Hyderabad	3686460	13.80	945	79.04	84.11	73.67
Visakhapatnam	969608	17.63	983	76.36	82.73	69.88
Vijayawada	870871	24.09	897	80.68	80.61	80.76
Warangal	528572	18.07	974	81.63	90.68	72.35
Rajahmundry	313347	-3.54	983	77.89	82.56	73.14
Kakinada	289920	3.55	1015	74.46	80.19	68.81
Kurnool	267739	13.07	971	72.41	79.52	65.10
Tirupati	227657	30.56	933	84.27	91.35	76.67

Infant Mortality: And Child Mortalities

Infant Mortality is a sensitive indicator of the health situations in a society. Infant mortality is very high in India. It was estimated to be more than 200 in 1901 and it has declined to 146, in 1951,129 in 1971, 110 in 1981, 80 in 1991 and 70 in 2001. Infant mortality is affected by both biological and environmental factors. Age of mother order of births spacing of children play a significant role in determining the level of infant mortality in a society. It is observed that infant mortality is very high among female children as compared to male children. This is attributed to neglect of girl child in terms of nutrition and health care. In India during the period 1971-1981, the male child mortality was 41 as against female child mortality of 44.8 Similarly during 1989-91, the child mortality was 26.3 as against 26.9 among females in India.

Son Preference

In a patriarchal society, there is strong preference for son. It is a reflected in the health care of the children. The birth of a male child is a cause of celebration where as birth of female child is a state of commensuration. Son preference to lead to foeticide. Thus son preference is one of the reasons for gender inequality in the country. There is a lot of difference in the adoption of family programme in India. Most of the adopters of family planning programme (permanent methods) are women. Similarly, because of poverty, women are becoming victims of prostitution, which indirectly affected women health leading to higher mortality and morbidity.

Undercounting

Undercounting of women is very high in India. Women are undercounted because of social stigma associated with gender. Widowed, divorced women are not counted properly. Similarly, families having only large number of female children will not provide full information which leads to undercounting of women. Thus, undercounting is one of the reasons for gender inequality in the country.

All the factors mentioned above such as mal nutrition, deceases, high maternal mortality and morbidity, high infant and child mortality, foeticide, abortion, infanticide, undercounting of women because of social stigma led to gender inequality in the country. However the expectation of life is a sensitive indicator of the living standards of a population in any country gives a different picture on the health status of women in India.

On the contrary the expectancy of life in India is almost equal between both the sexes in India. The Table 1 provides information on expectation of life in India both for males and females. The tables reveal that during 1901-10, the life expectancy for males was estimated as 22.6 years as against 23.3 years for females. During 1921-30, the life expectancy for males was estimated as 26.9 years as against 26.6 years for females, and then onwards the expectancy of life was higher for males as compared to females up to 1991. During 1991 the expectancy of life for males was 58.1 years as against 58.6 years for females. 1994 the life expectance for males was 61.1 years as against 61.4 years for females. On the hole, during 1901-1994 the expectation of life increased by 38.5 years among males 38.1 years among females. During 1951-94 the increased life span was 28.7 years among men and

29.7 years among females. This indicates that women progressed on par with men especially after independence. In many advanced countries the expectation of life has crossed more than 80 years (higher for females), and there is every need to increase life span in India, keeping the debate whether the rate in higher or lower between sexes in India.

7

An Analysis of Size of Population, Literacy Rate and Sex Ratio of A.P. in 2001 Census

*Dr. B. Kusuma Kumari**
Prof. V. Gandhi Babu

India is one of the very few countries in the world which has the proud history of holding census every ten years uninterruptedly since independence. The data generated by the Census of India, 2001 will provide benchmark statistics relating to socio-economic and demographic conditions of the people of India (constituting about 1/6th of the human population on this planet) at the beginning of this millenium. The main aim of this paper is to analyse the Census data, 2001 relating to Andhra Pradesh. The specific objectives are (1) to analyse the changes in rural and urban population of the districts in the three regions of A.P. by computing simple percentages in State population and by calculating percentage decadal growth rates during 1991-2001, (2) to investigate the changes in the literacy rates of males and females in all the districts of A.P., (3) to study the impact of adult literacy rate on infant mortality rate and life expectancy at birth by using regression analysis for the data relating to 10 Asian countries for 1997 and (4) to bring out the changes in sex ratio which is a crucial indicator of the population analysis. The analysis provides a fair idea of "the quantitative and qualitative aspects of the population" in the different districts of the State.

I

Stagnation of the rural economy acts as a major driving force for migration from rural to urban areas and urbanization of any region in determined by the indicators like percentage of urban population, percentage decadal growth rate of urban population and urban-rural growth differential. Table 1 shows that percentage of urban population has been on the rise in the State since 1961 and by 2001 it has reached to 27.08 % as against 26.90 % in 1991. Percentage of urban population is low in Mahabubnagar (10.6%), Srikakulam (11.00%), Medak (14.4%) and Prakasam (15.3%) districts. If one excludes the capital city of Hyderabad and Rangareddy District, the highly urbanized districts in AP are Visakhapatnam (39.9 %) and Krishna (32.4 %).

The figures relating to percentage decadal growth rate of rural and urban population are also computed and in Table 1. for the State, the percentage increase in total population is worked out to be 13.9% during 1991-2001 as against 24.20% during 1981-1991. The corresponding percentage figures for urban and rural AP are 14.6% and 13.6% respectively. With the exception of Rangareddy district, higher percentage decadal growth rate of urban population is observed for Adilabad (36.3%),. Nalgonda (26.9%) and Chittoor (25.4%). Among all the districts in the State, Srikakulam is the only district for which negative growth rate is observed for urban population. Low values of decadal growth rate are observed for Nizamabad (2.3%), West Godavari (2.6%) and Prakasam (2.8%) districts. For the rural AP, the highest decadal growth rate is observed for Kurnool (23.3%) followed by Rangareddy (21.7%) and Krishna (21.1) districts.

Region-wise analysis presented in Table 2 reveals that among the three regions of AP, coastal region contains 43.2% of the State population in 1991. Interestingly, its share is declined to 41.7% in 2001. The share of Telangana region is increased from 39.2% to 40.5% in 2001 while there is a slight

Table 1: Changes In Urban and Rural Population of Different Districts of A. P During 1991 and 2001

District	Percentage in 1991 Total population		Percentage in 2001 total population		Change in % of Pop during 1991 and 2001		% rate of increase during 1991 and 2001		
	Urban	Rural	Urban	Rural	Urban	Rural	Tot. Pop.	Urban	Rural
Andhra Pradesh	26.9	73.1	27.1	72.9	0.2	-0.2	13.9	14.6	13.6
Adilabad	23.1	76.9	26.5	73.5	3.3	-3.3	19.1	36.3	13.9
Nizamabad	20.3	79.7	18.0	82.0	-2.2	2.2	15.0	2.3	18.2
Karimnagar	20.6	79.4	19.5	80.5	-1.0	1.0	14.5	8.7	16.0
Medak	14.5	85.5	14.4	85.6	0.0	0.0	17.3	17.1	17.3
Hyderabad	100.0	0.0	100.0	0.0	0.0	0.0	17.2	17.2	-
Rangareddy	47.2	52.8	53.3	46.7	6.0	-6.0	37.4	55.0	21.7
Mahbubnagar	11.1	88.9	10.6	89.4	-0.5	0.5	14.0	8.5	14.6
Nalgonda	11.9	88.1	13.3	86.7	1.4	-1.4	13.5	26.9	11.7
Warangal	19.4	80.6	19.2	80.8	-0.2	0.2	14.6	13.6	14.9
Khammam	20.2	79.8	19.8	80.2	-0.4	0.4	15.8	13.4	16.4
Srikakulam	12.5	87.5	11.0	89.0	-1.5	1.5	8.9	-4.1	10.8
Vizianagaram	17.2	82.8	18.4	81.6	1.1	-1.1	6.4	13.4	4.9
Visakhapatnam	39.8	60.2	39.9	60.1	0.1	-0.1	15.4	15.5	15.3
East Godavari	23.8	76.2	23.3	76.7	-0.5	0.5	7.3	5.2	8.0
West Godavari	20.7	79.3	19.7	80.3	-1.0	1.0	7.9	2.6	9.3
Krishna	35.8	64.2	32.4	67.6	-3.4	3.4	14.0	3.1	20.2
Guntur	28.9	71.1	27.9	72.1	-0.9	0.9	7.3	3.8	8.7
Prakasam	16.5	83.5	15.3	84.7	-1.2	1.2	10.7	2.8	12.3
Nellore	23.8	76.2	22.7	77.3	-1.1	1.1	11.2	6.1	12.8
Cuddapah	24.0	76.0	23.3	76.7	-0.7	0.7	13.5	10.2	14.5
Kurnool	25.8	74.2	22.6	77.4	-3.3	3.3	18.1	3.2	23.3
Anantpur	23.5	76.5	25.3	74.7	1.8	-1.8	14.3	23.0	11.6
Chittoor	19.8	80.2	21.7	78.3	1.9	-1.9	14.5	25.4	11.8

Source: Census of India 2001 Series-29, Andhra Pradesh, Provisional Population Totals & Statsticl Abstract of A.P Different Issues.

Table 2: Changes in The Size of Population in the Three rgions of A.P

Region	No of Districts	1991			2001		
		Population	% in State Population	C.V	Population	% in State Population	C.V
Telangana	10	26089074	39.23	16.52	30696566	40.54	16.4
Coastal	9	28733209	43.21	26.63	31570722	14.68	26.31
Rayalaseema	4	11685725	17.57	15.49	13420253	17.78	15.91
State	23	66508008	100	36.48	75727541	100	37.06

Source: Census of India 2001, Series–29, Andhra Pradesh, Provisional Population Totals & Statstical.

increase (0.2%) in the share of Rayalseema. The coefficient. of variation (C.V) computed for the districts relating to the three regions is highest in the case of Coastal districts of AP (26.3%) in 2001 while the corresponding values for Telangana and Rayalseema are 16.4% and 15.9% respectively.

Among the three regions, Telangana region has registered a higher decadal growth rate of 17.66% during 1991-2001 as compared to 15.19% in Rayalaseema and 9.88% in Coastal Andhra. All the districts in Telangana except Nalgonda have recorded a higher growth rate than the State average. All districts in Coastal Andhra except Visakhapatnam and Krishna have recorded a lower growth rate than the State average. With regard to urban population, five districts in Telangana, namely Adilabad (36.33%), Medak (17.1%), Hyderabad (17.2%) Rangareddy (55.0%) and Nalgonda (26.9%); only one out of ten districts in coastal Andhra, namely, Visakhapatnam (15.5%) and two out of four Rayalaseema districts, namely, Visakhapatnam (15.5%) and two out of four Rayalaseema districts, namely, Anantapur (23.0%) and Chittoor (25.4%) have recorded a higher growth rate than State average. Thus, 9 out of 10 districts in Coastal Andhra depicted a lower decadal growth rate than State average of urban population (14.6%). With regard to rural population, all the districts in Telangana, except Nalgonda have recorded a higher growth rate than the State average (13.6%). On the other hand, all the districts in coastal Andhra, except Visakhapatnam (15.3%) and Krishna (22.2%) have recorded a lower growth rate than the State average. In Rayalseema, 2 out of 4 districts, namely, Cuddapah (14.5%) and Kurnool (23.3%) have shown higher growth rate of rural population than the State average.

II

The literacy rate for A.P. is continued to be lower than the all India figure during 1991-2001. The figures relating to the State and the Nation are 61.11% and 65.38% respectively in 2001 as against 44.08% and 52.21% respectively in 1991. Figures pertaining to literacy rates of persons, males and females for all the districts of the State are given in Table 3. In 2001, the literacy rate of males in A.P. is 70.9% as against 51.2% among females. Only eight out of 23 districts have recorded higher female literacy rate when compared to State average female literacy rate. The highest percentage decadal growth rate in literacy of both persons and males is observed for Medak (62.4% and 45.53% respectively). Females have shown highest decadal growth rate in Medak district (111.3%) which is followed by Adilabad (100.9%). Four out of ten Coastal districts have recorded low decadal growth rate of female literacy when compared to the average female literacy of the State. These districts are Viskahapatnam (44.48%), East Godavari (44.34%), Krishna (42.84%) and Nellore (54.74%). On the other hand, all the districts in Telangana and Rayalaseema with the exception of Hyderabad (15.92%), have higher decadal growth rate than the average figure of the State. Low literacy rate among females (especially in rural areas of AP) might be one of the main reasons for high child malnutrition, infant mortality rate, child death rate and maternal mortality rate.

III

The impact of adult literacy rate on infant mortality rate and life expectancy at birth is studied for the data relating to 10 Asian countries, namely, India, Bangladesh, China, Indonesia, Korea, Malaysia, Pakistan, Philippines and

Table 3: Literacy-Absolute increase And Percentage Decadal Growth Rate (1991-2001)

District	Literate Persons		Literate Males		Literate Females		Absolute Increase in %			% decadal growth rate in literacy		
	1991	2001	1991	2001	1991	2001	Persons	Males	Females	Persons	Males	Females
Andhra Pradesh	44.08	61.11	55.12	70.85	32.72	51.17	17.03	15.73	18.45	38.63	28.54	56.39
Adilabad	32.96	53.51	45.05	65.56	20.6	41.38	20.55	20.51	20.78	62.35	45.53	100.87
Nizamabad	34.18	53.26	47.33	66.27	21.35	40.57	19.08	18.94	19.22	55.82	40.02	90.02
Karimnagar	37.17	56	50.79	67.86	23.37	44.19	18.83	17.07	20.82	50.66	33.61	89.09
Medak	32.41	53.24	45.15	65.52	19.25	40.68	20.83	20.37	21.43	64.27	45.12	111.32
Hyderabad	71.52	79.04	78.9	84.11	63.55	73.67	7.52	5.21	10.12	10.51	6.60	15.92
Rangareddy	49.07	66.31	60.43	75.02	36.31	57.03	17.24	14.59	20.72	35.13	24.14	57.06
Mahbubnagar	29.58	45.33	40.8	57.87	18.03	32.83	15.75	17.07	14.8	53.25	41.84	82.09
Nalgonda	38	57.84	50.53	70.19	24.92	45.07	19.84	19.66	20.15	52.21	38.91	80.86
Warangal	39.3	58.41	51.68	70.01	26.08	46.54	19.11	18.33	20.46	48.63	35.47	78.45
Khammam	40.5	57.72	50.04	67.04	30.53	48.16	17.22	17	17.63	42.52	33.97	57.75
Srikakulam	36.22	55.94	49.14	67.9	23.52	44.19	19.72	18.76	20.67	54.45	38.18	87.88
Vizianagaram	34.19	51.82	45.93	63	22.47	40.73	17.63	17.07	18.26	51.56	37.17	81.26
Visakhapatnam	45.51	59.45	56.13	68.84	34.6	49.99	13.94	12.71	15.39	30.63	22.64	44.48
East Godavari	48.79	65.49	55.32	69.97	42.26	61	16.7	14.65	18.74	34.23	26.48	44.34
West Godavari	53.38	73.95	55.75	78.43	43.3	69.45	20.57	22.68	26.15	38.54	40.68	60.39
Krishna	53.16	69.91	60.55	74.57	45.54	65.05	16.75	14.02	19.51	31.51	23.15	42.84
Guntur	46.35	62.8	56.54	71.32	35.85	54.17	16.45	14.78	18.32	35.49	26.14	51.10
Prakasam	40.3	57.86	53.14	69.78	27.06	45.6	17.56	16.64	18.54	43.57	31.31	68.51
Nellore	47.61	65.9	58.04	74.45	36.99	57.24	18.29	16.41	20.25	38.42	28.27	54.74
Cuddapah	48.12	64.02	63.14	76.98	32.35	50.76	15.9	13.84	18.41	33.04	21.92	56.91
Kurnool	39.97	54.43	53.24	67.36	26.04	41.07	14.46	14.12	15.03	36.18	26.52	57.72
Anantpur	42.18	56.69	55.92	68.94	27.61	43.87	14.51	13.02	16.26	34.40	23.28	58.89
Chittoor	49.75	67.46	62.61	78.29	36.44	56.48	17.71	15.68	20.04	35.60	25.04	54.99

Source: Census of India 2001. Series – 29, Andhra Pradesh, Provisional Population Totals & Statistical.

Thailand for 1997. The data presented in Table 4 shows that Republic Korea is on top among the 10 Asian countries with high life expectancy at birth (72.4 years), adult literacy rate (97%) and low infant mortality rate (6 per 1000 births). Low values of life expectancy at birth is found for Bangladesh (58.1 years) and India (62.4 years). Poor adult literacy rate is noted for Bangladesh (39%) and Pakistan (41%) and India (62%). Infant mortality rate, on the other hand, is higher in Pakistan (95 per 1000 births), Bangladesh (81 per 1000 births) and India (71 per 1000 births).

Table 4: Indicators of Human Development for some Asian Countries-1997

Country	*Life Expectancy At birth (years) LEB (X)*	*Infant Mortality rate (per thousand births) IMR (X)*	*Adult Literacy rate (Per cent) ALR (Z)*
India	62.4	71	62
Bangladesh	58.1	81	39
China	69.8	38	83
Indonesia	65.1	45	85
Korea, Republic	72.4	6	97
Malaysia	72.0	10	86
Pakistan	64.0	95	41
Philippines	68.3	32	95
Thailand	68.8	31	95

Note: For Kerala State (India), the corresponding figures are 72.0, 12 and 93

Source: Economic Survey, 1999-2000.

Correlation and Regression Analysis:

$r_{xy} = -0.89$, $r_{xz} = 0.84$ and $r_{yz} = -0.92$

1. LEB = 53.65* + 0.1729* ALT $R^2 = 0.6970$
   (15.38) (4.01)

2. IMR = 139.36* - 1.2376* ALT $R^2 = 0.8396$
   (8.64) (6.05)

*indicates significant at 1 per cent level.

The results of correlation analysis reveal that there is a significantly high positive correlation between life expectancy and adult literacy rate. On the other hand, high negative correlation is found between life expectancy at birth and infant morality rate as well as between adult literacy rate and infant mortality rate. The results of regression analysis shows that adult literacy rate is one of the important explanatory variables in explaining the variation in life expectancy at birth. Nearly, 70% of the variation in life expectancy at birth is explained by adult literacy rate. The Students t-ratio of the regression coefficient is significant at one per cent level. From the results of regression equation (1), one can conclude that for every one per cent increase in literacy rate, the life expectancy at birth increases by 0.17 years (nearly 61 days). A similar analysis is done for investigating the impact of adult literacy rate on infant mortality rate. The value of simple correlation coefficient reveals that the two variables are negatively correlated. About 84% of the variation in infant morality rate is explained by adult literacy rate. The t-value of the regression coefficient is significant at one per cent level. Every one per cent increase in adult literacy rate causes a decline in infant mortality rate 1.24%. The analysis reveals significant impact of literacy rate on the above said variables.

IV

Sex ratio is a crucial indicator of population analysis. Women are fewer than men in most States in India and the state A.P is no exception. The State has a consistent higher sex ratio than the rest of the country. The number of females for every 1000 males in 2001 was 978 in AP as against a National average of 933. District-wise analysis for sex ratio is carried out by computing average sex ratio, standard deviation, coefficient of variation and growth rates for the data relating to 6 census years 1951-2001. Results are presented in Table 5. It is interesting to note that in the tribal dominated districts like Nizamabad, Khammam, Srikakulam and Vizianagaram, the sex ratio exceeded 1000. However it is worth to mention that the sex ratio declined in Krishna, Guntur, Mehbubangar as well as in East and West Godavari Districts. One of the possible reasons for the lower proportion of females might be strong preference for the male child. The coefficient of variation is the higehst for Hyderabad and Rangareddy districts. The analysis reveals significant negative growth rate in sex ration for the State as well as for the

Table 5: Sex Ratio-Coefficient of Variation and Growth Rates

District	1951-2001							Change in sex ratio in 2001 over 1991
	Average	S.D	C.V	Linear		Exponential		
				Growth Rate	t-ratio	% Growth Rate	t-ratio	
Andhra Pradesh	978	4.88	0.5	-1.97	2.31	-0.2	2.31	6
Adilabad	986	11.74	1.14	-2.69	0.94	-0.26	0.93	9
Nizamabad	1012	7.55	0.75	0.83	0.42	008	0.42	-1
Karimnagar	990	7.39	0.75	2.11	1.27	0.21	1.27	14
Medak	984	9.59	0.98	-4.49	3.62	-0.46	-3.62	6
Hyderabad	939	25.98	2.77	-5.74	0.91	-0.59	0.89	12
Rangareddy	963	21.32	2.22	-11.06	7.95	-1.15	8.04	0
Mahbubnagar	986	12.85	1.3	-6.43	5.32	-0.65	5.36	3
Nalgonda	960	9.15	0.95	3.97	2.78	-0.42	2.78	5
Warangal	960	7.61	0.79	3.77	4.96	0.39	5	11
Khammam	960	7.53	0.72	3.25	2.75	0.34	2.77	14
Srikakulam	10.32	19.84	1.92	-10.28	7.99	-0.99	8.13	1
Vizianagaram	1011	11.62	1.15	-5.54	3.95	-0.55	3.98	4
Visakhapatnam	994	16.85	1.7	-7.03	2.49	-0.7	2.49	16
East Godavari	997	3.78	0.38	-1.6	2.59	-0.16	2.6	-6
West Godavari	994	3.25	0.33	-1.06	1.53	-0.11	1.53	-2
Krishna	966	4.2	0.43	-0.34	0.31	-0.03	0.31	-8
Guntur	975	4.75	0.49	0.89	0.74	0.09	0.74	14
Prakasam	980	8.43	0.86	-3.48	2.44	-0.36	2.45	1
Nellore	984	4.26	0.43	-1.57	1.9	-0.16	1.9	3
Cuddapah	959	8.07	0.84	3.14	2.12	0.33	2.13	20
Kurnool	968	9.71	1	-4.26	2.87	-0.44	2.85	12
Anantpur	948	4.85	0.51	1.97	2.34	0.21	2.35	11
Chittoor	964	10.33	1.07	5.09	4.74	0.53	4.79	17

Source: Census of India 2001. Series–29, Andhra Pradesh, Provisional Population Totals.

districts like Medak, Rangareddy, Mehbubnagar, Nalgonda, Srikakulam, Visakhapatnam and Chittoor.

Summary

The main aim of this paper is to analyse the Census data, 2001 relating to Andhra Pradesh (A.P). The specific objectives are: (1) to analyze the changes in the sizes of rural and urban population of the districts in the three regions of A.P by computing simple percentages in State population and by calculating percentage decadal growth rates during 1991-2001, (2) to investigate the changes in the literacy rates of males and females in all the districts of A.P. (3) to study the impact of adult literacy rate on infant mortality rate and life expectancy at birth by using regression analysis. The analysis is expected to provide a fair idea of "the quantitative and qualitative aspects of the population" in the different districts of the State.

In order to analyze the changes in rural and urban population of the districts, percentages of district population in State population as well as the decadal growth rates during 1991-2001 are computed. The results show that the highly urbanized districts in A.P are Visakapatnam and Krishna districts if one excludes the capital city of Hyderabad and Rangareddy district. Among all the districts in the State, Srikakulam is the only district for which negative growth rate is observed for urban population. For rural A.P, then highest decadal growth rate is observed for Kurnool. The region wise analysis reaveals that the share of Coastal Andhra region declined from 43.2% in 1991 to 41.7% in 2001. This decline is compensated by the increase in the share of Telangana and Rayalaseema regions. The districts in Coastal Andhra region have also shown the highest coefficient of variation in the size of population. Further 9 out of 10 districts in Coastal Andhra region depicted a lower decadal growth rate than the State average decadal growth rate of urban population. With regard rural population, all the districts in Telangana (except Nalgonda) have recorded a higher growth rate than the State average growth rate, while all the districts in Coastal Andhra (except Visakhapatnam and Krishna) have shown a lower growth rate than the State average.

1. With regard to literacy rate, the State is continued to be lower than the All India figure during 1991-2001. Only 8 out of 23 districts have recorded higher female literacy rate when compared to the female literacy rate of the State. Further 4 out of 10 Coastal districts recorded low decadal growth rates of female literacy when compared to the average literacy rate of the State. On the other hand, all the districts in Telangana and Rayalaseema (except Hyderabad) have higher decadal growth rate than the State average.

2. The regression analysis carried out for investigating the impact of adult literacy rate on infant mortality rate (IMR) and life expectancy at birth brought out some interesting results. For every one per cent increase in adult literacy rate, life expectancy at birth increases by 0.17 years (nearly 61 days). On the other hand, every one per cent increase in literacy rate causes a decline in infant mortality rate by 1.24%.

3. The time series analysis carried out for the crucial indicator, sex ratio reveal that the ratio is exceeded 1000 in four tribal dominated districts, namely, Nizamabad, Khammam, Srikakulam and Vizianagaram. Further the results depict that the sex ratio is declined in Krishna, Guntur, Mahabubnagar as well as in East and West Godavari districts. The trend analysis carried out for six Census years 1951-2001 results in significant negative growth rate for sex ratio in the case of State as well as for seven districts, namely, Medak, Rangareddy, Mehabubnagar, Nalgonda, Srikakulam, Visakhapatnam and Chittoor. The results also reveal that the coefficient of variation in sex ratio is the highest for Hyderabad and Rangareddy districts.

8

Rural Out-Migrants in A Low Population Growth Setting

Dr. Ch. Appa Rao
Prof. G. Ramachandrudu
Dr. N. Subba Rao

Introduction

Migration is one of the basic three domographic components which influence the size and structure of population of a given place. Thus, migration takes place in the differentials of rural-urban wage rates, and the modern urban informal sector attracting the ruralites to the urban areas. In developing countries, the process of rural-urban migration is a positive sign during the 19th and 20th centuries. The link between rural-urban migration leads to urbanization, industrialization and economic development. There has been a wider gap between supply of labour and the availability of job opportunities in urban areas. The ruralities are slowly attracted towards urban areas as they earn higher wage rates than in the rural areas. They also change their quality of life in the towns then before. The social scientists, economists, researchers and the policy makers need to pay much attention on this important subject of migration.

Review of Literature

A few broad findings based on migration data collected during the 38th (1983), 43rd (1987-88) and 49th (1993) Rounds of NSS are noted hereunder. The absolute number of migrants, the number of male, female and total migrants in the rural sector increased by 9.5 per cent, 18.9 per cent and 17.2 per cent respectively during the period 1983 and 1987-88. Similarly, percentage increase of 6.2, 12.6 and 9.9 was noticed in case of males, females and persons respectively during the period 1988-93. The migration of males have shown negative trends in the urban areas during the period 1983-88 but the trend reversed in the period 1988-93 (Narasimhan, R.L. and Harish Chandra, 1998).

A Research Study on Rural-out-migration in Srikakulam District observed that age-wise migrants are overwhelmingly young, more than half of the seasonal migrants and two-thirds of other migrants left the village at the early working age of 15-34 years. Marital status of the migrants was married males. One-half of the total migrants were literates with 29 per cent possessing high school and higher level of education when compared to residents in the place of origin. The workforce shows that two-thirds of total migrants were from agriculture of the migrants who are currently employed/working as 32 per cent doing jobs, 19 per cent in constructive work and only per cent in agriculture (Sree Rama Murty, S. 1990).

The percentage of literacy is higher in migrant families compared to non-migrants. Among the migrants, the education level of permanent migrants was considerably higher than that of seasonal migrants. More than 50 per cent male and female members of age group of 16 to 35 years were migrating both seasonally and permanently (Gupta, S.P. and B.L. Prajapati, 1998).

A Study in Visakhapatnam Slums found that a large number of migrants are in the middle aged group and long distance migrants belong to the neighbouring Srikakulam District. Rural-Urban migration and its effects depend upon the levels of educational differences of the migrants. The Study concluded that the stress of economic situation not only singled out families and married couples to migrate to urban areas in large numbers in search of livelihood (Ranga Rao, K., K. S. Rani, and K. R Murty, 1977).

In the plains, intra-district migration is higher than that of hilly areas, where as in the hills inter-district migration is relatively higher. Out of total males who migrated from village to urban area, 70 per cent are literates while in case of females it was only 34 per cent (Singh, S.P. and R.K. Aggrawal, 1998)

A study of occupation and earnings of the migrants at the time of migration shows that 35 per cent of the migrants were employed in the agricultural sector. Nearly, 13 per cent of them were self-employed and only 3 per cent worked as non-mannual workers and 20 per cent were unemployed or students. Migration is the out-come of the relative strength of the 'push' and 'pull' factors. Among the various push and pull factors of migration, the economic factors are the important ones in determining the migration process. Most of the urban migrants maintain links with their native place in the rural areas through regular visits (Solucis Santhapparaj, 1998).

The Confederation of Indian Industry (CII) has conducted a Study on urban India, and found that urban population is growing very fast at three pr cent. Further, slum population is growing at an alarming nine per cent. This shows that massive rural-urban migration. If India urbanises properly, rural Indian will depopulate and there will be no population pressure on land (Economic Times, 2001).

The Study Area

Srikakulam is one of the drought prone districts in the State of Andhra Pradesh whose agricultural growth rate is stagnant with the lowest population growth rate and almost a zero industrial growth. According to the Census of India-2001 (Provisional Population Totals A.P), Srikakulam District has recorded the fifth lowest population growth rate among all the districts. The percentage growth of population in the District during 1991-2001 is only 8.93 as against 13.86 for the

State. In case of literacy rate, the District is lagging far behind. The District's literacy rate is 55.94 per cent where as for the State it is 61.11 per cent. The proportion of rural to urban migrants to the total population of the District has increased in 1991 compared to 1981, 1971 and 1961.

Objectives

The objectives of the study are:

1. To compare the total population of the selected village as per the census with household enumeration.
2. To estimate the proportion of out-migrants from the village and
3. To analyse the differences in socio-economic status of migrant and non-migrant households.

Methodology

We have chosen Jagannadhapeta village in Santhakaviti Mandal of Srikakulam District as a Case Study and the data were collected through a structured questionnaire with the reference date of 1-3-2002, exactly one year after the 2001 Population Census reference date of 1-3-2001.

Demographic Features of Sample Mandal and Village

Santhakaviti Mandal comprises of 52 villages. This Mandal, according to 2001 Census, has a total population 66,605, out of which 33,486 are males and 33119 are females. There are 29020 (43.6%) literates in the Mandal, out of which 18,030 (53.%) are males and 10,990 (33.2%) females. The total workers consist of 34,364 farmers. The percentage of agricultural labour is accounted for 17,196 (50%), while the percentage of cultivators and other workers constitute 26.3 per cent and 18.5 per cent respectively. (See Table 1).

According to the 2001 census, the total population of the sample village is 417, out of which 208 are males and 209 are females. The total literates in the Village is 185 (44.4%). The percentage of male literates is (58.2%) which is

Table 1: Demographic Features of sample village and Mandal

Sl. No.	*Item*	*Jagannadhapeta Village*	*Santhakaviti Mandal*
A.	**Population**		
	Total	417	66,605
	Male	49.9	50.3
	Female	50.1	49.7
B.	**Literacy**		
	Total	185	29,020
	Male	58.2	53.8
	Female	30.6	33.2
C.	**Composition of workers**		
	Cultivators	46.5	26.3
	Agriculture Labour	33.5	50.1
	Household Industry	0.0	5.1
	Other workers	20.0	18.5
	Total	**215 (100.0)**	**34,364 (100.0)**

significantly higher compared to females i.e. 30.6 per cent. The total number of workers are 215, out of which 100 (46.5%) are cultivators, 72 (33.5%) are agricultural labour and 43 (20.0%) are the other workers.

The percentage of total as will as male literates of the sample Village is higher compared to the Mandal average. In case workforce the percentage of cultivators is also significantly higher in the sample Village compared to the Mandal average (See Table 1).

The total population of the village was 449 as on 1.3.2002, as against 417 according to 2001 Census as on 1-3-2001. Out of 449, 133 (29.62%) were migrants and 316 (70.38%) were non-migrants. More than one-half of the migrants who left the Village are in the age group of 15-35. In the case of 36 years and above age-group the trend is otherwise (See Table 2).

Marital Status

Information was elicited on the marital status from the migrants and non-migrants of the sample Village. The

Table 2: Distribution of sample population by age-group and sex

Sl. No.	*Age Group*	*Migrants*						*Non-Migrants*					
		Male		*Female*		*Total*		*Male*		*Female*		*Total*	
1.	0 - 6	11	13.7	5	9.4	16	12.0	11	6.8	10	6.5	21	6.6
2.	7 - 14	8	10.0	3	5.7	11	8.3	17	10.5	25	6.5	42	13.3
3.	15 - 35	41	51.3	34	64.1	75	56.4	58	35.8	47	16.2	105	33.3
4.	36 - 49	12	15.0	8	15.1	20	15.0	35	21.6	34	30.5	69	21.8
5.	50 - 60	8	10.0	3	5.7	11	8.3	22	13.6	19	22.1	41	13.0
6.	61 & Above	-	-	-	-	-	-	19	11.7	19	12.3	38	12.0
	Total	**80**	**100.0**	**53**	**100.0**	**133**	**100.0**	**162**	**100.0**	**154**	**100.0**	**316**	**100.0**

percentage of married males and females among migrants are much higher between the age groups of 15-35, 36-49 and 50-60 years compared to non-migrants. Between 15-35 age-group, unmarried males among migrants are much lower than that of non-migrants (See Table 3).

It is interesting to note that, on the whole, the percentage of male married migrants is 51.3 and it is 53.7 among non-migrants. The male married non-migrants are higher compared to migrants, while it is reverse the case of unmarried females.

Literacy Level

Literacy plays a vital role of all the social factors. The children in the age group 0-6 are years excluded from the literacy rate. On the literacy front, all the non-migrants are lagging behind the migrants. The percentage of illiterates is higher (40.7) among non-migrants compared to migrants (12.0). In case of primary education, the non-migrants is in the forefront. Among the migrants, there are wide variations between males and females. Secondary education among females (39.5 per cent) is higher compared to males (21.7 per cent). Regarding college, higher secondary and technical education the males among migrants accounted for 39.1, 10.1 and 2.9 per cent respectively. Table 4 clearly shows that people with higher qualifications are attracted to the cities followed by those, having secondary education.

Occupation

Occupation-wise, cultivation occupies a dominant place, next to cultivation, agricultural labour accounted for 22.8 per cent among non-migrants. Among migrants, the percentage of male was 13.0 The highest percentage of male employees (37.0) are working in government agencies and 30 per cent of employees are working in the private organisations among migrants while it is almost negligible in non-migrants showing greater variation n workforce of females between migrants and non-migrants (See Table 5).

Table 3: Percentage Distribution of sample population by marital status

Sl. No.	Age-group	Male				Female			
		Married	*Unmarried*	*Widow*	*Total*	*Married*	*Unmarried*	*Widow*	*Total*
					MIGRANTS				
1.	0-6	—	100.0	—	100.0	—	100.0	—	100.0
2.	7-14	—	100.0	—	100.0	—	100.0	—	100.0
3.	15-35	53.7	46.3	—	100.0	82.4	17.6	—	100.0
4.	36.49	100.0	—	—	100.0	100.0	—	—	100.0
5.	50-60	87.5	—	12.5	100.0	100.0	—	—	100
6.	61 and above	—	—	—	—	—	—	—	—
	Total	51.3	47.5	1.2	100.0	73.6	26.4	—	100.0
					NON-MIGRANTS				
1.	0-6	—	100.0	—	100.0	—	100.0	—	100.0
2.	7-14	—	100.0	—	100.0	—	100.0	—	100.0
3.	15-35	29.3	70.7	—	100.0	53.2	44.7	2.1	100.0
4.	36-49	94.2	—	5.8	100.0	94.0	—	6.0	100.0
5.	50-60	90.9	—	9.1	100.0	73.7	—	26.3	100.0
6.	61 and above	89.5	—	10.5	100.0	52.6	—	47.4	100.0
	Total	53.7	42.6	3.7	100.0	52.6	36.4	11.0	100.0

Table 4: Percentage distribution of sample population by literacy status

Sl. No.	Literacy Status	Migrants			Non-Migrants		
		Male	Female	Total	Male	Female	Total
1.	Illiterate	10.1	14.6	12.0	27.6	54.5	40.7
2.	Literate	6.0	18.8	11.1	19.7	12.0	16.0
3.	Primary	10.1	20.8	14.5	15.1	22.3	18.6
4.	Secondary	21.7	39.5	29.1	17.1	9.8	13.6
5.	Higher Secondary	10.1	4.2	7.7	6.5	0.7	3.7
6.	College	39.1	2.1	23.9	10.0	0.7	5.4
7.	Technical	2.9	—	1.7	4.0	—	2.0
	Total	**100.0 (69)**	**100.0 (48)**	**100.0 (117)**	**100.0 (152)**	**100.0 (143)**	**100.0 (295)**

Table 5: Percentage distribution of migrants and non-migrants by main occupation

Sl. No.	Occupation	Migrants			Non-Migrants		
		Male	Female	Total	Male	Female	Total
1.	Cultivation	—	—	—	53.3	34.0	44.2
2.	Agricultural Labour	2.0	3.6	2.4	24.7	21.0	22.8
3.	Construction Labour	13.0	7.1	11.0	—	—	—
4.	Employees (Govt.)	37.0	—	24.4	1.0	—	0.5
5.	Employees (Private Organisation)	30.0	—	19.5	—	—	—
6.	House Wives	—	89.3	30.5	—	38.0	17.8
7.	Others	18.0	—	12.2	21.0	7.0	14.7
	Total	**100.0 (54)**	**100.0 (28)**	**100.0 (82)**	**100.0 (105)**	**100.0 (92)**	**100.0 (197)**

Occupation of Migrants in the Village Before their Migration

Information was collected on occupation of migrants before leaving village. The data on this show that there is a wider difference in the workforce between their native place and place of destination. There is more diversification in the workforce among migrants. All the migrants were working in their native village as agricultural labour (42.6 per cent), unemployed (24.1 per cent), students (18.5 per cent) and cultivators 14.8 per cent. After leaving their village none of them worked in the same occupations at the destination. Field observations showed that many rural people i.e. younger generation are attracted to the cities and they would like to enjoy different life style of living in urban areas (See Table 6).

Table 6: Distribution of sample migrants by occupation (before migration)

Sl. No.	*Occupation*	*No. of Migrants*	*Percent*
1.	Cultivation	8	14.8
2.	Agricultural Labour	23	42.6
3.	Unemployed	13	24.1
4.	Student	10	18.5
	Total	**54**	**100.0**

Destination of Migrants

The destinations of the migrants show far off places like other states, Hyderabad, Visakhapatnam and near by Vizianagaram. Visakhapatnam accounted for 50 per cent of the destinations, followed by other states by 16.7 per cent, Srikaulam by 15 per cent, Hyderabad by 11 per cent and Vizianagaram by 7 per cent. This clearly shows that Lee's Distance Theory of migration holds good in this case also.

Among the non-migrants, 17 members are seasonal migrants working as brick making workers in West Godavari District. They stay for four months in an year in this District (See Table 7).

Table 7: Distribution of sample migrants by destination

Sl. No.	District	No. of Migrants	Percent
1.	Srikakulam	8	14.8
2.	Vizianagaram	4	7.4
3.	Viskahapatnam	27	50.0
4.	Hyderabad	6	11.1
5.	Other States	9	16.7
	Total	54	100.0

Note: 17 Seasonal Migrants as Brick making workers migrate to West Godavari District in Andhra Pradesh.

Type of Housing

Housing is one of the basic inputs which influences the quality of life of the people. Majority of the sample migrants are living in pucca houses i.e. 66.6 per cent whereas 70.5 per cent are living in semi-pucca houses among non-migrants. In case of Kutcha houses, non-migrants is accounted for 26 per cent while it is 20 per cent among migrants. Non-migrants living in semi-pucca and kutcha houses are much higher compared to migrants (See Table 8).

Table 8: Percentage Distribution of Migrant and non-migrants by type of house

Sl. No.	Type of House	Migrants	Non-Migrants
1.	Pucca	66.6	3.4
2.	Semi-Pucca	13.0	70.5
3.	Kutcha	20.4	26.1
	Total	100.0	100.0

Summary of Findings and Implications

To sum up, according to the 2001 census, the total population of the sample Village is 417, out of which 208 are males and 209 are females. As per the survey conducted by us the total populations of the village was 449 as on 1-3-2002, out of which 133 were migrants and 316 were non-migrants. More than one-half of migrants who left the Village are in the age-group of 15-35. The study clearly shows that people with higher qualifications are attracted to the cities followed by those having secondary and above educational level. The highest percentage of male employees (37.0 %) are working in government agencies and 30 per cent of employees are working in the private organizations among migrants, while it is almost negligible in non-migrants. Field observations showed that many rural people i.e. younger generation are attracted to the cities and they would like to enjoy different life style of living in urban areas. The destination of the migrants show far off places like other states, cities and towns in the State like Hyderabad, Visakhapatnam and nearby Vizianagaram. Thus, the major reason for low population growth rate in the backward districts like Srikakulam appeared to be non-enumeration seasonal migrants along with higher mortality rate.

Large-scale out-migration has to be stopped by starting industries based on local natural resources like Jute, Sugarcane etc.

Post-Census Enumeration check has to be conducted so as to find out the reasons for low population growth rate in the District.

References

Census of India, 2001 Provisional Population Totals, Andhra Pradesh, Registrar General, Government of India.

Economic Times, 2001 'India's Urban Future', The Economic Times, 28-7-2001.

Gupta, S.P. and B.L. Prajapati 1998 "Migration of Agricultural Labourers in Chhatisgarh Region of Madhya Pradesh: A Micro Level Study", The Indian Journal of Labour Economics, Vol. 41 (4).

Narasimhan, R.L. and Harish Chandra, 1998 "Sources of Data on Migration and Recent Trends", The Indian Journal of Labour Economics, Vol. 41 (4).

Ranga Rao, K., K.S. Rani and K.R. Murty, 1977 "Migration Experience of Urban Slum Dwellers", The Indian Journal of Social Work, Vol. 38 (1).

Santhapparaj Solucis 1998 "International Migration, Remittance and Determinants of Remittance: An Empirical Analysis", The Indian Journal of Labour Economics, Vol. 41 (4)

Singh, S.P. and R.K. Aggarwal, 1998 "Rural-Urban Migration: The Role of Push and Pull Factors Revisited", The Indian Journal of Labour Economics, Vol. 41 (4).

Sree Rama Murty, S 1990 "A Study of Rural out-Migration in Srikakulam District of Andhra Pradesh", unpublished Thesis submitted to The Andhra University, Visakhapatnam, Andhra Pradesh.

9

Census 2001: A Critical Analysis of Sex Ratio in India

Dr. B. Ratna Kumari
Mrs. A. B. Santha Rajyam

"Gender position may not change unless gender relations are altered"

Introduction

A census is more than head count and it is vital tool for policy making and planning. It is the right time to analyze critically the sex ratio in gender perspective as India is marching towards women empowerment by making women as active participants in the developmental programmes.

The census 2001 has revealed some interesting and worrying features with regard to sex ratio which calls for some critical analysis and explanation. With a population count of 1,027 million as of zero hours of March 1,2001, India has completed its first census of the 21st Century. The census has been counted 531 million males and 496 million females giving rise to an overall sex ratio of 933 females per 1000 males, which is a matter of some satisfaction. But a matter of deep concern is the decline in sex ratio of population in 0-6 age group (hence forth called child sex ratio) from 945 in 1991 to 927 in 2001. Several questions have been raised from time to time with regard to the trend in overall sex ratio and particularly about the child sex ratio. In order to answer many questions pertaining to sex ratio the present study has made an attempt to study the following objectives as given below:

Objectives

1. to examine the trend sex ratio (BIMARU and DEMARU) and conditions that are responsible for changes in trend of sex ratio in India in general and Andhra Pradesh in particular.
2. to analyze how can 'gender' implicate for human poverty and also find out quarries involved in the census enumeration; and
3. to suggest strategies for gender empowerment in India as well as in Andhra Pradesh so that the sex ratio will be favourable to girl child and human dignity or enriched with harmony and solidarity between men and women in the society.

What are BIMARU & DEMARU States?

Ashish Bose (2001) and Agnihotri (2001) states that census has given a shocking aspect, namely a sharp decline in the female-male ratio in several states. He further states that migration can not explain this phenomenon which must be the consequence of female foeticide on a massive scale, if not female infanticide and higher female child mortality rates. It is unfortunate that even in the progressive Indian states, except Kerala, the sex ratio has been declined (see Table 1).

Sex ratio is defined as the member of females per 1000 male population. During 1980s, Ashish Bose had classified demographically backward states as Bihar, Madhya Pradesh, Rajasthan, and Uttar Pradesh (BIMARU) which is an acronym generally accepted 2001 census results to fully validate of his diagnosis of Indian population problems in terms of adverse role of these 4 BIMARU states. (see Table 2).

Table 2 gives a note of the alarming decline in the child sex ratio in 2001. Bose like to coin another acronym DEMARU when D stands for daughters and MARU stands for killing

Table 1: Sex ratio in India and Andhra Pradesh 1901-2001

Year	The rate of sex ratio (females for 1000 males)	
	India	Andhra Pradesh
1901	972	985
1911	964	992
1921	955	993
1931	950	987
1941	945	980
1951	946	986
1961	941	981
1971	930	977
1981	934	975
1991	929	972
2001	933	978

Source: Government of India, Census of India, 2001.

in English 'E' will denote 'elimination'. Daughters elimination by killing. Maithreyi and Vina Mazumdar (2001) have classified DEMURU as Daughters Elimination Men Aspiring Range for Ultrasound. On the basis of statistical cut off point of 60 points decline in the child sex ratio, Bose has classified Punjab, Haryana, Himachal Pradesh and Gujarat states as "DEMARU' Sates and questioned the whole country, except Kerala as becoming 'DEMURU'?

Analysis of Sex Ratio in India and Andhra Pradesh

The age distribution of population in the Indian census follows five yearly groupings like 0-4, 5-9, 10-14 and so on. In 1991, it was decided to calculate literacy rates for the population seven years and over. Therefore a new category of 0-6 was introduced in the primary census abstract, and literacy data for the age group seven and above were sorted out. Besides 0-6 was convenient age group to study the import of the Integrated Child Development Services (ICDS) etc. In keeping with this practice, the 2001 census tables give data on literacy after excluding 0-6 age groups. In this process separate figures are available for th sex composition of the 0-6 age group. It goes to the credit of the 2001 census commissioner that he could at once see a shocking aspect of

Table 2: Sex ratio in states and Union Territories of India: 1991-2001 census

S. No.	*India/States/UT*	*Sex ratio (number of females per 1000 males)*	
		1991	*2001*
	India	927	933
1	Jammu & Kashmir	896	900
2	Himachal Pradesh	976	970
3	Punjab	882	874
4	Chandigarh	790	773
5	Uttaranchal	936	964
6	Haryana	865	861
7	Delhi	827	821
8	Rajasthan	910	922
9	Uttar Pradesh	876	898
10	Bihar	907	921
11	Sikkim	878	875
12	Arunachal Pradesh	859	901
13	Nagaland	886	909
14	Manipur	958	978
15	Mizoram	921	938
16	Tripura	945	950
17	Meghalaya	955	975
18	Assam	923	932
19	West Bengal	917	934
20	Jharkhand	922	941
21	Orissa	971	972
22	Chatisgarh	985	990
23	Madhya Pradesh	912	920
24	Gujarat	934	921
25	Daman & Diu	969	709
26	Dadra & Nagar Haveli	952	811
27	Maharastra	934	922
28	Andhra Pradesh	972	978
29	Karnataka	960	964
30	Gao	967	960
31	Lashadweep	943	947
32	Kerala	1036	1058
33	Tamilnadu	974	986
34	Pondicherry	978	1001
35	Andaman & Nicobar Island	818	846

Source: Govt. of India, Census of India 2001, Series 29, paper 1, pp. 43-44.

this century namely, 'a sharp decline in the sex ratio of the under 0-6 population in the last 40 years, i.e., 976 in 1961, 962 in 1981, 945 in 1991 and 927 in 2001, a decline of 18 points in this last decade.

The decline is most pronounced in Punjab where the sex ratio in the age group 0-6 years fall from 875 to 793 (a decrease of 82 points), in Haryana (59 points) in Himachal Pradesh and Chandigarh (42 points) and Gujarat (50 points). These declines are in areas which had already been flagged as showing low sex ratio among children and as regions which were seeing a rapid growth of sex determination clinics (pre-natal Diagnostic Techniques, PNDT) and questionable abortions, with a high likelihood of female foeticides. Some historical evidences of female foeticide in Northern India indicate that certain castes had followed female foeticide since 1789. The castes with a new lower projections of female children compared to males were: the Rajputs, Jats, Khutois and noyal Brahmins, aturs, gujars (Viswanath, 2001). Lower the impact of modernity and modern education enhanced the price of dowry but may not be created the awareness of discrimination against females and other social evils. There is a need to study the impact of Green Revolution in Punjab and Haryana as it has worsened the female sex ratio among certain centres. The landless men and displacement due to mechanization had a negative impact on the female sex ratio in DEMARU states. The Indian census must also address certain quarries about caste domination, access to shared earned income, status of their levels of participation at decision making levels. Surprisingly even Maharastra, the first state who have been passed the pre-natal Diagnostic Techniques (regulation and prevention) act (PNDT act) also registered a decline in the under-6 sex-ratio, from 946 to 917 (29 points). In fact all states except three Kerala, Mizoram and Tripura who had impact of Christian Missionaries have reported fewer girls than boys under six years.

Andhra Pradesh

The sex ratio in Andhra Pradesh was 985 in 1901 and 986 in 1951, 981 in 1961, 977 in 1971, 975 in 1981, and 972 in

Table 3: Andhra Pradesh-Sex-ratio since 1901 for State and Districts

Sl. No.	State/District	Sex-ratio (Number of females per 1000 males)										
		1901	1911	1921	1931	1941	1951	1961	1971	1981	1991	2001
28	Andhra Pradesh	985	992	993	987	980	986	981	977	975	972	978
1	Adilabad	991	976	955	956	974	1,008	981	976	980	980	989
2	Nizamabad	1,006	1,006	1,016	990	994	1,019	1,007	999	1,013	1,017	1,016
3	Karimnagar	918	931	949	958	966	981	996	985	994	986	1,000
4	Medak	977	976	977	979	967	991	996	986	982	970	976
5	Hyderabad	944	948	956	925	944	988	929	918	920	933	945
6	Rangareddi	944	948	956	925	944	990	986	963	956	941	941
7	Mahbubnagar	980	971	976	969	969	996	1,003	988	983	973	970
8	Nalgonda	892	946	955	953	945	946	952	965	969	962	967
9	Warangal	907	938	947	946	943	953	954	956	964	962	973
10	Khammam	921	944	951	950	947	954	958	957	957	961	975
11	Srikakulam	1,076	1,098	1,093	1,078	1,059	1,062	1,047	1,033	1,023	1,012	1,013
12	Vizianagaram	1,061	1,082	1,086	1,068	1,048	1,032	1,017	1,009	1,006	1,000	1,004
13	Viskahapatnam	1,045	1,064	1,079	1,057	1,037	1,023	1,000	992	981	975	991
14	East Godavari	1,038	1,040	1,043	1,026	1,010	1,002	999	996	993	998	992
15	West Godavari	1,032	1,035	1,032	1,028	1,006	1,000	992	994	991	994	992
16	Krishna	975	979	980	972	965	969	962	964	971	969	961
17	Guntur	976	978	981	976	969	974	976	974	973	970	984
18	Prakasam	996	998	992	994	983	981	991	987	978	970	971
19	Nellore	985	994	983	993	988	987	989	986	978	980	983
20	Cuddapah	976	969	964	962	953	+952	957	958	959	955	975
21	Kurnool	972	977	964	968	974	979	977	969	962	953	965
22	Anantapur	952	950	943	947	942	943	946	947	946	946	957
23	Chittoor	971	968	959	957	952	954	957	960	966	966	983

1991 and was showing a decreasing trend. It is 978 in 2001 and for the first time the sex ratio has increased after 1951. The sex ratio in Andhra Pradesh is higher than the all India figure which is 933.

The district profile shows that the sex ratio continues to be favourable to women in Nizamabad (raises 1), Srikakulam and Vizianagaram. As per 2001 provisional population, Karimnagar has recorded a sex ratio of 1000 as against 986 in 1991, Hyderabad, Rangareddy, Ananthapuram, Kurnool and Cuddapah districts show lowest sex ratio in the state. (see Table 3).

Among the North Coastal District viz, Srikakulam (1012) and Vizianagaram (1000) ranks for higher sex ratio and noted that the figures for the seven and above age group are influenced by migration while the coastal districts viz., East Godavari and West Godavari and Prakasam, among the coastal districts of the state, the sex ratio is higher than the state average of Rayalaseema, all the districts except Chittoor have recorded a lower sex ratio then the state average. In Telangana out of 10 districts, 6 districts have recorded a lower sex ratio than the state average (Govt. of India, Census of India, 2001). This trend analyze the importance of research study on sex ratio in depth.

According to findings of the study by Devi Prasad (1994) that the cultural norms and attitudes which are affecting the status of several girl children viz., attitudes of son preference and family size, marriage practices like female foeticide proceeded by prenatal diagnostic techniques especially in Kurnool and Prakasam distrits and it is evident in the 2001 census also.

This phenomenon must be the consequence of female foeticide on a massive scale if not female infanticide and higher female child mortallity rates. The census commissioner rightly says in his report "one thing is clear-the imbalance that has set in this early age group is difficult to be removed and would remain to be haunt the population for a long time to come to say the least, demographically the sex ratio of 927 of the population in the age group 0-6 does not appear to angus well for the future of the country (2001)".

On the whole this decline trend has to be stressed, implies an irreversible change in the demographic picture. Children under 0-6 age group will be the adults of a decade and a half from new and there will be far fewer women than men in the adult population. Krishna Raj (2001) has rightly commented that "This is a sad status of the improvement that has occurred in the adult sex ratio across the country over the decades". He further stated that it is a grave indictment of the family planning programme that demographic concern has been to reduce the number of children per couple, often through for female social education in the provision of livelihood opportunities. The small family norms also help inevitably to devalue daughter. But in Andhra Pradesh, the Government has been initiated a number of programmes like Kishore Balika Pathakam (Scheme), girl child protection scheme and ICDS and Balika Samrudhi Yojana etc., to bring attitudinal changes of people (2001) and it helps to increase the sex ratio in future.

How Gender can Implicate Human Poverty in the Country?

The term 'gender' to the social differences and relations between men and women which are learned, changeable over time, and have wide variatins both within and between cultures. These differences and relationships are socially constructed and are learned through the socialization process (ILO, 2000). Gender roles are learned behaviour in a given society, community or social group, in which people are conditioned to perceive activities, tasks and responsibilities as male and female. These perceptions are affected by age, class, race, ethnicity, culture, religion and other ideologies. They are context specific and can be modified. During census operations enumerators are used to collect data regarding sexual differences between men and women which are biologically determined but based on femininity and masculinity. Gender therefore plays a predominant role in selection of a child sex in Indian family.

The Indian family institution is renounced for its family ties and to a large extent it is guided by customary gender norms and values based on patriarchal and hierarchical ideology (Agnihotri, B. 2001). In the Indian society human rights are heavily stacked against women such as attitudes towards son preference, intra-household discrimination of daughters in the allocation of food, medical care, health care, childcare, and in levels of education derived for boys and girls. Reflections of such ideology are also seen in the nature of marriage, dowry demands, dowry dealths, sati, and violence against women. If these, the most specific forms of manifestations of patriarchy and of contemporary challenges identified for decline sex ratio are female feoticide and infanticide. Such discrimination against girls child has not only lowered the status of girls but also was partly responsible for unequal sex ratios with men outnumbering women in the population of the country. Moreover this leads to extreme manifestations of power inequality between men and women constitute gross violation of girl child survival, protection and development.

In some societies the lower value assigned to women and girls translates into excess mortality (World Bank, 2000). Estimates based an official national census find that as a result of excess female mortality, about 7 per cent of girls under age five are 'missing' in China and Korea and more then 4 per cent in India and other parts of South Asia (Sen and Dreze 1989, Coale 1991, Klasen 19914, World Bank, 2000). Without such discrimination there would be an estimated 60-100 million more women in the World (Das Gupta and others 1997; Zeng and others, 1993). Gender inequality has strong repercussions for human poverty in the next generation because the decline sex ratio gives threat to the human natural life cycle.

Some of the social customs and traditions, beliefs and practices such as dowry, marriage expenditure, puberty rituals and lack of social and economic opportunities for girls have led to a general aversion among parents to have girl children in the family in DEMARU and BIMARU states. At the same time the unscrupulous medical practitioners have sought to exploit to make money by misusing prenatal SD tests against this prejudice. Later such test have wide spread all over India and this helps not only declining sex ratio but also silently propagate the nation that girls are a dispensable commodity. Since the survival chances of girl child start from the conception in mother's womb to delivery. On the whole the women are discriminated from womb to tomb in many ways and it leads to dangerous trends in the harmonial relationship between men and women. The implementation and enforcement of prenatal diagnostic Act was initiated in 1994 throughout the country. But the 2001 census gives a witness of declining sex ratio in spite of the above acts implementation. Therefore, any serious attempt to improve the status and survival chances of girl children in our society must deal firstly with gender bias of discrimination that have an impact on the lower sex ratio.

The estimates of percentage differentials among the child sex ratio, differential undercount, sex differential in mortality and sex ratio at birth directly affects the population in the 0-6 age group. (Mahendra K. Premi, 2001). In India and in fair other countries of South Asia and West Asia there is unfavourable situation towards females at almost all ages. But sex ratio at birth (SRB) becoming more favourable to males has however, influenced the overall sex ratio in the opposite direction, which is reflected in the adverse child sex ratio. Here also we can identify how gender roles, relations can implicate human poverty.

At the moment child sex ratio is available only at the district level for all the states, it would be possible to point those districts which have registered child sex ratio below 850. There would be several districts showing worse sex ratio and their identification would be quite important.

The available data with rural urban break down should not be able to identify whether the practice of female feoticide is basically an urban problem or rural? Further analysis is needed in this direction. There is a need of detailed problem or rural? Further analysis is needed in this direction. There is a need of detailed probing to understand the factors behind the declining sex ratio phenomenon as some of the DEMARU states, has fairly high literacy rate and economically developed. This is contrary to expectation, hence one needs to examine the various issues at length during the census operations.

Of course, Andhra Pradesh is a first state to declare its Population Policy and marching towards women empowerment. And also A.P. has gained prominent place in forming self-help groups and this group strategy helped to some extent so that its sex ratio increased in the 2001 census. Women are aware about their rights viz., health, education, employment and they are stakeholders of many governmental programmes like SHGs, Janma Bhoomi, Adult Education, non-formal education and many self employment programmes etc. on one side it reflects a favourable environment towards the survival of girl child, on the other side the rate of violence against women is growing day by day in terms of rape, molestation, dowry death, sexuality and physically harassment, domestic violence, violence at work spots are causing the declining trend of sex ratio. The women movement must take care of the gender issues involved in their life and it is the right time to work for sustainable development of women along with NGOs.

Strategies

However, in India, especially northern India has occupied top rank of lower sex ratio inspite of many developmental programmes initiated by the government of India. Therefore, there is a need for strategies which can certain human development through equalizing the sex ratios.

1. Conduct gender awareness workshops/seminar frequently to that particular areas where is necessary.

2. Develop vigilance committees to watch the activities of medical and non-medical practitioners against the foeticide.
3. District wise study is essential to get fair details for low sex ratio.
4. Media has to play a positive role in brining positive attitudinal changes of the community.
5. Autonomy of northern Indian women in socio-economic conditions will decide the fate of the girl child. Hence, number of socio-economic programmes must be initiated to achieve gender empowerment.
6. Provide literacy, education and employment to the process of the poor women to sustain themselves from the gender bias.
7. The role of state and social capital must be increased in order to give voice towards their problems and make powerful and vibrant.
8. It is absolutely necessary to bring about an attitudinal change among castes and communities which resort female foeticide and infanticide through a different kind of formal and informal education in rural areas.

Conclusion

On the whole what are the causes of female foeticide? The answer is simple: girls are liabilities and boys are assets. Girls mean dowry and with growing greed in Indian society and the mindless consumerism propagated by TV channels for 24 hours, the demand for dowry will increase further, why not make the girls assets? Why not establish women's polytechnics and train million of young girls in modern skills so that they can earn income and stand on their own feet and resist dowry. Why not reserve 50 per cent of jobs for women? e.g. the Kerala women nurses are reputed for their excellent services all over the world but there is an implicit saying that they have to save the money in order to buy husbands. Where does the so-called empowerment of women lead us to?

Ashis Bose (2001) rightly concluded that if the child sex ratio is very likely to go down future in the years to come the shortage of women will distort the society, the curve against women will increase, polyandry will emerge on the scene and there will no growing conflict and violence. It is so horrendous scenario and leads to social disaster. Isn't it time that the public policy put other issues on hold and got down to effectively and urgently pushing the agenda of changing social perceptions and value girl children and stamping out the practice of pre-natal sex determination and related female feoticide?

References

Agnihotri. S. B. (2001), "Rising sons and setting daughters provisional results of the 2001 census, in Vina Mazumdar and M. Krishnaji (eds.) Enduring Conundrum: India's Sex Ratio, Centre for Women's Development studies, Rainbow publishers, Delhi.

Ashish Bose (2001), "Census of India 2001 and After" Economic and Political weekly, May 19, PP. 1685-87.

Ashish Bose (2001), India's Billion Plus People, 2001 census. Highlight, methodology and media coverage, BR publishing corporation, New Delhi.

Ashish Bose (2001), Fighting Female Foeticide: Grouping Greed and shrinking child sex ratio, EPW, Sept. 8, 2001, PP. 3427-29.

Coale. A. (1991), "Excess Female Mortality and the Balance of the sexes: An estimate of the number of Missing Females" population and Development Review", 17, PP.517-23.

Das Gupta and others (2000), "State policy and women's autonomy in China, South Korea and India, 1950-2000: Lessons from contrasting experience".

Devi Prasad (1994), "A study of the declining sex ratio in Andhra Pradesh", unpublished research project, Andhra University.

Klasen. S. (1994), "Missing women" reconsidered, World Development 22(7), PP. 1061-71.

Krishna Raj (2001) "Editorial on population policy" central task, EPW, May, 12, PP. 1567-68.

Mahendra K. Premi (2001), "The Missing Girl Child", EPW, May 26, PP. 1875-80.

World Bank (2000), "World Development Report", Attacking poverty, Oxford University Press, New York, PP. 118-119.

Zeng and others (1993), "Causes and implications of the recent increase in the reported sex ratio at birth in China", population and development review, 19(2), PP. 283-302.

Government of India (2001), "Series 1, India, Provisional Population Totals, Paper 1 of 2001, controller of publications, Delhi.

Government of India (2001), SRS Bulletin, vol. 35, No. 1, Registrar General, New Delhi.

Government of India (2001), "Census of India 2001", series-29, Andhra Pradesh paper 1 of 2001, provisional population totals.

ILO (2000), Gender, bureau for Gender Equality, Geneva.

10

Changing Profile of Labour Composition—A study of Tanuku Municipality

Smt. K. Radha Pushpavathi
Sri D.V.V.S.Varma

Labour being a primary factor of production. The size of labour force is of great importance for the level of economic activity in a country. In the determination of the size of the labour force, it is customary to exclude children below the age of 15, and old people above the age of 60, though in India, poverty forces people belonging to these groups to work for bare substance. The work force participation rate in a country, i.e., proportion of working population to total population depends upon such factors as age and sex composition, attitude to work, availability of work, etc.

Broadly we divide occupations into three types. Agriculture, animal husbandry, forestry, fishing, etc., are collectively known as primary activities. They are primary because their products are essential or vital for human existence. They are carried with the help of nature. Manufacturing industries both small and large scale are known as secondary activities. Transport, communications, banking, finance and services are territory activities, which help the primary and secondary activities in the country.

Colin Clark, in his work 'conditions of economic progress' argues that there is a close relationship between development of an economy on the one hand, and the occupational structure on the other hand. Economic progress is generally associated with certain distinct necessary and predictable changes in occupation structure. Unfortunately India's labour force composition is static behaviour of the occupational structure. In this paper an attempt has been made to present changing profile of labour composition in Tanuku municipal area during the period 1981-2001. The analysis limited only to the workforce composition change over the years due to data constraints. Historically Tanuku is a part of Mogaltur paragana of Peddapuram Samstanam under the rulers of Rajahmundry. Tanuku also happened to be the birth place of "Adikavi" Nannayya who undertook the taste of translation of Mahabharatam from Sanskrit into Telugu.

Tanuku town was constituted into a Municipality in October, 1979. It is one of the eight municipalities in West Godavari District. The strength of council was 32.

The area of Tanuku town is 16.70 sq.km.over ¾ area of the extent of the town is covered Agricultural land. Residential area accounts only 16 per cent of total area. It has good educational and medical facilities. It has a Railway station and Bus terminal. It is agriculturally rich because of location in the midst of very fertilizer land producing abundant quantities of paddy and sugar cane besides banana and other garden crops. The town has both industrial and commercial importance.

The town is located on National highway No. 5 connecting Chennei & Calcutta. There are parks and play grounds. Nine Cinema theatres and library maintained by Zilla Grandhalya Samithi and a second library run by the Government.

The financial position of the Tanuku Municipality is sound. The Municipality income is greater than expenditure. However, the expenditure towards salaries due to pay revision will hamper developmental works. There is a need to increase the financial resources of the Municipality.

It is proud to say that Tanuku Municipality is the first literate town in the state by achieving 100 per cent literacy.

Demographic Patterns

According to 1981 census the total population Tanuku Municipality is 53,618 comprising 27,473 male and 26,145 females. During the census year 1991 the total population was 62,913 comprising 31,542 males and 31,371 females. The census year 2001 it has 68,224 persons comprising 33,928 males and 34,296 females.

Growth Table 1 represents the Growth of population in Tanuku Manicipality.

Table 1: Growth Population in Tanuku Manicipality (1981-2001)

Census Year	*Population*	*Decadal Growth*	*Males*	*Decadal Growth*	*Female*	*Decadal Growth*
1981	53618	-	27473	-	26145	-
1991	62913	17.33	31542	14.81	31371	19.98
2001	68224	8.44	33928	7.56	34296	9.32

Source: Census Reports & Municipal Records

During the period 1981-91 growth rate of population decreased from 56.79 per cent to 17.33 per cent. Again it has decreased to 8.44 per cent during the period 1991-2001. One interesting feature in Tanuku Municipality i.e., growth rate of female population is greater than growth rate male population.

During the census year the sex ratio of Tanuku Municipality is 952 females per 1000 males. It has increased to 1010 females per 1000 males. The sex ratio has increased due to the longevity of the women. The decades 1971-81 and 1981-91 can be turned as the period of rapid urbanization of the states. The decade 1991-2001 which presented a period of demographic transaction by way of a decline in population growth rate, has also exhibited a trend of stagnation urban population growth. There can be two probable reasons for decrease in the growth rate of urban population. Development Rural Growth centres can be a principal factor. After formation of 1125 Revenue Mandals, replacing the erstwhile taluks in 1985 as a measure for decentralization of administration, all the mandals head quarters become centeres of socio economic activities and as a result arresting the migration of people to town areas. Because of this the decadal growth rate of Tanuku Municipality. Population decreased 1981 to 2001.

Work Force

Every person counted the census gets classified as a main worker, marginal worker or non-workers. Main workers are those who had worked for the major part of the year i.e., 6 months or more. Marginal workers are those who had not worked for major part of the year i.e., less than 6 months.

Table 2 reveals that total work participation percentage in total population has shown an increase from 1981-2001. Work participation was 32 per cent in 1981. It improved to 33.65 per cent in 1991 and further improved to 34.18 per cent in 2001. It is not significant.

The work participation percentage for female has increasing 12.71 per cent to 13.84 per cent during the decade 1981-1991. The same decade work percentage for male has increasing 50.33 per cent to 53.36 per cent. During the decade 1991-2001 the percentage of male participation in work force has increased to 55.71 per cent. During the same period the percentage of female in work force has a slight decline ie., 12.83 per cent.

The percentage of non-workers in total population has decreased from 68 per cent to 65.82 per cent during the period 1991-2001. The percentage of non-workers in total population has decreased only 2.18 per cent during 20 years period. The reasons for the decrease of percentage of non-workers may be attributed to (a) Higher percentage of old people in total population as a result of increase in life expectancy rate, (b) increase in school enrollment and consequently decline in child perticipation rate.

Table 2: Total work Participation Percentage

	1981			1991			2001		
	Persons	*Male*	*Female*	*Persons*	*Male*	*Female*	*Persons*	*Male*	*Female*
Population	53618 (100.0)	27473 (100.0)	26145 (100.0)	62913 (100.0)	31542 (100.0)	31371 (100.0)	68224 (100.0)	33928 (100.0)	34296 (100.0)
Total Workers	17153 (32.0)	13828 (50.33)	3325 (12.71)	21173 (33.65)	16831 (53.36)	4342 (13.84)	23324 (34.18)	18923 (55.77)	4401 (12.83)
Non-Workers	36465 (68.0)	13645 (49.67)	22820 (87.29)	41740 (66.35)	14711 (14.64)	27029 (18.16)	44900 (65.82)	15005 (44.23)	29895 (87.17)

Source: Census Reports & Municipal Records.

Main Labour Force

Based on the data available the workforce is identified in (i) Primary sector (ii) other sectors.

Primary sector comprises cultivated agriculture labourers and animal husbandry, forestry, fishing etc., other sectors comprises secondary sector and territory sector. Secondary sector comprises trade and commerce, transport, storage and communications and other services.

Table 3 reveals that the composition of labour force during the period 1981-2001.

Table 3: Occupational Structure

	1981	*1991*	*2001*
Primary Sector	54.98 (32.75)	7374 (34.94)	6109 (28.57)
Other Sectors	11287 (67.24)	13725 (65.66)	15271 (71.43)
Total Workers	16785	21099	21380

An obvious conclusion from table 3 is that the changing profile of labour force of Tanuku reflects clearly shows urbanization of land of the Tanuku Municipality. Over the last two decades the proportion of primary sector workers in working population has decreased from 32.75 per cent to 28.57 per cent

The proportion of workers in other sectors in total population has increased from 67.24 per cent to 71.42 per cent during the period 1981-2001

The labour force in other sector swelled because of rapid industrialisation and the consequent growth of service sector institution wise banking finance, trade and commerce which provide more employment but are generating the process of occupational shift in favour of secondary and territory sectors. This is a clear indication of the growth of urbanization of Tanuku Municipality.

Reference

1. Colin Clark: Conditions of Economic progress
2. Vision 2020 of Tanuku Municipality
3. Municipality Administrative Report
4. Census of India 2001 Provisional Population
5. Census of India 1981 and 1991.

11

Demographic Transition in Developed and Developing Countries

Ch. Subramanyam
B. Ch. Krishna Murty

At some stage in the history of a country high growth of population and as a result over population was a reality for both developed and developing world. The causative factors could be same or different or even if the same magnitude could vary. It is germane to examine the relative performance of developing countries like India Vis-à-vis developed countries, although the time periods are different. The object of this paper is to explain the factors responsible for over population in developing countries like India when compared to the developed west.

The Theory of Demographic Transition

The historical experience of demographic transition recorded three stages of modern population growth where stages corresponds with high birth rate and high death rates having stable or slow growing population. Stage two began to occur when modernization, associated with improved public health methods, better diets, higher incomes, etc., led to a marked reduction in mortality that gradually raised life expectancy from under 40 years to over 60 years. However, the decline in death rates was not immediately accompanied by a decline in fertility. This trend is attributed to "The agrarian peasant economy characterized by high death and birth rates. The death rates usually fluctuate in response to the variations in harvests and the incidence of epidemics. They are high because of poor diet, primitive conditions of sanitation and lack of preventive and curative medical and public health programmes. The birth rates in such economies are high and are a functional response to high mortality. The ideals of prollfic fertility are, therefore, ingrained in the social systems, customs and bellefs of such societies. These ideals are reinforced by the economic advantages of having a large number of children. As the agrarian economy starts undergoing changes, it becomes inter-dependent on other economies, has high levels of production, and becomes highly industrialized, market oriented and urbanized. When this happens, death rates register striking reductions a consequence of better a regular supply of food as well as improved medical knowledge and care. At a somewhat later stage, birth rates also begin to fall. The acceptance of the ideal of a small family size comes about initially in urban grounds at the higher end socio-economic scale, and then spreads to small cities, lower-income groups and eventually to rural areas[1]. As a result, the growing divergence between high birth rates and falling death rates led to a sharp increase in population growth compared to past centuries. Finally, stage three was entered when the forces and influences of modernization and development caused the beginning of a decline in fertility leading to falling birth rates converging with lower death rates leaving little or no population growth. This type of demographic transition is the general historical experiences of almost all developed countries. In case of developing countries this transition stopped at the second stage with the spread of modern knowledge the death rates, particularly infant mortality declined significantly and raising birth rates resulted in population explosion. Even the developed countries have surplus population before the third stage set in after a long time.

The three Phases of demographic transition are also represented in the diagram. It shows that high birth and death

DIAGRAM

Karl Sax Model of Demographic Transitions

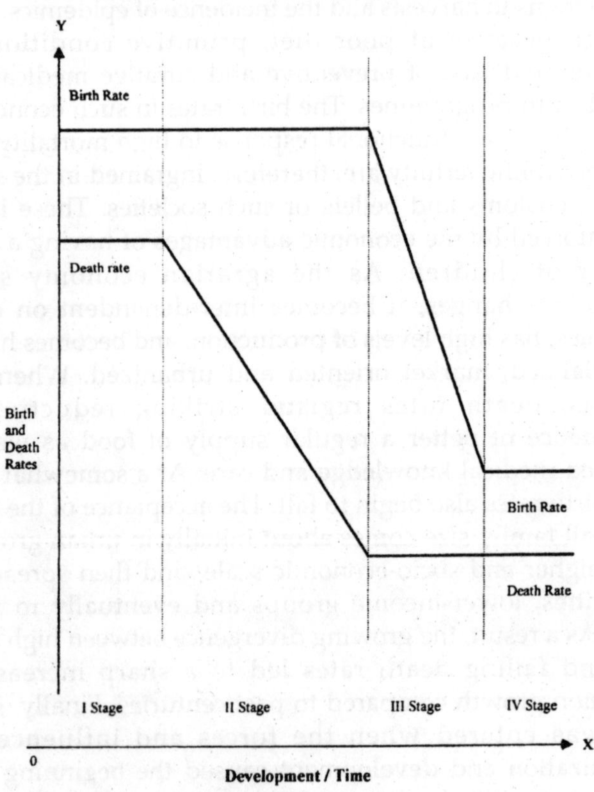

rates mark the first stage accompanied by rather long period of second stage with high birth rates and declining death rates. The third stage is marked by stable death rates and declining birth rate and after that the birth and death rates remain stable at low levels. From here onwards the population growth is expected to be around 1 per cent or even less for year and this could be labeled as desired population for a country.

Experience of Developed Countries

International migration played a dominant role in reducing the surplus population of the developed countries by encouraging migration to new worlds like Americas and

Australia or other colonies they occupied as the vanguards of their capitalism and colonialism. This migration took place on permanent basis reducing the population pressure on homelands.[2] If we see the changes that took place in the migration policies of England, one can find how the surplus population was transferred gainfully. English mercantilism emphasized the 'utility of poverty'—the doctrine, which viewed the poverty of lower classes as desirable and profitable. It argued that poverty would make them industrious and keep wages down. Since a large population would keep the labourers poor, immigration should be encouraged and emigration should be restricted[3]. Adam Smith and later John Stuart Mill advocated the 'Laissez faire' doctrine according to which apart from reducing State's role and absolute individual freedom, internal migration and colonial emigration and settlement are encouraged. Marx[4] argued that the resultant free flow of labour fulfilled the rapidly expanding industrial capitalism's rising labour needs.

But, ironically, accelerating industrial capitalism was later accompanied by increasing unemployment and poverty. Malthus explained these phenomena of increasing unemployment and poverty as direct manifestations of over population whereas Marx and Engels argued that the unemployment was a direct consequence of increasing capital intensification in the process of production. Whatever the reasons of their arguments, it was evident that the accelerated industrial revolution generated labour surplus and unemployment in developed countries in the early phases of modernization whether it was due to over population or displaced labour due to capital intensification. Consequently, migration to, and settlement in, colonies emerged as a logical solution to both satisfying Europe's resources and market demands and meeting the growing problem of unemployment and poverty by turning domestic supplicants for public handouts into international imperial guards[5]. Thus the developed nations got rid off the surplus population of early stages of modernization and the resultant unemployment by international migration and colonizing new worlds like America and Australia. Later when the process of development attained the stage of self sustained and full employment, the third stage of demographic transition was set in with stable population growth in these countries.

Experience of Develping Countries Like India

But it appears that the population growth in developing countries is never crossing the second stage of historical demographic transition. Day by day they are becoming more and more populous. In the last 50 years (1950-2000) world population has almost increased three times bringing the total figure to above 6 billion. More alarming is that 3/4 of total world population live in developing countries or every year 80 million people are added to world population of which 70 million are from the third world developing countries.[6] Every one is interested to know why there is such population explosion in developing countries and what are the main factors contributing for it? It is mainly due to the socio-economic, religious and other traditional institutions prevailing in these countries. Early and universal marriages are responsible for longer fertility giving opportunity for more births. Wide spread poverty tends to sustain high birth-rates for obvious reason that families living without adequate incomes, employment, health, education and social services have little security for the future other than reliance on their off springs (children). Apart from these institutional factors there are the modern factors, which are generated through colonial legacy and later through regular contact with western developed civilization. As a result, there is rapid improvement in health condition throughout the Third world countries. Modern vaccination campaigns against malaria, small pox, yellow fever and cholera as well as the proliferation of public health facilities like protected water supplies, improved nutrition and public education have all worked together over past 50 years to lower death rates by as much as 80 per cent in Asia and Latin America and by over 50 per cent in Africa and Middle East.

Generally, in the absence of outward migration, the population growth is mainly influenced by the difference in the birth rates and death rates. Due to the aforesaid factors the human mortality is so low during the last 50 years than at any other point in human existence. So, the significant reduction in human mortality, particularly infant mortality, coupled with improved life expectancy the population is increasing in these countries at an increasing rate.

Empirical Evidence

The empirical data for India also reveals that high population growth in spite of population control measures implemented over period. Table 1 shows that the decennial population growth increased continuously between 1931 to 1981 peaking 25.1 per cent growth for the decade 1971-1981. Between 1981-91 and 1991-2001 though decline in the growth is visible, it is not substantial. However, in case of Andhra Pradesh the peak growth recorded is for the decade 1981-91 and decline for the decade 1991-2001 is substantial.

Table 1: Trends in Population Growth in India and Andhra Pradesh

Year	*All India Population Size (Millions)*	*Percent Variation*	*A.P Population Size (Millions)*	*Percent Variation*
1901	238.9	-	19.07	-
1911	252.0	5.7	21.45	12.4
1921	251.2	-0.3	21.42	-0.1
1931	278.9	11.0	24.20	13.0
1941	318.5	14.2	27.30	12.9
1951	361.0	13.3	31.12	14.0
1961	439.1	21.6	35.98	15.7
1971	547.9	24.8	43.50	20.9
1981	685.2	25.1	53.55	23.1
1991	846.3	24.2	66.51	24.2
2001	1027.0	21.4	75.73	13.9

Table 2 shows the trends in the important indicators for all India and Andhra Pradesh. It shows that crude birth rate started declining from 1995 onwards for India. Same is the case with the other indicators. In the case of Andhra Pradesh the decline started from 1995 onwards.

Table 2: Trends in CBR, CDER, IMR In A.P and all India

Year	*All India*			*Andhra Pradesh*		
	CBR	*CDR*		*CBR*	*CDR*	*IMR*
1941-51	45.2	31.2	192	43.1	29.3	126
1951-61	39.9	27.4	140	39.7	25.2	111
1961-71	41.7	22.8	114	34.9	17.6	109
1971-81	41.2	19.0	113	33.2	14.5	100
1981-91	37.2	15.0	87	31.2	10.8	80
1991	29.5	3.8	80	26.0	9.7	73
1992	29.2	10.1	80	24.5	9.2	71
1993	28.7	9.3	79	24.3	8.6	64
1994	28.7	9.3	74	23.8	8.3	65
1995	28.3	9.0	74	24.2	8.4	67
1996	27.4	8.9	74	22.7	8.3	66
1997	27.2	8.9	72	22.5	8.3	63
1998	27.0	9.0	71	22.4	8.2	62
1999	26.1	9.1	70	21.7	8.0	61

It may be asked as to why the birth rates are not declining in developing countries as it is done in the developed west. The answer is that the birth rates may be declining with modernization, but it takes longer time to find its impact on population growth, as it is evident from the experience of European nations. Todaro argues "Population growth has a built-in tendency to continue, a powerful momentum which, like a speeding automobile when the brakes are applied, tends to keep going for sometime before ceasing (coming to stop). In the case of population growth this momentum can persist for decades after birth rates drop".[7]

Contrast

The foregoing discussion brings forth the fact that the developing countries are already over populated and more and more numbers will be added in future. More importantly there is very little scope for reducing the pressure of over population in the third world countries today through massive international emigration. It is due to the very restrictive nature of immigration laws existing in modern developed countries.

As a matter of fact significant number of people with high technical skills are migrating from poor countries to developed West mostly on permanent basis whom in fact the home countries cannot afford to lose. This pervasive 'brain drain' not only represents a loss of valuable human resources but could prove to be a serious constraint on the future economic progress of third world nations.[8] Thus the fundamental point remains that the possibility of legal international migration of unskilled workers on a scale resembling that of the nineteenth and twentieth centuries no longer exists to provide an effective 'safety valve' for the contemporary surplus population of Africa, Asia and Latin America.

The main problem of developing countries is to accommodate these millions of unskilled people who constitute very high proportion and live in perpetual poverty, unemployment and underemployment. Nearly half of the total population is estimated to be living below 'poverty line'- poor people having below a specified level of minimum income which supposed to keep the body and soul alive alone.[9] The incidence of such wide poverty indicates large scale inequality in income distribution which is contrary to the popular notion that secular rise in income will lead to secular decline infertility.[10]

It is evident that some countries like South Korea, Taiwan etc., which attained more equitable pattern of income distribution with higher rates of GNP growth, are able to reduce fertility significantly. Therefore, it can be concluded that countries that strive to lessen the inequality in their distribution of income, or, alternatively, attempt to spread the benefits of their economic growth to a wider segment of the population may be better able to begin to lower their birth rates than countries where the benefits of growth are more unmanly shared, were though these later countries may have both higher levels and faster growth rates of per capita income.[11]

Conclusion

It may thus be concluded that in the absence of free international migration for unskilled labour reduction in fertility is the only viable solution for overcoming poverty and unemployment in the developing countries like India. Fertility reduction centric policies like education, social institutional changes and ultimately equity in income distribution need to be targeted.

References

Ansely J. Coale and Edgar M. Hoover, Production Growth and Economic Development in Low-Income Countries, Princeton University Press, 1958, pp. 9-13.

Todaro, M.P., 'Economic Development in the Third World' Orient Longman Ltd., 1985. P. 122.

Todaro, M.P., Op. Cit., PP. 179-192.

Todaro, M.P., Op. Cit., PP. 179-192.

Todaro, M.P., Op. Cit., P. 190.

Todaro, M.P., Op. Cit., P. 123.

For measurement of poverty line in case of India, see V.M. Dandekar and Rath, No., 'Poverty in India', EPW, Jan. 9, 1971 and for estimates of people living below poverty line in India, see Dandekar V.M., (1986) 'Agriculture, Employment and Poverty', E.P.W. Sept. 20-27, PP. A 90.

Perlman, M., 'Population and Economic change in Developing Countries: A Review Article', in Journal of Economic Literature, Vol. XIX, No. 1, March 1981, PP. 74-82.

Todaro, M.P., Op.Cit., PP. 187-190: For empirical support of that reducing income inequality will tend to lower fertility level in developing nation, see A.K. Bhattacharya 'Income inequality and fertility: A comparative view'. population studies 29. No. 1 (1975). 5-19: David Morawer. Basic needs policies and population growth, 'World Development 6. No. 11 12 (1978); 1251-1259 and Robert Repetto. Economic Equality and Fertility in Development Countries (Balumore: Johns Hopkms University Press. 1979)

12

Migrant Construction Labour in Visakhaptnam City

Dr. M. Bhavani Shankar Rao

Rural urban migration, because of its socio, economic, political, demographic, ecological and environmental implications, has attracted attention of academicians, policy makers and administrators through out the world. India is one of the developing countries which is experiencing apart from high population growth, large scale rural-urban migration affecting basic demographic features of both rural urban areas. Indian rural economy is basically peasant economy typically characterized by (1) ever declining man land ratio due to population pressure (2) employment opportunities declining sharply (3) lack of adequate non-form employment opportunities sizeable proportion of rural population migrate to urban areas in search of employment. In the beginning migration was more a male dominated phenomenon, but in recent past proportion females in migrant labour is considerable. Most of the migrant labour find of employment in informal sector. Construction activity is one such activity, which is absorbing a sizeable proportion of migrant labour. This paper is an attempt to outline the nature, characteristic features of migrant construction Labour in Visakhapatnam city. The specific objectives are:

1. To outline the general characteristic features of migrant labour,

2. To examine the incidence of employment and earnings and
3. To analyse the living conditions.

Data Base

The study area is Visakhapatnam city, the second populous city in Andhra Pradesh next to Hydrabad. The study is based on primary data collected with predesigned questionnaire by applying purposive sampling technique. Generally migration studies are either origin or destination based. The present study is destination based as it is considered relevant to ascertain information from those who have taken decision to migrate. Migrant Labour in construction is of two streams (a) those who migrate individually on individual decision (b) who migrate in a group with the help of a mediator locally known as "maistry" (a Labour contractor). Sufficient care is taken while selecting the sample, that the two groups are represented in the sample. A total of 200 migrant workers are selected.

Sample Distribution

Table 1 presents details of the sample distribution of migrant construction workers. As per the details, there are more number of workers who have migrated as a group. This is noticed in case both male and female workers. This may be due to individual's attitude to move along with a group for security and support at a new place. Further, it is also noticed that majority of these workers have directly migrated from rural areas.

Table 1: Sample Distribution

Sl.No.	*Type of Migration*	*Male*	*Female*	*Total*
1.	As a Group	93(56.70)	24(66.70)	117(58.50)
2.	As a Individual	71(43.30)	12(33.33)	83(41.50)
3.	Total	164(100.00)	36(100.00)	200(100.00)

Figures in brackets are percentages to total.

Age and Sex Distribution of Workers

A majority of the workers are in the age group of 16 to 30 years followed by 31 to 45 years. This pattern is noticed in case of male workers (Table 2). Construction work is unskilled work demands hard physical labour, this may be the reason why there are more number of workers in the age group 16 to 45 years. The distribution pattern of female labour indicates all little different picture. Lower number of workers are in the age group of 16 to 30 years. The probable reason may be that generally females in rural areas get married between 14 to 18 years, the age group 16 to 30 years is normally child bearing period which prevent them to take up hard physical work and migrate to distant places.

Table 2: Age and sex Compostion of Sample Workers

Age-Group	*Males*	*Females*	*Total*
0-15 years	6-(3.66)	8(22.22)	14(4.00)
16-30 years	84(51.22)	7(19.44)	91(55.50)
31-45 years	43(26.22)	21(58.33)	64(25.00)
40-60 years	23(14.02)	-	23(1.50)
61 above	8(4.88)	-	8(4.00)
Total	**164(100.00)**	**36(100.00)**	**200(100.00)**

Figures in brackets are percentages total.

Place of Origin

Table 3 presents the details of origin place of migrant labour. A majority of migrant labourers in both the sexes are from Visakhaptnam district followed by Srikakulam district. There are workers belonging to neighboring East and West Godavari districts also. In migration studies it is important to know the place of origin, at the same time it is also much more important to know the distance these workers have covered in the process of migration. Table 4 presents these details. Fifty per cent of sample workers covered as about 200 Kms. (some workers are from Ichapuram region in Srikakulam district and Palkollu region of West Godavari district). Among the two sexes, relatively female workers are found to cover shorter distances then males as is revealed from the details

Table 3: Place of Origin

Sex Group	*Visakhapatnam Dt*	*Srikakulam Dt*	*Vigianagaram Dt*	*East-Godavari Dt*	*West-Godavari Dt*	*Total*
Males	60(36.58)	56(34.15)	38(23.17)	6 (3.66)	4(2.44)	164(100.00)
Female	18(50.00)	14(38.89)	4(11.110)	-	-	36(100.00)
Total	**78(39.00)**	**70.35.00)**	**42(21.00)**	**6(3.00)**	**4(2.00)**	**200(100.00)**

Figures in brackets are percentages to total.

Table 4: Distance between Native Place and Destination

Category	*0-25Km*	*26-50Km*	*51-100Km*	*101-200Km*	*202Km above*	*Total*
Male	22(13.4)	40(24.4)	50(30.5)	31(18.9)	21(12.8)	164(100.00)
Female	12(33.3)	10(27.8)	8(22.2)	6(16.7)	-	36(100.00)
Total	**34(17.0)**	**50(25.0)**	**58(29.0)**	**37(18.5)**	**21(10.5)**	**200(100.00)**

Figures in brackets are percentage to total.

given in the table. The findings of the study on who helped the migrants to come to Visakhapatnam, revealed that for a majority of workers friends, relatives and fellow villagers helped or instrumental in their migration. Since the construction activity is presently in unorganised market, the predominance of informal channels in supply market is obvious.

Levels of Literacy

The literacy levels of the migrant workers are given in Table 5. Most of these workers are illiterates, in case of females the incidence of illiteracy is relatively high, obviously the sample also reflects the same phenomenon. Among literate male labour, they had education unto middle school while in case of females it is just up to primary schools. Further, a little over 90 per cent of these workers are unskilled. Skilled workers include masons, carpenters and plumbers. These skills are informally acquired and not through formal training.

Type of Work

Information regarding the occupations these migrant workers were pursuing at the time migration is ascertained

Table 5: Levels of Literacy

Level	*Male*	*Female*	*Total*
Illiterate	106 (64.63)	31 (86.11)	137
Primary	27 (16.46)	5 (13.89)	32
Middle	29 (17.68)	-	29
Secondary	2 (1.22)	-	2
Skilled	14 (8.54)	-	14
Unskilled	159 (91.46)	36 (100.00)	186

Figures in brackets are percentages.

and compared vis-a-vis they are pursuing at destination place. About 73 per cent of male workers and all the female workers were pursuing cultivation work at the time of migration. While at the place of migration 72 per cent of males and the entire female workers are working as simple labourers in construction (table 6). The type of work includes weight-carrying, digging, dust clearing and watering etc.; the other

Table 6: Type of Work

Type of Work	*Male*		*Female*		*Total*	
	Origin	*Destination*	*Origin*	*Destination*	*Origin*	*Destination*
Carpenter	13 (7.9)	13 (7.9)	-	-	13 (6.5)	13 (6.5)
Plumber	2 (1.2)	2 (1.2)	-	-	2 (1.0)	2 (1.0)
Mason	29 (17.7)	29 (17.7)	-	-	29 (14.5)	29 (14.5)
Tile Fitter	-	12 (14.5)	-	-	-	12 (6.0)
Simple laborer	-	108 (65.9)	-	36 (100.00)	-	144 (72.0)
Cultivation Work	120 (73.2)	-	(100.00) 36	-	156 (78.0)	-
Total	164 (100.00)	164 (100.00)	36 (100.00)	36 (100.0)	200 (100.0)	200 (100.0)

Figures in brackets are percentages to total.

important work for few workers is mason. More number of workers working as simple labourers is simply because most these workers have peasant background (either land poor or land less agricultural labour) with no other skills and hence they are prepared to take up labour work at the place of destination. This way suggests proletarisation of peasantry. This obviously because (a) the places of their origin do not create/provide employment opportunities to earn to maintain a minimum existing standard of living and (b) change in the attitude of rural workers towards agricultural labour mainly in the age group of 16-30 years.

Incidence of Employment

Before we explain the incidence of employment a brief description of the methodology adopted in this regard is given below. The sample data as indicated earlier consists of two streams. (a) those who migrate as group (b) those who migrate on individual decision for purpose of present analysis the first stream is termed as 1st group and second stream as 2nd group.

The incidence of employment is estimated on current status. The incidence of employment is expressed in terms of number of days each worker is gainfully employed during the preceding fortnight of enquiry. In case of 1st group, for nearly 50 per cent of the workers the maximum number of days of employment is ten days for the reference period, for females it is just nine days (Table 7). In case 2nd group for male workers it is just only seven days and six days for females. The difference in the incidence of employment is attributable to middlemen on whom 1st group of workers depend on maistry who generally goes round the city and fix the work. Another factor is most of these labourers are engaged in apartment projects where duration of employment is longer. The security and duration of employment in case of 1st group is more assured than that of 2nd group. However, one fact can't be bypassed here, that the attachment of labourers as group to maistry ensures security and length of employment, but this form of attachment of labourers may result in the long run some nature of bonded labourers.

Table 7: Percentage of Workers Reporting Number of Days of Employment

(Figures are in percentages)

No of days	*1*	*2*	*3*	*4*	*5*	*6*	*7*	*8*	*9*	*10*	*11*	*12*	*Total*
Category													
1st group													
Male	-	-	-	-	2.0	5.5	6.5	11.6	16.9	49.5	3.8	4.2	100.0
Female	-	-	-	5.9	3.2	4.6	22.2	10.4	53.7	-	-	-	100.0
2nd group													
Male	-	-	1.7	3.2	11.6	12.6	33.4	16.1	9.4	3.2	4.2	41.2	100.0
Female	-	-	-	-	-	100.0	-	-		-	-	-	100.0

Earnings

There is no wage difference between the two group of workers. However, in case of 1st group of workers some amount of money is paid as advance to meet the case of transport from the place origin to destination. The amount is later adjusted to wage. The wage is fixed by the maistry and the workers have little say. The workers of this group receive wages once in a week i.e., on Saturday. While in case of 2nd group the receive the wage on the evening itself. The working hours is generally eight hours and additional amount is paid for extra hours of work. Table 8 gives details of eargings. A majority of male workers in both the groups received

Table 8: Distribution of Workers on the Basis of Earnings During the Reference period

Category	*First Group*		*Second Group*	
	Male	*Female*	*Male*	*Female*
Rs 0-250	+6(180)	6(120)	5(180)	4(120)
Rs 251-500	30(420)	9(360)	18(420)	8(320)
Rs 501-750	49(640)	9(560)	41(560)	-
Rs 751-1000	6(680)	-	5(480)	-
Rs 1001-Above	2(1200)	-	2(1150)-	
Total	**93((580)**	**24(360)**	**71(510)**	**12(280)**

Figures in brackets are average earnings in Rs. Per worker during the reference period

income ranging between Rs. 501-750 during the period of reference. While females received income lass than Rs. 500. The variation in the average incomes as revealed by the figures in the table is due to differences in the duration of employment of each worker.

Living Conditions of Migrant Labour

Table 9 presents details of the living conditions. Provision of basic facilities of living is not taken proper care either by the labour contractor or by the building contractor. Workers who have migrated through maistry have to share accommodation along with the fellow labourers, which are mostly make shift huts either at the work site or on government wasteland. In case of the other group they have to share accommodation with friends and relatives.Many of these workers have illegally constructed their huts in vacant private, municipal or government land. These workers have in fact developed their own colonies in different places resulting in the spread of slums. These slums are filthy, lack basic sanitary and hygienic facilities, needless to mention that this has become breeding grounds of a number of diseases.

Table 9: Details of Living Conditions

Details	*Yes*	*No*	*Total*
	32	168	200
	60	140	200
	60	-	60
	60	-	60
	18	-	18
	14	-	14
	4	-	4
	5	-	5
	13	-	13
	-	18	18

Information regarding the health hazards, the arrangement of social security is also ascertained. This information is elicited from the sample workers for the last one year. 30 per cent of the workers have complained about illness of some sort, they have received routine treatment for which financial assistance is received from the maistry in the form of the advance which is later adjusted to the wage. 18 out 200 sample workers have met accidents while working. Out of these for persons sustained major injuries like fractures. These workers are given treatment and were sent back to native villages till such time they are physically fit. Only five workers out of these 18 have received total assistance and the rest were to satisfy with partial assistance. The discussion with sample workers revealed that the present arrangement of social security is only informal mostly depends on the attitude of the labour contractor and bargaining strength of the worker or some middlemen on behalf of the worker.

Conclusions

As economic development proceeds there will be a gradual shift of labour from rural subsistence agricultural sector to expanding urban secondary and teritary sectors. One such urban sector, which absorbs this labour, is construction. The migration process in fact helped the urban sector by supplying the necessary labour to the increase in the demand for unskilled construction labour. However, the living conditions of these workers are highly deplorable. The social security is highly informal and insufficient suggesting for the Government's intervention in this regard. The scheme of group insurance "Janashree Bima Yojana" introduced in the budget for the year 2000-2001 as a measure to extend some social security cover to the poorest sections of out society will go a long way in solving the social security problems of these poor construction labour.

References

Todero, M.P., (1969), " A model of labour migration and urban unemployment in the developed countries", American Economic Review, Vol. 59, No.1.

Joshi and Joshi, V. (1976), "Surplus Labour and the City" a study of Bombay.

Amitab Kundu (1986), "Migration, urbanisation and the regional inequality the emerging challenges", Economic and Political weekly, September.

Mitra, A., (1993), "Urban employment, migrant labour and structural adjustment", Indian Journal of Labour Economics, Vol. 36, No.4.

13

Literacy and Life Expectancy in India An Empirical Analysis

K.Madhu Babu
K. Siva Prasad

Introduction

The quality of population in a given country is a pre-requisite for country's economic development. No period in the history of economic thought has gained more importance to improve the quality of population than the present period. The quality of population in a country to a large extent depends on education and life expectancy attained by the population of that country. Education, more particularly, influences the demographic pattern and health practices besides resulting in political and economic development of a country. The rate of literacy, in short, is considered to be a good indicator of development in any given society. "Spread and diffusion of literacy is generally associated with essential traits of today's civilisation such as modernization, urbanization, industrialisation, communication and commerce"[1] . It is also widely believed that education, more particlulary women's education, is closely related to the health status of a family. "There is also large evidence to show that children of educated mothers live healthier and have longer lives, as the more a mother is educated, higher is the

1. Census of India, 2001

probability of her taking good health care of the family, and her providing better nutritional food. Nutrition is after all an important determinant of survival rates"[2]

Hence, all possible efforts must be made to educate all the children, both males and females, there be enabling them to participate more effectively in the process of economic development, when they grow up. In India Article 45 of the Directive Principles of the constitution urges the state to provide free and compulsory education for all children until they complete fourteen years of age. Education is included in the concurrent list in our country and as such both the centre and states assumed joint responsibility to promote education. The success of the government policies in this direction is reflected in the literacy rates obtained in the census.

In this paper an attempts is made (i) to analyse the inter-state disparities in literacy rates of males and females and (ii) to identify the effect of literacy on life expectancy in India towards the 21st century.

Literacy Rates in India

The literacy rates for the country and the gap in male-female literacy rates are given in Table 1.

Table 1: Literacy Rate In India: 1951-2001

Census Years	*Person's*	*Males*	*Females*	*Males-Females Gap in literacy rates*
1951	18.33	27.18	8.86	18.30
1961	28.30	40.40	15.35	25.05
1971	34.46	45.88	21.97	23.81
1981	43.57	56.38	29.76	26.62
1991	52.21	64.13	39.29	24.84
2001	65.38	75.85	54.16	21.70

Note: Literacy rates for 1951, 1961 and 1971 census relate to population aged five years and above. The rates for the 1981, 1991 and 2001 census relate to the Source: Census of India 2001.

2. Jandhyala B.G. Tilak," Education, health, Nutrition and Demographic changes: A Review of Evidence on Asia" The Journal of Labour Economics, vol 35, No.2, p. 116.

As can be seen from the table, India has achieved a remarkable progress in improving the literacy rate, since India attained independence. By 2001, the literacy rate for the country as a whole stands at 65.38 per cent. The corresponding figures for males and females indicate that three fourth of male (75.85%) and more than half of the female population (54.16%) aged seven years are literates by 2001. It can also be seen from the table that India has improved its literacy rate very impressively by jumping from 52.21 in 1991 to 65.38 in 2001.

But if we look at the gap in male-female literacy rates it is understood that the gap has increased from 18.30 percentage points in 1951 to 26.62 in 1981, though the gap in male-female literacy rates is observed to be reducing from 1981, it still constitutes 21.70 percentage points by 2001. If this gap is only due to the continuing backlog of past legacy of a large number of adult illiterate women and not due to the preferences of parents to educate the male children, the literacy rates of 2001 augurs well for the country. From the above table it is understood that the increase in literacy rates during 1991-2001 in respect of persons, males and females have been highest recorded when compared to earlier decades. With the exception of males during 1951-61. But this improvement in literacy rates is to be sustained.

Inter-State Disparties in the Literacy Rates

Now an attempt is made to analyse the inter-state disparities in the literacy rates for person's, male and female at census of India, 2001. The State-wise information on literacy rates for person, males and females is presented in Table 2.

As can be seen from the above Table, Kerala tops the list with 90.82 per cent of literacy rate, while Bihar takes the last position with a literacy rate of 47.53. It is noticed that Jammu and Kashmir in North, Rajasthan in West, Andhra Pradesh in south, Madhya Pradesh, Chattisgarh and Uttar Pradesh in Central, Bihar, Jharkand and Orissa in East and Arunachal Pradesh, Assam and Meghalaya in North-East

Table 2: State-Wise Literacy Rates by Sex-2001

Sl. No	*State*	*Total persons*	*Male literacy*	*Female literacy*	*Gap in literacy*
1	Andhra Pradesh	61.11 (22)	70.85(22)	51.17(20)	19.66
2	Arunachal Pradesh	54.24(25)	64.07(27)	44.24(24)	19.88
3	Assam	64.28(18)	71.93(20)	56.03(18)	16.90
4	Bihar	47.53(28)	60.32(28)	33.57(28)	28.75
5	Chattisgarh	65.18(17)	77.86(12)	52.40(19)	25.46
6	Goa	82.32(3)	88.88(3)	75.51(3)	18.97
7	Gujrat	69.97(9)	80.50(9)	58.60(15)	21.90
8	Haryana	68.59(14)	79.25(10)	56.31(17)	22.94
9	Himachal Pradesh	77.13(5)	86.02(5)	68.08(4)	17.94
10	Jammu & Kashmir	54.46(26)	65.75(26)	41.82(26)	23.93
11	Jharkand	54.13(27)	67.94(24)	39.38(27)	28.57
12	Karnataka	67.04(16)	76.29(17)	57.45(16)	18.84
13	Kerala	90.82(1)	94.20(1)	87.86(1)	6.34
14	Madhya Pradesh	64.11(19)	76.80(14)	50.28(22)	26.52
15	Maharastra	77.27(4)	86.27(4)	67.51(5)	18.75
16	Manipur	68.87(13)	77.87(11)	59.71(14)	18.17
17	Meghalaya	63.31(21)	66.14(25)	60.41(11)	5.73
18	Mizoram	88.49(2)	90.69(2)	86.13(2)	4.56
19	Nagaland	67.11(15)	71.77(21)	61.92(9)	9.85
20	Orissa	63.61(20)	75.95(18)	50.97(21)	24.98
21	Punjab	69.95(10)	75.63(19)	63.55(8)	12.08
22	Rajasthan	61.03(23)	76.46(16)	44.34(23)	32.12
23	Sikkim	69.68(11)	76.73(15)	61.46(10)	15.27
24	Tamil Nadu	73.74(7)	82.33(7)	64.55(7)	17.78
25	Tripura	73.66(6)	81.47(8)	65.41(6)	16.06
26	Uttar Pradesh	57.36(24)	70.23(23)	42.38(25)	27.25
27	Uttranchal	72.88(8)	84.01(6)	60.26(12)	23.75
28	West Bengal	69.22(12)	77.80(13)	60.22(13)	17.35

Source: Census of India 2001
Figures in brackets indicate Rank.

parts of the country fall below the national average of literacy rate (65.38 per cent).

On the basis of literacy rates of males and females the following observations are made. Kerala occupies the first rank among the states both in male literacy with 94.20 per cent and female literacy with 87.86 per cent. Kerala is closely followed by Mizoram and Goa, which have occupied second and third ranks respectively. Of the total 28 states in our country, Andhra Pradesh takes 22nd position with 70.85 male literacy, though its position is relatively better in the case of female literacy with 51.17 per cent taking the 20th position. Bihar takes the unceremonious position of the last rank in respect of literacy rates for both males and females.

New it is interesting to analyse the gap in literacy rates in the states of India. As can be seen from the Table 2, the minimum gap in male-female literacy is seen in Mizoram with 4.56 percentage points followed by Meghalaya (with 5.73 percentage points) and Kerala (with 6.34 percentage points). The maximum gap in male-female literacy rate is observed for Rajasthan (with 32.12 percentage points). The state of Andhra Pradesh stand better in respect of gap in male-female literacy rate with 19.69 percentage points as compared to the national average which is 21.70 percentage points.

Life Expectancy and Literacy rates:

Now, it is interesting to study the relationship between life expectancy and literacy rates. 15 major states have been selected for this purpose. Table 4 presents the projected values of the state-wise expectation of life at birth by sex for the period 1996-2001.

It is interesting to notice that Kerala, which happened to occupy the first position in literacy rates for males and females also occupied the first rank in respect of life expectancy of males and females.

For analytical convenience these states are devided into top, middle and lower categories on the basis of the ranks obtained in the expectancy. Accordingly the top five states in respect of males life expectancy are (1) Kerala (2) Punjab (3) Haryana (4) Karnataka and (5) Maharashtra, while the lower five states are (1) Rajasthan (2) Orissa (3) Madhya Pradesh (4) Assam (5) Uttar Pradesh. The remaining states belong to the middle category. Similarly the top five states in respect of females' life expectancy are (1) Kerala (2) Punjab

Table 3: Projected values of the exception of life at Birth by sex & Literacy rates

State	M/F	Projected Values of 1996-2001	Literacy Rates
Andhra Pradesh	M	63.40(8)	70.85(13)
	F	65.93(6)	51.17(10)
Assam	M	61.14(14)	71.93(12)
	F	61.18(12)	56.03(9)
Bihar	M	62.81(10)	60.32(15)
	F	62.78(11)	33.57(15)
Gujarat	M	62.94(9)	80.50(4)
	F	65.59(7)	58.60(6)
Haryana	M	66.21(3)	79.25(5)
	F	65.94(5)	58.31(7)
Karnataka	M	65.55(4)	78.29(6)
	F	66.55(3)	57.45(8)
Kerala	M	68.23(1)	87.86(1)
	F	73.62(1)	94.20(1)
Madhya Pradesh	M	61.50(13)	76.80(8)
	F	60.81(14)	50.28(12)
Maharashtra	M	65.45(5)	86.27(2)
	F	66.31(4)	67.51(2)
Orissa	M	62.13(12)	75.95(10)
	F	61.15(13)	50.97(11)
Punjab	M	67.61(2)	75.63(11)
	F	67.80(2)	63.55(4)
Rajasthan	M	62.50(11)	76.46(9)
	F	63.59(10)	44.34(13)
Tamil Nadu	M	64.85(6)	82.33(3)
	F	65.20(8)	64.55(3)
Uttar Pradesh	M	60.09(15)	70.23(14)
	F	56.09(15)	42.98(14)
West Bengal	M	63.95(7)	77.58(7)
	F	64.19(9)	60.22(5)

M-Male F-Female

The figures in brackets indicates ranks

Source: Report of the Expert committee on Population Projections. Census of India 1981, Occasional Paper No 4 of 1988.

(3) Karnataka (4) Maharashtra and (5) Haryana, while the lower five states are (1) Bihar (2) Assam (3) Orissa (4) Madhya Pradesh (5) Uttar Pradesh. The remaining states belong to

the middle category. It is interesting to observe that states like Kerala, Maharashtra, Haryana which are the top states in literacy rates are also the top states in life expectancy in respect of males. On the other hand, the states like Uttar Pradesh, Assam obtained the lower ranks not only on literacy rates but also in life expectancy in respect of males.

The analysis of literacy rates and life expectancy in respect of females reveals that states like Kerala, Maharashtra and Punjab are the top states not only in literacy rates but also in life expectancy. On the other hand, Bihar Orissa, Uttar Pradesh, Madhya Pradesh are the states which have obtained lower ranks both in literacy rates and life expectancy.

Hence, education seems to have strong influence on life expectancy. We have examined the impact of literacy rates of males on their life expectancy. Similarly the relations between female literacy and female life expectancy is also investigated. Following are the regression results.

Table 4: Regression results: Literacy and life Expectancy

1.	$L.E_M$=48.40 +0.5745*MLIT	(7.880)	R^2=0.3300
2.	$L.E_F$=51.51+0.7904*FLIT	(18.032)	R^2=0.6246

Notation: $L.E_M$=Life Expectancy of Males
$L.E_F$=Life Expectancy of Females
MLIT=Male Literacy Rate
FLIT=Female Literacy Rate
*Significant at 1 per cent level
Figures in brackets are t-values

Female literacy is explaining 62 per cent of the variation in female life expectancy, whereas only 33 per cent of variation in male life expectancy is explained by male literacy rates.

The regression co-efficient corresponding to male literacy reveals that for every one per cent increase in male literacy, life expectancy of males increases by 0.58 Similarly from the results of the second equation life expectancy of females increases by 0.79 time for every one per cent increase in female literacy. Both the regression co-efficient are significant at one per cent level. The regression results in the above table demonstrate that there exists a strong relationship between the life expectancy of females and literacy rates of females.

Conclusion

In conclusion, it may be pointed out that the improvement in the literacy rates for males and females in India is impressive by 2001. However, this improvement in literacy rates is to be sustained. Moreover, as the effect of female literacy is found to be dominant on life expectancy, greater fillip is also to be given to educate the fairer sex.

14

Inter-Tribe Variations in Literacy Levels—A Study of Tribes in Srikakulam District, AP.

Prof. M. Sundara Rao
Prof. D. Rambabu

Introduction

Education has been recognized as a key factor in tribal development to bring in economic and social transformation among the tribals. The government of Andhra Pradesh spends approximately 50 per cent of tribal sub-plan allocation on education. The ITDAs right from their inception have been putting tremendous effort in the provision and spread of both formal and non-formal education among tribal people. The enormous expenditure on education in the tribal areas expected to have positive impact on the literacy rates of the tribal people. The tribal literacy is very low in Andhra Pradesh. Also one can find lot of variations in the literacy levels of various tribes in different regions. The literacy levels are generally found at very low level among the hill tribes when compared to the tribes in plains.

Against this background an attempt is made in the present study to examine the inter tribe variations in the literacy levels, while selecting different tribes in the Srikakulam district. The details pertaining to methodology and collection of data are presented first (section 1.1), afterwards the general literacy trends in the study area (section 1.2) and estimated education scores relating to formal and informal education are presented (section 1.3). The conclusions are given at the end (section 1.4).

Methodology and Collection of Data

Multi stage stratified random sampling method is used in the present study. The selection process is carried out in four stages, they are relating to district, mandal, villages and households. Srikakulam district is selected for the study due to the fact that the district has drawn worldwide attention through the tribal movement in the political upheavel of 1969-'71. The Seethampeta mandal is selected for the study because it is the only tribal mandal that is having a high proportion of (89.54 per cent) tribal population and also the ITDA is placed at Seethampeta. The villages are selected depending upon the higher concentration of specific tribes. With a stratification procedure based on the specific tribe population concentration, the panchayats are classified into three categories. From the Konda Savara tribes concentrated panchayats the villages Vaijjayyaguda and Mutyalu are selected from very interior hill areas. From the plain Savara tribe concentrated panchayats Dibba guda and Keesari Jodu villages are selected and from Jatapu tribe concentrated panchayats Goidi and Gadiguddi Villages are selected.

The Konda Savara, Plain Savara and Jatapu tribes are equally proportioned in the Seethampeta Mandal. To examine the inter tribe variations in their socio economic conditions 60 households are selected from each tribe from their concentrated selected villages based on the random sampling procedure. The selected 180 households are further classified into the stratification of size class groups in accordance with their proportion in total tribal population of the district. Hence the 180 households consist of 90 medium farms (less than 2.50 acres), 60 small farms (2.51 acres to 5.00 acres), 24 medium farms (5.1 acres to 10 acres) and 6 large farms (10 acres above) and the analysis is carried out separately.

Information relating to the literacy levels of the selected households is collected while canvassing a pre-designed and structured household schedule in the selected villages during April 1998 to March 1999 in different visits. Secondary data has been obtained from Annual Reports and Action Plans of ITDA Seethampeta, District hand book of statistics of different years published by the Chief Planning Officer, Srikakulam, MRO and MDO offices of Seethampeta Mandal.

Literacy Trends in the Study Area

The tribe and size group wise distribution of head of the households literacy level presented in table 1 reveal that only 32.22 per cent households have completed primary education and 6.11 per cent completed secondary education and 61.67 per cent are illiterates. Though majority of the households are illiterate (61.67 per cent) in the study area they take care more for their word of promises than for any written document. Their ways of behaviour towards moneylenders, traders, GCC salesman, GCC purchasing agents are very cautious. Due to political awareness among them particularly, the plain tribes Jatapu and Kapu Savaras, they are facing police, revenue officials, government officials and extension officers with out any fear. They are participating in the regular ITDA darbars and presenting their problems time to time to the officials. the field observations shows the older generation realized the importance of education from which they are deprived. They are rearing the new generation in the Ashram Schools. Polytechnics and professional colleges since last one and half decades. Due to this the new generation are leaving their isolation and becoming part of the open society of India.

It is clear that majority of the educated heads of households are having education up to primary level only. Further there is considerable variation of the education status of the heads of households among the tribes and size groups. However, the literacy level of the heads of households partially reflects the status of tribals. To have a complete picture, one has to examine the literacy levels among all the members of the family, which are presented in table 2. The table shows that out of total family members only 40.72 per cent are literates. The adult literacy rates are very low and it is 36.12 per cent in case of male and only 6.27 per cent in case of women. However the children literacy rates are very encouraging in the tribal areas. Out of the total male children 70.07 per cent are literates and it is interesting to note that in the total female children 60.74 per cent of female children are literate. The differences between the adult female literacy and female children literacy level indicate the changing position in the tribal areas. The female literacy level is extremely low, particularly among the adults because in olden days in villages female members are not sent to school, due to social inhabitions or restrictions.

A comparison of sex-wise literacy levels of children population shows a different picture. The levels of literacy among the children are very high in both males and females. This reflects the change in the attitude of the elders towards education, which is the main reason for increasing the incidence of literacy among children. Increasing educational facilities particularly, separate ashram schools for girls students, scholarships to girl students coupled with favourable change in parental attitude has resulted in more and more girls attending schools.

Normally in the villages, the number of dropout children is expected to be more. Hence an attempt is made to study the pattern of dropouts and data are presented in table 3. It can be noticed from the table that among school drop-out children the proportion of female children is more than that of male children. Most of the children are dropouts at the primary education level. The number of dropout children is more in the remote hilly tracts rather than in plains. The dropouts are high among the children of Konda Savara and marginal and small farms and very less among the children) of Jatapu and Kapu Savara tribes and medium and large farms. The positive change on education is very high in the plain tribes. Generally in the tribal economy children are used as wage earners. But in the present period, children are being sent to schools by foregoing the present income for their future prosperity. This is one important change in the value system of tribal economy that parents are accepting the importance of education of their children for the future prosperity of the children by diverting them from the traditional rural activity to other urban activities.

Estimation of Educational Scores

An attempt is made to ascertain the views of the heads of the households regarding various aspects relating to education. The foregoing analysis reveals that the efforts of the governmental and non-governmental organizations in the development of education among tribals for the last three decades have became successful in raising the literacy levels among tribals. 86 per cent of the tribal people are satisfied over the development of education facilities only 4 per cent of the households are not satisfied and the remaining 10 per cent are not responded. In preparation of the educational scores of the households both their formal schooling and informal learning are taken account.

In preparing the formal educational scores of the households the following cardinal numbers are allotted for different formal schooling status of the households. Zero for illiterate, 1 for primary level and 2 for higher education. The formal educational scores of the tribal households across tribes and size groups are presented in Table 4. From the table it is noticed that 72.50 per cent of the educational score is obtained from primary education and only 27.50 per cent is obtained from secondary education. The total score of all the tribes and farms are estimated at 80. Across tribes Konda Savaras proportion is only 22.50. Jatapus contributed relatively high of 41.25 to the educational score. Across size groups of farms marginal farms constitute 50 per cent of total households have their educational score consist only 3.75 per cent. On the other hand though the small, medium and large farms are in lower proportion in total households, their contribution to educational score is relatively significant.

The informal learning is identified with head of the households contact with village level, mandal level and district level government officials and non-governmental agencies. The following cardinal numbers are allotted for different informal status and zero is given to those heads of households who are not having any contacts with even village level and mandal level (ITDA) officials. One is allotted to households who are having contracts with village level and mandal level (ITDA) officials and who visit frequently Seethammapeta and attend ITDA darbars and mandal revenue and development offices located in Seethammapeta. Two is allotted to those heads of households who visit Palakonda R.D.O. office and Srikakulam district head quarters to meet and contact various governmental offices and non-government agencies. The field data pertaining to their informal learning status are collected and presented in Table 4.

The informal learning status of the heads of the households presented in the table reveal that at the level of all households, tribes and size group of farms the informal learning score is relatively recorded much higher than their formal education score. This situation indicates that simple reading and writing may not have meaning as part of literacy among tribals. They take care more for their word of promise than for any written document. Formal learning may give them more simple elementary calculations, but that is not even the informal learning changes their ways of behaviour towards moneylenders, trader, GCC salesmen GCC purchasing agent and government officials. Across tribes the informal learning status of Konda Savara tribe is recorded relatively lower (41) than Savara is plains (58) and Jatapu (68). Similarly the proportion of informal learning status across different size groups of farms shows they are relatively high in case of large, medium, and small farms. The marginal farms are lagging very behind on this front.

The combined formal education score and informal learning score which reflect the total education score of all the households and it is recorded as 242. The relative position of formal, informal and total education score, formal education score contributed only 33.06 per cent and informal learning score contributed very high of 66.94 per cent. Across tribes the Konda Savara tribe recorded with a low total education score (59) when compared to Savara in plains (87) and Jatapu (96). On the front of different size groups of farms the proportional distribution of total education scores are relatively very high in cases of large medium and small farms when compare to the marginal farms.

Conclusion

The overall picture regarding literacy indicate that the literacy rate is very high among Jatapus and Savara tribes and medium and large farms those who are living in plain areas. At the same time the level of education is comparatively low among Konda Savara tribe and marginal and small farms who are living in hilly and remote areas. This is very important point on which the policy makers can give serious thought as part of overall improvement in the levels of living of the tribal people in fulfilling the objectives of tribal development.

The analysis of educational score pattern reveal that still the Konda Savara tribe and marginal farms needed more emphasis to promote both formal and informal learning. Much emphasis may be given by the governmental and non-governmental agencies on providing more informal learning facilities to Konda Savara tribe and marginal farms who live in the hilly and remote areas through providing more informal learning measure. They must be made more conversant with the functioning of banks, co-operative societies, health centers and the government offices. The further promotion of informal learning will improve their rational understanding of social and economic values. They appreciate the good values of life and they will come into close contact with the main stream of Indian life such that they strive to desire modern amenities of life and the benefits of new agricultural technology.

References

Thurston, E, 1987, "Castes and Tribes of Southern India", Vol. VI, p. 305, Vol III.

Verma, R.C., 1990, "Tribes of India Through the Ages", Delhi Publications Division, Ministry of Information and Broadcasting.

Mohan Rao K., 1990, "The Kolams a primitive tribe in Transition", Hyderabad, Book Links Corporation.

Bhowmic, P.K., 1991, "Tribes in the Changing Circumstances of India", Man in India, Vol. 71, No. 1.

Janah, Sunil, 1993, "The Tribals of India", Calcutta, Oxford University Press.

Doshi, Saryu, 1993, "Tribal India", Bombay, Marg Publications.

Vidyarthi & Roy, "Tribal Culture of India", Concept Publishing Company, New Delhi, 1977.

Nag, D.S., "Tribal Economy-An Economic study of the Baiga", Bharatiya Adimajati Sevak Sangh, Kingsway Camp, New Delhi, 1958.

Sexena, R.P., "Tribal Economy in Central India", Calcutta.

Ramaiah, P., "Tribal Economy of India", Light Life Publishers, New Delhi, 1981.

Patnaik, N., "Tribals and their Development" National Institute of Community Development, Hyderabad, 1972.

Singh, S.K., "Economics of the Tribals and their Transformation", New Delhi, 1982.

Jain, L.C., "Emancipation of Scheduled Castes and Tribes: Some suggestions", Economical Political Weekly, February, 28, 1991.

Bhowmic, P.K., 1991., "Tribes in the Changing Circumstances of India", Man in India, vol. 71, No. 1

Imam Bulu, 1993, "Cultural Spatial Concepts Inflict in Tribal Art and Identity in Hazaribagh District", Man in India, vol. 73 and No. 2.

15

Primary Education of Tribals in a Backward Region in Andhra Pradesh—A Case Study of Vizianagaram District

Prof. K. Sreerama Murthy
Mr. K.V. Jagannadha Rao

Introduction

Education is the key factor in accelerating the pace of development of any society. The importance of education in the process of economic growth has been emphasised by several economists.[1] (HLA. Mint 1954, Theodore W Schuttz 1962, Panchamukhi, P.R. 1965, Ambashat N.K., 1966, Richard A Musgrave 1966, Mark Blaugh 1968, Christaper Colclough 1982, Jandhyala B.G. Tilk, 1987). The World Bank's education Sector policy paper (1980) also observes that "Studies have shown that economic returns on investment in education seem, in most instances, to exceed returns to alternative kinds of investment, and that developing countries obtain higher returns than the developed area". In view of this, Education is considered as a pre-requisite for socio-economic development, particularly for the weaker sections of the society who have been long subjected to deprivation and discrimination (Sachchidananda 1994). Thus, education is recognised as a basic human right and is conceived as an instrument of liberation which endows deprived groups with confidence, courage and ability to resist exploitation.

Tribal Education in India

The benefits of the education to individuals and to society are widely known (Amartya Sen and Dreze 1995)[2]. Literacy as an indicator of socio-economic status, is highly essential for the economic development as well as social development of scheduled tribes. According to the Article 46 of the Indian Constitution special emphasis is laid on the educational development of tribals. It says that "The state shall promote with special care the educational and economic interests of the Weaker sections of the people and in particular of the scheduled castes and scheduled tribes, and protect them from social injustice and all forms of exploitation". Educational policies in respect of the tribals have changed from time to time during the post-independence period. During the First Five Year plan[3] special funds were provided for opening special tribal institutions in tribal areas. As a result, by the end of the first plan about 4000 schools were established in the tribal areas of Bombay, Bihar, Orissa and Madhya Pradesh states. This includes more than 1000 Ashram and Sevashram schools and about 650 Samskar Kendras, Balwadis, Community Centres etc., in Bombay, Bihar, Madhya Pradesh and Rajasthan. The establishment of Ashram schools in tribal areas in all the states was taken up as a major programme during the second plan. Accordingly the expansion of education facilities in tribal areas was speeded up. The Ministry of Education has earmarked Rs.11.38 crores for post-metric scholarships for scheduled tribes and accorded permission to open 3, 178 schools and 398 hostels particularly for tribal students. During the Third Five Year Plan, it was observed that the tribals living outside the tribal development blocks did not get educational benefits which were available to those living in the block area. This led to wide gap in educational development of different tribal communities. The Fourth Five Year Plan laid emphasis on a system of education geared to the socio-economic development of the tribals, and recommended that the primary schools be located nearer to tribal villages while middle and secondary schools be located at a central place. However, the plan allocations for tribal education were lower than in the Third plan. A significant change in the approach to the development of tribals has been made during the fifth Five Year Plan. In order to reduce the gap between the level of development of tribal and other areas the sub-plan approach was implemented during this plan.[4] The plan emphasised the importance of quantitative as well as qualitative improvement of education for tribal communities. During this plan a number of Ashram Schools, Hostels and book banks were established and efforts were also made to provide remedial coaching, counselling and guidance to tribal students. Another notable feature of this plan is that voluntary agencies were provided with huge funds to run adult education programmes in the tribal areas. During the sixth Five Year Plan emphasis was laid on the Universalisation of elementary and spread of non formal education among the tribals. The syllabi was streamlined in the light of cultural ethos and assimilating power of tribal child.

Special emphasis was laid on the female literacy besides strengthening the intrastructural base of the tribal education during seventh Five Year Plan. Steps were also initiated to prevent high percentage of dropouts and stagnation in the tribal schools. Recognising the importance of universalisation of elementary education the Eight Five Year Plan accorded high priority to primary education of tribals. Following the National Policy of Education 1986 (revised in 1992) District Primary Education Programme (DPEP) and mid-day meal programmes were introduced during the Eight Five Year Plan. Further, the Ninth five year plan set the goal to make the Nation fully literate by the year 2005.

Though a number of programmes were implemented for promoting education among tribals over years, India presents a bleak picture with regard to levels of literacy among tribals. According to 1991 census, while the National Literacy is estimated as 65.35 per cent, literacy among tribals is found to be a meagre 29.06 per cent. Similarly at the National level literacy among males is estimated as 63.83 per cent and for females as 39.9 per cent, the corresponding figures with regard to tribal males and females are found to be as 40.65 per cent and 18.19 per cent. More over the situation is one of the low overall literacy combined with large variations across states, Rural Urban regions, Communities and sexes (V.K Ramachandram, 1997).[5] While states like Mizoram, Nagaland, Sikkim and Kerala achieved high literacy level among tribals, it is found to be very low in the case of Andhra Pradesh and Rajasthan. Added to this, it is held that investment in education remained grossly inadequate as compared to other developed countries and developing countries of the world. (Draze and Sen 1995). While advanced countries like Japan and the USA are spending more than 6 per cent of their Gross National Product on education, public expenditure on education is around 3.7 per cent of the GDP in India (Tilak, 1999). This problem is much more acute in the case of elementary education. Public expenditure on elementary education is found to be only 1.8 per cent of the Gross Domestic Product (Tilak 1995). As such, it is argued that the investment on elementary education should be increased to a minimum of 3 per cent of GDP in order to realise the goal of universal primary education in the country (Ramachandran and others 1997). Though several studies have examined the problem of education in terms of investment, investment gap, scope and constraints, most of the studies were silent about the problem of wastages-particularly in the case of investment on primary education. As such, any attempt to analyse the problem of wastages in primary education would be useful to the policy formulation on education.

Primary Education of Tribals in the Vizianagaram District

Vizianagaram District extends over an area of 6,300 sq. kms. With a total population of 22,15,103 (2001 Census). The scheduled tribes constitute around 9 per cent and schedules castes constitute around 10 per cent of the total population of the district (1991 Census). The district can be divided into two distinct natural divisions viz., plains and hilly regions. The integrated tribal development agency covers eight mandals in the hilly region under its sub-plan area viz., G.L. Puram, Kurupam, Panchipenta, Komarada, Salur, Makkuva, Jiyyammma valasa and Parvathipuram. However, a predominant section of tribal population is also living outside the sub-plan area in the mandals such as Mentada, Ramabhadrapuram, S. Kota, Vepada of Vizianagaram District. The major sub-castes of tribals living in the district include Savara, Gadaba, Jatapu, Kondadora and Mannedora.

According to 2001 census, the total literacy in the state of Andhra Pradesh is estimated as 61.11 per cent as compared to the national literacy rate of 65.38 per cent. In the case of Vizianagarm district, the total literacy is estimated at 51.82 per cent as against the state literacy level of 61.11 per cent. Literacy among the tribals of Vizianagaram district is estimated at meagre 9.01 per cent of the total literates in 1991 of which males account for 51.90 per cent and females account for 34.20 percent*.

This shows that the literacy rate is not only very less in the district compared to the state level but also very meagre in the case of tribals. Available data shows that as on August 1998 there are 2,411 primary schools including DPEP schools to cater to the needs of primary education in the district. At the primary level, the enrolment of students of 6-11 years of age group is about 2.38 lakhs of which boys accounts for 1.21 lakhs, girls account for 1.17 lakhs.

Since 1979, the Integrated Tribal Development Agency (ITDA) has been playing an important role in the development of tribal education in Vizianagaram district. The ITDA has been largely engaged in looking after the educational needs of the tribal children. In order to promote education at the

* In view of the lack of availability of 2001 Census data with regard to the literacy level of a tribals we are constrained to present 1991 census figures with regard to tribal literacy.

primary level a number of Ashram Schools were opened in the tribal areas. Besides providing free education, boarding and lodging facilities were also provided to the tribal children who inhabit the inaccessible hills and forests without proper communication facilities. To cater to the educational needs of tribal children, 32 Ashram elementary schools, 6 Ashram upper primary schools, 11 Ashram high schools were started by ITDA in 1980. In addition to these 384 single teacher schools (Girijana Vidya Vikas Kendras) were established in 1986 to reduce dropout problem among tribal children.

Further, in 1995, 63 (Maabadi) schools were also started but ITDA for improving enrolment in the 1st standard in tribal areas and their number has increased to 156 by 1999. ITDA has also established Ashram schools outside the sub-plan area viz., Nimmalapadu in Bobbili Mandal, Andra in Mentada Mandal, Konda Gangupudi in Vepada Mandal, Nerallavalsasa in Remabhadrapuram Mandal. A total of 53.130 students are studying in all these ITDA institutions during academic year 1999-2000. Of these, 43,025 (i.e., 81 per cent) of the scheduled tribe students are studying 1 to Xth class as Day Scholars and 10,105 (i.e., 19 per cent) are studying as boarders in the ITDA institutions. These students are provided with free boarding and lodging facilities, besides other incentives such as free text books, note books and dress etc.

Need for the Study

Education is considered as an indispensable 'passport to life (Jacque Delors, 1996) not only to enable to people to choose their occupation but also to eradicate the inequalities between different sexes and different groups within and between countries. In India during the last five decades several strategies and approaches for educational development of tribals were adopted. The sub-plan area approach adopted since the fifth Five Year Plan, has classified tribal areas into three broad categories i.e., (i) tribal concentrated areas (ii) tribal dispersed areas (iii) primitive tribal pockets. The tribal concentrated area is called sub-plan area where tribals constitute more than 50 per cent of the total population of a mandal or block. The sub-plan area approach is aimed at integrating various developmental activities besides flexibility in planning and resource allocation. It is significant to observe that primary education, among other things, is accorded high priority in the sub-plan strategy.

The strategy is expected to boost up the level of primary education among the tribals living in the sub-plan area while the same advantages of the programme are not within the reach of tribal children living outside the sub-plan area. It is in this context, it may be noted that there is no proper evaluation of the educational development of tribals living outside the sub-plan area. As such an intensive study of primary education among the tribals living in the sub-plan area vis-a-vis outside the sub-plan area would provide useful insights into the educational development of tribals. Hence an attempt is made to examine the pattern of education among the tribal children in the sub-plan area as well as outside the sub-plan area. Specific objective of this paper is to make a comparative study on the level of enrolment and dropouts in primary education of tribal children in the sub-plan area vis-a-vis out-side the sub-plan area. The present study pertains to Vizianagaram district, one of the backward district in the state of Andhra Pradesh.

Methodology

Data for the present study were collected by canvassing a pre designed questionnaire in the selected villages from the sub-plan and out-side the sub-plan area. As mandal primary schools (MPP schools) and Ashram schools are located in both areas, 6-11 years age group children going to these schools formed the unit of sampling. In the first stage, for the purpose of our study, we have selected at random 6 Tribal villages from the sub-plan area and 7 villages from out side the sub-plan area in Vizianagaram District. After an exhaustive survey of all the households in selected villages, we got a sample of 232 households in the sub-plan area and 201 households out side the sub-plan area having children of school going age i.e., 6-11 years. At the second stage, we have canvassed a pre-designed questionnaire to collect primary data from the parents of the school-going children of each village and the Head Masters of the Selected schools for the purpose of our study.

In the sub-plan area, we selected Duddukhallu, Regidi, Kottaguda, Jollaguda, Babbidi and K.D. Colony of G.L. Puram mandal in Vizianagaram district. We have canvassed questionnaire among 41 sample households in Dukkukhallu, 72 households in Regidi, 26 households in Kottaguda, 7 households in Jallaguda, 41 households in Babbidi and 44 households in K.D. Colony. The total number of sample households thus-covered in the sub-plan area is 232 with a total household population of 942.

Similarly, in the case of Out side the sub-plan area 7 villages with more than 95 per cent of the Scheduled Tribe population and also having Ashram schools and M.P.P. Schools are purposefully selected from 2 mandals viz., S. Kota and Vepada in Vizianagaram District. The villages covered under the category are Punyagiri, Cheediplem, Ammapalem, Addateegala, Bandavalasa, Dorlapalem in S. Kota mandal and K.G. Pudi colony in Vepada mandal. K.G. Pudi S.T. Colony is selected from Vepada mandal because of the location of Ashram school in that village. And the household questionnaire is canvassed among a sample of 21 households in Punyagiri, 17 households in Cheeedipalem, 67 households in Ammapalem, 16 households in Addateegala. 18 households in Bandavalasa, 19 households in Dorlapalem and 43 households in K.G. Pudi S.T. Colony. The total number of the sample households, thus covered out-side the sub-plan area are 201 with the total population of 825.

Primary Education Among Tribal Children in the Study Area

Data relating to the Distribution of Children of Primary school going age (6-11 years) among the sample households in the sub-plan area and out side the sub-plan area are presented in Table 1. It may be observed from the table that out of the total population of the sample households (942) children of 6-11 years age group account for 35.1 per cent in the sample villages of the sub-plan area. Of these children, Boys account for 54.7 per cent and Girls account for 45.3 per cent. Among the selected sample villages, K.D. colony accounts for highest proportion of children (46.4 per cent) followed by Kottaguda (40.2 per cent), Regidi (37.9 per cent), Jollaguda (30.6 per cent). Duddukallu (30.2 per cent) and Babbidi (26.8 per cent) in that order. It may also be observed that the proportion of Boys in the school going age group is comparatively more than the proportion of girls in that age-group in all the sample villages except Babbidi village in the sub-plan area.

Similarly, in the case of Out-side the Sub-plan area, out of total population (825) of the sample households, 6-11 years age group children account for 35.6 per cent. Of these children, Boys account for 57.5 per cent and Girls account for 42.5 per cent. Among the sample villages out side the sub-plan area Ammapalem accounts for the highest proportion of children (47.4 per cent) followed by K.G. Pudi (35.1 per cent), Dorapalem (34.7 per cent), Cheedipalem (32.9 per cent), Punyagiri (31.5 per cent), Addateegala (25.6 per cent) and Bandavalasa (24.7 per cent) in that order.

It may also be observed that the proportion of boys in the schools going age is comparatively more than the proportion of Girls in the entire sample villages out-sides the sub-Plan area.

Enrolment

Data relating to the enrolment of tribal children (6-11 years) of the sample households in the sub-plan area and out side the sub-plan area are presented in Table 2. From the table, it may be observed that the proportion of the children (6-11Years) enrolled in the primary education in the sub-plan area is relatively high (87.6 per cent) compared to that of out side the sub-plan area (85.0 per cent). Even within the sub-

Table 1: Distribution of Primary School Going Children (6-11 years) in the Sample Households

S.l. No.	Sample Village	No. of Household	Total Population	No. of Boys	No. of Girls	Total Children (6-11)Ys	S.l. No.	Sample Village	No. of Households	Total Population	No. of Boys	No. of Girls	Total Children (6-11) ys
1.	Luddukhallu	41	172	29 (55.8)	23 (44.2)	52 (30.2)	1.	Punyagiri	21	95	19 (68.3)	11 (36.7)	30 (31.5)
2.	Regidi	72	298	65 (57.5)	48 (42.5)	113 (37.9)	2.	Cheedipalem	17	79	18 (69.2)	8 (30.8)	26 (32.9)
3.	Kottaguda	26	102	24 (58.5)	17 (41.5)	41 (40.2)	3.	Ammapalem	67	219 (51.9)	54 (48.1)	50 (48.1)	104 (47.4)
4.	Jollaguda	7	36	7 (63.6)	4 (36.4)	11 30.6)	4.	Addateegala	16	82	13 (62.0)	8 (38.0)	21 25.6)
5.	Babbidi	42	209	26 (26.4)	30 (53.6)	56 (26.8)	5.	Bandavalasa	18	93	14 (60.9)	9 (39.1)	23 (24.7)
6.	K.D. Colony	44	125	30 (51.7)	28 (48.3)	58 (46.4)	6.	Dorlapalem	19	72	18 (72.0)	7 (28.0)	25 (34.7)
7.							7.	K.G. Pudi	43	185	33 (50)	32 (49.2)	65 (35.1)
	Total	**232**	**942 (100.0)**	**181 (54.7)**	**150 (45.3)**	**331 (35.1)**		**Total**	**201**	**825 (100.0)**	**169 (57.5)**	**125 (42.5)**	**294 (35.63)**

Source: Sample Households Data.

Table 2: Enrolment of Tribal Children in Primary Education

Sub-plan Area								*Out side the sub-plan area*							
							(percentage)								*(percentage)*
S.l. No.	*Sample Village*	*Total 6-11 years age Children*			*Total enrolled*			*S. No.*	*Sample Village*	*Total 6-11 years age children*			*Total enrolled*		
		Boys	*Girls*	*Total*	*Boys*	*Girls*	*Total*			*Boys*	*Girls*	*Total*	*Boys*	*Girls*	*Total*
1.	Duddukhallu	55.8	44.2	30.2	60.0	40.0	86.5	1.	Punyagiri	68.3	36.7	31.5	65.2	34.8	76.7
2.	Regidi	57.5	42.5	37.9	57.5	42.3	92.0	2.	Cheedipalem	69.2	30.8	32.9	47.6	52.4	78.0
3.	Kottaguda	58.5	41.5	40.2	62.2	37.8	90.2	3.	Ammapalem	51.9	48.1	47.4	52.7	47.3	87.5
4.	Jollaguda	63.6	36.4	30.6	77.8	22.2	81.8	4.	Addateegala	62.0	38.0	25.6	57.9	42.1	90.4
5.	Babbidi	26.4	53.6	26.6	51.2	48.8	76.7	5.	Bandavalasa	60.9	39.1	24.7	68.8	31.2	86.9
6.	K.D. Colony	51.7	48.3	46.4	54.5	45.5	89.6	6.	Dorlapalem	72.0	28.0	34.7	64.7	35.3	76.0
								7.	K.G. Pudi	50.8	49.2	35.1	57.6	42.4	90.7
	Total	**54.7**	**45.3**	**100.0**	**57.7**	**42.3**	**87.6**		**Total**	**57.5**	**42.5**	**35.63**	**56.9**	**43.1**	**85.0**

Source: Sample Households Data.

plan area the proportion of boys is high compared to girls in the 6-11 years age group. Of the total children enrolled 57.7 per cent are boys while 42.3 per cent are girls in the sub-plan area. Similar pattern may be observed with regard to all the selected villages in the sub-plan area.

In the case of out side sub-plan area also the proportion of boys enrolled in primary education is found to be high (56.9 per cent) compared to the girls (43.1 per cent) of 6-11 years age group. However, data reveals variations in the enrolment of boys and girls in different selected villages. Of the selected villages Cheedipalem village accounts for higher enrolment of the girls (52.4 per cent) compared to the boys (47.6 per cent) in the case of all other village boys out number the girls in terms of enrolment in the primary educational institutions out side the sub-plan area.

Dropouts

Data relating to the dropouts among the primary school going children in the sub-plan area and out side the sub-plan area are presented in the Table 3. From the table, it may be observed that the percentage of the dropout is high among the primary school going tribal children (6-11years) in out side the sub-plan area (49.6 per cent) compared to the school going children in the sub-plan area (42.7 per cent). Further, among the dropouts the proportion of girls is high in the sub-plan area as well as out side the sub-plan area. However, data reveals significant variations of dropouts among boys and girls in different selected villages in both sub-plan area and out side the sub-plan area. In the case of sub-plan area the proportion of girls dropped out in the primary education is high compared to boys in Duddukhallu, Kottaguda, Babbidi and K.D. colony villages. On the other hand, the proportion of dropouts among boys is high in Regidi village in the sub-plan area. The proportion of dropouts among boys and girls is equal in Jollaguda village in the sub-plan area.

In the case of out side the sub-plan area also there are significant variations in dropouts among boys and girls in

Table 3: Dropout among Tribal Children in Primary Education

Sub-plan Area								Out side the sub-plan area							
							(percentage)								(percentage)
S.l. No.	Sample Village	Total Dropped out			Total Dropped out			S. No.	Sample Village	Total enrolled			Total Dropped out		
		Boys	Girls	Total	Boys	Girls	Total			Boys	Girls	Total	Boys	Girls	Total
1.	Duddukhallu	60.0	40.0	86.5	38.5	61.5.	40.0	1.	Punyagiri	65.2	34.8	76.7	63.6	36.4	47.8
2.	Regidi	57.7	42.3	92.0	53.8	46.2	41.3	2.	Cheedipalem	47.6	52.4	73.0	50.0	50.0	47.3
3.	Kottaguda	62.2	37.8	90.2	44.4	55.6	40.5	3.	Ammapalem	52.7	47.3	87.5	31.3	68.7	49.4
4.	Jollaguda	77.8	22.2	81.8	50.0	50.0	44.4	4.	Addateegala	57.9	42.1	90.4	40.0	60.0	47.3
5.	Babbidi	51.2	48.8	76.7	44.4	55.6	46.5	5.	Bandavalasa	68.8	31.2	86.9	57.1	42.9	554.0
6.	K.D. Colony	54.5	45.5	89.6	38.1	61.9	46.1	6.	Dorlapalem	64.7	35.3	76.0	50.0	50.0	42.1
7.								7.	K.G. Pudi	57.6	42.4	90.7	4.29	57.1	52.5
	Total	57.7	42.3	87.6	45.0	55.0	42.7		Total	56.9	43.1	85.0	43.4	56.6	49.6

Source: Sample Households Data.

the selected villages. It is pertinent to observe that the proportion of dropout is high in boys compared to girls in Punyagiri and Bandavalsa villages, while the boys and girls account for equal percentage of dropouts in the case of Cheedipalem and Dorlapalem villages.

Reasons for Dropouts

The withdrawal of the child from the school depends on variety of factors. However, for the purpose of our study we have considered the most prominent determinants of dropout such as location of the school, lack of facilities at the school, Teacher absenteeism, lack of hostel facilities, assistance to parents, need to look after the young siblings and the need to collect forest produce etc.,

Data relating to the reasons for dropouts of tribal children from primary education are presented in Table 4 From the table, it may be observed that lack of adequate hostel facilities has been the major reason for dropout among tribal children in the sub-plan area as well as out side the sub-plan area. In the sub-plan area, next to inadequate hostel facilities, collection of forest produce, and assistance to parents and to look after the young siblings are found to be the major causes for dropout of children from primary schools. On the other

Table 4: Reasons for Dropout of Tribal Children from Primary Education

S. No.	*Reasons*	*Sub-Plan Area*	*Out-side the sub Plan Area*
1.	Location of school at a distance	-	-
2.	Lack of adequate school facilities	4.8	7.5
3.	Teacher's absenteeism	-	-
4.	Lack of Hostel facilities	31.05	51.7
5.	To help the parents in domestic and agricultural activity	25.4	20.9
6.	To look after the young siblings	11.6	8.5
7.	To collect forest produce	27.2	11.4
	Total	**(100.0)**	**(100.0)**

Source: Sample household data.

hand, assisting the parents in domestic and agricultural activity is found to be the second major cause for dropout of children from primary schools out side the sub-plan area. It is interesting to observe that teacher absenteeism and location of school are not found to be influencing dropout among tribal children in the sub-plan as well as out side the sub-plan area.

Our study reveals that enrolment of tribal children (6-11 years age group) is comparatively low in out side the sub-plan area compared to sub-plan area. Further, the proportion of tribal boys enrolled in primary education is relatively high than the tribal girls. It is significant to observe that the proportion of dropouts from primary education is found to be high among tribal girls compared to tribal boys in the sub-plan area as well as out side the sub-plan area. Our study also reveals that inadequate hostel facilities, collection of forest produce, assistance to parent in domestic and agricultural activity are the major reasons for dropouts of children from primary education.

In view of this, in order to attain the goal of hundred per cent literacy by 2005 the Government should evolve appropriate policy packages to arrest the dropouts rate among tribal children.

References

HLA Myint (1954), "An Interpretation of Economic Backwardness", Oxford Economics Papers June, 1954, pages 132 to 163.

Theodore W. Schultz (1962), "Investment in Human Capital in Poor Countries". In Foreign trade and human capital, edited by P.D. Zook pages 3 to 4.

Richard A Musgrave (1966), "Note on Educational investment in Developing Nation," Financing of education for economic growth, Paris 1966, petitioner. 31 to 39.

Christopher Colclough (1982), "The impact of Primary schooling on Economic Development. A review of the evidence" World Development, March 1982.

Sachchidananda (1994), "Tribal education—New Perspectives and Challenges, Journal of Julian Education March' 1994.

Dreze, J. and Amartya Sen (1965), "Indian Economic Development and Social Opportunity", Oxford University Press, New Delhi.

Planning Commission: The Seventh Five Years Plan, Planning Commission, Govt. of India.

Planning Commission: The First Five Year Plan, Planning Commission, Govt. of India.

V.K. Ramachandran and Vikas Rawal (1997), "Investment Gaps in primary Education, Economic & Political Weekly", Jan. 14-21, 1997.

Dreze and Sen (1995), "Indian Economic Development and Social Opportunity", Oxford University Press, New Delhi, 1995.

Jandyala B.G. Tilak (1995), 'Costs and Finances of Education in India'—Studies in Human Development in India, Discussion paper-5, Economic and Political Weekly, Jan. 1995.

Jandyala B.G. Tilak (1999), "National Human Development Institute—Education in the Union Budget, Economic and Political Weekly, March' 1999.

Vizianagaram District hand book, District Planning Officer, Vizanagaram.

16

Trends in the Growth of Primary Education in East Godavari District of Andhra Pradesh

Dr. D. Pull Rao

Introduction

Education plays a vital role in the process of development of human resources. For an overall development of the economy, development of education in general and universalization of literacy and elementary education in particular, are given a very high priority in India in line with the other developing countries of the World. Primary education constitutes a very important part of the entire structure of education. It is at this stage, the child starts going to a formal institution and formal education starts. Education which he receives at this juncture provides the basic foundation for his physical, mental, emotional, intellectual and social development. Primary education deserves the highest priority, not only on grounds of social justice and democracy, but also for raising the competence of the average worker and for increasing the national productivity.

Article 45 of the Indian Constitution guarantees provision of free and compulsory education to all children up to the age of 14. Apart from being a Constitutional obligation, the provision of universal elementary education is crucial for spreading mass literacy, which is a basic requirement for economic development, modernization of the social structure and effective functioning of any democratic Institution. It also represents an indispensable first step towards the provision of equal opportunity to all citizens.

East Godavari lies in the north-eastern part of Andhra Pradesh. The population of the District is 48.73 lakhs as per 2001 census and this constituted 6.43 per cent of the population of the state. There are 28.13 lakhs literates forming 57.73 per cent of total population of the District. Among the total literates male literates constitute 69.97 per cent while female literates constitute 61.00 per cent. As the focus of the study is on the development of primary education in East Godavari District, we confine ourselves to the same examining the trends of primary education in East Godavari District, which is one of the most developed districts of the Coastal Andhra Pradesh.

Objectives

This paper has two main objectives namely,

(a) To examine the trends of primary education in East Godavari District during 1988-89 to 1997-98, and

(b) To estimate the pupil teacher ratio.

The Data

The Secondary data relating to the number of schools, enrolment and number of teachers working in primary and upper primary schools for the decadal period 1988-89 to 1997-98 are obtained from the offices of the commissioner and Director of School Education, Hyderabad and the District Educational Officer, Kakinada, East Godavari District. It was however found that there are some discrepancies in the data supplied by these offices particularly with respect to the primary education. Suitable adjustments were made wherever necessary. There is a difference between enrolment in primary schools and enrolment at primary stage. Therefore we have taken to enrolment of the primary schools as a proxy to enrolment in primary stage, similar is the case with upper primary schools. This difference is to be kept in mind while understanding the trends in the growth of primary education in East Godavari District.

The Results

(a) Growth of Primary Education

In Table 1 the growth in the number of schools and the enrolment into primary education for selected years during the period 1988-89 to 1997-98 are provided. The rate of enrolment to the corresponding age group and the number of children per school are also presented. There were about 2800 primary schools in the District during 1988-89. The number has increased to around 3,000 by 1997-98 recording a decadal growth rate of 7.32 per cent. The annual growth of the schools and the number of children in 6-11 years age group are calculated with the help of index number of taking 1988-89 as the base year. It is observed that the increase in the number of schools is higher when compared to the growth of children of school going age (6-11 years).

The total enrolment in primary education in the year 1988-89 was 3.80 lakhs and it has increased continuously to 4.33 lakhs up to 1992-93. In 1993-94 it has decreased to 3.91 lakhs and marginally increased to 3.95 lakhs by 1994-95. Further, it has decreased to 3.83 lakhs for two years 995-97 and again increased to 4.08 lakhs in 1997-98.

Growth of enrolment and the achievement in universalization of elementary education in the district can be discovered only in terms of the achievement with respect to the corresponding age group, as the number of enrolment alone does not convey its proportion to the population. Therefore, we have estimated the proportion of school going children enrolled into the primary schools to find out how many of them are still left. It is interesting to find that the District has an enrolment rate of 66.81 per cent in 1988-89 and the proportion has increased to 72.60 in 1990-91. Later from 1991-92 onwards the rate of enrolment has been on the decline.

The figures in Table 1 further suggest that the District still has a back log of more than 30 to 40 per cent towards universalisation of elementary education. A peculiar trend that may be noted is that the number of students in each school has been decreasing substantially during the period of the study because of decreasing number of enrolled children and increasing number of schools due to various schemes like Andhra Pradesh Primary Education Project (APPEP), Operation Black Board (OBB), etc. In addition to the mushroom growth of private unregistered convents in the district.

(B) *Growth of Upper Primary Education*

Article 45 of the Indian constitution guarantees free and compulsory education up to elementary stage to the children up to the age group 6-14. In order to find out the achievement of the targets, the enrolment figures and the number of schools available in the District during the period 1988-89 to 1997-98 are presented in Table 2.

It is observed that there were only 309 upper primary schools in 1988-89 and this number has increased to 374 by 1997-98.

The enrolment of students in the upper primary schools has recorded a slower growth compared to number of upper primary schools during 1988-98. But a peculiar trend could be seen from the table that the enrolment in 1992-93 was the highest when compared to the enrolments during other years. Total number of students enrolled in upper primary schools were 1,14,901 in 1988-89. But this number has declined to 94,159 in 1989-90, registered on increase up to 1992-93 and again this number has decreased to 1,07,848 in 1993-94. The enrolment has increased to 1,14,754 in 1995-96 and thereafter number has been on the decline. Thus, there were severe fluctuation in respect of school enrolment.

Table 1: Growth of Primary Education in East Godavari District

Year	*School age population (6-11) years*	*Index*	*No. of schools*	*No. of children enrolled (6-11) years*	*Index*	*Rate of enrollment to corresponding age group (%)*	*No. of children per school*
1988-89	5,68,149	100.00	2,773	3,79,607	100.00	66.81	137
1989-90	5,79,909	102.07	2,788	4,15,348	109.42	71.62	149
1990-91	5,91,914	104.20	2,882	4,29,718	113.20	72.60	149
1991-92	6,04,241	106.35	2,873	4,32,311	113.88	71.55	150
1992-93	6,16,730	108.55	3,031	4,32998	114.06	70.21	143
1993-94	6,29,477	110.79	2,970	3,90,734	102.93	62.07	132
1994-95	6,42,488	113.08	2,897	3,94,521	103.93	61.41	136
1995-96	6,55,768	115.42	2,918	3,90,752	102.94	59.59	134
1996-97	6,69,322	117.80	2,966	3,83,202	100.95	57.25	129
1997-98	6,83,156	120.24	2,976	4,08,456	107.60	59.79	137

Source: Commissioner & Director of School Education, Hyderabad and District Educational Officer, Kakinada.

Table 2: Growth of Upper Primary Education in East Godavari District

Year	*School age population (11-13) years*	*Index*	*No. of schools*	*No. of children enrolled (11-13 years)*	*Index*	*Rate of enrollment to corresponding age group (%)*	*No. of children per school*
1988-89	2,12,735	100.00	309	1,14,901	100.00	54.01	372
1989-90	2,17,139	102.07	309	94,159	81.95	43.36	305
1990-91	2,21,634	104.18	311	1,11,543	97.08	50.33	359
1991-92	2,29,860	108.05	311	1,12,600	98.00	48.99	362
1992-93	2,34,611	110.28	348	1,27,110	110.62	54.18	365
1993-94	2,39,460	112.56	337	1,07,848	93.86	45.04	320
1994-95	2,44,409	114.89	363	1,14,635	99.77	46.90	316
1995-96	2,49,460	117.26	362	1,14,754	99.87	46.00	317
1996-97	2,54,616	119.69	362	1,10,070	95.79	43.23	304
1997-98	2,59,879	122.16	374	1,14,022	99.23	43.88	305

Source: Commissioner & Director of School Education, Hyderabad and District Educational Officer, Kakinada.

The rate of enrolment in upper primary schools in terms of rate of enrolment to the corresponding age group has shown a dismal picture recording less than 45 to 50 per cent. In 1988-89 the rate of enrolment for the corresponding age group was 54.01 per cent. It has declined to 43.36 per cent in 1989-90, again it has increased to 50.33 per cent in 1990-91 but it has declined to 48.99 in 1991-92 and since 1992-93 onwards it has been on a decline. This is very unfortunate particularly, when governments are boasting of universalization of Elementary Education. A more or less similar picture has emerged from the number of children per school during the period under study. Despite the fact that the number of children enrolled in schools has been on the decline and the number of schools is on the increase, the number of children per school has been on the decline. This calls for an examination of the pupil teacher ratio.

(c) *Pupil Teacher Ratio*

The pupil teacher ratio shows the quality of education. Here, we will examine the number of teachers employed in the primary schools in the District and the rate of growth of number of teachers during the period under study. The data are presented in table 3. It is observed that there were 6,588 teachers employed in primary schools in 1988-89, of which 1980 are women, constituting 30.05 per cent of the total. The number has increased to 7557 in 1991-92 and increased further to 8040 by 1997-98. The number of women teachers were 2922 in 1997-98. It was high during the study period and constituted 36.34 per cent of the total teachers, indicating that women teaching community is on the increase in the area of primary education.

The trends in the growth of teachers show a peculiar feature with irregular ups and downs. The index of growth of male teachers has increased to 110 in 1991-92, went down and increased again to 111 by 1997-98. However, there is some positive change in the case of female teachers. Their index has been rising almost continuously but for the setback during 1993-94 to 1996-97. It reached to 148 by 1997-98 an all time high for the period under study. The index of female teachers' is higher than that of the male teachers in general. This may

Table 3: Number of teachers appointed in the primary schools of East Godavari District during 1988-89 and 1997-98

Year	*Men*	*Index*	*Women*	*Index*	*Total*	*Index*	*Pupil teacher ratio (no. of pupils per teacher)*
1988-89	4608	100	1980	100	6588	100	57.62
1989-90	4608	100	1980	100	6588	100	63.05
1990-91	5018	109	2505	127	7557	112	58.23
1991-92	5052	110	2505	127	7557	115	57.21
1992-93	4867	106	2644	134	7511	114	57.65
1993-94	4501	98	2480	125	6981	106	55.97
1994-95	4206	91	2297	116	6503	99	60.67
1995-96	4725	103	2504	126	7229	110	54.05
1996-97	4716	102	2455	124	7171	109	53.44
1997-98	5118	111	2922	148	8040	122	50.80

Source: Commissioner & Director of School Education, Hyderabad and District Educational Officer, Kakinada.

be due to the implementation of 33.33 reservation policy of the government in favour of women.

During the period of our study, the increase in the number of teachers was around 1500. But the enrolment in primary schools showed a decreasing trend except for 2 or 3 intervals over the period of time. This resulted in a change in pupil teacher ratio. It is observed that there are 57.62 pupils per teacher in 1988-89 and it was declining continuously except in two years i.e., 1989-90 and 1994-95. It is finally reached to 50.80 pupils per teacher in 1997-98. Though, the Government has been insisting on a pupil teacher ratio of 40 students per teacher particularly, for aided schools it may not be possible for the government to achieve this objective. In fact school wise pupil teacher ratios are less favourable to the students. This adversely affects the quality of education at the primary level, where the teacher does not find any motive to teach such a huge number of students let alone the much needed individual attention at the stage of primary education. This may be one of the reasons for the large number of dropouts at the elementary level.

The Conclusions

This paper analyses the trends in the growth of primary

and upper primary education during the period 1988-89 and 1997-98. In terms of its proportion to the corresponding school going age group the enrolment rate is found to be below the objectives of the constitution. The rate of enrolment to the corresponding age group (6-11) has been stable except in a few cases during the study period. The number of children per school has been decreasing substantially at primary level because of increasing number of schools boosted by various incentives of the government of Andhra Pradesh. The mushroom growth of the unregistered convents is another reason for this tremendous growth of schools. However, the rate of enrolment of children in the age group of 11-13 years (at upper primary level) has been decreasing which suggest heavy drop outs at the primary level. This resulted in the lower per school enrolment that made the upper primary education economically unviable for the private management. The pupil teacher ratio though declined from 57.62 in 1988-89 to 50.80 by 1997-98 still is very high. This resulted in poor quality of education. Thus the universalization of elementary education is, yet, a distant dream.

Reference

1. East Godavari District Handbook, District Planning Officer, Kakinada.
2. George Psacharopoulous (1987): "Economics of Education Research and Studies", Pergamon Press, Oxford.
3. Gopinathan Nair, P.R. (1981): "Primary education, Population growth and socio-economic change", Allied Pub., New Delhi.
4. Govinda, R. and Varghese (1992): "Quality of Primary Education: an empirical study", Journal of Educational Planning and Administration, Vol. 6, No. 1, January New Delhi.
5. Naik, J.P. (1971): "Elementary education in India—a promise to keep", Allied Pub., Bombay.
6. Rajaiah, B. (1987): " Economics of Education", Mittal Pub., New Delhi.
7. Ray, Ash Narain (1993), "Education for all: an exclusive dream", The Hindustan Times, December 13, New Delhi.
8. Singh and Surdarshan (1996), "Primary Education", H.P. Bhargava Book House, Agra.

17

Gender Disparity in Literacy Rates in Andhra Pradesh with Special Focus on Visakhapatnam District

Prof. T. Nirmala Devi
K. Subhashini

Population growth is influenced by many complex factors of which literacy level, particularly female literacy plays a pivotal role. Female literacy provides decision making power, increases labour productivity, leads to later marriage which will induce a desire for a small family, besides reducing the child bearing period and ultimately leads to lower fertility. In other words, female literacy is well recognised as a *sine quo non* for demographic, economic and social change in a country. In India, sufficient attention has not been paid to improve the education of women, despite the striking evidence of its socio-economic and demographic benefits. Although India has raised the female literacy rate over the decades, it still has a long way to go. The level of female literacy has begun to increase considerably from the last two decades. As per the 2001 Census, all the four southern States, viz., Kerala, Tamil Nadu, Karnataka and Andhra Pradesh figure among the leading States with the lowest population growth rates, reflecting reasonable levels of human development as the south leads in the literacy level of India with 78 per cent against the East and Central (65 per cent),

North (69.57 per cent) and West (72 per cent), being the national average at 65.35 per cent. In the south, Kerala continued to top the literacy rate at 90.92 per cent followed by Tamil Nadu (73.47 per cent), Karnataka (67.04 per cent) and Andhra Pradesh (61.11 per cent). Though Andhra Pradesh ranked eighth in the ten least literate States of India, it registered a decline in the decadal population growth from 24.2 per cent to 13.86 per cent as well as in the exponential growth of population from 2.17 per cent to 1.31 per cent in the past and present Censuses respectively. The State has recorded an increase of 17.03, 15.73 and 18.40 percentage points in total, male and female literacy rates from 1991 to 2001 respectively. Despite the relatively high increase in female literacy in the current Census, a significant gender gap of 19.73 percentage points persists in the State, revealing the lagging performance of females in literacy in some of the backward districts. Likewise, the gender gap was highly significant in a majority of mandals in Visakhapatnam district. Viewed against this background, the present paper aims at assessing the variations in female literacy in Andhra Pradesh at district level with special focus on Visakhapatnam district and also examining the gender disparity in literacy at district level of the State and at mandal level of Visakhapatnam.

Female-Male Gap in Literacy

The increase in female literacy rate of India in the current Census registered the highest, in comparison with the earlier decades starting from 1951. The female male gap-the difference between male and female rates-in literacy in India was at 18.30 percentage points in 1951 due to abysmally low male and female literacy rates. The gap, viz., 25.05, 23.99, 26.62 24.84 and 21.69 percentage points in 1961, 1971, 1981, 1991 and 2001 respectively[4] has not showed any consistent decline over the years, with the exception of the latter two Censuses. Till 1991 Census, a gradual increase in female-male gap was experienced by Andhra Pradesh, however, it was erased in the current Census.

In regard to female-male gap in Andhra Pradesh at district level, as seen from Table 1, two districts viz., West Godavari and East Godavari registered a low gap of less than 15 percentage points in 1991 while Krishna and Hyderabad followed by Khammam were having a variation of 15 to 20 percentage points. On the other hand, a high gap of more than 25 percentage points was recorded in 11 districts, being Cuddapah at the bottom of female literacy. The remaining seven districts showed a significant gap in literacy, as they varied between 20 to 25 percentage points. In the 2001 Census, the situation had not changed markedly. Krishna and Hyderabad were the only two districts of low gap in the current Census besides the two districts recorded in 1991. Guntur and Nellore followed by Rangareddy, Khammam and Visakhapatnam districts showed a medium variation in literacy between males and females. A high gap of more than 25 percentage points was registered in Kurnool, Cuddapah, Nizamabad, Nalgonda and Ananthapur districts in the current Census. Surprisingly, the gap increased from 22.77 in the past to 25.04 percentage points in the present Census in the backward literate district, Mahaboobnagar, reflecting the sluggishness of female literacy relative to male literacy. The decadal change in the gap is insignificant in five districts-Adilabad, Niramabad, Nalgonda Khamman and Kurnool because they have not showed an increase of even one percentage point. A significant reduction was noticed in the gap in literacy in six districts, particularly Ranga Reddy, Cuddapah and Chittoor, apart from Krishna, Hyderabad and East Godavari.

Table 2 shows the female-male gap in literacy in the mandals of Visakhapatnam district at total, rural and urban levels in 2001. Only five mandals of the total 43 mandals, viz., Nakkapale, Payakaraopeta, Visakhapatnam-urban, Visakhapatam-rural and Gudem Kothaveedhi displayed a low gap in total literacy, i.e., 10 to 15 variation between male and female literacy rates. The three least gender gap mandal registered at the rural level also constituted a part of the total.

Table 1: Male-Female Gap in Literacy Rates (in per cent) in Andhra Pradesh at District Level

	1991		*2001*	
Low Variation (10 to 15)	West Godavari	12.77	East Godavari	8.97
	East Godavari	13.06	West Godavari	8.98
			Krishna	9.52
			Hyderabad	10.44
Medium Variation (15 to 20)	Krishna	15.01	Guntur	17.15
	Hyderabad	15.34	Nellore	17.21
	Khammam	19.51	Ranga Reddy	17.99
			Khammam	18.88
			Visakhapatnam	18.88
High Variation (25 and above)	Cuddapah	30.79	Kurnool	26.29
	Anantapur	28.31	Cuddapah	26.22
	Karimnagar	27.42	Nizamabad	25.70
	Kurnool	27.20	Nalgonda	25.12
	Chittoor	26.17	Anantapur	25.07
	Prakasam	26.08	Mehbubnagar	25.04
	Nizamabad	25.98		
	Medak	25.92		
	Warangal	25.90		
	Srikakulam	25.62		
	Nalgonda	25.61		

Source: Calculated from *Population Education cell of SRC*, Hyderabad.
Note: Gap is the difference between the literacy rates of males and females.

Along with the two mandals—Visakhapatnam-rural and Visakhapatnam-urban which were also shown in the overall category, Bheemunipatnam, Pendurthi and Anakapalle also displayed least gender gap at the urban level. By contrast, a high gender gap of 25 per cent and above was recorded in eight mandals of Visakhapatnam district, the highest being K. Kothapadu with more than 30 per cent gap in literacy at the overall level. These eight mandals were also under rural division showing high gender gap along with Gajuwaka. At the urban level, a high gap of more than 25 per cent, in Gudemkothaveedhi not only contrary to the general norm of prevalence of high literacy rate at urban level but also pointed out the need for adequate provision of institutional facilities as well as public action. Thus in Visakhapatnam district,

Table 2: Male-Female Gap in Literacy Rate in Visakhapatnam at M ndal level in 2001

(in per cent)

	Total		*Rural*		*Urban*	
Low Variation (10 to 15)	1. Nakkapalle	11.23	1. Nakkapalle	11.23	1. Visakhapatnam-rural	12.63
	2. Payakaraopet	11.96	2. Gudem Kothaveedhi	11.96	2. Visakhapatnam-urban	12.85
	3. Visakhapatnam-urban	12.85	3. Payakaraopeta	11.81	3. Bhemunipatnam	14.27
	4. Visakhapatnam-rural	14.04			4. Pendurthi	14.49
	5. Gudem Kothaveedhi	14.21			5. Anakapalle	14.75
High Variation (25 and above)	1. K. Kottapadu	30.23	1. K. Kottapadu	30.23	1. Gudem Kothaveedhi	27.14
	2. Peda Bayalu	29.34	2. Peda Bayalu	29.34		
	3. Devarapalli	28.13	3. Devarapalli	28.13		
	4. Pedagantyada	28.13	4. Pedagantyada	28.13		
	5. Cheedikada	27.62	5. Cheedikada	27.62		
	6. Dumbriguda	27.28	6. Dumbriguda	27.28		
	7. Araku Valley	25.86	7. Gajuwaka	25.48		
	8. Chodavaram	25.18	8. Araku Valley	25.22		
			9. Chodavaram	25.18		

Source: Calculated from *Census of India*, 2001, Provisional Population Totals, Paper-2, Andhra Pradesh, Table 5

gender gap persisted largely in nine mandals displaying the poor social structure and weak management in terms of the literacy. Only five mandals recorded a low gap, i.e., less than 15 per cent of variation between males and females in literacy. The rest of 29/30 mandals fell under the category of 15 to 25 per cent gap which was also considered as large.

Gender Disparity in Literacy

There are large differences in female literacy attainment across the States in India. A huge variation was also seen among the southern States, as Kerala topped at 86.17 per cent of female literacy and Andhra Pradesh lagged behind at 32.72 per cent in 1991 with a gap of 53.45 per cent. However, the gap between the two States was narrowed to 36.7 per cent in 2001. Table 3 presents the gender disparity in literacy rates in India and in the southern States in 1991 and 2001 Censuses. Gender disparity is denoted by f/m ratio-a proportion of females to males. The gender disparity in literacy had considerably reduced in India from the past to the present Census, reflecting the change in the socio-economic scenario in the 1990s. The marginal change in gender disparity in Kerala over a decade may be attributed to the high base existed in the past. The improvement in Karnataka and Tamil Nadu was not highly significant in comparison with Andhra Pradesh, which recorded an appreciable surge in the current Census, notwithstanding of the moderate increases in the past Censuses-0.40, 0.47, 0.52 and 0.59 percentage points in 1961, 1971, 1981 and 1991 respectively (not shown in the Table). However, the present growth has been attributed to the low base of female literacy in the past, besides the other institutional factors.[6]

The rural-urban variation in literacy declined modestly in Andhra Pradesh at the district level in 2001, but not to the significant level. Rural literacy in the State reflected more or less the same scenario of total literacy in the present Census, as the three high literate districts, viz., West Godavari, Krishna and Chittoor were categorised in both total and rural level

Table 3: Gender Disparity in Literacy Rates in Southern States (in per cent)

	f/m in1991	*f/m in 2001*
India	0.61	0.71
Andhra Pradesh	0.59	0.72
Karnataka	0.66	0.75
Kerala	0.92	0.93
Tamil Nadu	0.70	0.78

Source: Calculated From *Census of India*, 1991 and 2001.

Note: Gender Disparity is measured by ratio of females to males (f/m) literacy level. High (f/m) ratio indicates less difference between males and females *vice-versa*..

while Hyderabed ranked the first at the total level. Out of the least literate districts at the total level, viz., Mehboohnagar, Vizianagaram and Medak, the latter was substituted by Adilabad at rural level. Urban literacy of over 80 per cent was registered in Nalgonda, Warangal, besides Chittor, which represented a high overall literacy. The lowest urban literacy was recorded in Kurnool, Ananthapur and Adilabad districts. In sum, the rural-urban variation in female literacy rate was at 24.98 percentage points, being the rural and urban female literacy rates at 44.36 and 69.34 percentage points respectively, whereas the rural-urban variation in males was at 17.08 percentage points.[7]

Gender Disparity in Literacy in Andhra Pradesh

The gender disparity is generally significant in low literate districts and *vice-versa*. The encouraging fact is that the gender discrimination in backward districts is declining over the decade, however, it is still considered as significant and causing concern. The gender disparity in low female literate districts and high female literate districts in Andhra Pradesh are presented in Table 4. Some districts have recorded significant success in reducing the gender disparity over time, while others showed a slow progress, reflecting the regional backwardness. Hyderabad, West Godavari, East Godavari and Krishna continued to be the least gender disparity districts in both the Censuses. Significant improvement was visible in these four districts and particularly pronounced in the latter three districts in the present Census. Of late, Ranga Reddy, Nellore and Guntur had improved their female literacy and showed low gender disparity as seen from their f/m ratio of 0.75 per cent and above in the current Census. On the other hand, Medak, Karimnagar, Srikakulam, Adilabad, Vizianagaram, Nizamabad, Nalgonda and Ananthapur which experienced a high gender disparity in 1991 census have now displayed a better picture of f/m of more than 0.60 per cent due to the sizeable increase in female literacy. However, Mehboobnagar was being left as the least female literate district in the current Census.

Table 4: Gender Disparity in Literacy Rates in Andhra Pradesh at District level (in per cent)

Sl. No.	*Districts*	*(f/m) in 1991*	*(f/m) in 2001*
1.	Adilabad	0.45	0.63
2.	Nizamabad	0.45	0.61
3.	Karimnagar	0.46	0.65
4.	Medak	0.42	0.62
5.	Hyderabad	0.80	0.87
6.	Ranga Reddy	0.61	0.76
7.	Mahaboobnagar	0.44	0.56
8.	Nalgonda	0.49	0.64
9.	Warangal	0.50	0.66
10.	Khammam	0.61	0.71
11.	Srikakulam	0.47	0.65
12.	Vizianagaram	0.48	0.64
13.	Visakhapatnam	0.61	0.72
14.	East Godavari	0.76	0.87
15.	West Godavari	0.78	0.88
16.	Krishna	0.75	0.87
17.	Guntur	0.63	0.75
18.	Prakasam	0.50	0.65
19.	Nellore	0.63	0.76
20.	Cuddapath	0.51	0.65
21.	Kurnool	0.48	0.60
22.	Anantapur	0.49	0.63
23.	Chittor	0.58	0.72

Source: Calculated from the data provided by the *Population Education Cell of SRC*, Hyderabad.

Note : As in Table 3.

Gender Disparity in Literacy in Visakhapatnam District

Gender disparity in literacy rates at mandal level in Visakhapatnam is shown in Table 5. Out of the 43 mandals in the district, only six mandals, viz., Visakhapatnam-urban, Visakhapatnam-rural, Gajuwaka, Payakaraopeta, Nakkapalle and Pendurthi showed least gender displarity at the overall level, as the female-male ratio was more than 0.75. Payakaraopeta and Nakkapalle were the only mandals showing low gender disparity at the rural level, while another nine mandals, are showing signs of improvement in terms of female literacy. Least gender disparity at the urban level has been visualized in eight mandals out of 10 mandals. In the remaining two, especially in Gudem Kothaveedhi, the female literacy rate had not increased significantly, resulting in sizeable disparity in socio-cultural factors. On the other hand, gender disparity at the total level (also at the rural level) was highly significant in six mandals-Dumbriguda, Peda Bayalu, G. Madugula, Munchingipattu, Ananthagiri and Gudem Kothaveedhi-and another ten mandals also showed a f/m ratio of less than 0.60 (not shown in the Table). By and large, gender disparity is considered to be high in nearly 30 mandals in Visakhapatnam district, showing the lack of adequate institutional and infrastructure facilities as well as the poor public action.

Conclusion

It is evident that several socio-economic and cultural factors are influencing the female literacy, particularly at rural level. In order to attain a significant level of female literacy/ education in developing societies, a firm commitment and implementation are required on the part of the government as the sustainable development of the economy is intricately related to the empowerment of women. At large, the initiatives taken by the Government of Andhra Pradesh during the last decade have been giving encouraging results in female literacy. The sluggishness in female literacy in some of the districts and in the mandals of Visakhapatnam district

Table 5: Gender Disparity in Literacy Rates (percentage) in Visakhapatnam at Mandal level in 2001

(in per cent)

Visakhapatnam 0.73		*Total*	0.47		*Rural*	0.63		*Urban*	0.83
Low Disparity (above 0.75 of f/m ratio)	1.	Visakhapatnam-urban	0.85	1.	Payakaraopeta	0.80	1.	Visakhapatnam-urban	0.84
	2.	Visakhapatnam-rural	0.83	2.	Nakkapalle	0.78	2.	Visakhapatnam-rural	0.84
	3.	Gajuwaka	0.82				3.	Pendurthi	0.83
	4.	Payakaraopeta	0.50				4.	Arakuvalley	0.83
	5.	Nakkapalle	0.78				5.	Anakapalle	0.82
	6.	Pendurthi	0.75				6.	Gajuwaka	0.81
							7.	Bheemunipatnam	0.81
							8.	Narsipatnam	0.78
High Disparity (Below 0.50 of f/m ratio)	1.	Dumbriguda	0.39	1.	Dumbriguda	0.39			
	2.	Peda Bayalu	0.42	2.	Peda Bayalu	0.42			
	3.	G. Madugula	0.42	3.	G. Madugula	0.42			
	4.	Munchingipathu	0.46	4.	Munchingipattu	0.46			
	5.	Ananthagiri	0.48	5.	Gudem Kothaveedhi	0.47			
	6.	Gudem Kothaveedhi	0.49	6.	Ananthagiri	0.48			

Source: As in Table 2.
Note: As in Table 3.

underscores the need for overcoming the institutional and infrastructure bottlenecks and also the weakness in government towards the spread of education. In view of the striking importance of female education, in social, economic and demographic sectors, the share of public spending towards the gender specific policies and programmes should be strengthened and sustained to allow the women to avail the basic human right to education. Finally, it is believed that the determination and drive of the state government is the ultimate in promoting female literacy.

References

G. Rambabu, "South Leads the Way on Demographic Front" in *Business Line,* March 28, 2001.

P.R. Brahmananda, "Population: Green and Red Signals", in *Business Line,* April 4, 2001.

Population Education Cell of SRC, Hyderabad.

Ruddar Dutt, "2001 Census: Encouraging and Discouraging Features", in *Business line,* October 14, 2001.

Census of India, 1991 and 2001

Ibid.

Census of India, 2001, Provisional Population Totals, Paper 2, Andhra Pradesh, p. 80.

18

Literacy Scenario–with Special Reference to West Godavari District of Andhra Pradesh

K. Parameswara Rao

India ranks second in the world next only to China in terms of the size of the population. India's land scape is just 2.4 per cent of the total world area, whereas population is nearly 16.7 per cent of the world population. India accounted for 19.6 per cent of the estimated population of developing countries in 1998 (5.01 billion). These facts clearly indicate that the pressure of population on the land in this country is very high. How alarming is the situation in this country can be easily followed from the fact that the national income of India is presently even less than 1.2 per cent of the total world income.

India's population, according to the latest census of 2001 was 102.70 crores. According to the census of 1901, the population of the country was just 23.83 crores. Since then, in a period of 100 years, the population of the country increased by 78.87 crores. If viewed in the context of a relatively slow economic growth, this growth is really an alarming situation.

The National Literacy Mission (NLM) in 1988, aims at attaining functional literacy for 100 million persons in the age group of 15-35 (including the age group of 9-14 where Non-formal education is not in operation) in a time bound manner. The most important development that has taken place under the NLM is the near ascendancy of the campaign mode in the adult education programmes in the country.

Today, literacy campaigns, being area-specific, time bound, volunteer-based, cost-effective and outcome-oriented, are the dominant strategy of the NLM for the eradication of illiteracy. Skill up gradation is an important component of post-illiteracy. The adult education programme aims at the creation of a learning society through continuing education programmes. The continuing education package offers a host of programmes viz., the equivalency programme, income-generating programme, quality of life improvement programme and individual interest promotion programme etc.

In this paper, an attempt has been made to study the literacy scenario in general and with particular reference to West Godavari District of Andhra Pradesh.

Literacy

The most important characteristic of population is literacy which is a pre-requisite for the overall development of the country both socially and economically.

For the purpose of census, a person is deemed as literate if he or she can read and write any language with understanding. The definition of literate for census of India 2001 is the same as was adopted in 1991 census. In the 1991 census, the question on literacy was canvassed only for population aged seven years and above, unlike earlier census which took into account population of five years and above for this purpose.

The preliminary results of population 2001 reveal that there has been an increase in literacy in the country. The literacy rate in the country is 65.4 per cent with 76.9 for males and 54.2 for females. The steady improvement in literacy rate is apparent from the table on next page.

Table 1: Literacy Rate in India 1951-2001

Year	*Persons*	*Males*	*Females*	*Male-Female Gap in Literacy Rate*
1951	18.3	27.2	8.9	18.3
1961	28.3	40.4	15.4	25.0
1971	34.5	46.0	22.0	24.0
1981	43.6	56.4	29.8	26.6
1991	52.2	64.1	39.3	24.8
2001	65.4	76.9	54.2	22.7

Literacy: States Performance

Kerala retained its position by being on top with a 90.9 per cent literacy rate in the country. The rate among males was 94.2 per cent and among females it was 87.9 per cent. Bihar stood at the bottom with a literacy rate of 47.5 per cent (60.3 per cent for males and 33.6 per cent for females). Among the three new states Uttaranchal has the highest literacy rate of 72 per cent for the total population, male literacy of 84 per cent and female literacy rate of 60 per cent. Chattisgarh has an overall literacy rate of 65 per cent (male 78 per cent and female 52 per cent), Jharkhand has an overall literacy rate of 54 per cent (68 per cent male and 39 per cent female).

Six out of the 28 states in India have a female literacy rate of less than 50 per cent. These states are Rajasthan (44 per cent), Jammu & Kashmir (42 per cent) Jarkhand (39 per cent) and Bihar (34 per cent). The female literacy rate in Madhya Pradesh is 50 per cent.

The gap between male and female literacy rate is the highest in Rajasthan (32 per cent), followed by Uttar Pradesh (27 per cent), Madhya Pradesh (27 per cent) Jarkhand (27 per cent), Chattisgarh (26 per cent) and Bihar (26 per cent). It is distressing to note that the male-female literacy gap is high in Gujarat (22 per cent). Maharashtra and West Bengal (18 per cent each) indicating social backwardness. In Andhra Pradesh female literacy rate was only 51 per cent and the male-female gap is 20 per cent points.

In terms of progress on the female literacy front during the last decade. Chhatishgarh has the best record (the increase in the literacy percentage by 25 points between 1991-2001), followed by Rajasthan (24 per cent) Madhya Pradesh (21 per cent). In the case of males, Rajasthan has the best record (increase of 21.5 points) followed by Chhattisgarh (20 points) and Madhya Pradesh (18 points). There is no doubt that special programmes launched by the government and NGOs in Rajasthan and Madhya Pradesh have succeeded in stepping up literacy rates mostly among males.

In 2001, Andhra Pradesh had a population of 75.7 million constituting about 7.4 per cent of India's population Andhra Pradesh is the fifth most populous state in India. In terms of geographical area, Andhra Pradesh is also the fifth largest state in the country. The density was 275 (persons per sq. km). for the State as compared to 324 for the country and the state ranked 19 among the major states in this respect.

Literacy Rate in Andhra Pradesh by Sex 2001

Among the districts Hyderabad is at the top with a literacy rate of 79.04 per cent followed by West Godavari District with 73.95 per cent. Krishna District with 69.91 per cent and Chittoor District with 67.46 per cent. The least literate district is Mahabubnagar with 45.33 per cent followed by Vizianagaram District with 51.82 and Medak District with 53.24 per cent.

Among the rural population West Godavari District stands first in rural literacy rate with 72.48 per cent followed by Krishna District with 65.56 per cent and Chittoor District with 63.67 per cent while the least rural literacy was recorded in Mahabubnagar District with 41.72 per cent followed by Adilabad District with 46.74 per cent and Vizianagaram District with 46.86 per cent.

Among the urban population, Nalgonda District ranks first with a literacy rate of 81.89 per cent followed by Warangal District with 80.95 per cent and Chittor District with

80.94 per cent. The last three districts are Kurnool with 66.48 per cent. Ananthapur with 70.23 per cent and Adilabad with 71.70 per cent.

Among the males, the literacy rate was 70.85 per cent as against 51.17 per cent among females. Among the rural males the literacy rate is 66.13 per cent as against 44.36 per cent among rural females. Among the urban males, the literacy rate is 83.21 as against 69.34 per cent among urban females.

The literacy rate of Andhra Pradesh (61.1 per cent) is lower than the all India literacy rate (65.4 per cent) and difference in literacy rate between rural and urban and between male and female is very wide.

West Godavari district is one of the agriculturally prosperous districts of Andhra Pradesh. It is also known as rice bowl of Andhra Pradesh. As per 2001 census, the West Godavari district population is 37.96 lakhs and constitutes about 5.01 per cent of Andhra Pradesh population. In this district literate persons are 73.95 per cent. In urban areas it is 79.8 per cent and in rural areas it is 72.18 per cent. in urban areas 84.64 per cent of males are literates and 75.21 per cent of females are literates. in rural areas 76.91 males and 67.99 per cent of females are literates, which is above the state average.

Literacy plays a crucial role in socio-cultural and economic development of the people. The women folk in this district are innovative. In this connection *Akshara Mahila Literacy Programme* was launched. Akshara Mahila Programmes is a special literacy programme. It is mainly meant to make women literates through self-help groups. It is planned first for women groups but its impact on total literacy movement and created a new wave in literacy movement.

Akshara Mahila Programme is mainly based on self-help groups and it is a voluntary movement. These self-help groups are managed by the Akshara Mahila centers and they will fix the place and time. The educated members among them become volunteers and handle the classes. Books and volunteers training are not available locally and hence they will be provided by the outside agencies.

Basing on the experience of the previous literacy programmes they designed new texts and teaching methods to suit the changing needs of the literates. In this method, reading and writing are separated, and material is provided reading in such a way as to learn Telugu alphabet first and gradually Telugu language in 40 days. Another important thing one can mention is group reading. This created interest to the learners in the *Akshara Mahila Programme.* The creation of interest leads to their self-help groups thereby the self-help groups are motivated to become literates.

Akshara Mahila Programme was started on 2nd April 2000 in the District.

1. Those who are interested in Akshara Mahila Programme were identified and enrolled from self-help groups and volunteers. This was conducted with the hope of Mandal Literacy Organizers, Additional Village Sevikas. West Godavari Literacy Mission and District Rural Development Agency are actively involved in this activity.
2. At Mandal level, they conducted group leaders meeting to self-help groups to create awareness on literacy programmes.
3. Teaching methods and training provided are to the Mandal Literacy Organizers and resource persons at divisional level in this district.
4. To provide training to mandal volunteers in every mandal and M.L.O. in clusters and resource persons and
5. At Mandal level weekly reviews are conducted. On every Monday Mandal Development Officers and M.L. Os and Assistant Gram Sevikas review the meetings.

To strengthen this programme the following are highly essential:

Interest: Akshara Mahila Programme was spontaneously picked up from the women and self-help groups. In this district nearly 4,500 groups have undertaken this programme. They registered 37,283 illiterates. From among the groups 3697 are volunteers who come forward to actively participate in the programme. In no time easy learning methods were developed by them and created interest among learners.

Sponsors of the Akshara Mahila Centres: District Collector's plea to sponsor the Akshara Mahila Centres has created positive response from the individuals, institutions and retired teachers who come forward to take the responsibility and to maintain the Akshara Mahila Centres and developed the centers.

To strengthen the Akshara Mahila Programme a number of social workers and institutions have provided cash and kind to support the great cause of literacy movement.

Achievement of the Akshara Mahila Programme in West Godavari District

The Mandal Literacy Organizers have evaluated the performance of the programme in the District

Actuals		*Results*	
1. Participated Groups	4,500	Course completed learners	29,831
2. No. of volunteers participated	3,697	100 percent training centres	150
3. No. of enrolled learners	37,283	50 per cent marks obtained by learners	24,049
4. Actual training centres conducted	228		

From above table 1 it can be seen that 80 per cent of the learners have completed their course. In another study conducted by Sri N. Sanjeeva Rao N.S.S. Programme Co-ordinator, A.U. have revealed that in 144 centres 65 per cent literacy rate was obtained from the Akshara Mahila Programme. It is interesting to note that in his report he mentioned that within no time more results are obtained from this programme. In 90 days more than 60 per cent of illiterates become literates.

In addition to this Akshara Mahila Programme, those who have completed literacy programme, they will continue their education through continuing education. This programme was introduced by Hon. Chief Minister, Sri N. Chandra Babu Naidu on 19th July 2000. In this programme there are three aspects viz.

1. To stabilize the literacy rate and develop.
2. To generate additional income programmes, and
3. To improve the living standards.

A group of 15 housewives set a record by learning to read simple paragraphs in their mother tongue in 42 working hours. On learning about this, several women's groups in the villages volunteered to attend the 40-days school. The experts of Adult literacy Programme accept the Kotthapalli Model and the women as Neo-literates.

The success behind the Akshara Mahila Programme was then Collector of west Godavari, Smt. Poonam Malakondaiah, Chairman West Godavari Literacy Mission and Dr. Krishna Mohan, Deputy Director Adult Education and other officials who are interested in increasing literacy rate in this District and actively participated in this literacy mission.

From the discussion and analysis carried out in this paper, it is clear that, literacy programmes alone may not help to increase the literacy rate but also active participation of the Government is highly essential in every respect. On the other hand, adult education and consciousness of the learner is also essential for effective implementation of the literacy programmes. Government agencies, educational institutions, voluntary organizations through self-help groups, intellectuals etc., should collectively work to enhance the literacy rate. So wide publicity and people awareness campaign should be launched to reach the goal of universal literacy in this district in Andhra Pradesh.

References

1. Akshara Mahila: Mahilabhi Vrudhi Ki Tolemettu. West Godavari Akashara Samithi, Eluru.

2. Ashish Bose, (2001), Population of India, 2001 census results and Methodology, B.R. Publishing Corporation, Delhi.

3. Census of India 2001, Series 29, A.P. V.S. Bhaskar, of the I.A.S. Director of Census Operations, Andhra Pradesh.

4. India (2001), A Reference Annual Publishing, Ministry of I. & B. Government of India, New Delhi, pp. 97, 98.

5. Mishra S.K. & Puri V.K., 2001 Indian Economy, Its Development experience, Himalaya Publishing House, New Delhi, pp. 128, 129.

6. Sreenivasulu, D. 2000, Housewives' Group sets record in learning to read, The Hindu 29-1-2000.

APPENDIX 1

Lteracy Rate in States by Sex, 1991-2001

S.No.	State	Females			Males			Persons		
		2001	1991	Variation	2001	1991	Variation	2001	1991	Variation
1.	Andhra Pradesh	51.2	32.7	18.5	70.9	55.1	15.7	61.1	44.1	17.0
2.	Arunachal Pradesh	44.2	29.7	14.6	64.1	51.5	12.6	54.7	41.6	13.2
3.	Assam	56.0	43.0	13.0	71.9	61.9	10.1	64.3	52.9	11.4
4.	Bihar	33.6	22.0	11.6	60.3	51.4	9.0	47.5	37.5	10.0
5.	Goa	75.5	67.1	8.4	88.9	83.6	5.2	82.3	75.5	6.8
6.	Gujarat	58.6	48.9	9.7	80.5	73.4	7.1	70.0	61.6	8.4
7.	Haryana	56.3	40.5	15.8	79.3	69.1	10.2	68.6	55.9	12.7
8.	Himachal Pradesh	68.1	52.3	15.8	86.0	75.4	10.6	77.1	63.9	13.2
9.	Karnataka	57.5	44.3	13.1	76.3	67.3	9.0	67.0	56.0	11.0
10.	Kerala	87.9	86.2	1.7	94.2	93.6	0.0	90.9	89.8	1.1
11.	Madhya Pradesh	50.3	29.4	20.9	76.8	58.5	18.3	64.1	44.7	19.4
12.	Maharashtra	67.5	52.3	15.2	86.3	76.6	9.7	77.3	64.9	12.4
13.	Manipur	59.7	47.6	12.1	77.9	71.6	6.2	68.9	59.9	9.0

Appendix 1 Contd.

14.	Meghalaya	60.4	44.9	15.6	66.1	53.1	13.0	63.3	49.1	14.2
15.	Mizoram	86.1	78.6	7.5	90.7	85.6	5.1	88.5	82.3	6.2
16.	Nagaland	61.6	54.8	6.9	71.8	67.6	4.1	67.1	61.7	5.5
17.	Orissa	51.0	34.7	16.3	76.0	63.1	12.9	63.6	49.1	14.5
18.	Punjab	63.6	50.4	13.1	75.6	65.7	10.0	70.0	58.5	11.5
19.	Rajasthan	44.3	20.4	23.9	76.5	55.0	21.5	61.0	38.6	22.4
20.	Sikkim	61.5	46.8	14.7	76.7	65.7	11.0	69.7	56.0	12.8
21.	Tamil Nadu	64.6	51.3	13.2	82.3	73.8	8.6	73.5	62.7	10.8
22.	Tripura	65.4	49.7	15.8	81.5	70.6	10.9	73.7	60.4	13.3
23.	Uttar Pradesh	43.0	24.4	18.6	70.2	54.8	15.4	57.4	40.7	16.7
24.	West Bengal	60.2	46.6	13.7	77.6	67.8	9.8	69.2	57.7	11.5
25.	Chattisgarh	52.4	27.5	24.9	77.9	58.1	19.8	65.2	42.9	22.3
26.	Uttaranchal	60.3	41.6	18.6	84.0	72.8	11.2	72.3	57.8	14.5
27.	Jharkhand	39.4	25.5	13.9	67.9	55.8	12.2	54.1	41.4	12.7
28.	Jammu & Kashmir	41.8	NA	-	65.8	NA	-	54.5	NA	-

Source: Compiled from Population of India 2001, Census Results and Methodology by Ashish Bose, p. 115.

APPENDIX 2

Literacy Rates by Residence and Sex District Wise-2001

S.No.	District	Total			Rural			Urban		
		Persons	Males	Females	Persons	Males	Females	Persons	Males	Females
1.	Srikakulam	55.94	67.90	44.19	53.80	65.86	41.56	74.50	84.07	65.08
2.	Vizianagaram	51.82	63.00	40.73	46.86	58.57	35.21	73.36	82.45	64.47
3.	Visakhapatnam	59.45	68.84	49.99	47.73	58.72	36.78	76.60	83.46	69.59
4.	East Godavari	65.49	69.97	61.00	62.52	66.85	58.15	75.11	80.08	70.16
5.	West Godavari	73.95	78.43	69.45	72.48	76.91	67.99	79.87	84.64	75.21
6.	Krishna	69.91	74.57	65.05	65.56	71.34	59.64	79.00	81.15	76.88
7.	Guntur	62.80	71.32	54.17	58.84	67.88	49.67	72.88	80.14	65.59
8.	Prakasam	57.86	69.78	45.60	45.93	67.44	42.03	73.75	82.52	62.82
9.	Nellore	65.90	74.45	57.24	62.13	71.62	52.53	78.58	83.96	73.12
10.	Cuddapah	64.02	76.98	50.76	61.14	75.02	46.94	73.41	83.43	63.21
11.	Kurnool	54.43	67.36	41.07	50.83	64.72	36.50	66.48	76.22	56.41
12.	Ananthapur	56.69	68.94	43.87	52.04	65.13	38.31	70.23	80.10	59.99
13.	Chittor	67.46	78.29	56.48	63.67	75.36	51.85	80.94	88.62	73.04
14.	Adilabad	53.51	65.56	41.38	46.74	59.66	33.88	71.70	81.10	61.95
15.	Niamabad	53.26	66.27	40.57	48.90	62.68	35.60	72.91	81.91	63.66
16.	Karimnagar	56.00	67.87	44.19	51.23	63.59	38.99	75.36	84.36	65.59
17.	Medak	53.24	65.52	40.68	48.98	61.85	35.91	77.97	86.50	68.95
18.	Hyderabad	79.04	84.11	73.67	-	-	-	79.04	84.11	73.67
19.	Ranga Reddy	66.31	75.02	57.03	53.67	65.75	40.99	77.01	82.74	70.82
20.	Mahabubnagar	45.53	57.87	32.83	41.72	54.45	28.66	76.69	85.56	67.39
21.	Nalgonda	57.84	70.19	45.07	54.08	67.04	40.72	81.89	90.09	73.23
22.	Warangal	58.41	70.01	46.54	52.88	65.03	40.43	80.95	90.24	71.24
23.	Khammam	57.72	67.04	48.16	52.52	62.31	42.48	78.20	85.69	70.55
	Andhra Pradesh	61.11	70.85	51.17	55.33	66.13	44.36	76.39	82.21	69.34

Complied from Census of India 2001 Series 29A.P.
Director of Census Operation A.P.

Decennial Table of Literacy in West Godavari District

Year	*Males*	*Females*	*Total*
1901	9.07	0.78	4.84
1911	11.19	1.54	6.28
1921	10.89	2.29	6.52
1931	14.71	3.32	8.93
1941	-	-	-
1951	28.13	14.02	21.09
1961	38.12	23.35	30.76
1971	40.45	28.34	34.41
1981	41.50	31.59	36.57
1991	50.36	39.67	45.03
2001	78.43	69.45	73.95

N.B. Statistics for 1941 are not available.

Source: NIC, Eluru.

19

Literacy in 21st Century A Study of West Godavari District in Andhra Pradesh

Dr. L. Krishna Veni

Literacy is an important tool for communication, learning and information. Thus literacy is a virtual pre-condition for individual and national development. Such an important aspect of human development cannot be neglected. Hence efforts have been taking place in recent years to attain the objective of education to all.

In this context the definition proposed by United National Population Commission has been taken into consideration. As a matter of convenience literacy is defined as the ability to read and write one's name is one's own mother tongue.

The national policy on education aimed at making the effective instrument for taking the country into 21st century, accorded a high priority to the programme of education, particularly to the universalisation of elementary education. The national policy in education (1986) provides a broad policy frame work for total eradication of illiteracy and a commitment to make primary education free and compulsory up to 5th standard. India has decided to raise its investment to 6 per cent as Kothari Commission recommended as the gross domestic product.

There is a national political commitment to achieve the objective of eradicating illiteracy in the country. As a result of efforts intensified under the National Literacy Mission (NLM) literacy rate has shown a much sharper increase during 1990s as compared to the previous decades.

The total population of India as at 0.00 hours on 1st March 2001 stood at 1,027, 015,247 persons. With this India became only the second country in the world after China to cross the one billion mark. The number of literates stood as 566,714,995. Among this males are 339,969,048 and females are 226,745,947. Total literacy was returned to 65.38 per cent. Male literacy (75.85 per cent) was relatively higher than female literacy (54.16 per cent)

Against this background the present study aimed to examine the following objectives with a view to suggest a viable strategy to attain 100 per cent literacy in the country.

1. To examine the literacy rates of different states on population basis.
2. To examine the literacy rates of different states on Region basis.
3. To study the literacy trends in different districts of Andhra Pradesh.
4. To analyse the trend of literacy rate in different charges of West Godavari district.

The present study is mainly based on 1991 and 2001 census data. The male, female literacy rates also have been specially examined at various levels. Change in literacy rates during 1991-2001 also have been estimated in order to indicate the growth.

Literacy Trends During 1991-2001-Classification of States on Population Basis

Since we consider size to the most important factor in the context of population stabilisation we have classified the country as follows. The literacy trends of different states during 1991-2001 have been indicated in Table -1.

A. *Mega states (10) over 50 million and more than 5 Per cent of India's total population*

Among Mega states Maharastra recorded high literacy (77.3 Per cent) out of all states. During 1991-2001 the literacy rate has increased to 12.4 per cent. Similar trends are indicated both in male and female literacy rates also. Bihar recorded lowest literacy rate among Mega states with 47.5 per cent in 2001. However it has raised from 37.5 per cent to 47.5 per cent during 1991 to 2001. The literacy rate has indicated an increase of 10 per cent 1991-2001 Not only among Mega states, even in the entire country also Bihar occupied the lowest position. In female literacy also Bihar remained in the bottom place in 1991-2001

B. *Bigger states/Uts (10) over 10 millions and more than 1 per cent of India's total populations*

Among this group Kerala ranked the first position with 90.9 per cent literacy rate in 2001. But the increase in literacy of this state indicated only 1.1 per cent during 1991 to 2001. Jharkhand occupied the lowest position among the bigger states in terms of literacy with 54.1 per cent. However this State recorded an increase of 12.7 per cent in literacy rate during 1991-2001.

C. *Smaller states /UTS (16) Less than 10 million and Less than 1 per cent of India's total population*

In this group Mizoram occupied the first place in literacy rate with 88.5 per cent in 2001. But the increase of literacy rate in this State is only 5.2 per cent during 1991-2001 Arunachal Pradesh occupied the bottom place with 54.7 per cent. However it recorded 13.1 per cent increase during 1991-2001. On the whole the total literacy rate of the country has increased from 52.0 per cent to 65.4 per cent from 1991 to 2001.

Table 1: Literacy Rate: India—1991-2001

S. No.	State/UT	Persons	Males	Females	Persons	Change in Literacy Rate
A.	**Mega states (9) (population: over 50 million and more than 5 per cent of India's total population)**					
			2001		**1991**	**1991-2001**
1.	Uttar Pradesh	57.4	70.2	43.0	40.7	16.6
2.	Maharashtra	77.3	86.3	67.5	65.0	12.4
3.	Bihar	47.5	60.3	33.6	37.6	10.0
4.	West Bengal	69.2	77.6	60.2	57.7	11.5
5.	Andhra Pradesh	61.1	70.9	51.2	44.1	17.0
6.	Tamil Nadu	73.5	82.3	64.6	62.7	10.8
7.	Madhya Pradesh	64.1	76.8	50.3	44.7	19.4
8.	Rajasthan	61.0	76.5	44.3	38.5	22.5
9.	Karnataka	67.0	76.3	57.5	56.0	11.0
B.	**Bigger states/U.Ts. (10) (population: over 10 million and more than 1 per cent of India's total population)**					
1.	Gujarat	70.0	80.5	58.6	61.3	8.7
2.	Orissa	63.6	76.0	51.0	59.1	14.5
3.	Kerala	90.9	94.2	87.9	89.8	1.1
4.	Jharkhand	54.1	67.9	39.4	41.4	12.7
5.	Assam	64.3	71.9	56.0	52.3	11.5
6.	Punjab	70.0	75.6	63.6	58.3	11.4
7.	Haryana	68.6	79.3	56.3	56.8	12.7
8.	Chhatisgarh	65.2	77.9	52.4	77.8	3.9
9.	Delhi NCT	81.8	87.4	75.0	42.9	2.37
10.	Jammu & Kashmir	54.5	65.8	41.8	N.A.	N.A.

Table Contd.

Table 1: Contd.

C.	Bigger states/U.Ts. (16) (population: less than 10 million and less than 1 per cent of India's total population)					
1.	Uttaranchal	72.3	84.0	60.3	57.7	14.5
2.	Himachal Pradesh	77.1	86.0	68.1	63.9	13.3
3.	Tripura	73.7	81.5	65.4	60.4	13.2
4.	Manipur	68.9	77.9	59.7	59.8	9.0
5.	Meghalaya	63.3	66.1	60.4	49.1	14.2
6.	Nagaland	67.1	71.8	61.9	61.7	5.4
7.	Goa	82.3	88.9	75.5	75.5	6.8
8.	Pondicherry UT	81.5	88.9	74.1	74.7	6.7
9.	Chandigarh UT	81.8	85.7	76.7	77.8	3.9
10.	Mizoram	88.5	90.7	86.1	82.2	5.2
11.	Arunachal Pradesh	54.7	64.1	44.2	41.6	13.1
12.	Sikkim	69.7	76.7	61.5	56.9	12.6
13.	Andaman & Nicobarislands	81.2	86.1	75.3	73.0	8.1
14.	Dadra & Nagarhaveli UT	60.0	73.3	43.0	40.7	19.4
15.	Daman & Diu UT	81.1	88.4	70.4	71.2	9.9
16.	Lakshadweep UT	87.5	93.2	81.6	81.2	5.2
	India	65.4	75.9	54.2	52.0	13.4

It is evident from Table 1 that the literacy rate of the country has indicated 13.4 per cent increase during 1991-2001. As usual the male literacy was relatively higher than the female literacy to the extent of 21.7 per cent during 1991-2001.

Literacy Trends During 1991-2001-Classification of States on Region Basis

The country can be generally classified into Northern and Southern parts. The literacy trends of these State are provided in Table 2.

Table 2: Literacy Rate in South India (1991-2001)

S. No.	*State/UT*	*Literacy Rate in 2001 Percent*			*Literacy Rate in 1991*	*Increase in Literacy rate in 1991-2001*
		Persons	*Males*	*Females*	*Persons*	
1.	Andhra Pradesh	61.1	70.8	51.6	44.1	17.0
2.	Karnataka	67.0	76.3	57.4	56.0	11.0
3.	Kerala	90.9	94.2	87.9	89.1	1.1
4.	Tamil Nadu	73.5	82.3	64.5	62.7	10.8
5.	Goa	82.3	88.9	75.5	75.5	6.8
6.	Pondicherry	81.5	88.9	74.1	74.7	6.7

Among Southern States, Kerala occupied the top place in both 1991 and 2001. In fact Andhra Pradesh recorded lowest literacy rate out of all states/union Territories in 2001 also. Similar trends are noticed in both male and female literacy rates also. However it is very interesting to note that the literacy rate in Andhra Pradesh has recorded spectacular progress with 17 per cent during the decade 1991-2001. Karnataka (11. Per cent) and Tamil Nadu (10.8 per cent) also going in the same path during this decade. Though Kerala and Pondicherry recorded more female population than male population, they have recorded lower literacy rates than male.

According to 2001 census Kerala has the highest literacy rate (90.9 per cent) followed by Tamilnadu (73.5 per cent), Karnataka (67 per cent) and Andhra Pradesh (61.11 per cent). Union territories of South also recorded more than 80 per cent of literacy rate individually.

Among Northern states/Uts Mizoram occupied the top place with 88.5 per cent in 2001 as shown in Table 1. Bihar occupied the bottom place with 47.5 per cent. (Particulars are given in the above analysis). All Union Territories recorded higher literacy rates in 2001.

Literacy Trends in Districts of Andhra Pradesh

Andhra Pradesh has relegated to fifth most populous State in the country as against fourth returned at the previous Census. This has achieved substantial reduction in its decadal growth of population during 1991 to 2001. Andhra Pradesh also achieved spectacular progress in literacy rate during the decade 1991-2001 among the southern states and Union Territories. The literacy rate of Andhra Pradesh has increased from 44.8 per cent in 1991 to 61.11 per cent in 2001. For detailed analysis the entire Andhra can be divided into three regions. The literacy trends of Andhra Pradesh have been indicated in Table 3A.

In Telangana region (1 to 10 districts) Hyderabad district stood first with 79.0 per cent literacy rate. Mahaboobnagar indicated minimum literacy rate out of all districts in Telangana and even in the entire Andhra.

In female literacy also Hyderabad occupied the first place. Though the sex ratio in Nizamabad district was 1016 the female literacy rate has not revealed any significant progress.

In coastal Andhra (11 to 19 districts), West Godavari record 73.9 per cent literacy rate. In male, female literacy rates also west Godavari recorded maximum out of all coastal districts. It is very interesting to note that west Godavari district indicated significant improvement with 4 per cent additional growth over the neighbouring district Krishna during the decade 1991-2001 (Table 3B). Vizayangaram district indicated the lowest literacy rate in both male and female literacy rate. Srikakulam (1013) and vizianagaram (1004) District having high sex ratio have not recorded high female literacy rates.

Table 3A: Literacy Rate: Andhra Pradesh—1991-2001

S.No.	State/District	Literates			Literacy Rate					
		2001			1991			2001		
		Persons	Males	Females	Persons	Males	Females	Persons	Males	Females
	Andhra Pradesh	40,364,765	23,636,077	16,728,688	44.08	55.12	32.72	61.11	70.85	51.1
1.	Adilabad	1,134,631	696,240	437,391	32.96	45.05	20.60	53.51	65.56	41.3
2.	Nizamabad	1,075,644	661,001	414,643	34.18	47.33	21.35	53.26	66.27	40.5
3.	Karimnagar	1,699,577	1,027,826	671,751	37.17	50.79	23.37	56.00	67.86	44.1
4.	Medak	1,211,807	753,941	457,866	32.41	45.16	19.24	53.24	65.52	40.6
5.	Hyderabad	2,564,526	1,403,346	1,161,180	71.52	78.90	63.56	79.04	84.11	73.6
6.	Rangareddy	2,016,435	1,177,556	838,879	49.07	60.43	36.91	66.31	75.02	57.0
7.	Mahabubnagar	1,356,186	874,033	482,153	29.58	40.80	18.03	45.53	57.87	32.8
8.	Nalgonda	1,618,918	998,575	620,343	38.00	50.53	24.92	57.84	70.19	45.0
9.	Warrangal	1,632,868	990.389	642,479	39.30	51.98	26.08	58.41	70.01	46.5
10.	Khammam	1,285,948	756,068	529,880	40.50	50.04	30.53	57.72	67.04	48.1

Table Contd.

Table 3A: Contd.

11.	Srikakulam	1,235,418	743,113	492,305	36.22	49.14	23.52	55.94	67.90	44.1
12.	Vizayanagaram	1,017,536	616,143	401,393	34.19	45.93	22.47	51.82	63.00	40.7
13.	Visakhapatnam	1,981,214	1,151,086	830,128	45.51	56.13	34.60	59.45	68.84	49.9
14.	East Godavari	2,813,118	1,506988	1,306,130	48.79	55.32	42.26	65.49	69.97	61.0
15.	West Godavari	2,484,269	1,321,561	1,162,708	53.38	59.75	46.98	73.95	78.43	69.4
16.	Krishna	2,609,627	1,419,433	1,190,194	53.16	60.55	45.54	69.91	74.57	65.0
17.	Guntur	2,446,904	1,397,818	1,049,086	46.35	56.54	35.85	62.80	71.32	54.1
18.	Prakasam	1,552,382	949,411	602,971	40.30	53.14	27.06	5786	69.78	45.6
19.	Nellore	1,546,252	879,191	667,061	47.61	58.04	36.99	65.90	74.45	57.2
20.	Cuddapah	1,440,741	875,881	564,860	48.12	63.14	32.35	64.02	76.98	50.7
21.	Kurnool	1,629,213	1,024,282	604,931	39.97	53.24	26.04	54.43	67.36	41.0
22.	Anantpur	1,802,696	1,120,708	681,988	42.18	55.92	27.61	56.69	68.94	43.8
23.	Chittor	2,208,855	1,290,487	918,368	49.75	62.61	36.44	67.46	78.29	56.4

Table 3B: Growth Rate (%) of Literacy: In Andhra Pradesh—1991-2001

S.No.	District	Persons	Males	Females
	Andhra Pradesh	17.03	15.73	18.38
1.	Adilabad	20.55	20.51	20.7
2.	Nizamabad	19.08	18.94	19.15
3.	Karimnagar	18.83	17.07	20.73
4.	Medak	20.83	20.36	21.36
5.	Hyderabad	7.52	5.21	10.04
6.	Rangareddy	17.24	14.59	20.09
7.	Mahaboobnagar	13.95	17.07	14.77
8.	Nalgonda	19.84	19.66	20.08
9.	Warangal	19.11	18.08	20.42
10.	Khammam	17.22	17.00	17.57
11.	Srikakulam	19.72	18.76	20.58
12.	Vizayanagarm	17.63	17.07	18.23
13.	Visakhapatnam	13.94	12.71	15.30
14.	East Godavari	16.70	14.65	18.74
15.	West Godavari	20.57	18.68	22.42
16.	Krishna	16.75	13.88	17.46
17.	Guntur	16.45	14.78	18.25
18.	Prakasam	17.56	16.64	18.54
19.	Nellore	18.29	16.41	20.21
20.	Cuddapah	15.9	13.84	18.35
21.	Kurnool	14.46	14.12	14.96
22.	Ananthapur	14.51	13.02	16.19
23.	Chittor	17.71	15.68	19.96

In Rayalaseema (20 to 23 districts) Chittor recorded maximum literacy rate with 67.5 per cent. Similar trends are noticed in case of male and female literacy rated also. Kurnool district indicated minimum literacy rate.

The literacy rate of Andhra Pradesh has indicated 17 per cent increase during the decade 1991-2001. The growth of female literacy rate is 18.38 per cent, where as the male literacy rate was only 15.73 per cent during 1991-2001.

Literacy Profile of West Godavari District in Andhra Pradesh

West Godavari as its name indicates is a part of the Godavari Delta in Andhra Pradesh. This district occupied an area of 7742 sq. kms with density of population of 490 sq.k.m. The total population of the district is 3,796,144 lakhs of which 1,906,104 lakhs are males and 1,890,040 lakhs are females. The area covered by paddy cultivation is about 83 per cent. Above 70 per cent of the workers are engaged is agriculture and allied activities. About 68 per cent of the irrigated area and the cultivation are mainly under canals. The normal rainfall of the district is 1076.M.M. Against this glorious back ground, we Godavari district is known as 'The Granary of Andhra Pradesh'.

This district has 2,484,269 literates forming 73.95 per cent of the population of the district excluding 0-6 years age group. The male literates are 78.43 per cent and female literates are 69.49 per cent according to 2001 census.

Efforts are being made to achieve total literacy in west Godavari district. Akshara Mahila is the milestone in the literacy programmes launched by west Godavari to improve the literacy of women in the district. This scheme created a sensation with commendable progress in literacy campaign.

Many people both administrators and academicians have evinced keen interest in the programme and some districts are following this model. Against this background west Godavari district has received a certificate of application from National Literacy Mission, Ministry of Human Resource Development, Government, of India for commendable performance in the field of literacy during the decade 1991-2001 on National Literacy Day i.e. September, 8th, 2001.

Though west Godavari received the certificate of appreciation, there are some constraints in declaring it a totally literate state. This district has been always recording higher growth in literacy rate. But the decade wise literacy growth rates have indicated a different picture. The backward district of Telengana region Medak recorded the highest growth of 20.83 per cent, where as West Godavari district recorded only 20.57 per cent during this decade. Medak district recorded 0.26 per cent of additional growth than west

Godavari during 1991-2001. The backward district of Telangana region. Medak deserves this appreciation for the commendable progress during 1991-2001 in literacy growth. This illustration tells us that there is a need to examine the growth rates thoroughly before declaring any district for this meritorious certificate.

During 1991-2001 the male, female literacy rates also have been estimated separately to evaluate the progress of literacy (Table 3B). In male literacy Adilabad (20.51 per cent) and Medak (20.36 per cent) districts have occupied the first and second positions during 1991-2001. It is very disappointing to note that west Godavari recorded only 18.68 per cent growth in male literacy during 1991-2001. The female literacy growth during this decade indicated the supremacy of west Godavari district with 22.42 per cent among all districts. Medak, Karimnagar, Adilabad, Nalgonda, Rangareddy, Srikakulam and Nellore also have recorded more than 20 per cent in their respective districts during 1991-2001.

According to 2001 Census, Hyderabad (with huge urban population) being the Head quarters of Andhra Pradesh recorded highest literacy with 79.04 per cent. Among the remaining districts wet Godavari occupied the top position with 73.95 per cent in 2001.

The success behind the achievement of significant growth in female literacy of west Godavari can be attributed to Akshara Mahila Programme.

It has introduced unique design in teaching the Adult Women. Learning process is divided into reading and writing skills and the duration of the programme is three months. The number of letters in Telugu reduced to 34 out of which 29 are very important for purpose of improving reading skills.

According to Akshara Mahila Evaluation report (2000) 3697 groups have participated in this programme from 46 rural charges. The number of learner enrolled was 37,283. Out of this the successful learners were 29,831.

Literacy Trends in West Godavari-charge/Mandal Wise Analysis

In this connection the literacy rate in west Godavari district has been analysed separately. Charge/Mandal wise analysis also has been made with a special focus to study the rapid progress in literacy rate. Charge wise data has been presented in Table 4.

Table 4: Literacy Rate: West Godavari 2001

Name of the Charge/Mandal	*Charge No.*	*Persons (%)*	*Male (%)*	*Female (%)*
Rural				
Chintalapudi	1	62.15	67.37	56.84
Lingapalem	2	69.19	74.10	64.13
T. Narasapuram	3	64.83	64.23	59.10
Jeelugumilli	4	62.01	67.75	56.13
Buttaigudem	5	62.13	66.74	57.76
Polavaram	6	66.71	71.25	62.25
Tallapudi	7	71.05	75.55	66.47
Gopalapuram	8	65.69	68.81	62.57
Koyyalagudem	9	67.20	70.45	63.89
J.R. Gudem	10	66.84	71.80	[illegible]1.83
Kamavarapukota	11	65.66	70.33	60.84
Dwaraka Tirumala	12	67.26	67.44	67.07
Nallajerla	13	66.40	69.56	63.17
Devarapalli	14	66.86	70.38	63.24
Kovvur	15	67.09	71.23	62.93
Chagallu	16	67.81	72.34	63.18
Nidadavolu	17	71.85	75.24	63.43
Tadepalligudem	18	64.71	66.52	62.79
Unguturu	19	73.96	73.32	65.16
Bhimadolu	20	76.91	81.23	72.63
Pedavegi	21	69.13	73.98	68.73
Pedapadu	22	88.63	91.48	85.64
Eluru	23	79.48	84.70	74.15
Denduluru	24	67.76	73.06	82.48
Nidamarru	25	75.10	78.95	71.22
Pentapadu	26	72.92	76.91	68.92
Undrajavaram	27	84.34	86.95	81.67
Peravali	28	74.84	78.50	71.16
Tanuku	29	80.61	83.60	77.56

Attili	30	79.77	84.30	75.22
Ganapavaram	31	78.49	82.89	74.04
Akiveedu	32	79.26	83.19	75.25
Undi	33	74.47	78.76	70.27
Palakoderu	34	72.23	77.92	66.52
Penumantra	35	80.38	84.70	75.98
Irgavaram	36	76.98	82.03	71.87
Penugonda	37	75.31	81.95	68.60
Atchanta	38	78.19	84.21	71.39
Poduru	39	75.54	81.38	69.48
Veeravasaram	40	83.60	88.06	79.08
Bhimavaram	41	73.27	78.09	68.35
Kalla	42	67.14	70.55	63.68
Mogalturu	43	65.65	80.19	60.91
Narasapuram	44	73.70	79.45	67.74
Palakol	45	82.41	87.80	76.92
Ealamanchali	46	80.43	85.29	75.01
Rural Total		72.48	76.92	66.38
Kovvur	1	78.53	83.51	73.64
Nidadavolu	2	80.87	84.89	76.99
Tadepalligudem	3	72.18	77.27	67.28
Eluru	4	78.83	84.22	73.73
Tanuku	5	84.10	87.69	80.57
Bhimavaram	6	81.72	86.06	77.27
Narasapuram	7	83.60	87.79	79.53
Palakollu	8	83.06	88.12	78.04
Total Urban		80.31	84.33	75.73
Grand Total		73.95	78.43	69.49

In west Godavari district there are 46 rural charges or mandals and 8 urban charges. Among 46 rural charges of this district Pedapadu, Undrajavaram, Veeravasaram, Palkol, Elamanchili and Penumantra have recorded more than 80 per cent literates among the rural charges individually. But the agency areas like Jeelugumilli and Buttaigudem have indicated minimum literates among rural charges.

Out of 8 urban charge/Municipalities except Tadepalligudem, Kovvur and Eluru the remaining change have individually recorded more than 80 per cent literates. It is very unfortunate to note the Eluru Municipality being the head quarters of west Godavari district occupied the 6th place among 8 urban charge with 73.83 per cent.

On the whole 72.48 per cent from rural charge and 80.31 per cent from urban charge are literates. The west Godavari district as a whole indicated 73.95 per cent literacy in 2001.

Major Findings of the Study

1. The literacy rate of India has been sharply increasing due to vigorous efforts of National Literacy Mission. The literacy rate of our country has increased from 51.2 per cent to 65.4 per cent during the decade 1991-2001.
2. As usual male literacy rate recorded higher growth than the female literacy rate during this recent decade.
3. State wise analysis has concluded that there are extreme variations in literacy rate of different States in our nation. In the entire country and South India Kerala maintained the supremacy during 1991-2001.
4. All Union Territories of the country have recorded signification growth in literacy rate.
5. Bihar remained in the bottom place in literacy and female literacy of the country in 1991 and 2001.
6. Andhra Pradesh occupied the lowest position out of the all Southern State/union Territories in literacy terms. However it is very interesting to note that Andhra Pradesh has recorded a spectacular (Highest) growth with 17.01 per cent during 1991-2001.
7. West Godavari district known as "The Granary of Andhra Pradesh" received a certificate of appreciation from Government of India for its commendable performance in the field of literacy during 1991-2001.
8. But this study proved that Medak district of Telangana deserves this certificate of appreciation for its highest literacy growth during the decade 1991-2001.

9. Charge/Mandal wise analysis of west Godavari district indicated that Eluru (Municipality) being the Head quarters of west Godavari occupied the 6th place in literacy among 8 urban charge of the district. Some agency areas have been indicated minimum literacy among 46 rural charge.

In order to reduce the State-wise/Districtwise Variations in literacy rate, some Corrective steps are urgently needed.

Suggestions

1. Real socio-economic development is not possible without making women literate. Women empowerment through literacy has to be selected as a thrust area in the country.
2. Compulsory and free education to all upto 5th standard has to be implemented strictly.
3. The dropouts numbers has to be reduced through abolition of child labour.
4. There is a need to increase the number of primary schools for the universalisation of primary education.
5. School atmosphere must be inspiring to the children, with free food, play ground, pacca buildings, audio, visual equipment etc.
6. Teaching and learning has to be made lively and meaningful to the children.
7. Child and Adult education has to be concentrated in backward states/districts/charges of the country to improve the literacy rate of the country.
8. The Non Formal Education (NFE) programme has to intensify to cater the school dropouts, girls, working children and those belonging to Schedule Castes and Scheduled tribes.
9. Enrolment in the school must be made compulsory.

10. Stress has to be laid on promotion of primary education in backward and tribal areas.

Selected References

1. Census of India-1991.
2. Census of India-2001.
3. Census of West Godavari-2001.
4. Economic Survey-2000-2001.
5. Ashish Bose-Population of India 2001 Census Result & Methodology.
6. Akshara Mahil-Paschima Godavari Akshrara Samithi.
7. The Hindu-29-1-2000 & 19-5-200.
8. Deccan Chronicle-1-6-2002.

20

Literacy Trends and Variations in Tribal Sub Plan Area, Parvathipuram

D. Parinaidu

Tribal area is entirely different from that of plain are. Tribal needs, problems, environment, language and culture separate them from developing areas.

Plenty of nature resources are available there; lands fit for agriculture forests, minor (major) forest produces and rich water resources are found every where and is every nook and corner of agency. The only problem is, they are not put to proper use; because of lack of literacy, and because of variation of literacy in between plain areas, and tribal sub-plan area.

There are two talks/thoughts among officials, educationists and tribal leaders on the matter of control of population.

(a) Plenty of nature resources are available for usage of tribal population.

(b) if the population goes on increasing the natural resources decline gradually. The two talks/thoughts may be true or may not be true one thing is very true; illiteracy is the main reason for non development of tribal community both economically and socially.

The main object for the submission of this paper is to denote how the illiteracy in Tribal Area, leads/throw the poor in to poorest.

The following are the observations in Tribal Area, due to lack of literacy.

(a) Infact mortality rate

Infant mortality rate in the Tribal Area is 180 per thousand where as it is 60 per thousand in the district, due to many reasons like lack of health awareness.

(b) Medical Facilities

Adequate Medical Facilities are not available to the tribal people residing in the interior and hill top areas. Sub centers and primary health centers are very far to utilise. The density of population is very low in the Tribal area, in the because of small habitations scattered in the large extent of area.

(c) Blind Beliefs (Superstitions)

Due to lack of literacy, the blind beliefs creates/causes many problem. They don't prefer to go the Hospitals for any sickness. They approach, and seek the help of traditional country doctor "Janni" and act according to his directions to please the local goddness, like "Ammathalli", "Grama Devatha", "Goddalamma" etc. In some cases they offer cock sacrifices and goat sacrifices.

(d) Traditional and old Cultivation Methods

The traditional old and cultivation methods are still in vogue. They are not aware of new agricultural tectonics and methods.

(e) Marketing Facilities

The Tribals are not getting reasonable price for the agricultural and forest produces. The middle man like G.C.C. and local traders are cheating them in weighment and price fixation.

(f) Irregular Schools Habitations with no Schools

There are some schools in some habitations but may of them are not functioning regularly due to many reasons such as inaccessibility and lack of moral responsibility on the part of teachers. Still there are many habitations in the Agency area where there are no schools.

(g) There is not Separate Syllabus, Methods Impart in Tribal Areas

The above observations clearly reveal, that the Tribals are thrown into darkens, obstructed them in the process of developing.

The following are the suggestions to improve the way of life of tribals both economically and socially.

1. To organise awareness meetings frequently in all the tribal habitations.
2. To organise every habitation into need based groups and strengthen them by imparting trainings to them and by way of exposure visits.
3. To establish foot hill, miny ashram schools, and single teacher schools in the habitations where there are no schools and appoint dedicated persons and to organise strong monitoring machinery and monthly review meetings with the teachers along with the local community leaders.
4. Impart trainings to tribal beneficiaries on value additional programmes.

   Ex: Tamarind De-seeding, leaf plates making etc.
5. Educate the tribal people on resource development.

   Ex:-Land development, water management new tectonics on gumtaping etc.
6. Organise functional literacy centres regularly in every tribal habitation for aware them on several issues.

21

Demographic and Reproductive Health Indicators in Andhra Pradesh

P. Satya Sekhar

The International Conference on Population and Development (ICPD) in 1994 at Cairo came as a watershed in the field of population and development providing emphasis on individual needs of women and men rather than achieving demographic targets. India, being one of the signatory countries of ICPD Plan of Action, has been implementing the Reproductive and Child Health (RCH) programme since early 1997. The Ministry of Health and Family Welfare introduced significant strategic changes, moving away from target-oriented approach to target-free approach. The RCH programme gave emphasis on individual needs of men and women rather than achieving demographic targets (by removing incentives and disincentives to clients and health staff). The Government of India formulated national population policy (NPP, 2000). The states namely Andhra Pradesh, Madhya Pradesh, Rajasthan, Uttar Pradesh, Gujarat, Maharasthra formulated State Population Policy (SPP), which sharply divergent from the NPP and ICPD perspectives (Mohan Rao, 2001, 2002; Medico Friends bulletin, 2001). The National Commission of Population constituted by Government of India, recommended revamping of incentives and disincentives to family planning acceptors, as per local needs and implementation of 'two child' norm in 2002. In the haste to determine state level priorities, the SPP has not given adequate attention to the inter-district variations within a state (Editorial, EPW, 2002).

Andhra Pradesh State formulated the State Population Policy for the first time in the country. The Health and Family Welfare department identified four important areas for strategies (GOAP, 2002). The first strategy consists of reduction in maternal mortality rate through 100 per cent provision of comprehensive antenatal care, supply of iron and folic acid tablets and tetanus toxoid vaccine, weighing, urine and blood examinations and identification of high-risk cases among pregnant women. The second strategy addresses to increase institutional deliveries and provision of full immunization to reduce infant mortality (pre natal and neonatal). The third strategy addresses to increase contraceptive prevalence rate and encouraging male sterilization and spacing methods to low parity couples. The fourth strategy is to reduce total fertility rate in rural and backward sections of people by increasing female age at marriage.

The National Family Health Survey (1992, 1999) and multiple indicator Survey (2001) are the major data sets that provide programme impact and outcome indicators at state level. Unfortunately, at district level, the data on health and in particular RCH indicators are primarily based on infant mortality rate. The Rapid Household Survey (RHS) under RCH project is the first of its kind in the country conducted by Government of India, to generate basic data at the district level in order to monitor the implementation of RCH programme.

The state level indicators provide information about the implementation of national policies and district indicators provide utilization and accessibility of health services. The paper examines the performance of demographic and RCH initiatives in districts and state as a whole under four headings. Section 1 deals with demographic and RCH scenario at state level. Section 2 examines various components of district RCH indicators based on RHS-RCH surveys. The correlates of demographic and reproductive health indicators in the districts are discussed in Section 3. Summary and major findings are presented in Section 4.

Demographic and RCH Scenario in Andhra Pradesh

The population of Andhra Pradesh recorded 75.7 million according to 2001 census. The estimated growth rate of population in the 1991-01 recorded 1.30 per cent as compared to 2.17 per cent in 1981-1991. The percentage decline in growth rate between 1981-91 and 1991-01 was 40 per cent (51 per cent in Coastal Andhra, 27 per cent in Rayalaseema and 37 per cent in Telangana regions respectively). Due to non-availability of data on age-distribution by Census, 2001, we relied on the projections of Registrar General of India (young adults i.e., 15-59 years, grow from 45.3 million in 2001 to 59.2 million by 2015). It is also estimated that the age distribution of population in 15-49 years increase from 39.9 million in 2000 year to 49 million in 2010 and to a level of 50.2 million by the year 2015. The proportion of females to total population in 15-49 years remains around 50 per cent in the projected period (Fig. 1). These women in reproductive ages requires wide range of RCH services and curative care services. Due to

Figure 1: Projected Population by Board Age Groups Andhra Pradesh, 2000-2015

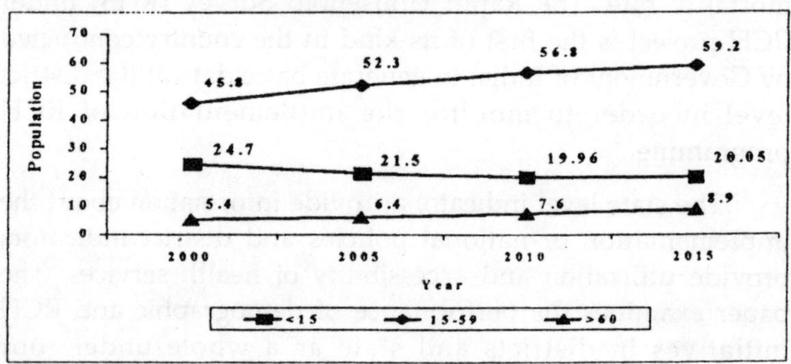

Registrar General of India, 1999

increase in female literacy rate and wider access to information through media, majority of women expect higher accessibility and quality care services namely maternal and child health care, contraceptive care, management of gynecological problems, RTI, HIV/AIDS management and control etc.

Demographic and RCH indicators at stage level presented in Table 1. The state recorded a striking decline in fertility since 1980s, despite no improvement in Human Development Index (HDI) in the last two decades (National Human Development Report, 2001). The NFHS-2 study estimated a total fertility rate of 2.25 (2.32 in rural and 2 in urban). The different data sources clearly indicate a rapid fertility decline in the state after mid-1980s. About six out of ten (64 per cent) women aged between 20-24 years married before legal age at marriage. The median age of marriage for girls was around 15 years. It is distressing to note that, more than one-fourth (27 per cent) of all births of order two occurred within 24 months of the earlier birth. The percentage increased marginally from 22.7 per cent in 1993 to 27.3 per cent in 1999. Antenatal care to pregnant women by trained personnel is a quick and useful measure of maternal health in the absence of data on maternal mortality and morbidity. Little over 90 per cent women who delivered, received at least one antenatal check-up. In contrast to higher utilization of antenatal services, the proportion of institutional deliveries remained at 50 per cent in 1999 (NFHS-2) improved from 33 per cent during 1992 (the other survey, MICS recorded around 56 per cent in 2000). The NFHS-2 and MICS studies confirm that 65 per cent of deliveries attended by health personnel. This reflects that majority of women have accessibility and quality prenatal and obstetric care services. In the state, 60 per cent (about 50 per cent reported in NFHS-2) of currently married women aged 15-49 reported that they or their husbands are following contraceptive methods (MICS, 2001). The median age at sterilization remained around 24 years between two NFHS survey periods and no significant

Table 1: Trends in Demograhic and RCH Indicators in Andhra Pradesh

Sl. No.	*H. Indicator*	*1992 (NFHS-1)*	*1999 (NFHS-2)*	*2000 (MICS)*
1.	Crude Birth Rate	24.1	22.3	23.2
2.	Total Fertility Rate	2.60	2.25	2.25
3.	Women in 20-24 married below 18 years	69.0	64.0	75.5
4.	Median Age at Marriage among women in 25-49 (years)	15.4	15.9	14.5*
5.	Higher Order Births of 3 and above (%)	41.0	31.4	-
6.	Percentage of births with antenatal care.	86.4	92.7	89.7
7.	Percentage of births with medical assistance at delivery.	49.3	65.2	67.9
8.	Percentage of institutional deliveries	32.9	49.8	56.0
9.	Per cent of births within 24 months of duration	22.7	27.3	-
10.	Per cent of children with full immunization	45.0	58.7	46.1
11.	Infant Mortality Rate	73.3	65.8	-
12.	Neo-natal Mortality Rate	47.7	43.8	-
13.	Contraceptive Prevalence Rate (any method)	45.3	49.6	60.0
14.	Median Age at Sterilization	24.5	23.6	-
15.	Male sterilization (%)	Below 9	Below 9	-
	Spacing Methods (%)	Below 5	Bew 5	-
16.	Woman with at least one symptom of RTI (%)		48.5	-

*Median age at marriage of women aged 15-49 years.

Source: 1. National Family Health Survey (MCH and Family Planning). Andhra Pradesh 1992, Bombay: PRC, Visakhapatnam and IIPS.
2. IIPS and ORC Macro (2000), National Family Health Survey (NFHS-2), Andhra Pradesh, Mumbai: IIPS.
3. UNICEF (2001), Multiple Indicator Survey (MICS-2000), Andhra Pradesh, Draft, July 2001.

improvement achieved in promoting male sterilization and temporary contraceptive (spacing) methods.

In a nut shell, the overall picture in the state indicate that women may at early ages, have desired fertility of children with short birth intervals (within 24 months) and adopt female sterilization in early age of 24 years. The Family Welfare Programme has to cater wider spectrum of RCH services to the growing adult population (15-49) in the state (Prema Ramachandran, 2002). It is also of important concern that these women in reproductive ages are sexually active for a longer period because of early age at marriage and may be at risk of RTI and gynecologic morbidities (GOI/UNFPA, 2001).

The state achieved remarkable results of low fertility and lower decadal growth rate in all districts due to successful implementation of family welfare programme. The other important interventions namely, strengthening of Round the Clock Primary Health Centers, Sukhibhava scheme to poor pregnant women for availing institutional deliveries (both in public hospitals and private nursing homes), formation of mother committees in each village (Janani) to strengthen routine immunization, inclusion of Hepatitis-B vaccine, provision of contingency funds and mopeds for better mobility of female health workers in the sub-center villages introduced as a catalyst in accelerating the decline in total fertility rate.

District Demographic and RCH Scenario

The districts are classified into three groups according to the estimated value of total fertility rate (TFR) in 1994-2001 (Table 2). In Group-I which consists of East Godavari, West Godavari, Krishna, Guntur, Nellore and Hyderabad, with a combined population of 23.7 million in 2001 (31.3 per cent to State). In the nine districts of Group II, which include 36.5 per cent of State's population, fertility is approaching replacement level. In Group III, the eight districts comprise 24.4 million population with TFR above 2.5 level. All the eight districts belong to Telangana region, a drastic reduction of TFR in these districts only can bring any reduction in fertility for the State as a whole.

Table 2. Classification of Districts According to the Level of Total Fertility Rate, 1994-2001

Group	*Total Fertility Rate (194-01)*	*Districts*	*Combined Population in 2001 ('000s)*	*Percent to State Population*
I	<=2.10	East Godavari, West Godavari, Krishna, Guntur, Nellore, Hyderabad	23.7	31.3
II	2.11-2.49	Srikakulam, Prakasam, Vizianagaram, Visakhapatnam, Anantapur, Cud dapah, Chittoor, Khammam, Karimnagar	27.5	36.5
III	>=2.50	Kurnool, Ranga Reddy, Nizamabad, Medak, Mahabubnagar, Nalgodna, Warangal, Adilabad	24.4	32.2

Source: Guilmoto and Rajan (2001)

The RCH programme consists of various aspects including maternal and child health, child immunization, adolescent health, contraception, reproductive health problems and HIV and AIDS. In the following paragraphs, a detailed picture of RCH indicators is discussed in districts/ regions respectively.

Marriage and Adolescent Child Bearing

Low age at marriage and the consequent adolescent child bearing had been a serious issue in Andhra Pradesh. Despite some evidence of increase in age at marriage indicated by nuptiality patterns, about three-fourths of women in all the regions except North Coastal Andhra, getting married before attaining legal age at marriage of 18 years. Though North Coastal Andhra performs better in this respect than other regions, the proportion of women married below legal age is as high as 61 per cent (Appendix). On the contrary, adolescent child bearing (in 15 19 age groups) is highest at 71 per cent in North Coastal Andhra as compared to 55 per cent in South Telangana. However, the performance is not uniform across districts in South Telangana region. While Visakhapatnam and Krishna districts recorded 94 per cent of childbearing adolescents followed by slightly above 70 per cent in Nellore, Mahabubnagar and Warangal districts respectively.

Another area of concern is unsafe abortions in the state. Prevention and management of unsafe abortions is one of the key interventions for safe motherhood under RCH programme. About 2 per cent of pregnancy outcome among women in 15-49 years ended as spontaneous or induced abortion with highest percentage (2.8 per cent) recorded in North Coastal Andhra. The proportion is higher in adolescent ages than in other ages. Among the regions, the incidence of abortions among adolescents is higher in Rayalaseema and lowest in South Coastal Andhra. This is a reflection of better accessibility to family planning services in South Coastal Andhra, which is reflected in the highest contraceptive prevalence rate in the State. Increase in the usage of spacing methods considerably reduces the need for induced abortion. The proportion of adolescent girls who had undergone abortions is above 9 per cent in the districts of Nellore, Kurnool, Chittoor and Nizamabad.

Antenatal Care

Complications during pregnancy can adversely affect women's health as well as pregnancy outcome. Early identification of the pregnancy-related complications and timely treatment are the important components of RCH programme. The results of NFHS-2 reveals that the most commonly reported pregnancy related problems are anemia (35 per cent), excessive fatigue (33 per cent) and swelling (25 per cent). More than 70 per cent of the pregnant women received medical check ups like recording of weight and blood pressure. There are not many regional variations in this aspect. However, wide regional variations are reported with respect to abdominal check up (45 per cent in Rayalaseema and 64 per cent in North Telangana). Among the districts, only one-third of pregnant women in East Godavari, Kurnool and Nalgonda districts received three or more abdominal checkups.

The RCH programme recommends that as part of antenatal care to pregnant women have to be given two doses of tetanus toxoid (TT) vaccine, adequate amounts (100 tables in general and 200 tablets in case of high risk) of iron and folic acid (IFA) tablets or syrup to prevent anaemia, and at least three antenatal check ups that include blood pressure and procedures to detect pregnancy complications (Ministry of Health and Family Welfare, 1998). At the state level, about half of the pregnant women received antenatal care during first trimester and three-fourths of the received three or more antenatal checkups (NFHS-2, 1999). According to the MICS survey conducted in 2000 reported that about 70 per cent of pregnant women received IFA tablets though only 62 per cent consumed all tablets received. The coverage is uniform across regions and in rural and urban areas. Some women avoid the IFA tablets due to side effects as gastric irrigation, constipation and black stools caused by iron.

Technically, full ANC coverage includes two doses of TT injections and consumption of IFA tablets and three antenatal care visits by pregnant women. The results show that about two-thirds of pregnant women in South Coastal Andhra and North Telangana regions received complete package of ANC services (the coverage in the remaining regions is around 50 per cent). In case of pregnant women who availed ANC in the first trimester are two-thirds in North Telangana and more than half in other regions. To our surprise, only a little over one-third (35-38 per cent) of women registered in the first trimester in developed districts of West Godavari, Ranga Reddy as well as in backward districts of Mahabubnagar and Adilabad.

The consumption of IFA tablets is found to be considerably low in all the regions and there are significant inter-district differences. For instance, only 18 per cent of women consumed the supplied tablets in Rayalaseema while the corresponding figures in South Coastal Andhra and North Telangana regions was 40 per cent. This clearly indicates huge wastage of resources due to poor extension services in backward districts.

Post Natal Care

An important thrust of the RCH programme is to encourage conduct of deliveries under proper hygienic conditions under supervision of a trained health worker. The result shows that only half of deliveries are conducted in medical institutions. In case of home deliveries, 65 per cent of deliveries attended by health personnel (NFHS-2, 1999). According to MICS (2001), about three-fourth of deliveries ended as normal (spontaneous) followed by 18 per cent by caesarian section. About half (58 per cent) of delivered babies were not weighted at birth. Out of those babies weighted, only 23 per cent were below 2500 grams (MICS, 2001). Among the regions, the proportion of hospital deliveries was highest in South Telangana (57 per cent) followed by South Coastal Andhra (54 per cent). This is due to the proximity of South Telangana to Hyderabad and high density of private medical institutions in South Coastal Andhra. About half of deliveries in North Telangana and 57 per cent of deliveries in North Coastal and Rayalaseema regions are domiciliary deliveries. About three-fifths of deliveries are conducted domiciliary in Srikakulam, Vizianagaram, Kurnool, Anantapur and Adilabad districts. Private health sector played a major role in conducting institutional deliveries in many districts.

About one-third of the women availed for postpartum care (whether they have delivered in a hospital or at home) or ANM visited house for a follow up service. Coastal Andhra and North Coastal regions recorded higher postpartum care of 40 per cent and 33 per cent respectively. The low percentage may be due to poor access, client disinterest or lack of understanding about the importance of postpartum care.

There is a need to develop postpartum care that accessible and valued by mothers, that provides support for infant care and opportunities to discuss family planning options.

Child Health

Breast-feeding improves the health of the child and increases birth interval. About three-fourths of infants of less than 3 months were exclusively breast fed in the state. In the age group of 6-9 months, about sixty per cent of the infants were breast fed along with supplementary feeding (NFHS-2, 1999). About half of the mothers reported that the practice of discarding colostrum and three-fourths of mothers did not breastfed with in two hours of infant birth. The results reveal significant variations across regions regarding the advice received on breast feeding. The highest proportion is found in South Coastal Andhra (70 per cent), which also recorded the highest proportion of deliveries conducted in hospitals. This clearly indicates that conducting deliveries at hospital not only ensures mother and child survival, but also provides indirect benefits like providing beast feeding and deriving associated benefits.

Another important aspect in childcare is immunization including Vitamin-A supplement. The NFHS-2 survey shows that only 59 per cent of child are fully protected against six vaccine preventable diseases i.e. tuberculosis, polio, diphtheria, whooping cough, tetanus and measles. However, the result of RHS survey indicates a very high percentage of full immunization with significant inter-district variations. Children who had incomplete/partial immunization recorded around 40 per cent in Visakhapatnam. Krishna, Guntur, Cuddapah and Nalgonda districts.

Vitamin-A deficiency can cause eye damage leading to total blindness among children. It can be easily prevented by Vitamin-A supplementation or dietary change. The MCS study in Andhra Pradesh recorded 33.8 per cent of children in the preceding one year of survey given Vitamin-A supplementation. But the RHS data shows that the districts Krishna Urnool. Nizamabad, Medak and Warangal reported about 40-50 per cent of coverage of Vitamin-A solution to infants.

Contraceptive Methods

The persistent efforts in the state since early seventies resulted in a sleep rise in couple protection rate (CPR). About three-fourths (59.6 per cent) of eligible couples are effective users of contraceptions (NFHS-2, 1999). The data indicates a total fertility of 2.25 births per woman, contraceptive prevalence of 50 per cent among currently married women with 90 per cent of female sterilzation. Majority of the districts recorded more than 50 per cent of CPR irrespective of regional imbalances. However, this was not resulted in the comensurate fall in crude birth rate (CBR). The CBR recorded above 30 births per 1000 population in the districts of Anantapur and Kurnool of Rayalaseema region and all districts of South Telangana and North Telangana except Nizamabad and Karimnagar (Figure 2).

Figure 2: Couple Protection Rate & Birth Rate In Districts of Andhra Pradesh

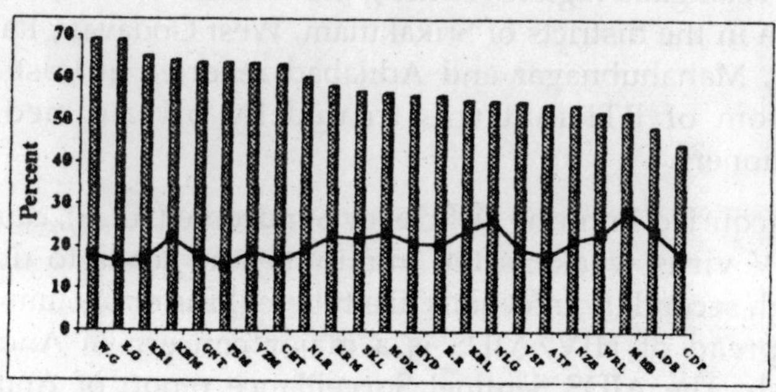

Source: RCH Rapid Household Survey, 1998-99

The unmet need for contraception (terminal methods and spacing methods) at state level reported below 10 per cent (NFHS-2, 1999). However, the districts recorded above one-fifth (20 per cent) of unmet need for contraception are Visakhapatnam, Krishna, Kurnool, Anantapur, Cuddapah, Hyderabad (urban), Nizamabad and Warangal respectively. The districts namely Krishna, Kurnool Cuddapah and

Nizamabad recorded higher unmet needed for spacing methods rather than terminal methods.

Reproductive Health Problems

Reproductive tract infections (RTI) are a serious threat to the reproductive health of women and men. More and more reproductive health programmes are being designed to address these problems in public health care. Research studies show that many Indian women suffer from RTI silently without seeking health care. The low acceptance of intra uterine device (IUD), a temporary method, among women was mainly due to high incidence of RTIs (Bang et al, 1989, Jeejeebhooy and Rao, 1992). About half (49 per cent) of currently married women in the state reported some type of reproductive health problem, including abnormal vaginal discharge, symptoms of urinary tract infection and pain or bleeding associated with intercourse. Among these women with one symptom of RTI, nearly 63 per cent have not sought any treatment (NFHS-2, 1999). The awareness of RTI among females recorded more than 60 per cent in South Coastal and South Telangana regions. Among the districts, four out of ten women in the districts of Srikakulam, West Godavari, Ranga Reddy, Mahabubnagar and Adilabad reported at least one symptom of RTI that was treated by private medical practitioners.

Acquried Immune Deficiency Syndrome (AIDS), caused by HIV virus weakens the immunity and leads to death through secondary infections like tuberculosis or pneumonia. The spread of HIV/AIDS is a major concern in Andhra Pradesh. The AIDS Sentinel Surveillance report of Andhra Pradesh reveals some startling observations. Andhra Pradesh is among the four states with higher prevalence of HIV infection in the country. According to MICS study, 71 per cent of women aged 15-49 have not head of HIV/AIDS. The awareness of HIV/AIDS is lower in rural areas, among poorer sections, and illiterate women. In Guntur district of South Coastal Andhra region slightly more than five out of every 100 women are HIV infected (Basu, 2002).

Studies in developed countries indicated that provision of antenatal education to perspective fathers significantly improves female antenatal care visits, lowers peri-natal mortality rate, meeting better nutritional needs during pregnancy, fight against STI/AIDS. The couple approach encouraged better safe motherhood interventions than counselling individual clients (Bhalerao et al, 1984; Raju and Leonard, 2000).

Correlates of Demographic and RCH Indicators

Data availability restricts for an in depth analysis of inter-district variations in demographic and RCH indicators. Table 3 presents the factors influencing infant mortality rate (IMR) in the districts of Andhra Pradesh. The independent variables having negative sign and statistically significant in reducing IMR were girls marrying below legal age, deliveries conducted in medical institutions, timely medical intervention

Table 3: Factors Influencing Infant Mortality Rate in Andhra Pradesh.

Dependent	*Model-1*		*Model-2*		*Model 3*	
Variable	*Coefficient*	*t-value*	*Coefficient*	*t-value*	*Coefficient*	*t-value*
% of girls married below 18 years	-0.8830	4.20	-0.9010	4.39	-0.8910	4.52
% of Institutional deliveries	-0.8570	2.49	-0.8470	2.50	-0.9070	3.36
% of women had delivery complications	-0.3180	1.69	-0.3440	1.89	-0.3520	2.01
% of pregnant woman with at least one ANC	0.0014	0.02	-0.1870	0.306	-	-
CMIE Infrastructure Index (1995)	-0.1050	0.68	-	-	-	-
Intercept	182.28	3.27	192.46	3.64	177.25	9.97
R-squre	0.83		0.84		0.87	
F-value	10.1		13.0		18.2	

Note: 1. Infant mortality rate refer to 1991 (Census of India (1991), District level estimates of fertility and child mortality for 1991 and their inter relations with other variables, Occasional Paper No. 1 of 1997, New Delhi: Registrar General of India).

2. Centre for Monitoring Indian Economy (2000), District Profiles.

during delivery by obstetrician and gynaecologist. Both the economic variable (CMIE infrastructure index, 1995) and the antenatal care during pregnancy have appropriate signs but are not statistically significant. In a nutshell, reduction in IMR very closely influenced by girl marriage above 18 years of age, widespread coverage of institutional deliveries and delivery related complications attended by skilled medical personnel.

Some districts in Andhra Pradesh need special attention because of their poor performance in demographic and RCH indicators. The top eight districts in the state with highest per cent of girls married below legal age, highest adolescents (15-19) gave child birth, lowest coverage of full ANC, lowest per cent of women registered in first trimester for ANC, lowest proportion of pregnant women (with minimum three abdominal checkups) reported in the districts, lowest coverage of full immunization of children, high unmet need for contraception, highest RTI symptoms among women, low knowledge of HIV/AIDS among women, high crude birth rate and high total fertility rate respectively compared in Table 4. Out of a dozen indicators, Mahabubnagar, Nalgonda figures in 9 indicators, Adilabad in 8 indicators and Warangal and Nizamabad in 6 indicators. Hence, these five districts have to be improved on a priority basis in the Tenth Five Year Plan period.

Summary and Conclusions

Over 45 per cent of females in Andhra Pradesh are in reproductive age group and will increase in next few decades due to population momentum. The sharp decline in total fertility rate was not backed by a comparable decline either in infant mortality, mobility or a rise in female literacy, age at marriage. Low age at marriage and consequent teenage pregnancies are predominant in all districts. Special efforts are also appropriate for addressing the needs of adolescent girls in case of un-formed reproductive health risks and ill effects of teenage pregnancies.

Tables 4: Demographic and Reproductive Health Indicators in the Districts of Andhra Pradesh

S.No.	Indicator	Districts
1.	Highest Per cent of Girls Married Below 18 Years	Mahabubnagar, Srikakulam, Nalgonda, Adilabad, Cuddapah, Medak, Nizamabad
2.	Highest Per cent of Adolescents Who Gave Child Births	Krishna,Visakhapatnam, Warangal, Nellore, Mahabubnagar, Kurnool, Nizamabad
3.	Lowest Per cent of Pregnant Women Received Full ANC	Adilabad, Nalgonda, Cuddapah, Mahabubnagar, Ranga Reddy, Kurnool, Srikakulam
4.	Lowest Per cent of Pregnant Women Received ANC in First	Trimester Ranga Reddy, Mahabubnagar, Adilabad, West Godavari, Nalgonda; Vizianagaram, Anantapur.
5.	Lowest Abdominal Check-ups (>3 times) During Pregnancy	Kurnool, East Godavari, Nalgonda, Vizianagaram, Srikakulam, Adilabad, Chittor.
6.	Lowest per cent of Institutional Deliveries	Srikakulam, Vizianagaram, Anantapur, Kurnool, Adilabad, Mahabubnagar, Nalgonda.
7.	Lowest per cent of child Immunization (Full)	Nalgonda, Cuddapah, Visakhapatnam, Adilabad, Krishna, Guntur, Mahabubnagar.
8.	High Unmet Need for Contraception	Cuddapah, Kurnool, Visakhapatnam, Warangal, Nizamabad, Krishna, Anantapur.
9.	Highest RTI symptoms among women	Adilabad, Mahabubnagar, Ranga Reddy, Srikakulam, Nalgonda, Warangal, Karimnagar.
10.	Lowest Knowledge of HIV/AIDS Among Females	Anantapur, Cuddapah, Visakhapatnam, Warangal, Karimnagar, Medak, Nizamabad
11.	High Crude Birth Rate	Mahabubnagar, Kurnool, Adilabad, Medak, Ranga Reddy, Nizamabad, Nalgonda, Warangal.
12.	High Total Fertility Rate (1994-2001)	Mahabubnagar, Kurnool, Medak, Ranga Reddy, Nalgonda, Warangal, Nizamabad, Vizianagaram.

Source: 1. Guilmoto, Christophe Z and S. Irudaya Rajan (2001)
2. Rapid Household Survey, 1998-99.

Despite good coverage of ante natal care services including supply of IFA tablets, the actual consumption of tablets by pregnant women is found to be very low. This is a matter of serious concern in view of high prevalance of anemia among pregnant women in the state. Though only a half of the deliveries conducted in medical institutions majority of the remaining half are attended by professional health workers. However, deliveries at hospital provide the advantage of popularizing the desirable practice of breast-feeding. There is a need to improve the practice of breast-feed the child with in two hours of birth and feeding of colostrum. The postpartum care after delivery by health personnel requires substantial improvement. The RHS data indicates high percentage of full immunization with inter-district variations. About 40 per cent of children in Visakhapatnam, Krishna, Guntur, Cuddapah and Nalgonda district were recorded incomplete/partial immunization. Only five districts (Krishna, Kurnool, Nizamabad, Medak and Warangal) recorded about 40-50 per cent of Vitamin-A dose coverage to children.

The higher proportion of young population in 15-49 age groups require an effective counselling on HIV/AIDS, which is in alarming scale in the state. The awareness of RTI, STI and HIV/AIDS is found to be poor in all regions except South Coastal Andhra and South Telangana. This is of serious concern in view of the magnitude of HIV/AIDS cases reported in general and pregnant mother in particular. In case of age at marriage, reproductive health problems and HIV/AIDS, all districts in the state need immediate intervention. Besides these, the eight Telangana districts require special emphasis on antenatal care, child immunization and postnatal care.

The analysis includes the data sources of 1998-99, the subsequent year after implementation of the State Population Policy. In the last five years a lot of inputs are introduced in health sector by way of infrastructure development, efficient drug policy, age at marriage campaigns etc. The district level

MICS surveys conducted by UNICEF (2001-02) provide valuable information regarding current improvement of maternal and child health aspects.

References

Basu, A (2002), HIV Nestles in Wombs of Guntur Moms, Deccan Chronicle, 8th March 2002.

Bhalerao Vijaya R, Medha Galwankar, Shobha S. Kowli, Rajesh Kumar and R.M. Chatirvedi (1984), Contribution of the education of the perspective father to the success of maternal health care programmes, Journal of post Graduate Medicine, 30(1), pp. 10-12.

Government of Andhra Pradesh (1999), Draft Vision 2020 Document, State Secretariat.

Government of Andhra Pradesh (1999), *Working Paper on Health and Family Welfare,* Health, Medical & Family Welfare Department, Government of Andhra Pradesh.

Government of Andhra Pradesh (2002), *Working Paper on Health and Family Welfare,* Health, Medical & Family Welfare Department, Government of Andhra Pradesh.

Government of India (1999), *Population Projections for India and States, 1996-2016,* Registrar General, Ministry of Home Affairs, Government of India, New Delhi.

Government of India (2000), *National Popualtion Policy,* 2000.

Guilmoto, Christophe Z and S. Irudaya Rajan (2001), District Level Estimates of fertility from India's 2001 Census, *Economic and Political Weekly,* Vol. 37, No. 7.

Mohan Rao, (2001), *Special Issue on Population,* Medico Friend Circle Bulletin, July-October, 2001.

Mohan Rao, (2002), State Population Policies, *Health for the Millions,* pp. 6-7, June-July 2002.

National Family Health Survey (MCH and Family Planning). Andhra Pradesh 1992. Bombay: PRC, Visakhapatnam and IIPS.

National Family Health Survey (NFHS-2), India, 1998-99: Andhra Pradesh. Mumbai: IIPS and ORC Macro.

Planning Commission (2002), *National Human Development Report-2001,* Government of India, Oxford University Press, 2002.

Prema Ramachandran (2002), *Reproductive and Child Health Initiative and Population Stabilisation,* National Seminar on Reproductive and Child Health and Family Welfare New Delhi, 25th-27th February 2002.

Raju, S. And Leonard, A (2000), 'Men as Supportive Partners in Reproductive Health: moving from Rhetoric to Reality, Population Council, New Delhi, India.

Rapid *Household Survey: Reproductive and Child Health Project, 1998/ 99*. Ministry of Health and Family Welfare, Government of India, New Delhi and Population Research Centre, Visakhapatnam (various district level reports).

The Word Development Report (1993), *World Development Report: Investing in Health,* Washington, DC.

UNICEF (2001), *Multiple Indicator Survey* (MICS-2000), Andhra Pradesh, Draft, July 2001.

APPENDIX

Reproductive and Child Health Indicators in the District of Andhra Pradesh, 1998 and 1999

District	% of Girls Married at age <18 years	% of Adolescents who gave child-birth (15-19) years	% of Abortion performed on adolescent girls	% of Women received				% of deliveries conducted at			% of deliveries under skilled personnnel	% women who had post delivery follow up visit by ANM
				ANC at least once	3 or more ANC Check ups	Full AMC	Two inj. of T.T.	% of Women received ANC in first trimester	Medical instruction	Home (Domi-cillary)		
1	2	3	4	5	6	7	8	9	10	11	12	13
Andhra Pradesh	72.65	61.49	5.63	94.22	87.84	59.22	56.5	52.4	50.94	48.9	71.48	30.22
North Coastal	61.1	71.5	5.52	91.1	83.8.	53.9	57.0	57	43.1	58.8	64.6	32.9
Srikakulam	83.5	45.7	6.7	87.4	79.7	48.5	82.2	50.8	26.2	71.7	50.2	40.2
Vizianagaram	40.4	62.3	2.0	91.7	84.5	56.3	84.9	48.5	34.9	65.0	57.5	45.4
Visakhapatnam	58.4	93.6	3.3	93.2	86.1	56.1	75.6	66.2	58.0	41.9	78.6	20.6
South Coastal	75.2	64.2	4.6	96.8	91.1	68.1	54.1	54.0	54.2	45.7	78.4	40.6
East Godavari	72.4	63.8	N A	97.9	90.3	66.5	88.3	54.8	48.7	51.2	76.1	49.7
West Godavari	78.4	60.4	8.6	95.2	87.8	52.7	87.8	38.0	49.4	50.5	71.5	36.9
Krishna	72.6	93.7	6.6	97.3	91.1	74.8	86.5	54.4	60.4	39.5	90.2	32.5
Guntur	78.7	40.9	N A	96.5	91.3	72.8	92.5	54.3	56.3	43.7	79.9	22.8
Nellore	72.6	70.7	9.7	98.1	93.1	71.5	85.3	63.3	63.3	36.7	78.4	53.6
Prakasam	77.0	57.5	4.0	95.8	94.4	71.0	87.9	64.1	49.6	50.3	72.5	56.2

Table Contd.

Appendix Contd.

1	2	3	4	5	6	7	8	9	10	11	12	13
Rayalaseema	70.4	61.2	7.6	93.7	84.9	53.9	55.9	55.9	43.1	56.9	62.4	25.2
Kurnool	71.2	69.4	10.0	92.0	78.6	48.0	83.7	53.1	38.8	61.1	64.3	7.3
Anantapur	73.2	47.6	5.1	90.6	79.0	51.2	88.0	49.8	36.1	63.9	51.2	10.8
Cuddapah	79.4	66.2	4.2	93.7	87.6	42.4	69.1	57.9	47.4	52.5	66.8	19.6
Chittoor	60.8	63.3	9.6	98.3	94.5	70.0	85.0	62.9	50.8	49.1	68.3	60.8
South Telangana	72.6	55.4	4.8	92.8	85.7	49.6	50.2	50.2	56.9	43.0	72.0	73.3
Hyderabad	46.6	53.3	N A	94.9	94.0	42.2	93.3	70.3	88.3	11.6	93.6	17.6
Ranga Reddy	73.1	47.0	8.3	92.1	83.3	48.1	84.2	34.9	55.3	44.6	60.0	18.8
Medak	79.3	49.5	2.0	95.1	92.0	80.4	92.3	67.7	50.8	49.1	65.1	12.2
Mahabubnagar	84.9	70.7	7.1	89.2	77.5	44.3	69.7	37.8	41.9	58.0	61.2	39.5
Nalgonda	82.5	54.8	2.9	93.5	82.4	39.7	76.6	42.9	44.7	55.2	78.0	26.3
North Telangana	77.5	58.5	6.6	94.1	90.1	63.9	63.6	67.7	50.7	49.2	72.1	34.5
Nizamabad	79.0	65.1	10.7	97.2	93.2	72.2	83.9	72.5	53.0	46.9	80.8	17.9
Warangal	73.4	71.7	5.2	98.9	93.5	65.0	81.4	78.9	52.1	47.8	72.1	22.1
Khammam	77.6	56.1	2.1	97.6	90.4	63.2	81.6	57.4	52.7	47.2	74.4	42.1
Karimnagar	77.4	50.4	3.3	99.6	97.5	75.9	92.9	84.8	54.7	45.2	76.6	16.9
Adilabad	81.4	48.2	7.5	79.9	72.2	38.3	66.6	35.1	38.9	61.0	55.1	26.8

Table Contd.

Appendix Contd.

Reproductive and Child Health Indicators in the District of Andhra Pradesh, 1998 and 1999

District	% of Women who sought treatment for pregnancy complication	% of Women by type of complications				% of pregnant woman got services					
		Premature labour	Obstructed labour	Prolonged labour	Others	Weighed measure	B.P. measure	IFA tablets give	IFA tablet regularly	Two tablets regularly	Abdominal checkup (>=3 times)
	14	**15**	**16**	**17**	**18**	**19**	**20**	**21**	**22**	**23**	**24**
Andhra Pradesh	67.7	19.2	9.4	9.4	6.2	81.7	84.1	73.0	37.0	32.1	54.8
North Coastal	72.8	17.1	9.1	9.7	8.2	75.4	79.9	72.9	28.6	37.7	49.0
Srikakulam	72.1	11.7	3.4	5.7	5.1	82.5	83.4	66.2	30.0	32.0	40.5
Vizianagaram	73.0	12.4	6.3	8.6	4.8	83.4	82.3	74.4	34.2	37.2	40.2
Visakhapatnam	73.2	23.6	14.6	13.1	12.3	65.9	76.0	76.17	24.3	41.9	59.9
South Coastal	62.1	27.8	11.6	9.1	4.5	86.3	89.1	80.2	39.2	38.5	55.9
East Godavari	52.7	23.3	5.5	11.1	4.5	83.7	85.7	78.6	40.6	36.5	35.5
West Godavari	73.7	6.6	6.2	6.6	4.0	86.7	89.6	65.3	31.0	33.2	54.2
Krishna	76.3	49.3	27.4	12.5	7.4	85.1	92.5	88.3	37.6	46.5	66.0
Guntur	58.3	38.9	18.9	3.9	5.1	88.9	89.7	81.1	41.3	38.1	64.1
Nellore	52.1	17.4	5.0	10.5	1.8	85.3	86.7	86.2	45.4	38.0	58.7
Prakasam	57.8	24.8	2.0	11.0	2.7	89.6	90.3	84.1	41.0	38.6	62.4

Table Contd.

Appendix Contd.

	14	15	16	17	18	19	20	21	22	23	24
Rayalaseema	66.0	16.1	9.0	8.0	4.7	71.5	72.0	67.8	44.7	17.7	44.7
Kurnool	6.14	1.5	1.9	1.9	3.5	71.0	72.2	59.8	37.9	18.1	28.6
Anantapur	81.1	14.0	13.7	5.0	5.7	65.7	60.2	63.5	45.4	9.3	55.6
Cuddapah	59.6	23.5	18.5	12.7	3.0	62.1	68.7	58.6	31.6	17.7	48.6
Chittoor	60.0	26.6	4.5	13.3	6.2	84.1	85.4	85.8	59.5	25.4	46.6
South Telangana	71.2	11.8	7.1	8.7	6.7	83.0	85.17	62.1	34.4	24.2	56.8
Hyderabad	86.7	1.8	2.2	17.3	14.5	92.4	94.3	43.5	34.0	8.2	83.6
Ranga Reddy	67.0	7.5	6.6	5.9	7.2	86.1	86.4	61.6	30.1	30.5	53.1
Medak	51.3	19.6	11.6	5.6	4.6	82.7	90.0	84.7	48.5	33.8	74.4
Mahabubnagar	69.5	12.4	4.6	8.0	3.4	78.5	80.7	71.2	40.2	28.7	47.8
Nelgonda	76.4	20.4	12.2	5.5	2.9	74.2	77.1	54.9	21.6	23.3	25.7
North Telangana	70.9	17.8	8.9	11.5	8.3	85.9	87.6	78.7	34.5	40.2	63.4
Nizamabad	65.4	16.6	12.9	4.3	9.5	85.8	91.3	84.2	40.4	34.5	79.0
Warangal	91.4	22.8	11.0	13.2	10.7	90.7	94.6	84.2	35.0	42.5	68.2
Khammam	64.4	28.5	6.1	13.2	2.7	90.4	91.1	87.0	32.9	51.0	67.6
Karimnagar	54.7	12.3	7.7	14.1	10.9	96.8	98.2	83.0	34.2	48.0	62.1
Adilabad	38.9	9.1	6.7	10.9	5.9	68.7	67.2	57.8	31.8	24.7	44.8

Table Contd.

Appendix Contd.

Reproductive and Child Health Indicators in the District of Andhra Pradesh, 1998 and 1999

District	*Immunization*			*% Eligible women having unmet need for*		*Awarness of RTI Female (%)*	*% of Respondents with at least one symptom of RTI*		*Awareness of HIV/AIDS among*	
	Fully Immunized	*Incomplete Immunized*	*Not Immunized*	*Limiting*	*Spacing*		*Male*	*Female*	*Male*	*Female*
	25	**26**	**27**	**28**	**29**	**30**	**31**	**32**	**33**	**34**
Andhra Pradesh	74.5	23.6	1.8	7.1	7.6	54.8	9.9	21.0	67.1	59.5
North Coastal	71.3	28.0	0.7	9.3	5.5	56.2	33.0	41.2	57.0	54.1
Srikakulam	78.0	22.0	0.0	6.5	2.2	56.0	18.8	36.6	60.4	49.6
Vizianagaram	86.0	13.0	1.0	4.9	1.0	59.5	13.2	24.1	56.7	58.8
Visakhapatnam	58.0	41.0	1.0	13.9	10.3	17.7	7.9	11.7	45.8	31.3
South Coastal	74.7	24.8	0.6	5.1	4.2	66.2	6.1	16.6	71.3	75.6
East Godavari	85.0	13.0	2.0	4.7	0.4	72.8	1.7	10.6	71.0	83.0
West Godavari	79.0	20.0	1.0	4.8	1.5	73.2	22.8	33.4	79.4	80.9
Krishna	61.0	39.0	0.0	6.3	12.4	43.9	2.3	17.5	58.9	66.5
Guntur	65.0	35.0	0.0	5.0	8.3	60.2	4.2	14.1	79.0	73.7
Nellore	83.0	17.0	0.0	6.9	0.5	79.9	2.9	17.1	73.0	79.6

Table Contd.

Appendix Contd.

	25	26	27	28	29	30	31	32	33	34
Prakasam	78.0	22.0	0.0	3.3	N A	74.2	2.8	6.9	68.6	68.6
Rayalaseema	77.5	21.1	1.4	7.7	16.9	36.9	4.3	10.2	62.2	45.3
Kurnool	77.0	21.0	2.0	5.7	31.2	44.6	7.8	16.9	69.2	51.1
Anantapur	81.0	17.0	2.0	9.0	9.1	10.0	4.7	4.1	49.9	19.1
Cuddapah	58.0	40.0	2.0	12.3	33.1	11.9	1.4	5.3	50.5	28.4
Chittoor	88.0	12.0	0.0	5.0	0.1	72.9	2.7	13.1	75.4	76.8
North Telangana	71.8	24.8	3.4	7.7	7.7	61.9	7.9	24.0	76.7	62.1
Hyderabad	85.0	13.0	2.0	12.0	18.5	56.0	0.2	8.7	83.5	77.9
Ranga Reddy	74.0	25.0	1.0	6.4	1.9	72.9	17.0	35.2	76.1	66.7
Medak	85.0	13.0	2.0	5.0	6.7	65.3	0.6	15.2	66.7	43.7
Mahbubnagar	65.0	32.0	3.0	8.1	1.5	55.0	16.2	34.1	75.8	52.6
Nalgonda	51.0	40.0	9.0	5.8	9.3	61.6	3.7	25.8	73.9	64.9
South Telangana	76.6	20.1	3.1	7.6	5.5	43.7	9.2	22.2	61.2	46.9
Nizamabad	79.0	18.0	3.0	8.7	11.7	47.5	4.0	42.5	68.1	47.7
Warangal	81.0	18.0	1.0	11.0	10.8	13.2	13.0	24.6	66.6	32.4
Khammam	81.0	18.0	0.0	5.2	0.5	65.4	3.3	9.9	58.7	62.6
Karimnagar	86.0	12.0	2.0	5.0	5.6	25.1	8.4	24.6	52.1	35.9
Adilabad	59.0	32.0	9.0	9.0	1.8	55.7	17.4	38.9	62.2	49.1

Note: Full ANC include 2 doses of T.T.+ iron folic acid tables + at least 3 ANCs

N.A. Not available

Source: Rapid Household Survey, 1998-99

22

Cost of Treatment, People's Choices and Health Sector Reforms in Andhra Pradesh

Prof. G. Ramachandrudu
Dr. (Mrs.) G. Kamalamma
Dr. G. Vinay Kumar

Introduction

Andhra Pradesh is the fifth most populous state in India with a population of about 76 million in 2001, of which 23.1 per cent are below Poverty line (BPL) in 1993-94 (Planning Commission) and majority of the people (73 per cent) live in the rural areas. The state has a vast network of health care services. In 1994-95, there are 10,555 Sub-centres/1306 Primary Health Centres (PHCs), 175 Community Health Centres (CHCs), 150 area and district hospitals, 22 dispensaries, 38 tertiary hospitals attached to 9 Medical colleges, and 2 super Speciality Hospitals. In addition, there are 23 district T.B. centres, 25 T.B. clinics and 194 Leprosy Control Units which provide primary and secondary care. Distribution of hospital beds among three levels of care is skewed towards tertiary care with 31, 32 and 37 per cent in primary, secondary and tertiary care respectively.

The state spends about Rs. 6.45 billion on health, which constitutes 5.4 per cent of the total revenue budget during 1996-97. The percentage share has declined steeply over the years from 13.74 per cent during 1955-56 to 7.88 per cent during 1975-76 and 5.8 per cent during 1993-94. While Kerala, another Southern state spends about Rs. 122 per capita on health, Andhra Pradesh spends only Rs. 69 per capita where as all India average is even higher at Rs. 85 per capital.

The World Development Report (1993) recommended that about US $ 12, (Rs. 432) per capita are required in low-income developing countries to meet the requirements of preventive and promotive services including minimum package of essential public health and clinical services. There is an urgent need to step-up public health expenditure in Andhra Pradesh.

The Directive Principles of the State Policy in the Constitution of India provide that the "State shall regard the level of nutrition and standard of living of its people and improvement of public health as among its primary duties'. Keeping in tune with the goal, the First Five Year Plan (1951-56) set its objectives as "to initiate a process of development which will raise living standards and open up to the people, new opportunities for a richer and more varied life.

Several Health Committees offered valuable recommendations for Health Sector reforms in India. The Committee headed by Bhore during preindependence period (1946) emphasised that health service should be available to all citizens irrespective of their ability to pay for it and as near the location of the people as possible in order to ensure the maximum benefits to the communities to be served (Bhore Committee Report, 1946). Other Committee Reports, Mudaliar (1959), Mukherjee (1965), Junjunwala (1967), Kartar Singh (1973), Srivastava (1974) and Krishan (1984) have made far reaching recommendations for expanding Health and Medical Infrastructure with a view to improve the accessibility of services in both rural and urban areas. The W.H.O. sponsored Alma Ata declaration in 1978 has made remarkable change in the thinking of all the governments towards health sector reforms.

The World Bank has focused on health care financing in developing countries as one of its central areas of interest since it started to take an active role in the health sector in the 1980s. In 1987 the World Bank published its policy paper "Financing Health Services in Developing Countries: An Agenda for Reform" and the World Development Report of 1993 focused on "Investing in Health". The World Bank agenda for Health Sector Reform proposed four policy recommendations: (a) to charge user fees at government health facilities (b) to promote health insurance (c) to promote the private sector and (d) to decentralise government health services.

The objectives of the paper are: (a) to analyse the changes in the health expenditure and health status in A.P. (b) to present morbidity pattern and cost of treatment from household survey, (c) to examine the people's choices and client satisfaction and (d) to discuss the implications of the on-going health sector reforms in A.P.

The paper used both primary and secondary data sources. All the available health satisfies from Govt. publications are used to analyse the public expenditure and overall morbidity pattern. The primary data have been taken from the research project done by the Population Research Centre (PRC), Andhra University, Visakhapatnam, during 1995-96.

Health Infrastructure and Expenditure in A.P.

The role of the government in providing basic services including health care is very critical in developing countries like India. Public health expenditure is a necessary social investment without which the large mass of working classes can not realise good health and contribute to the economy. In the process of liberalisation in India, though the state has a large stake in the health sector, government appear to be pushing the growth of private sector, which is unchecked and unregulated.

Health Infrastructure

This section presents a comparative picture of the health infrastructural development in Andhra Pradesh, Kerala and all India.

Table 1 presents the growth of number of government hospitals (Allopathy in Andhra Pradesh over a period of 34 years) (1957-58 to 1991-92). The total number of hospitals, dispensaries and specialised hospitals had increased from 569 in 1957-58 to 1878 in 1991-92. The growth during the period was 230 per cent. There was a big jump in the number of medical institutions during the period between 1957-58, 1967-68, 1983-84 and 1990-91.

Revenue Expenditure on Health

Table 2 presents the growth of public revenue expenditure on health in Andhra Pradesh, Kerala and All India. While Andhra Pradesh spends about Rs. 5 billion (5.6 per cent of the total budget) on health during 1994-95, Kerala spends about Rs. 3.8 billion (7.4 per cent of the total budget). This public health spending is Rs. 69 per capita in Andhra Pradesh, Rs. 122 in Kerala and Rs. 85 in All India. Thus Andhra Pradesh is lagging behind even All India average. It can be observed from the table that the percentage of public health expenditure was nearly 14 during 1955-56 in Andhra Pradesh, while in Kerala the percentage was only 9. Thus there is a need to step up the public health expenditure in Andhra Pradesh.

Changes in the Health Status in Andhra Pradesh

Health status has become an important component of human development measure. This section analyses briefly the changes in the health status of A.P. Population. A detailed sketch of health status in A.P. is represented by Kamalamma. G. (1996).

Health Status is generally measured in terms of mortality indicators like Crude Death Rate, Infant mortality Rate, Expectation of Life at Birth among others. Morbidity rate is

Table 1: Growth of Number of Government Hospitals (Allopathy) in Andhra Pradesh 1957-58 to 1991-92

Year	*Hospitals*	*Dispensaries*	*Specialised Hospitals (TB, Eye, Mental, etc.)*	*Total*
1957-58	-	-	-	569
1958-59	-	-	-	852
1959-60	-	-	-	940
1960-61	-	-	-	998
1961-62	323	637	90	1050
1962-63	-	-	-	1094
1963-64	-	-	-	1094
1964-65	-	-	-	1124
1965-66	326	711	90	1127
1966-67	258	1024	27	1309
1967-68	263	1106	27	1396
1968-69	263	1111	27	1401
1969-70	268	1107	27	1402
1970-71	-	-	-	1404
1971-72	272	1106	27	1405
1972-73	-	-	-	1412
1973-74	272	1113	27	1412
1974-75	276	1115	27	1418
1975-76	278	1118	27	1423
1976-77	268	1118	38	1424
1977-78	276	1110	39	1424
1978-79	-	-	-	1469
1979-80	292	1161	39	1492
1981-82	295	1101	39	1435
1982-83	300	1105	39	1444
1983-84	300	1117	40	1457
1984-85	303	1161	40	1504
1985-86	304	1615	40	1959
1986-87	304	1640	39	1983
1989-90	291	1666	39	1996
1990-91	289	1680	39	2008
1991-92	315	1556	49	1920
1992-93	294	1547	39	1880

Source: Directorate of Health, Govt. of A.P.

Table 2: Revenue Expenditure on Health

Year	Andhra Pradesh			Kerala			All India		
	A	B	C	A	B	C	A	B	C
1950-51	—	—	—	—	—	—	218.55	2.69	0.61
1955-56	39.83	3.74	0.60	16.67	8.46	1.09	809.83	4.36	1.27
1960-61	75.57	8.89	2.10	44.49	9.67	2.63	1076.82	5.13	2.45
1965-66	124.99	7.83	3.15	85.18	10.41	4.45	1685.90	3.28	3.41
1970-71	259.39	8.74	5.96	150.11	9.26	7.03	3351.18	3.84	6.11
1975-76	398.02	7.88	8.20	337.75	9.51	14.43	611.66	3.49	9.91
1980-81	876.22	7.55	16.36	570.92	8.5	22.43	11888.12	3.29	17.35
1985-86	1837.60	6.61	30.66	1133.97	7.82	41.64	27153.91	3.39	35.52
1991-92	3752.55	5.82	55.09	2226.61	6.92	76.86	62039.06	2.71	70.15
1992-93	4221.63	5.87	60.51	2301.31	6.29	76.86	62039.06	2.71	70.15
1993-94 (R.E.)	4648.96	5.75	65.06	3131.60	7.13	103.77	71825.18	2.1	79.44
1994-95 (B.E.)	5043.53	5.63	68.91	3759.77	73.44	122.07	78666.34	2.63	85.10
1995-96 (R.E.)	5459.40	4.99	82.10	—	—	—	—	—	—
1996-97 (B.E.)	6451.60	5.35	97.01	—	—	—	—	—	—

Note: RE = Revised Estimate, B.E. = Budget Estimate

Source: Upto 1985-96 combined finance and revenue account controller and auditor General of India, Respective Years, other years, demand for grants respective states.

A = Amount in Rupees million;

B = As percentage of total government revenue expenditure

C = Expenditure on Health per capita in Rupees.

another dimension of health status measurement, because of the emerging health situation in India is the fall in the death rate and raise in morbidity rate. The most important constraint in measuring morbidity is lack of reliable data. Mortality data presented in this section are drawn from the Sample Registration System (SRS).

Table 3 presents trends in the Crude Death Rate (CDR), Infant Mortality Rate (IMR) and expectation of life at birth in India and Andhra Pradesh during 1901-94. Crude Death Rate in India has declined from 42.6 in 1901-11 to a low of 9.0 in 1995, where as that of Andhra Pradesh from 43.1 in 1941-51 to a low of 8.3 in 1995. Infant mortality in India has declined from a high 278 in 1911-21 to a low of 74 in 1995 and that of Andhra Pradesh from 111 in 1951-61 to 66 in 1995. Male life expectancy has increased from 22.6 years in 1901-11 to 60.6 years in 1991-96 and that of females has increased from 23.3 to 61.7 years during the same period in All India. the increase in life expectancy in Andhra Pradesh is from 48.4 year in 1970-75 to 61.4 in 1991-96 for males and from 49.3 to 64.5 for females during the same period.

The mortality indicators show that the health status in Andhra Pradesh is better than that of All India.

Methodology and Sample Design

The planning and design of a hospital is a systematic process which involves stages moving progressively from the macro-level of epidemiological surveys of the needs and demands of populations in catchment areas to the micro-level of specific location and space in a building designed for a particular function of human activity. It is a multi-disciplinary activity that requires the active participation of professionals in various roles; it also requires continual interaction between the users and the professionals who are to translate functional requirements into physical forms.

The PRC study is basically a multi-disciplinary one. Experts in medical and health, demography, health economics

Table 3: Health Status Indicators of Andhra Pradesh and All India

Year	All India Life Expectancy				Andhra Pradesh Life Expectancy			
	CDR	IMR	Male	Female	CDR	IMR	Male	Female
1901-11	42.6	—	22.6	23.3	—	—	—	—
1911-21	47.2	278	19.3	20.9	—	—	—	—
1921-31	36.3	228	26.9	26.6	—	—	—	—
1931-41	31.2	207	32.1	31.4	—	—	—	—
1941-51	27.4	192	32.4	31.7	43.1	—	—	—
1951-61	22.8	140	41.9	40.6	39.7	111	—	—
1961-71	19.1	114	46.4	44.7	34.9	109	—	—
1970-75	—	—	—	—	—	—	48.4	49.3
1976-80	—	—	52.5	52.1	—	—	52.2	54.2
1971-81	15.0	—	50.9	50.0	33.2	—	—	—
1991-96	—	—	60.6	61.7	—	—	61.4	64.5
1982	11.9	105	—	—	10.9	79	—	—
1983	11.9	105	—	—	10.7	77	—	—
1984	12.6	104	—	—	10.7	78	—	—
1985	11.8	97	—	—	10.5	83	—	—
1986	11.1	96	—	—	9.9	82	—	—
1987	10.9	95	—	—	9.9	79	—	—
1988	11.0	94	—	—	10.2	83	—	—
1989	10.3	91	—	—	9.5	81	—	—
1990	9.7	80	—	—	9.1	70	—	—
1991	9.8	80	—	—	9.7	73	—	—
1992	10.1	79	60.8	—	9.3	71	—	—
1993	9.3	74	—	—	8.4	64	—	—
1994	9.3	74	—	—	8.3	65	—	—
1995	9.0	74	—	—	8.3	66	—	—

Source: SRS, 1995.

and management and social anthropology, were associated with the study, which was financed by Ministry of Health and Family Welfare, Govt. of A.P. The field work was conducted during August-November, 1996.

The sample design adopted is a multi-stage random sample. There are three stages for selecting the sample for the study. In the first stage all the districts in Andhra Pradesh are subdivided into six contiguous regions according to their geophysical characteristics, each representing one or more of the 1991 census regions. The district composition of the regions is as follows:

Region I : Srikakulam, Vizianagrarm and Visakhapatnam

Region II : East Godavari West Godavari, Krishna and Guntur.

Region III : Prakasam and Nellore

Region IV : Chittoor, Cuddapah, Anantapur, Kurnool.

Region V : Mahaboobnagar, Rangareddy, Hyderabad, Medak, Nizamabad, Adilabad, Nalgonda.

Region VI : Karimnagar, Warangal, Khammam

In the second stage/in each region/all the referral hospitals are ranked according to a composite index taking into consideration the population served by each bed/ infrastructure available/utilisation of the facilities and health personnel currently working and vacancy position.

After dividing them into two groups: Less developed and more developed hospitals/one hospital from each group is randomly selected for the study. Thus we have 12 referral hospitals for the purpose of our study. Corresponding to each selected hospital/one private nursing home in the same town/village with similar facilities is selected for the purpose of comparison. Thus the number of sample institutions covered in the study is 24. A detailed institutional questionnaire has been designed for getting comprehensive picture of the functioning of the FRUs. In the third stage a household survey is conducted to estimate the demand for referral health care system by assessing the morbidity pattern in different socio-economic groups. Using the WHO's cluster sample methodology/200 households (50 in urban wards and 150 in rural areas) from randomly selected villages that predominantly utilise the health services (basing on the inpatient registers) in each hospital region are selected. Apart from morbidity pattern, cost of treatment and referral practices/demographic and socio-economic particulars are collected through the household questionnaire. The total sample size has come to 2404 households.

The List of Selected First Referral Units Region

Region I : 1. Palasa in Srikakulam District

2. Bheemunipatnam in Visakhapatnam District

Region II : 1. Rampachodavaram in East Godavari District

2. Thadepalligudem in West Godavari District

Region III: 1. Giddalur in Prakasam District

2. Kavali in Nellore District

Region IV: 1. Srikalahasthi In Chittoor District.

2. Dharmavaram in Anantapur District.

Region V : 1. Vikarabad in Rangareddy District.

2. Sirpur in Adilabad District

Region VI: 1. Peddapalli in Karimnagar District.

2. Kothagudem in Khammam District.

Background Characteristics of the Sample Households

Table 4 presents the background characteristics of the sample household. Out of the total households (HHs) (2,404), 77 per cent are from rural areas and 23 per cent from urban areas.

Table 4: Background Characteristics of the Sample Households (Per cent Distribution of Households by Selected Characteristics of Households Head and Size According to Residence, 1996)

	Residence					
	Rural		Urban		Total	
	No.	%	No.	%	No.	%
No. of	1841	76.6	56.3	23.4	2404	00.00
Households Religion						
Hindu	1734	94.2	495	87.9	2229	92.7
Muslim	104	5.6	61	10.8	165	6.9
Christian	3	0.2	7	1.2	10	0.4
Total	**1841**	**100.00**	**63**	**100.00**	**2404**	**100.00**
Caste						
S.C.	295	16.0	125	22.2	420	17.5
S.T.	228	12.4	28	5.0	256	10.6
B.C.	889	48.3	241	42.8	1130	47.0
Others	107	5.8	68	12.1	175	7.3
O.C.	322	17.5	101	17.9	423	17.6
Total	1841	100.0	563	100.0	2404	100.00
Monthly Income						
1000	815	44.3	220	39.1	1035	43.1
1001-2000	754	41.0	198	35.2	952	39.6
2001-3000	142	7.7	85	15.1	227	9.4
3001-4000	66	3.6	27	4.8	93	3.9
400≤ & above	56	3.0	26	4.6	82	3.4
Missing	8	0.4	7	1.2	15	0.6
Total	**1841**	**100.0**	**563**	**10.0**	**2404**	**100.0**

As regards the religious composition of households, 94 per cent in rural areas and 88 per cent in urban areas belong to Hindu; 6 per cent in rural and 11 per cent in urban belong to Muslim and 0.2 per cent in rural and 1.2 per cent in urban belong to Christians.

A predominant proportion of the sample households belong to Backward Classes (47 per cent) Scheduled Castes comprise 17 per cent and Scheduled Tribes 11 per cent, others 7 per cent and Forward Castes (FCs) comprise 18 per cent.

The respondents were asked to mention the monthly Household income. Out of 2404 households 15 (0.6 per cent) have either not respondent or do not know their income. Out of the total sample, majority 43.1 per cent of the households are reported to have their monthly incomes below Rs. 1,000/-. About 40 per cent are in the income group of Rs. 1001-2000 and 3.4 per cent are in the highest income group of Rs. 4001 and above. Thus the sample consists of predominantly low income households. There are no marked rural-urban differentials except that the highest income bracket has a higher proportion of urban respondents.

Table 5 gives percentage distribution of sample household population aged 7 years and above. Among the sample households, 34 per cent of male and 54 per cent of female are illiterates. The illiteracy rates in the rural areas are 36 per cent for male and 58 per cent for females. It can observed from the table that one fourth of the people have primary education (27 per cent for males and 22 per cent for females).

Prevalence of Disease Based on Household Survey

The respondents were asked to report whether during the 30 days period preceding the date of survey, any body in the household suffered with illness and during the past one year whether anybody was admitted in the hospital and inpatient. In the rural population of 8290, a total of 1113 cases of outpatients and 344 cases of inpatients are reported (See

Table 5: Educational Level of the Household Population (Age 6+)

Education level	Rural			Urban			Total		
	Male	Female	Total	Male	Female	Total	Male	Female	Total
Illiterate	36.17	57.80	46.87	26.05	43.29	34.63	33.60	54.21	43.85
Literate but no formal schooling	4.82	3.78	4.31	3.86	5.45	4.65	4.59	4.20	4.39
Primary	27.50	22.31	24.93	25.11	21.99	23.56	2.91	22.23	24.59
Middle	12.10	8.31	10.23	14.14	12.03	13.09	12.60	9.23	10.93
Secondary	9.87	4.87	7.39	12.00	8.57	10.29	10.39	5.78	8.11
Higher Education	9.45	2.90	6.21	18.7	8.66	13.74	11.74	4.33	8.07
Missing	0.08	0.03	0.06	0.09	0.00	0.04	0.08	0.02	0.05
Total (Age 6+1)	0.0	100.0	100.00	100.00	100.00	100.00	100.00	100.00	100.00
Population (Age 6+)	3586	3514	7100	1167	155	2322	4753	469	9422
Population (Age <6)	57	603	1190	174	158	332	71	761	1522

Tables 6 and 7). Thus in the rural areas of Andhra Pradesh, the prevalence rate of morbidity is 13.42 per cent during one month period as outpatients and 4.15 per cent of the population seek hospital care (as inpatients). In the urban areas the corresponding rates of sickness are 14.05 per cent and 4.30 per cent respectively.

The significant Morbidity pattern of 1113 persons reported sickness (as outpatient) in the rural areas is Rheumatic fever (4.6 per cent). Nervous and general debility (3.7 per cent), skin diseases and accidents and injuries (3.4 per cent each), diarrhoea (3.2 per cent). Typhoid (2.9 per cent), Malaria (2.7 per cent) and whooping cough (2.6 per cent). A detailed morbidity pattern of outpatients for 50 diseases is presented in Table 6.

In urban areas, out of 373 persons reported sick and sought outpatient care, the mobility pattern of significant cases is injury and accidents (5.4 per cent), nervousness and debility (5.1 per cent). Rheumatic fever (3.8 per cent), Malaria (3.2 per cent), whooping cough, heart disease, age disease and skin disease (2.9 per cent), typhoid and high blood pressures (2.7 per cent each). For more details see Table 6.

The morbidity pattern of inpatients is also presented in Table 7. In the rural areas, out of 344 persons reported sick, the morbidity pattern is gastritis (10 per cent), pregnancy related cases (8 per cent) injury and accidents (7.8 per cent), typhoid (6.1 per cent), diarrhoea and gastro-enteritis (5.8 per cent), nervousness and debility (3.8 per cent) and heart and eye disease (3.5 per cent each).

In the urban areas, out of 114 persons reported impatient care, the morbidity pattern is ailment related to pregnancy (7 per cent). Malaria, Typhoid, Diarrhoea, Injury and accidents (6 per cent each), high blood pressure (5 per cent). Gastric ulcer (4.4 per cent) and Cancer (3.5 per cent).

Morbidity pattern in rural and urban areas is almost similar except that malaria, typhoid, cancer and high blood pressure are more prevalent in the urban areas.

Table 6: Morbidity Pattern of Outpatients by Rural and Urban

Code	Name of the Disease	Rural No.	(N = 1113) %	Urban No.	(N=373) %	Total No.	(N=1486) %
1	2	3	4	5	6	7	8
01	Chicken Pox	4	0.4	2	0.4	6	0.4
02	Cholera	2	0	2	0.5	4	0.3
03	Influenza	+1	0.09	1	0.3	2	0.1
04	Diphtheria	2	0.2	2	0.5	4	0.3
05	Encephalitis	-	-	-	-	-	-
06	Filariasis	4	0.4	1	0.3	5	0.3
07	Leprosy	15	1.3	1	0.3	1	1.1
08	Malaria	30	2	12	3.2	42	2.8
09	Measles & German Measles	1	0.9		0.3	2	0.1
10	Mumps	-	-	-	-	-	-
11	Poliomyelitis	4	0.35	0	-	4	0.3
12	Rheumatic Fever	51	4.6	14	3.8	65	4.4
13	Tetanus	1	0.9	-	-	1	0.1
14	Typhoid & Para typhoid fever	33	2.9	10	2.7	43	2.9
15	Whooping Cough	29	2.60	11	2.9	70	2.7
16	Tuberculosis	14	1.2	3	0.8	17	1.1
17	Sexually transmitted disease	1	0.9	1	0.3	2	0.1
18	Asthma, bronchitis	22	1.9	5	1.3	27	1.8
19	Pleuriary	4	0.4	-	-	4	0.3
20	Pneumonia	3	0.3	-	-	3	0.2
21	Epilepsy	3	0.3	-	-	3	0.2
22	Other mental disease	5	0.4	2	0.3	6	0.4
23	Cancer	4	0.4	2	0.5	10	0.7
24	Diarrhoea & Gastro-enteritis	36	3.2	6	1.6	42	2.8
25	Dysentery	8	0.7	2	0.5	10	0.7
26	Food Poisoning	2	0.2	-	-	2	0.1

Table Contd.

Table 6: Contd.

1	2	3	4	5	6	7	8
27	Gastritis/gastric peptic/duodenaulcer	26	2.3	5	1.3	31	2.1
28	Jaundice, disease of liver	8	0.7	-	-	8	0.5
29	Disease of kidney	3	0.3	1	0.3	4	0.3
30	Arthritis, gout, rheumatism	14	1.3	9	2.4	23	1.5
31	Diabetes	1	0.09	-	-	1	0.1
32	Goitre, disease of thyroid gland	4	0.4	1	0.3	5	0.3
33	Cerebral blood pressure	-	-	1	0.3	1	0.1
34	High blood pressure	4	0.4	3	0.8	7	0.5
35	Low blood pressure	4	0.4	3	0.8	7	0.5
36	Heart disease & coronary thrombosis	26	2.3	1	2.9	37	2.5
37	Nerves & general debility	19	1.7	5	1.3	38	2.5
38	Anaemia	-	-	1	0.3	1	0.1
39	Beri Beri	1	0.09	-	-	1	0.1
40	Epidemic dropsy	1	0.09	-	-	1	0.1
41	Rickets	-	-	-	-	-	-
42	Scurvy	-	-	-	-	-	-
43	Other Mal-nutritinal disease	-	-	-	-	-	-
44	Disease of mouth, teeth and gum	10	0.9	3	0.8	13	0.9
45	Disease of eye	28	2.5	11	2.9	39	2.6
46	Disease of ear, nose and throat	12	1.1	8	2.1	20	1.3
47	Disease/ailment relating to pregnancy & child birth (exclude delivery)	35	3.1	12	.2	47	3.2
48	Skin disease	38	3.4	11	2.9	3	0.2
49	Piles	3	0.3	-	-	3	0.2
50	Injury due to accident and viole	38	3.4	20	5.4	58	3.9
90	Other diagnosed ailment	485	43.6	154	41.3	639	43.0
99	Ailment not diagnosed or not known	31	2.8	11	2.9	42	2.8
00	Missing	6	0.5	5	1.3	11	0.7

Table 7: Morbidity Pattern of Inpatients by Rural and Urban

Code	Name of the Disease	Rural No.	(N = 1113) %	Urban No.	(N=373) %	Total No.	(N=1486) %
1	2	3	4	5	6	7	8
01	Chicken Pox	2	0.58	-	-	2	0.4
02	Cholera	-	-	-	-	-	-
03	Influenza	-	-	-	-	-	-
04	Diphtheria	2	0.58	1	0.9	3	0.7
05	Encephalitis	-	-	-	-	-	-
06	Filariasis	1	0.29	1	0.9	2	0.4
07	Leprosy	2	0.58	-	-	2	0.4
08	Malaria	7	2.03	7	6.1	14	3.0
09	Measles & German Measles	-	-	-	-	-	-
10	Mumps	-	-	-	-	-	-
11	Poliomyelitis	4	1.16	-	-	4	3.0
12	Rheumatic Fever	5	1.45	5	4.4	10	2.2
13	Tetanus	2	0.6	-	-	2	0.4
14	Typhoid & Para typhoid fever	21	6.10	7	6.1	28	6.1
15	Whooping Cough	10	2.9	3	2.6	30	2.8
16	Tuberculosis	11	3.2	1	0.9	12	2.6
17	Sexually transmitted disease	-	-	-	-	-	-
18	Asthma, bronchitis	8	2.3	3	2.6	11	2.4
19	Pleuriary	1	0.3	1	0.9	2	0.4
20	Pneumonia	1	0.3	1	0.9	2	0.4
21	Epilepsy	-	-	-	-	-	-
22	Other mental disease	8	2.3	-	-	8	1.7
23	Cancer	8	2.3	4	3	12	2.6
24	Diarrhoea & Gastro-enteritis	20	5.8	7	6.1	27	5.9
25	Dysentry	3	0.9	2	0.8	5	1.1
26	Food Poisoning	-	-	-	-	-	-

Table Contd.

Table 7: Contd.

1	2	3	4	5	6	7	8
27	Gastritis/gastric peptic/duoldenaulcer	33	9.6	5	4.4	38	8.3
28	Jaundice, disease of fiver	6	1.7	2	1.8	8	1.7
29	Disease of kidney	5	1.5	3	2.6	8	1.7
30	Arthritis, gout, rheumatism	2	0.6	3	2.6	5	1.1
31	Diabetes	3	0.9	-	-	3	0.7
32	Goitre, disease of thyroid gland	2	0.6	-	-	2	0.4
33	Cerebral blood pressure	1	0.3	-	-	1	0.2
34	High blood pressure	-	-	6	5.3	6	1.3
35	Low blood pressure	1	0.3	-	-	1	0.2
36	Heart disease & coronary thrombosis	12	3.5	2	1.8	14	3.1
37	Nerves & general debility	13	3.8	3	2.6	16	3.5
38	Anamia	1	0.3	-	-	1	0.2
39	Beri beri	-	-	-	-	-	-
40	Epidemic dropsy	-	-	-	-	-	-
41	Rickets	-	-	-	-	-	-
42	Scurvy	-	-	-	-	-	-
43	Other Mal-nutritional disease	1	0.3	-	-	1	0.2
44	Disease of mouth, teeth and g	1	0.3	-	-	1	0.2
45	Disease of eye	12	3.5	3	2.6	15	3.3
46	Disease of ear, nose and throat	2	0.6	-	-	2	0.4
47	Disease/ailment relating pregnancy & child birth (exclude delivery	29	8.4	8	7.0	37	8.1
48	Skin disease	6	1.7	1	0.9	7	1.5
49	Piles	2	0.6	-	-	2	0.4
50	Injury due to accident and viol	27	7.8	7	6.1	34	7.4
90	Other diagnosed ailment	15	14.5	16	14.0	66	14.4
99	Ailment not diagnosed or not k	12	3.5	6	12.3	18	3.9
00	Missing	7	2.0	6	12.3	13	2.8

Cost of Treatment and Willingness to pay

Backett, M. (1977) argues that in health services poor may actually face a triple penalty for poverty. They are poor, and partly as a result of this they have worse health and more sickness than other groups; and yet they tend to get less or worse medical care than other groups. This section presents the total cost of medical treatment per each illness episode.

Costs represent the resources given up in a particular situation in order to carry out an activity. For the sake of convenience and comparability they are usually expressed in terms of money. Costs are not the same as prices, which reflect a market rate of exchange. As a result of the concept of scarcity, economists refer to the opportunity costs' of an action. By this, they mean the alternative actions (by implication the next best), that could have occurred if one had not gone ahead with the chosen action. For example, the opportunity cost of training one doctor might be the alternative of training two nurses.

The concept of opportunity cost has not been used in the present analysis, since the opportunity cost of an illness of a rich man (Utility of mandays lost) may be many times more than that in the case of a poor man. In the present study, we have enquired about the actual amount spent on treatment of the illness under the heads of tests, medicines/fees, transport, nursing home changes for inpatients and other expenditure. We have also asked the respondent how much he was willing to pay to treat the patient vis-a-vis actual expenditure incurred.

Table 8 presents the cost of treatment per illness episode (both in-patient and out-patient) and willingness to pay for the treatment. While the cost of treatment as outpatient is Rs. 288/- in rural areas, it is Rs. 230/- in the urban areas. However, the Urbanites are willing to pay 86 per cent of the cost incurred, while the rural people are willing to pay only 63 per cent. This is understandable because the average income levels of the urban population are higher than those of rural people and hence ability to pay will be more. The cost of treating in-patients in rural areas is Rs. 1954 as against Rs. 911 in urban areas. The rural people are willing to pay a higher proportion of the costs than their urban counter parts (72% as against 68%).

People's Choices

In order to ascertain the people's choices regarding the type of doctor consulted during the first and referral visits, the respondents were asked to state's whether the patient is taken to some other doctor, prior to coming to this doctor (current visit). All those visited two doctors/centres are asked to state the type of doctor (Govt. Private, Indian system of medicine, traditional/Unqualified that they had consulted then and now.

Out of 1486 illness episodes (non-hospitalisation cases) 945 (63.6 per cent) have reported to have consulted another doctor before consulting the present one. A turn over table is presented for the 945 cases. The table 9 clearly brings out the people's choices for consultation at the primary as well as the referral levels.

The peoples' choices at the first as well as the secondary level consultation is clearly towards the private doctors. While only 71 per cent of the out-patients consulted private doctors at the first level, the percentage increased to 78 per cent at the secondary level. While 69 per cent shifted from one private hospital to another private hospital, 8 per cent shifted from government to private one, and the remaining changed from other types of doctors.

As regards the use of referral systems in the government hospitals, while 25 per cent approached government hospitals in the first visits, only 17 per cent visited them in the current visit. Only 16 per cent retained the referral status with the government hospitals.

Table 8: Cost of Treatment and Willingness to pay (Rupees)

		Impatients	*Outpatients*
Cost of Treatment	Rural	2703.00	288.00
	Urban	1343.00	230.00
	Total	363.00	273.00
Willingness to pay	Rural	1954	181.00
	Urban	911.00	199.00
	Total	1694.00	186.00
Percentage in the cost	Rural	72.00	63.00
	Urban	68.00	86.00
	Total	72.00	68.00

Table 9: Turnover Table for Outpatients

Current Visit *First Visit*	*Govt. Doctor*	*Private Doctor*	*ISM Doctor*	*Traditional/ Unqualified Doctor*	*Total*
Govt. Doctor	150 (15.9)	78 (8.3)	1 (0.1)	3 (0.3)	232 (24.6)
Private Doctor	9 (0.9)	654 (69.2)	3 (0.3)	2 (0.2)	668 (70.7)
ISM Doctor	-	1 (0.1)	6 (0.6)	-	7 (0.7)
Traditional/ Unqualified Doctor	1 (0.1)	7 (0.7)	-	30 (3.2)	38 (4.0)
Total	**160** **(16.9)**	**740** **(78.3)**	**10** **(1.1)**	**35** **(3.7)**	**945** **(100.00)**

Table 10: Turnover Table for In-Patients

Current Hospitalization *Doctor Consulted before hospitalization*	*Govt.*	*Private*	*Others*	*Total*
Govt.	26 (5.15)	68 (16.10)		94 (2.2)
Private	23 (5.44)	287 (57.85)	7 (1.65)	317 (74.94)
Others	1 (0.24)	9 (2.13)	2 (0.47)	12 (2.84)
Total	**50** **(1.82)**	**364** **(86.05)**	**9** **(2.13)**	**423** **(100.00)**

The turnover table 10 also presents a similar picture with regard to the inpatients. While 75 per cent visited private hospital earlier to the hospitalisation, 86 per cent have been admitted in them now. About 16 per cent have shifted from government to private hospitals. In the government hospitals only 5 per cent have retained the referral status.

In this scenario, there is an urgent need to strengthen the government referral hospitals for achieving equity in health care delivery system and providing quality care to the poor people.

Client Satisfaction

The inpatient household respondents are asked whether they are satisfied with the services provided by both public and private institutions in which the patients are treated. They are asked to give codes for very poor (Code-I). Poor (Code-2), Satisfactory (Code-3), good (Code-4), very good (Code-5). The data are presented in Table 11.

A higher number of respondents have reported very poor and poor services in Govt. hospitals than Private hospitals. In Govt. hospitals the behaviour of compounder, technician and Class-IV employees are the most dissatisfaction part of client satisfaction. Cleanliness and doctor's examination are also found to be the causes of dissatisfaction.

In Private hospitals, most of the services are found to be satisfactory or good. Cleanliness and behaviour of the nontechnical staff are the causes of dissatisfaction.

Reasons for Client Dissatisfaction

The inpatient household respondents are asked "What is the level of satisfaction of the services provided by the hospital?", accordingly codes are given as follows: 1-very poor, 2-poor, 3-satisfactory, 4-good and 5-very good. Those who give codes 1 and 2 were asked to state the reasons for dissatisfaction. The data are presented in Table 12.

Out of 458 inpatients, 240 (52 per cent) reported that they have very poor and poor levels of satisfaction. Out of

Table 11: Client Satisfaction (Government)

S.No.	Client Satisfaction	Satisfaction Codes					
		Very Poor	*Poor*	*Satisfaction*	*Good*	*Very Good*	*Missing*
1.	Admission Procedure/OP Counter	3 (5.0)	10 (6.7)	30 (50.0)	8 (13.3)	5 (8.3)	4 (6.7)
2.	Facilities at Waiting room	2 (3.3)	15 (25.0)	33 (55.0)	9 (15.0)	-	1 (1.7)
3.	Doctor's Examination	2 (3.3)	6 (10.0)	523 (86.7)	-	-	-
4.	Behaviour of the compounder at Injections/Medicines counter	3 (5.0)	16 (26.7)	21 (35.0)	1 (20.0)	- (13.3)	8
5.	Behaviour of Technician at	1 (1.7)	12 (20.0)	22 (36.7)	8 (13.3)	1 (1.7)	16 (26.7)
6.	Behaviour of Class IV employees Thoties/Wardboys)	3 (5.0)	19 (31.7)	18 (30.0)	5 (8.3)	-	14 (23.3)
7.	Cleanliness in the hospital	3 (5.0)	3 (5.0)	17 (28.3)	28 (46.7)	5 (8.3)	4 (6.7)
8.	Cleanliness in Lavatory/Bathroom	3 (5.0)	23 (38.3)	16 (26.7)	9 (15.0)	2 (3.3)	7 (11.7)

Table 11: Contd.

	Client Satisfaction (Private)						
1.	Admission Procedure/OP counter	1 (0.3)	6 (1.6)	239 (62.6)	57 (14.9)	30 (7.9)	49 (12.8)
2.	Fecilities at Waiting room	1 (0.3)	5 (1.3)	123 (2.2)	230 (60.2)	22 (5.6)	1 (0.3)
3.	Doctor's Examination	-	-	-	161 (42.1)	221 (57.9)	- -
4.	Behaviour of the compounder at Injections/Medicines counter	1 (0.3)	4 (1.1)	241 (63.1)	94 (24.6)	32 (8.4)	10 (2.6)
5.	Behaviour of Technician at	1 (0.3)	5 (1.3)	193 (50.5)	88 (23.0)	15 (3.9)	80 (20.9)
6.	Behaviour of Class IV employees (Thorites/Wardboys)	2 (0.5)	15 (3.9)	123 (32.2)	172 (45.0)	17 (4.5)	53 (13.9)
7.	Cleanliness in the hospital	5 (1.3)	39 (10.2)	178 (46.5)	70 (18.3)	24 (6.3)	66 (17.3)
8.	Cleanliness in Lavatory Bathroom	5 (1.3)	39 (10.2)	178 (46.50)	70 (1.3)	24 (6.3)	66 (17.3)

240,136 (57 per cent) have been treated in Govt. hospitals and 104 (43 per cent) in Private hospitals. The three most important reasons for dissatisfaction in Govt. hospitals are unhelpful attitude of paramedical and other staff 47 per cent), inadequate supply of drugs (15 per cent) and unhelpful attitude of doctors (6.6 per cent). The corresponding percentages in Private hospitals are 34 per cent. 17 per cent and one per cent respectively. Thus it is clearly established that client friendly relationship between health staff and patients has to be improved in Govt. hospitals for achieving higher levels of client satisfaction.

World Bank's Health Sector Reforms—A Critical View

The title of the World Development Report 1993 "Investing in Health" perhaps gives a wrong focus on health policy of the developing countries because it may consider health expenditure as an investment. Illness may affect overall production, either, through absenteeism or by lowering productivity through its & debilitating effects. Such a view of health, as primarily an investment good or means to an end rather than as an end in itself, persists in some quarters, although its influence has been reduced by a variety of factors. First is the recognition that growth in GNP does not by itself lead to the form of development, but often, instead to a widening of inequalities in a society, with little alleviation of the condition of the poorest. Second comes the recognition that the health state of an individual, particularly within an agricultural economy affected by seasonal variations with periods of under-employment and family based labour system, may not have the expected effect on production levels. And third is the fact that the effects of such a strategy, 11 taken to its logical conclusion, on provision for health for non-productive groups, such as the elderly, could be unacceptable (Green, 1992).

In the on-going structural adjustment process (SAP) health sector obviously is affected by cutbacks in public spending, privatisation of government enterprises; freezing

Table 12: Reasons Reported by the Respondents for Very Poor and Poor Client Satisfaction Level.

Sl. No.	Reasons	Govt. Hospitals			Private Hospital		
		Rural (N=85)	Urban (N=51)	Total (N=136)	Rural (N=80)	Urban (N=24)	Total (N=104)
1.	Admission Procedure/OP Counter	3 (3.5)	8 (15.7)	11 (8.1)	3 (3.7)	1 (4.2)	4 (3.8)
2.	Facilities at Waiting room	6 (7.0)	3 (5.9)	9 (6.6)	1 (1.3)	- -	1 (0.9)
3.	Doctor's Examination	43 (50.6)	21 (41.2)	64 (47.1)	25 (31.3)	10 (41.7)	35 (33.7)
4.	Behaviour of the compounder at Injections Medicines counter	3 (3.5)	1 (1.9)	4 (2.9)	6 (7.5)	2 (8.3)	8 (7.7)
5.	Behaviour of Technician at	3 (3.5)	-	3 (.2)	3 (3.7)	-	3 (2.9)
6.	Behaviour of Class IV employees (Thoties/Wardboys)	17 (20.0)	4 (7.8)	21 (15.4)	18 (2.5)	- -	18 (17.3)
7.	Cleanliness in the hospital	2 (2.4)	4 (7.8)	6 (4.4)	-	6 (25.0)	6 (5.7)
8.	Cleanliness in Lavatory Bathroom	8 (9.4)	9 (17.6)	17 (12.5)	24 (30.0)	5 (20.8)	29 (27.9)

of wages and freeing of prices; increase of production for export rather than for local consumption; creating incentives to attract foreign capital and reducing government deficits by changing user fees for social services (Wermer, D., 1995). The World Bank has recently conceded that the SAP may cause temporary hardships for low income families, but in the long run the benefits will somehow trickle down to the poor. But, the evidence appears to be very much adverse in the Third World health (Danher, K., 1994), Poor and socially disadvantageous sections in the developing countries should not be deprived of quality of health care under any circumstances, just because of their lower productivity in the economy.

Health Sector Reforms in Andhra Pradesh

In recent years there was a rapid decentralisation of public health care management system in Andhra Pradesh, Prior to 1967, there were only two Directorates-one for Medical Services and Drug Control, and the other for Public Health and Food (Health) Authority and family planning. In November 1976, a separate department headed by Drugs Controller and Food (Health) Authority was created for effective implementation of Food Adulteration Act. In 1979, two separate departments were created for Medical and Health and Family Welfare. In 1981, a separate directorate for Medical Educational has been formed, which looks after Medical Colleges, teaching hospitals, specialist hospitals and nursing colleges. During 1986-87, the State Government has created an autonomous body called the Andhra Pradesh Vaidya Vidhana Parishad (APVVP) (Commissionerate) for improving the infrastructure in various hospitals at the secondary level by augmenting its resources through mobilising donations and external funding. Recognising the potential for developing a model for health sector reforms in Andhra Pradesh, the World Bank has sanctioned a Project called A.P. First Referral Health System Project which has to be implemented during 1994-95 to 2001-02 with an estimated cost of 159 million US$ of which 133 million US$ is the World

Bank assistance and 26 million US$ is the share of the Government of Andhra.

The state Medical and Health Department has four major Directorates Medical, Health, Family Welfare and APVVP. In addition there are six smaller Directorates-AIDS Programme, School Health Programme, Preventive Medicine. Employees State Insurance (ESI), Indian System of Medicine (ISM) and Drug Control.

In 1987-88, University of Health Sciences has been established by affiliating all Medical Colleges in the state with a view to achieve uniformity in the standards of Medical Education.

In February 1997, an expert committee headed by Dr. K. Subba Rao, former Health Advisor to the Government of Andhra Pradesh submitted a report for streamlining the health care delivery, development and management system in Andhra Pradesh. The main purpose of setting up this Expert Committee, constituted by this Government in its G.0. Rt. No. 1419 dated 16.08.1996, was to examine how health care services could be better delivered within the state, with specific reference to the scope for improvement of the Government Health Systems.

The following are some of the recommendations for the Health Sector Reforms.

1 The medical code should be finalised as quickly as possible in the interest of improving the quality of health care.

2. It shall be the duty of the Hospital Development Committee to review and supervise all aspects of the functioning of the hospital including budgeting and raising of additional resources.

3. The proposal of the previous committee constituted to go into the issue of neutralised drug purchase be accepted into.

4. A strong referral system should be put in place for improving the cost effectiveness of health care being provided.
5. A regulatory authority should be set-up to inspect, certify and regulate private health facilities.
6. Adequate incentives in the form of subsidy for infrastructure and interest rebate should be provided to doctors willing to set-up facilities at remote and uncovered areas.
7. The private sector must be encouraged to set-up training institutions for delivering more para-medicos and technicians to the medical sector.
8. Efforts should be made through the Hospital development societies to explore avenues to raise revenues through better use of common facilities.
9. User changes should be levied after certain minimum basic services are provided at the hospitals.
10. In view of the critical nature of Hospital services not only should strikes be banned but employees should be governed only by CCA rules and not covered under the Industrial Disputes Act.
11. Every Government health institution should clearly display all facilities available at the hospital, the broad range of treatments available and also the drugs available prominently.
12. Privatize the cleaning services.
13. University of Health Services be given the task of developing and monitoring the introduction of a course in Family Medicine in all teaching institutions.

Policy Recommendations

Most of the people are willing to pay for better quality medical care services. This obviously paves the way for promoting health insurance scheme. On a trial basis, all public and private sector employee families should be brought under Health Insurance Scheme by making mandatory for employers to pay 50 per cent of the premium. This reduces pressure on government hospitals, so as to enable the government to focus on informal, unorganised and rural sectors. The health insurance scheme certainly promotes competition among private hospitals and help improve the quality of health care. Unfortunately health care needs are greater among those with least ability to pay. At any cost the targeted poor should be provided free health care at all levels. The star hospitals in private sector should be enforced to treat the poor, the stipulated 10 per cent of their patients, since they get huge concessions in land, capital and equipment costs. Governments, should be regulating authorities, but not regularising bodies.

Doctors in government hospitals are the most influential section of the society. Any attempt of strict enforcement of service rules are either stalled or diluted. In consultation with the staff associations, a code of conduct has to be designed so as to ensure doctors to stay at the places of work and attend to the work with greater commitment. If government fails to reform the public health sector, the institutions may be leased out for a specified period to prominent NGOs with good track record of working in the health aspects by adopting social control on user charges.

The study clearly brings out that the preferences of people towards referral services are for private medical care. These who can afford certainly prefer private hospitals and those who cannot afford only go to government hospitals. Thus users of the existing health facilities are the very poor and the FRUs amply demonstrate this with poor environmental sanitation, maintenance of buildings and equipment and the non-availability of drugs. The situations requires immediate attention of the government.

Introduction of user charges for selective services may be necessary. China has experimented this and reported to have succeeded in achieving quality of care even to the poor (Bogg et al. 1996). Wards in FRUs may be divided into paid and free Wards. Paid wards generate surplus funds to meet the costs of poor patients in free wards.

Unfortunately Health Transition Research in India as well as in Andhra Pradesh is almost non existent Government should encourage research in Health Transition Processes, if necessary, through action research for developing feasible strategies for improving health status and also reducing inter-regional and intergroup variations.

References

Backett, M. (1977), Health Services in F. Williams. Why the poor pay more, Macmillion.

Bhore Committee Report (1946).

Bogg, L. et al. The cost of coverage: Rural Health Insurance in China/ Health Policy and Planning, Vol. 11(3).

Danher, El. (1994), *Fifty years is enough: The case against the World Bank and* IMF, South End Press, Bosen, MA.

Gopalakrishna Kumar, B. (1993), Low Mortality and High Morbidity in Kerala *Reconsidered, Population and Development Review,* Vol. 19, No. 1.

Gopalan, C. et. al. (1977), *Nutritive value of Indian Foods,* NIN, ICMR.

Green Andrew (1992), *An Introduction to Health Planning in Developing* Countries, Oxford University Press.

Kamalamma, G. (1996), *Health and Nutrition Status in India,* APH Publishing Corporation.

NCAER (1995), Household Survey of Health Care Utilisation and Expenditure, Working Paper No. 53.

Nirmala, A. and Parthasarathy. G. (1995), Human Development Policies and Strategy in Urban Slums—A Case Study of Two slums in Visakhapatnam City, IDPS, Visakhapatnam.

Planning Commission (1993), The report of the expert group on estimation of Proportion and number of poor. Perspective Planning Division, Govt. of India, New Delhi.

Ramachandrudu, G. et. al. (1992), National Family Health survey-Andhra Pradesh, Population Research Centre (PRC), Waltair & IIPS Bombay.

Rani Gopal K. (1987) Economic of Health and Nutrition-Some aspects of Growth and Welfare, Chug Publications.

Swarajya Laximi, B. et al. (1992), Evaluation of Primary Health Care Delivery Systems in Visakhapatnam City, IDPS, Visakhapatnam.

Wermer, D. (1995), Turning Health into an Investment-Assaults on third world Health Care, Economic and Political Weakly, January 21, 1995.

World Bank (1993), World Development Report, Oxford University Press.

23

Health Implications of the Census of India-2001

Prof. (Smt) Rani Gopal

Introduction

The Census of India, 2001 throws light on literacy which has tremendous impact on life expectancy and infant mortality rate. These two factors are indicators of health status and the literacy is one of the crucial non-health care determinants of the health status of the people. The shifts in these variables and the relationship between the literacy rate and the other two parameters clearly shows the existing health standards of the people, so as to adopt required policies and measures.

Literacy and Health Status

We are all aware of the fact that the Directive Principles of the Indian Constitution lay emphasis on the provision of educational facilities. Literacy rate is one of the social characteristics, about which information is collected in every census. The increase in the literacy rate influences the decisions at the micro level regarding the utilization of health services, as it leads to health consciousness. In fact intake of nutritious food, income earning capacity, success of immunization programmes, maternal and child health population control and better utilization of available basic services, i.e., water supply and sanitation are all influenced by the variations in literacy rate.

The Human Development Report 1990 brought out by UNDP, highlighted the link between literacy and health status, while presenting the comparative profile of India. Pakistan and Sri Lanka. It has been observed that the literacy rate was 43, 30 and 87 per cent in these countries and the life expectancy at birth was 59, 58 and 71 in the respective nations. It clearly shows that health status as indicated by life expectancy is high, where literacy rate is high.[1]

The agreement adopted at the International Conference on population and Development (ICPD) at Cairo in 1994, focused on improving health, educational opportunities and individual rights, especially for women as a way to stablize growth of population and promote sustainable development The ICPD goals for 2015 include reduction of IMR to below 35 infant deaths per 1000 live births and increasing life expectancy at birth to more than 75 years and to achieve Universal access to and completion of primary education and to ensure the widest and earliest possible access by girls and women to secondary and higher levels of education. The UN sponsored ICPD remains the largest international population conference to date. At the ICPD 11000 representatives from Governments, non-governmental organizations and inter-governmental agencies forged to comprehensive agreement that provided a new vision for future population and development policies.[2] The UN Millennium Declaration indicated collective responsibility to uphold the principles of human dignity equality and equity at the global level. The balance sheet of human development goals, achievements and unfinished path emphasized enrolment of children in primary school, so as to achieve universal completion of Primary Schooling and reduction of IMR besides other important goals.[9] The above-mentioned facts clearly indicate the

1. UNDP Human Development Report, 1990.
2. Population Reference Bureau, *Measure Communication*. Washington, USA, January 2000, p. 1.
3. *Human Development Report 2001*. UNDP, New York, Oxford University Press, 2001, pp. 21-22.

necessity to view literacy and health status together, as they are complementary to each other. Even if we provide excellent health facilities, it may not lead to an enhancement in the health status of the people, if the utilization of the health services is not up to the mark (particularly regarding rural areas and low income groups). Here lies the crucial role of literacy because literacy leads to awareness of the existing health services—both preventive and curative i.e., health consciousness.

Impact of Literacy on health Status

An attempt has been made to find the relationship between literacy rate (Z) i.e., independent variable and the indicators of health status i.e., life expectancy (X) and IMR per 1000 births (Y). The correlation coefficient of X and Z is 0.99, indicating positive and almost perfect correlation between the two variables. A similar high negative association is found between Y and Z. The correlation coefficient is –0.97.

As the variables are highly correlated, a two variable linear relationship is estimated, for studying the impact of literacy rate on the other two variables.

(1) $X = 21.57^{*} + 0.6710^{*} Z \qquad r^2 = 0.9738$
$\quad (9.06) \qquad (12.19)$

(2) $Y = 188.92^{*} - 1.8676^{*} Z \qquad r^2 = 0.9363$
$\quad (17.93) \qquad (7.66)$

* Significant at 1 per cent level.

From the first regression equation, one can conclude that for every one unit of increase in literacy rate, life expectancy at birth increases by 0.67 units. The regression coefficient is significant at 1 per cent level. It is also seen from F2 that 97 per cent of the variation in life expectancy at birth is explained by the literacy rate.

The second regression analysis revealed that for every one unit increase in the independent variable literacy rate, the dependent variable IMR declined by 1.87 units. The regression coefficient in significant at 1 per cent level. Moreover, the value of goodness of fit depicts that 94 per cent of the variation in IMR is explained by the literacy rate. On the basis of above analysis, it may be pointed out that literacy, a non-health care determinant of health status is quiet crucial.

Table 1: Basic Indicators of Human Development—India

Year	*Life Expectancy at Birth (years)* X	*Infant Mortality Rate (per thousand births)* Y	*Literacy Rate (per cent)* Z
1951	32.1	146	18.3
1961	41.3	146	28.3
1971	45.6	129	34.5
1981	50.4	110	43.6
1991	59.4	80	52.2
2001	63.2	70	65.4

Source: Economic Surveys, 1999-2000 and 2000-2001.

In this context it is worth mentioning about health transition. India is still in the second stage of health transition characterized by low mortality and high morbidity. In the words of Dr. C. Gopalan we are only prolonging the lives of these who are in the substandard state of Health.[4] It has been rightly pointed out by Director WHO in his address that 'health Expectancy' is more important and that life expectancy without health expectancy is an empty prize.[5] In our country one has to concentrate on the enhancement of life expectancy and health expectancy. In this context literacy has got to play a key role. Of course we have achieved some success regarding life expectancy as visualized from (Table 2) the changes in the percentage of population in the three major age groups i.e., 0-14, 15-59, and 60+. The composition in 1981 was 3970, 54.09 and 6.21 and in 2001 it is 31.87, 60.50 and 7.63. Table 3 also throws light on indicators of health, which clearly reveal that mortality has gone down significantly. But

4. C. Gopalan Population Problem, Need for a total View, *Economic and Political weekly*, Vol. XXV No. 33, August 18, 1990, pp. 1827-28.
5. Director, WHO, *WHO Report*, 1997, p. 1.

Table 2: Percentage of Population in Three Major Age Groups 1981-2001

	1981			1986			1991			1996			2001		
	Persons	*Males*	*Females*	*Persons*	*Males*	*Females*	*Persons*	*Males*	*Females*	*Persons*	*Males*	*Females*	*Persons*	*Males*	*Females*
0-14	39.70	39.60	47.71	37.70	37.50	37.90	35.55	35.43	35.69	33.93	33.90	33.97	31.87	31.86	31.88
15-59	54.09	54.26	46.84	56.03	56.33	55.72	57.91	58.13	57.67	59.03	59.17	58.89	60.50	60.64	60.35
60+	6.21	6.14	5.45	6.27	6.17	6.38	6.54	6.44	6.64	7.03	6.93	7.14	7.63	7.50	7.78

Source: Census Data.

Table 3: Selected Health Indicators

	Parameter	*1951*	*1981*	*1991*	*Current Levels*
1.	Crude birth Rate (per 1000 population	40.8	33.9 (SRS)	25.5* (SRS)	26.1 (SRS 99)
2.	Crude Death Rate (P = 1000 population)	25.1	12.5 (SRS)	9.8* (SRS)	8.7 (SRS 99)
3.	Total Fertility Rate (Per woman on average)	6.0	4.5 (SRS)	3.6* (SRS)	3.2 (SRS 98)
4.	Maternal Mortality Rate (per 100,000 live births)	NA	NA	437 (1992-93)	407 (1998)
5.	Infant Mortality Rate (Per 1000 live births)	146 (1951-1961)	110 (SRS)	80* (SRS)	70.0 (SRS 99)
6.	Child Mortality Rate (0-4 Years, per 1000 children)	57.3 (1972)	41.2 (SRS)	26.5 (SRS)	22.5 (SRS 98)
7.	Couple Protection Rate (%)	10.4 (1971)	22.8	44.1	46.2 (31.3.2000)
8.	Life Expectancy at birth (in years) Male Female	37.2 36.2	54.1 54.7	59.2 60.9 (1991-95)	60.4 61.8 (1993-97)

* Excludes J.&K.

SRS = Sample Registration System of Office of Registrar General, India (Except for the year 1951)

Source: Office of Registrar General, India.

Source: Economic Survey 2001-2002, p. 257.

still there is a long way to go to achieve higher levels of life expectancy. Greater access to quality health care, technological advances and the development of infrastructure facilities have all lead to a decline in mortality.

But still morbidity or burden of sickness continues to be high. Although communicable diseases constitute the important cause for mortality and morbidity, with increase in life expectancy the epidemiological transition is underway resulting in an increase in non-communicable diseases. Though a substantial infrastructure for providing primary health care has been created in rural and urban areas, the issues of inequitable distribution of existing institutions and manpwoer, poor functioning due to mismatch between personnel and infrastructure, requirement of skill upgradation of personnel and lack of appropriate referral system need to be paid attention. These have been emphasised during the ninth five year plan. Strengthening of secondary health care infrastructure i.e., district hospitals to cater to referrals, from community health centers/first referral units and provision of adequate diagnostics, consumable and drugs etc., are other priority areas.[6]

India is the second country in the world to cross the one billion mark, but the health status is low due to high morbidity. Malaria continues to be a major public health problem with 1.91 million (prov) cases being reported during 2000. TB is a major problem and nearly one third of global TB incidence is in India. Leprosy is now at an incidence of one per 1000 population in 13 states. HIV/AIDS emerged as a serious problem besides others like Kala Azar and Blindness.[7]

We need to do a lot to raise health expectancy. Unfortunately ample and accurate morbidity data is not available. As primary health care approach found to be defective, now the trend is towards vertical disease care programmes. In the context of health for all by 21st century, technological medicine in emphasised.[8]

Conclusion

The principal goal of development policy is to create sustainable improvement in the quality of life for all people. Besides enhancing per capita income and consumption, concentration must also be on other objectives like expanding access to health services and educational levels.[9]

In fact the 1990's has seen important changes in the overall development paradigm and there is growing

6. *Economic Survey 2001-2002*. Government of India, Ministry of Finance, Economic Division, p. 259.
7. *Economic Survey 2001-2002*. Govt. of India, Ministry of Finance, Economic Division, p. 259-260.
8. EMMEL, "Health for all in the 21st Century" *Economic and Political Weekly*, March 14, 1998.
9. Entering the 21st Century *World Development Report 1999-2000*, p. 13.

international consensus that development cannot be merely equated with growth, but must aim at the triple objectives of income expansion, social development and environmental protection and regeneration. It is only then sustainable development can be attained.[10]

In conclusion it may be pointed out that for sustainable human development and economic development, it is highly essential to concentrate on the spread of literacy, which is a prominent non-health care determinant of health status.

10. Sudhir Anand and Lincoln Chen *Health Implication of Economic Policies*. A Frame work of Analysis UNDP discussion paper series 1999-2000, p. 5.

24

Structural Changes in the Indian Industry in Terms of Pollution Intensity

Dr. M. Sudha
Prof. C. Ratnam

Introduction

Industrialization is an engine for economic growth. Though economic growth is the concern of policy makers and economists, now a days every individual is paying attention to this problem. This is because, in the process of growth, the major part of the national resources are used to develop a technically upto-date, diversified national industry for a high rate of growth. But it also involves in production of wastes as a by-product, on the other hand, for which there is no market. Because of absence of market, these wastes simply thrown into the environment. When such non-assimilative and non-degradable wastes are thrown into the environment, causes environmental pollution and further threatens the balance of the eco-system.

According to Lester Brown, "as human pressures build the relationship between people and their natural support systems can cross key thresholds, leading to a breakdown. So policies that are economically successful in short run, can be ecologically disastrous in the long run."[1] In this context, the structure of the industry, with given technology, plays a crucial role.

According to the experiences of some industrialised nations, as economy's develop, the structure of the industry changes and its impact on its environmental quality also changes. Its relation-ship follows an inverted U-shape pattern[2]. A growing economy, in the first phase of industrialization consume large quantities of energy and uses increasing quantities of raw materials, thereby experiences increasing per capita income and consumption. It also experiences a rise in pollution levels. In the next phase, the industrial structure shifts from less pollution intensive to more pollution intensive industries. After this phase, the industry move towards technological changes, which works in lowering pollution intensity. In brief, in the process of development, many pollutants show an increasing tendency along with the raise in income levels. Further, there will be a declining trend in pollution intensity as the level of income increases.

These changes in the industrial structure and corresponding environmental pollution/problems are found consistent from the experiences of some of East-Asian Countries. The studies by Prof. Lucas (1992) and Prof. Lu (1992) examined the pollution intensity of industries with the changed structure of industrial sector due to development, for the five East Asian Countries-Taiwan, Thailand, Japan, Korea and Indonesia.

The study is concluded by following general observation, "In all countries mentioned above, the pace of industrial transformation has been rapid. The East and South-East Asian economies (excluding Japan) rank highest of any group of countries in the world on an index of structural change in industrial sector between 1975 and 1991, and suggest that types and volumes of pollutants discharged have also been changing rapidly. This change may further lead to increase in industrial production further in large quantities. Because of this the pollution may also become more concentrated".

For all industrialising nations mentioned above, the

environmental problems of prosperity are going to increase much more due to—automobile pollution, solid waste disposal, hazardous waste generated by new industries in the third phase of development.

Purpose of the Study

India is one among the countries where industrialization is taking place at a rapid rate. This status of industrializing nation is an outcome of deliberate and conscious planning, especially from second five-year plan. To achieve still higher growth and more real benefits out of industrialization, India is moving more rapidly on this selected path of industrialization. But, how far this race helps Indian economy to remain on the path of sustainable development in the long run, is an issue to be examined. This is because, the extent of environment deterioration depends on the size, structure, and growth of the industry and technology used in the industry coupled with the effectiveness of the government policies.

Many studies indicate that Indian industry experienced drastic changes in its structure and growth over the years. All these studies analyzed the structural changes on the basis of one or more of the factors i.e., size, ownership, use of the products and the type of inputs used, thereby to suggest a policy for promoting growth of the economy.

But by considering economic costs and benefits and excluding the factor like impact of industrial growth on the environment in the growth models/policies, a time may come when social costs surpasses the social benefits. Therefore, what is required is not just the higher growth of the industry in general, but the higher growth of the environmentally viable industries/industries using cleaner technologies.

For promoting industries on the path of sustainable development and articulate a policy accordingly, there is a need to study the structural changes in the industry in relation to its pollution intensity. The present study is a modest attempt to analyse the structural changes in the Indian industry in relation to its pollution intensity, to suggest, whether there is a need for regulation of changes that are occurring in the industry, or it can be left free to the economic forces, to determine the growth of economy.

Objective

To substantiate the necessity of this study in this direction, a brief explanation is made here in Section 2 about the types of pollutants released by various industries and their likely impact on environment and health, using the secondary information sources. The analysis and results of the study follows later.

1. To study the structural changes in the Indian industrial sector in terms of pollution intensity.
2. To give a brief account of type of industrial pollution and effects of pollution, on some life supporting systems.

Methodology

The main focus of this study is on the assessment of the pollution intensities caused by structural change of the industrial sector in the process of industrialization. Accordingly, industries are classified following the definitions given by the Pollution Control Board as (i) Red (the most pollution intensive industries); (ii) Orange (the medium pollution intensive industries) and (iii) Green (the least pollution intensive and eco-friendly industries). The lists of industries under these groups are furnished in Annexure. The distribution of industries falling under the Red, Orange and Green categories is the basis of the study of structural changes.

Accordingly, the structural changes are analysed in terms of the variation in the share of the one or more variable parameters viz., number of factories, number of employees, capital invested, value added, fuels used, raw materials used and total inputs used of all the above said variables. The conclusions are drawn based on the divergence in the results across these variables. The final conclusions are drawn especially on the basis of fuels consumed, raw materials used and total inputs used. Because, the pollution levels are more closely associated with the fuels used, raw material used and total inputs used (i.e. pollution intensity indicators), than with the other variables, with given technology.

Sources of Data

This study is based on the time series data drawn from secondary sources. The major secondary sources for the data on industries in India are CMI and ASI. The CMI data was available upto 1959. The ASI data are available from 1960. The NIC changed descriptions from 1973-74. As there are some variations in the definitions adopted by CMI and ASI, the two sets of data are not comparable. Therefore, this study is based only on the ASI data covering the period 1973-74 to 1993-94. The choice of the period is restricted mainly by the data availability. However such a choice may in no way stand as a limitation for the study of structural changes, because the period chosen is fairly large.

The study of structural changes comparing the values of the variables across the periods/points of time chosen (viz.) 1973-74, 1980-81, 1990-91 and 1993-94, broadly covers three periods i.e., the seventies, the eighties and the early nineties. Basing on various variables, the structural changes are studied in terms of the variations in percentages indicating the share of an industry/group of industries in the total of all industries.

Types of Industrial Pollution

According to the report of the Environmental Pollution Panel of the U.S. President's Science Advisory Committee (1965), Environmental Pollution can be defined as "the unfavourable alteration of our surroundings, wholly or largely, as a by-product of man's actions, through direct or indirect effects, of changes in energy pattern, radiation levels, chemical and physical constitution and abundance of organisms.[3]

In other words, pollution may be defined as the addition

of materials to air, water and soil. Which affects the quality of the environment adversely. So the environment gets polluted, may be due to a solid waste, radioactive waste, heat from thermal plants, gaseous pollutants, metals and other organic and inorganic compounds. Mostly, the industries are the major source.

Many industries like paper and pulp, distillery, steel and iron, sugar, inorganic chemicals, textiles, electroplating and heat treatment, hydrogenated oil and soaps, oils, tanneries, dairy and dairy products, fertilizers, petroleum refinery, rubber, cement, explosives, metal containers, paints, and varnishes, plastic, food processing units, beverages, synthetic, bakeries, brass, cane manufacturing, plywood manufacturing, phosphorous mining, coal mining, photographic processing, antibiotics, wood turpentine, fluorine, cyanide compounds and thermal plants—release various pollutants like CO_2 (carbondioxide), CO (carbon monoxide), dust, SPM (suspended particulate matter), dust silica, sulphur dioxide (SO_2), nitrogen dioxide (NO_2), nitrous oxides (NO_x), fluorine, sulphur oxides (SO_x), cadmium, chlorine, chromium, copper, iron, lead, zinc, manganese, mercury, oil and grease, phenol, phosphates and silver through effluents and emissions[4]. Some of these pollutants are released into air, some, in water and some, on the soil. Thus industrialization causes air, water and soil pollution.

Air Pollution

According to WHO, substances put into air by the activity of mankind into concentration sufficient to cause harmful effect to his health, vegetables, and property or to interfere with the enjoyment of his property is known as air pollution.[5]

In other words, air pollution is "the presence in the outdoor atmosphere of one or more air pollutants in such quantities and duration which tend to be injurious to human health or welfare, animal or plant lives, or would unreasonably interfere with the enjoyment of life and property."[6]

An air pollutant does not have to be inhaled; it becomes a pollutant merely by being in air. Major sources of air pollution are transportation, domestic heating, electric power generation, refuse burning, industrial fuel burning and process emissions. Out of these, industries are one of the major sources.[6] Industry pollutes the environment by emissions of hazardous gases and industrial dust. The chemical composition of these emissions in different industries depends on the type of fuels, raw materials and technology used.

Among the various industries, major sources of air pollution are nuclear power plants, thermal power plants, cement industry, basic metal and alloys industries, sulphuric acid plants, nitric acid plants, foundries, chloralkalin industries, plastic industry, kraft, paper & pulp, coal cleaning and refuse, grain mills and grain handling.[8] There are 5 primary air pollutants causing 90 per cent of global air pollution. They are Carbon monoxide (CO), nitrogen oxides (NO_x), hydrocarbons (HC), sulphur oxides (SO_x) and particulate matter. Apart from these, polluted air consists of, constituents of flyash of silica, aluminium, iron oxide and carbon.[9] Air pollution also consists of some major trace metals like arsenic cadmium, chromium, iron and steel, manganese, nickel, lead, vanadium, zinc, which comes from smelters processing these metals, herbicides, pesticides, metals, paints and pigments Units, iron and steel industry, alloy industries, galvanizing units etc.[10]

Water Pollution

Water is regarded polluted, when it is changed in quality or composition directly or indirectly as a result of human activities. So that it renders water less suitable for drinking, domestic, agricultural and recreational purposes as well as for fisheries etc. For which it would other wise be quite suitable in its natural form.[11]

In other words "The addition of an excess material or heat to water that is harmful to humans, animals and aquatic life or surrounding environment" as such is known as water pollution.[12]

In general water pollutants can be classified as organic or oxygen demanding wastes, disease causing wastes, toxic substances which are not biodegradable, sediments or silt, radioactive substances and heat form power and manufacturing plants using water for cooling purposes.[13]

The major sources of water pollution are industrial effluents, community wastes, ground storage of solid refuse, air pollutants settled on the lakes and their catchment areas, storms and agricultural run off, ground water pollution, distribution system.[14] Among all these sources, the trade effluents and wastes of industry play a significant role in pollution of water. Almost all industries release effluents either in the water stream or on the soil. If they are released on the soil, it results in soil pollution and ground water pollution. If they are released in water streams, it pollutes the surface water.

The quality of the water can be judged by the composition and concentrations of pollutants. Some of the major indicators of water pollution are presented here. Some of the effluents released by some industries have high Biological Oxygen Demand (BOD). When such effluents are released into the water, the oxygen levels in the water will decline. Some of the effluents have high Chemical Oxygen Demand (COD). When they are released into the water, oxygen levels decrease due to chemical reaction. The effluents of some industries will have high pH value and they increase the alkaline content in the water. Some times, effluents with low pH value convert the water into acids. Apart from these parameters, the other indicators of water pollution are oil and grease (O&G), and suspended solids (SS). These pollutants also change the colour and odour of the water. Thus the effluents released by the industries into water, cause water pollution due to high BOD/COD, high/low pH, and change in colour/odour.[15]

Soil Pollution or Solid Wastes

Soils are among the most important of man's natural resources and as vast as the land area of the world. Its soils are finite enough to suffer deleterious modification through environmental contamination.[16] Solid wastes are unwanted materials disposed off by man, which can neither flow into streams nor escape immediately into the atmosphere. These non-gaseous and non-liquid residues cause soil pollution.[17]

In other words, when derelict materials from industries, agriculture, mining, domestic, powerhouse and demolition and construction are discharged on land the process is known as land, soil, garbage or solid refuse pollution.[18]

The greatest portion of solid waste is from wood factory, cardboard and papers etc., which arises as a result of packing operations. Always a threat of fire hazard is associated with this. In case of metal industry the waste is unused metal, metal oxide and other compounds. Other materials such as chemicals, plastic, rubber, textile, and polymers and organic materials of many descriptions from various industries are the other sources of solid waste. The major threat comes from disposal of radioactive waste, which has a far-reaching effect. For instance radioactive waste—strontium, when it is absorbed by plants enters into food chain of milk cattle, from there man.[19]

Effects of Pollutants

If we observe water pollutants and air pollutants we can identify a number of pollutants common for many industries. So it is the pollutant which cause the damaging effect to the environment, but not a specific industry. This necessitates us to know about the pollutants and their impact on living and non-living things in general. Broadly they are categorized as water pollutants and air pollutants.

Air Pollutants

The major effects of air pollution are health hazards, ecological imbalances in plant and animal life and climatic changes. In the long run it leads to the extinction of species.

Air pollutants like Carbondioxide (CO_2), Choloflourocarbons (CFCs), Methane (CH_4), Nitrous Oxides (NO_x), to some extent Ozone (O_3), smog made up of these gases and particulate matter in large quantities form a blanket which shields some of the sun's radiation so necessary to life on the earth. This blanket changes the heat absorption pattern on the surface of the earth and can stop radiation of the earth's heat to the sky. This results into "green house effect", which ultimately hangs weather and temperature patterns across the entire surface of the planet (therefore these gases are known as "green house gases"). If this effect continued for a long time, the ice caps in the Antarctica and Arctic belt would melt and the sea level would rise. This may damage many major cities and the coastline of earth will also change drastically.[20]

Another impact of air pollution is due to the clouds made up of pollutants like SO_2 and NO_x. These clouds result into acid rain. Acid rain is the deposition on the earth of dilute solutions of acids (sulphuric and nitric) with rainfall. Its acid precipitation generally ranks between a pH value of 5.6 and 3.5. It effects deleteriously many life supporting systems like lakes and rivers, soil fertility, plants and forests which are sensitive to acidity, building materials, paper, leather, streams and other aquatic life.[21]

Another common air pollutant is dust particle. Dust particle increases the dustiness and reduces the amount of solar energy that reach earth, and results in cooling of the atmosphere more than required levels. So any imbalance in heat and cold atmosphere leads to disturbance in the earth's heat balance and climate.[22]

Water Pollutants

Water is a scarce commodity. If this gets polluted, the first and foremost effect is the reduction in the amount of pure water for basic necessities like drinking, irrigation, cleaning etc. The next effect is health hazard, because of its nature as a vehicle for transmitted diseases. It is estimated that 2/3rds of illnesses in India are related to water borne diseases.[23] The major source for this type of pollution is industrial wastewater, which is being released without any treatment. These waters affect the aquatic food resources and kill the fish, when released into rivers or sea. They also increase the temperature of the water and affect the breeding of aquatic organisms. Some times consumption of fish as food from these waters cause health hazards. Due to this the market value of such fish will decline. Some times, these fish causes fatal effects. One such example is Minimata Tragedy. In 1960's, forty-one people died and seventy more were seriously ill after consumption of fish caught in Japan's Minimata Bay. This is due to high concentration of mercury in the fish (upto 1.5-mg. per kg), because of the river carrying wastewater from plastics, paint, chemical and paper industries, which flow into coastal water. The fish were caught in these waters. This disease is known as Minimata Disease.[24] Apart from these effects, these polluted waters affect negatively the quality and fertility of soil, when they released on the open lands. This will destroy the vegetation. Some times these waters will damage the water supply for municipal and industrial uses. If these waters turn into acids, it results in damages like corrosion of concrete and steel structures. Aesthetically, odour and floated materials affect the consumption of these waters.[25] Sometimes these waters flow from one country to another, they create trans-boundary pollution.[26]

When the polluted waters and gaseous emissions (through acid rain) fall or settle on the surface lands, through seepage of pollutants in the upperlayers of soil, they cause soil pollution and in deeper layers cause ground water pollution.[27]

The Results of the Study

The results of the structural changes in the industry, across the most pollution intensive (Red), medium pollution intensive (Orange) and least pollution intensive (Green) industries and the structural changes within the most pollution intensive (Red) industries are analyzed hereunder.

Structural Changes in the Industry Across the Red, Orange and Green Industries

The data showing the shares of most pollution intensive (Red), medium pollution intensive (Orange) and least pollution intensive industries (Green) in the number of factories, number of employees, capital invested, net value added, fuels consumed, materials consumed and total inputs used, for the periods, 1973-74, 1980-81, 1990-91 and 1993-94 are presented in Table 1. Which enables a proper study of structural changes in the industry based on the variables under study.

Table 1: Distribution of Industries by Type According to Variables under Study Concerning the periods 1973-74, 1980-81, 1990-91 and 1993-94*

Variables	*Type*	*1973-74*	*1980-81*	*1990-91*	*1993-94*
	Red	44.23	41.88	42.01	41.25
Number of	Orange	6.64	7.54	4.05	3.91
Factories	Green	49.12	50.56	54.03	54.82
	Total	100.00	100.00	100.00	100.00
	Red	47.85	51.94	52.68	55.16
Number of	Orange	4.67	5.10	3.51	3.61
Employees	Green	47.46	42.94	43.8	41.21
	Total	100.00	100.00	100.00	100.00
	Red	79.42	79.56	72.34	80.42
Capital	Orange	2.20	2.34	1.99	2.50
Invested	Green	18.36	18.09	25.65	17.07
	Total	100.00	100.00	100.00	100.00
	Red	57.77	60.10	68.02	67.56
Net Value	Orange	3.56	4.46	3.26	3.11
Added	Green	38.66	35.43	28.71	29.32
	Total	100.00	100.00	100.00	100.00
	Red	77.77	79.03	82.40	81.90
Fuels	Orange	2.26	2.62	2.41	2.80
Consumed	Green	21.79	18.34	15.17	15.28
	Total	100.00	100.00	100.00	100.00
	Red	61.61	67.01	69.80	66.79
Materials	Orange	5.68	5.99	5.24	6.63
Used	Green	32.70	26.98	24.94	26.59
	Total	100.00	100.00	100.00	100.00
	Red	68.10	67.79	70.52	69.32
Total	Orange	4.27	6.18	4.78	9.12
Inputs	Green	27.66	26.01	24.69	21.55
	Total	100.00	100.00	100.00	100.00

*Own calculation based on ASI Data.

(i) In terms of number of factories, in 1973-74 the Green industries dominated the table with a share of 49.12 per cent followed by Red industries with a share of 44.23 per cent. The relative position of these industries in the dominance remained the same over time, however the share of the Green industries increased to 50.55 per cent in 1980-81, 54.03 per cent in 1990-91 and 54.82 per cent in 1993-94, with the decline in the shares of both the Red and Orange industries. Thus the industrial structure in India during the period 1973-74 to 1993-94 is changing in favour of the Green industries in terms of number of factories. This prompts us to believe that the structural changes that have taken place in the Indian industry during-seventies, eighties and early nineties are environment friendly. But it may not be meaningful to draw such a conclusion at this stage, because, the mere comparison of the number of factories with out their size and inputs consumed may not give a good indication of pollution intensity.

(ii) In terms of employment, (i.e.) number of persons employed in 1973-74, Indian industry was dominated by Red industries with a share of 47.85 per cent followed by Green industries with a share of 47.46 per cent. The relative position of the dominance of these industries remained the same during the periods 1980-81, 1990-91 and 1993-94. But, there was a decline in the share of Green industries and increase in the share of Red industries through 1993-94. Orange industries remained at the same place with a share of around 3 to 5 per cent throughout the study period. Thus, measurement in terms of the number of employees (which is a better indicator of the size of the industry rather than the number of factories), structural changes that took place in the Indian

Industry during the study period are in favour of Red industries.

(*iii*) In terms of capital invested, in 1973-74, the Red industries dominated the Indian industry with a share of 79.42 per cent, followed by Green industries with a share of 18.36 per cent. The dominance of Red industries continued till the end of the period 1993-94. Thus the total period under study indicated that the investments in Red industries are dominant and Green Industries investment are around 18 to 25 per cent and the investments in Orange industries formed around 2.5 per cent. This shows that, pollution intensive industries are receiving more investments along with more employees.

(*iv*) In terms of the measure of net value added, which is the most prominent measure of the size of industry (since the industries are established mainly for the purpose of producing the goods and generating income), in 1973-74, the Red industries dominated the Indian industry with a share of 57.77 per cent. These were followed by Green industries with a share of 38.66 per cent. The same trend continued till the end of the study period. The share of Red industry increased from 60.10 per cent in 1980-81 to 67.56 per cent in 1993-94. Where as the share of the Green industries decreased to around 10 per cent in the study period. The share of Orange industries revolved around 3.5 per cent, almost throughout the study period.

(*v*) In terms of fuels consumed, it was again; the Red industries dominated the Indian industry with the shares of 77.77 per cent, 79.03 per cent and 81.90 per cent during the period 1973-74 to 1980-81, and 1993-94 respectively. Green industries share was 21.79 per cent in 1973-74. This was declined to 15.28 per cent in 1993-94. The dominance of Red industries was found even in terms of fuels consumed, which is one of the major contributors in increasing pollution. The share of Orange industries increased from 2.2 per cent in 1973-74 to 2.8 per cent in 1993-94.

(vi) With respect to materials consumed (Which is another indicator to measure pollution intensity), in 1973-74 the Red industries dominated with 61.61 per cent followed by Green industries with a share of 32.70 per cent and Orange industries with a share of 5.68 per cent. As the time is moving, the gap between the shares of Green industries and Red industries widened from the range of 32% to 61% in 1973-74 to 27% to 67% in 1993-94. In seventies, eighties and even in early nineties the Red industries' share was more compared to Green industries. And Orange industries share increased to 6.6 per cent through 1993-94.

(vii) On the whole, if we take total inputs, in 1973-74 the Red industries share in total industrial sector was the highest at 68.06 per cent followed by Green industries with 27.66 per cent. Even in 1980-81, 1990-91 and 1993-94, the Red industries dominated the industrial sector with the shares of 67.79 per cent and 70.52 per cent and 69.32 per cent in the respective time periods. Whereas, the share of Green industries, decreased to 21.55 per cent through 1993-94. Meantime the share of Orange industries increased to 9.12 per cent.

On the whole the study of structural changes items of the variables which are more closely associated with the pollution intensities of the industries viz., fuels consumed, material consumed and total inputs, across the broad industrial groups (Red, Orange and Green) during the period 1973-74 to 1993-94 are in favour of pollution intensive industries. During this period the size of Green industries declined and the size of Orange industries increased slightly along with Red industries.

As the Red industries are more pollution intensive, if the industrialization in India is following the present trend with huge share of Red industries, it increases the pollution and causes environmental degradation, if proper pollution control methods are not adopted.

An attempt also made here to show, what are those industries within the Red category contributing for the growth of Red category averages, a separate analysis is undertaken the result of this analysis is presented in the following paragraphs.

Structural Changes in the Most Pollution Intensive (Red) Industries

It is observed that in India, the size of Most Pollution Intensive (Red) industries is increasing slightly. Where as the size of least pollution or eco-friendly (Green) industries is declining significantly over a period of time. Meantime the share of Orange industry also increased slightly. Here the main focus is on, studying the structural changes in the industry in relation to pollution intensities. It may be appropriate to study the structural changes within the Red industry at dis-aggregated level in a more detailed manner. Because the industries listed under Red group are not equally pollution intensive. Following the 2-digit level classification of industries by ASI and based on the information provided by CPCB, industries falling under the Red group of industries are: (1) Food products (2) Beverages, tobacco and related products (3) Silk, wool, manmade fibre textiles, (4) Paper and paper products, (5) Leather and fur products (6) Rubber, plastic, and coal products (7) Basic chemicals and chemical products, (8) Non-metallic minerals products, (9) Basic metal and alloys industries (10) Metal products; (11) Machinery and equipment (12) Transport equipment (13) Other manufacturing units and (14) Electricity generation and distribution.

Data showing the shares of manufacturing industries within the Most Pollution Intensive (Red) industrial sector under each of the above groups with reference to the terms of the number of factories, number of employees, capital invested, net value added, fuels consumed, materials consumed and

Table 2: Distribution of Most Pollution Intensive Industries by two Digit Classification of Industries According to Number of Factories Concerning the periods 1973-74, 1980-81, 19910-91 and 1993-94*

Industry Name	*1973-74*	*1980-81*	*1990-91*	*1993-94*
Food Products	39.26	35.82	34.60	33.54
Beverages & Related Products	0.75	0.44	0.60	0.62
Wool, silk and Textiles	3.25	4.17	2.96	2.75
Paper and Paper Products	3.00	4.05	2.00	2.08
Leather & Fur Products	1.08	1.71	2.17	2.59
Rubber, Plastic and coal products	2.76	2.88	3.78	4.01
Basic Chemicals and Chemical Products	11.34	13.41	15.21	14.53
Non-metallic Minerals	5.27	6.10	6.87	7.07
Basic Metal & Alloys	14.39	14.20	13.10	13.18
Metal Products	4.61	4.56	3.74	5.09
Machinery and Equipment	6.01	8.10	8.58	9.07
Transport Equipment	5.66	6.90	7.80	8.31
Other Manufacturing	0.56	0.42	0.36	0.43
Electricity	1.80	0.62	0.53	0.39
Total	**100.00**	**100.00**	**100.00**	**100.00**

* Own Calculations based on ASI Data.

total inputs used for the periods 1973-74, 1980-81, 1990-91 and 1993-94 are presented in the table 2 to table 8. Data in these tables are own calculations based on ASI Data.

(i) An analytical study of the data of the variables mentioned above on each group of industry enables a proper study of the structural changes and the pollution intensity. In terms of number of factories (Table 2) in 1973-74, food products industry dominated with a share of 39.26 per cent, followed by basic metal and alloys industry with a share of 14.39 per cent, and by basic chemicals and chemical products industry with a share of 11.34 per cent. All other industries under the variable-number of factories, accounted for a share of less than 6 per cent each. The three industries continued its domination during the remaining periods. Except in 1990-91, the same relative positions were maintained.

In 1990-91, chemical industry share was more than basic metals and alloys. However, the share of the basic chemicals and chemical products industry was on an increasing trend, food products industry's share was on a decreasing trend and basic metals and alloys industry's share remained more or less the same during the periods, 1973-74 to 1993-94. Chemicals Industry and Basic Metal Industry causes both air and water pollution, where as the food products industry even though ranked as relatively less pollution intensive, the pollution load will be very high with high BOD and COD etc. Generally these industries even with very less in number, affects the surrounding environment to a larger extent. Because, these industries release such pollutants, which are hazardous even in very less concentrations.

(*ii*) In terms of number of employees, (Table 3) another indicator for size, in 1973-74 electricity generation

Table 3: Distribution of Most Pollution Intensive Industries by two Digit Classification of Industries According to Number of Employees Concerning the period 1973-74, 1980-81, 1990-91 and 1993-94.

Industry Name	*1973-74*	*1980-81*	*1990-91*	*1993-94*
Food Products	16.91	24.07	18.16	17.00
Beverages & Related Products	0.71	0.77	0.92	0.90
Wool, silk and Textiles	2.38	2.35	3.81	3.45
Paper and Paper Products	3.01	2.80	2.90	2.82
Leather & Fur Products	0.96	0.89	1.19	1.10
Rubber, Plastic and coal products	2.00	2.09	2.45	2.70
Basic Chemicals and Chemical Products	12.52	12.62	13.28	14.35
Non-metallic Minerals	5.04	3.81	4.00	4.05
Basic Metal & Alloys	16.26	14.18	14.24	13.00
Metal Products	2.19	1.47	1.36	3.55
Machinery and Equipment	5.52	4.92	5.81	5.45
Transport Equipment	12.16	10.06	9.02	9.75
Other Manufacturing	1.06	0.74	0.84	0.95
Electricity	18.55	17.46	19.71	18.60
Total	100.00	100.00	100.00	100.00

and distribution industry got highest share 18.55 per cent, followed by food industry with a share of 16.91 per cent, further by basic metal industry with 16.26 per cent and chemical products industry with 12.52 per cent. The share of transport equipment was 12.16 per cent. All other industries under the variable of number of employees have a share of less than five per cent each. The relative position of the shares of the dominant four industries remained more or less the same throughout the study period. By employing more workers in such above mentioned hazardous industries with improper safety measures, will affect the health of the workers.

(iii) In terms of capital investment, (Table 4) in the year 1973-74 the electricity generation and distribution industry dominated with a share of 38.13 per cent, followed by basic metal and alloys industry with

Table 4: Distribution of Most Pollution Intensive Industries by two Digit Classification of Industries According to Capital Invested Concerning the Periods 1973-74, 1980-81, 1990-91 and 1993-94

Industry Name	*1973-74*	*1980-81*	*1990-91*	*1993-94*
Food Products	8.12	6.20	7.82	7.70
Beverages & Related Products	0.29	0.39	0.49	0.45
Wool, silk and Textiles	1.63	1.91	2.62	2.80
Paper and Paper Products	2.34	2.50	2.25	1.92
Leather & Fur Products	0.31	046	0.40	0.34
Rubber, Plastic and coal products	2.69	5.56	4.68	5.44
Basic Chemicals and Chemicals Products	14.92	16.51	15.65	14.84
Non-metallic Minerals	3.07	2.56	4.05	3.97
Basic Metal & Alloys	17.69	19.02	19.50	19.12
Metal Products	0.76	0.48	0.45	0.90
Machinery and Equipment	4.24	4.04	4.34	4.20
Transport Equipment	60.15	6.17	6.10	4.10
Other Manufacturing	0.41	0.25	0.30	0.42
Electricity	38.13	35.64	32.44	31.95
Total	100.00	100.00	100.00	100.00

17.69 per cent. Chemical products industry with 14.92 per cent occupied third place and this was followed by food products industry with 8.12 per cent. In the relative position of the dominance, the same trend continued till the end of the period, i.e. upto 1993-94. However, there was a decline in the share of electricity generation and distribution industry from 38 per cent in 1973-74 to around 31 per cent in 1993-94. The share of remaining dominant industries remained more or less the same. Except food products industry, all other industries under the variable of capital investment had a share of less than five per cent each. For food products industry, the share ranged between 7 and 8 per cent.

(iv) In terms of net value added (Table 5) the chemical industry topped with a share of 22.82 per cent in 1973-74, followed by basic metal industry with a share of 17.40 per cent and further by electricity generation and distribution industry with a share of 16.23 per cent and food products industry by 11.51 per cent. Even in eighties and in early nineties, the same industries dominated in a jumbled manner. In 1980-81 electricity generation and distribution industry moved to second position, in 1990-91 the same industry moved to first position. In 1993-94 again this industry moved to second place with a share of 20.87 per cent while replaced by chemical industry (occupied first position) with a share of 22.53 per cent. The basic metal and alloys industry occupied the third place with a share of 12.7 per cent followed by food products industry with a share of 9.93 per cent. All other industries under this variable, except rubber, plastic, coal and petroleum industry had a share of less than six per cent each. Rubber, plastic, coal and petroleum

Table 5: Distribution of Most Pollution Intensive Industries by Two Digit Classification of Industries According to Net Value Added Concerning the periods 1973-74, 1980-81, 1990-91 and 1993-94

Industry Name	*1973-74*	*1980-81*	*1990-91*	*1993-94*
Food Products	11.51	8.56	9.95	9.93
Beverages & Related Products	0.79	0.95	1.05	0.90
Wool, silk and Textiles	3.41	3.30	3.70	4.08
Paper and Paper Products	3.26	0.32	1.83	1.13
Leather & Fur Products	0.53	0.59	0.69	.60
Rubber, Plastic and coal products	3.70	5.09	7.75	7.56
Basic Chemicals and Chemical Products	22.82	20.86	17.57	22.53
Non-metallic Minerals	3.04	3.01	4.39	2.57
Basic Metal & Alloys	17.40	17.50	16.03	12.70
Metal Products	1.90	1.53	0.79	1.40
Machinery and Equipment	5.67	6.30	5.36	4.87
Transport Equipment	10.31	9.62	8.40	7.10
Other Manufacturing	0.70	0.68	0.64	0.76
Electricity	16.23	20.59	21.26	20.87
Total	**100.00**	**100.00**	**100.00**	**100.00**

industry had a share of about eight per cent. This is an indication of growing significance of other industries, which grow as the industrial growth moves into other advanced phases. If these industries are adding net value to the economy, obviously growth of such industry will be in the eyes of the policy makers. At this juncture, it is the duty of the policy makers to look into past history and to keep in mind the nightmare experiences of industrialized countries. So that, the hazards involved in the presence of such products can be tackled carefully along with growth.

(*v*) In terms of fuels consumed, (Table 6) in the year 1973-74, the basic metal and alloys industry dominated with a share of 25.25 per cent, while electricity generation and distribution industry occupied the second position with a share of 24.23

Table 6: Distribution of Most Pollution Intensive Industries by Two Digit Cl⋯ification of Industries According to fuels consumed concerning the periods 1973-74, 1980-81, 1990-91 and 1993-94

Industry Name	*1973-74*	*1980-81*	*1990-91*	*1993-94*
Food Products	7.29	5.49	4.85	5.90
Beverages & Related Products	0.44	0.54	0.56	0.49
Wool, silk and Textiles	2.07	2.10	2.69	3.12
Paper and Paper Products	4.54	4.29	4.14	3.87
Leather & Fur Products	0.12	0.15	0.18	0.16
Rubber, Plastic and coal products	3.09	1.91	3.21	3.15
Basic Chemicals and Chemical Products	18.49	20.61	19.33	19.48
Non-metallic Minerals	10.58	7.33	10.10	11.54
Basic Metal & Alloys	25.25	26.76	21.58	20.22
Metal Products	0.49	0.34	0.26	0.44
Machinery and Equipment	2.22	1.83	1.83	1.89
Transport Equipment	3.20	2.14	1.63	1.61
Other Manufacturing	0.14	0.08	0.09	0.42
Electricity	24.23	27.94	29.30	27.82
Total	**100.00**	**100.00**	**100.00**	**100.00**

per cent. Chemical industry occupied third position with a share of 18.49 per cent. Non-metallic minerals industry (an industry that grows along with industrial development, usually in the second phase of industrial development) occupied the fourth position with a share of 10.58 per cent. All other industries had a share of less than seven per cent each. Except food industry, the same trend continued in eighties and in early nineties with increased shares, except for Food industry, whose share was on a decreasing trend. The variable under study is mostly responsible for air pollution. So industries in the top position along with the more investments to produce more should pay necessary attention to control pollution. Electricity generation and distribution industry in terms of number of factories is not so significant and still managed to reach significant position in case of fuels consumed. This shows the importance of quantities used even by very less number of factories.

(*vi*) The analysis of structural changes in terms of materials consumed (Table 7) shows that in 1973-74, the share of food products industry was the highest at 33.87 per cent, followed by chemical industry with 18.59 per cent further by basic metal industry with 15.97 per cent. All other industries under the materials consumed had a share of less than eight per cent each. The same trend continued for the whole period with a surprising change in the share of rubber, plastic, coal and petroleum industry from eighties onwards. In 1980-81, this industry jumped into dominant industries list with a share of 18.09 per cent. Electricity generation and distribution industry is another industry whose

Table 7: Distribution of Most Pollution Intensive Industries by Two Digit Classification of Industries According to Materials Consumed Concerning the Periods 1973-74, 1980-81, 1990-91 and 1993-94

Industry Name	*1973-74*	*1980-81*	*1990-91*	*1993-94*
Food Products	33.80	18.97	19.68	19.38
Beverages & Related Products	0.44	0.56	0.76	0.69
Wool, silk and Textiles	3.77	3.65	4.08	4.20
Paper and Paper Products	2.67	1.86	2.05	1.86
Leather & Fur Products	1.70	1.34	1.13	0.97
Rubber, Plastic and coal products	7.20	18.09	16.37	11.34
Basic Chemicals and Chemicals Products	18.59	19.05	16.13	16.97
Non-metallic Minerals	3.13	3.09	2.24	2.21
Basic Metal & Alloys	15.97	16.14	16.37	15.77
Metal Products	1.01	1.01	0.15	1.06
Machinery and Equipment	3.83	3.73	4.11	4.28
Transport Equipment	8.1	7.0	7.6	7.6
Other Manufacturing	0.41	0.39	0.42	0.54
Electricity	2.43	3.72	6.49	10.40
Total	100.00	100.00	100.00	100.00

share increased from 3.43 per cent in 1973-74 to 10.4 per cent in 1993-94. The relative position of food products industry, chemical industry and basic metal industry remained almost the same, more or less with the same shares.

(vii) In terms of total inputs (Table 8), in 1973-74 food products industry dominated with a share of 33.8 per cent followed by chemicals products industry with a share of 22.73 per cent, and by basic metal and alloys industry with 19.81 per cent. The same trend continued till end of 1990-91, with the occurrence of a slight change due to increased share of rubber, plastic, coal and petroleum industry ranged between 7 and 15 per cent. Electricity industry share ranged between 6 per cent and 13 per cent. In 1993-94, the share of chemical industry was highest (17.48 per cent), followed by basic metal

Table 8: Distribution of Most Pollution intensive Industries by Two Digit classification of Industries according to Total Inputs Concerning the periods 1973-74, 1980-81, 1990-91 and 1993-94

Industry Name	*1973-74*	*1980-81*	*1990-91*	*1993-94*
Food Products	33.8	16.61	16.32	15.17
Beverages & Related Products	0.5	0.60	0.76	0.68
Wool, silk and Textiles	3.04	2.73	2.90	3.06
Paper and Paper Products	2.78	1.70	1.91	1.84
Leather & Fur Products	1.76	1.20	0.99	0.86
Rubber, Plastic and coal products	6.55	1.79	14.32	10.20
Basic Chemicals and Chemical Products	22.73	19.34	15.69	17.48
Non-metallic Minerals	4.24	3.12	3.48	4.32
Basic Metal & Alloys	19.81	18.25	18.76	17.06
Metal Products	2.13	1.22	1.03	1.68
Machinery and Equipment	5.16	4.87	5.05	5.15
Transport Equipment	7.9	7.4	6.9	6.8
Other Manufacturing	0.47	0.38	0.40	0.42
Electricity	5.42	7.84	9.97	12.89
Total	100.00	100.00	100.00	100.00

and alloys industry (17.06). In third place it was food products industry with 15.17 per cent, followed by electricity generation and distribution industry with a share of 12.89 per cent. All other industries under the variable of total inputs had a share of less than 7 per cent each. No matter the amount of inputs used, but the products produced by these industries, even in fewer quantities, are sufficient enough to cause the damage. Without proper care to control the negative externalises in the production process leads to disaster.

The above study of the data, of the most pollution intensive industries with reference to variables viz. number of factories, number of employees, net value added, capital invested reveals the size of the industries. And the variables like fuels consumed, materials used and total inputs reveals the intensity of pollution and pollution load of the industries.

Out of the Red industries, the highly pollution intensive and load generating industries are basic chemicals and chemical products, electricity generation and distribution, basic metals and alloys and food products. These industries having a share of more than ten per cent each, with respect to both pollution intensity indicating variables and size indicating variables. Industries having high pollution intensity and load, but whose share in the total value below ten per cent and above one per cent are rubber, plastic, petroleum and coal products, paper and paper products, leather and fur products, non-metallic minerals, wool, silk, synthetic textiles.

Industries which have medium pollution intensity and could generate high solid waste are machinery and equipment, transport equipment and metal products. Whose share is below one per cent in terms of size indicating variables and between one and eight per cent in terms of pollution intensity indicating variables.

Industries with relatively less pollution intensity and load in the Red industries group are beverages and tobacco products and other manufacturing units. Whose share is, also less than one per cent.

Structural changes in the industry are studied to assess its impact on environment. Therefore it is more appropriate to draw the conclusions on the structural changes basing on the variables which are more closely related to environment viz., capital invested, fuels consumed, materials used and total inputs used. Basing on these the foregoing analysis shows that the dominant industries in the Red industries group at the two-digit level of classification are food products, electricity generation and distribution, chemical products and basic metals and alloys. Over a period of time, the sizes of chemical industry and electricity generation is increasing and the size of food products is decreasing, while there is no significant change in the share of basic metals and alloys industry.

Sum Up

Industries are root cause for many types of pollution viz., air pollution, water pollution, and soil pollution. And through these various types of pollution, many pollutants will be released into the environment. These pollutants affect the environment negatively in many ways. The problem of pollution is accompanied in all phases of industrial development. This can be observed from the experiences of many industrialised and industrialising countries. The intensity of the pollution problem will change from one phase to another phase.

Generally, industrialized and industrializing countries' growth follows such a pattern, which transforms the economy from resource based economies to high techconomies. Along with this trend the pollution problems involved will also change with varied intensities. But no phase in this process of industrialization is free from environmental and related health risks, no matter whatever may be the pollution intensity. With this trend in industrialization, reduction in the impact of pollution intensive industries is not automatic. A deliberate and conscious planning along with technological change and public consciousness is necessary for such a change.

With regard to the situation in India, Indian industry is dominated by the most pollution intensive and load generating (Red) industries, and the structural changes that took place during the period 1973-74 to 1993-94 are in favour of pollution intensive industries as against Green industries. Among the Red industries group, the most prominent industries at the two-digit level of classifiation are food products, chemicals products, electricity generation and distribution and basic metals and alloys industries. Among these four, the highly pollution intensive industries are chemical products and electricity generation and distribution. The size of these industries is increasing over time. Thus the structural changes that are taking place in the Indian Industry are in favour of most pollution intensive industries.

As per the changing phases of industrialization with economic growth, approximately India is in the second phase. During this phase the highly pollution intensive industries will dominate the industrial structure. The experience of many countries shows that, in the next phase (i.e., third phase) medium pollution intensive industries will come up as a result of technological changes. So the movement from second phase to third phase, requires a deliberate policy pertaining to effective pollution control and technological development.

Even though, there is a well-defined policy for controlling pollution, to make it more effective certain extra measures have to be implemented vigorously, viz., fixing the rates of emissions, creating public awareness, promoting participation by groups, co-ordination between various departments with reference to land-use pattern and also the environmental laws should be user-friendly. Above all, there is dire necessity for a multi-disciplinary approach of introspection in this direction to make growth policies more upto date and effective.

References

1. Brown, Lester R. (1985): "By a False sense of Security", *State of the World. A World Watch Institute Report on Progress toward sustainable society,* ed by Linda Starke et al., Prentice-Hall of India Pvt. Ltd., New Delhi, pp. 5.
2. O. Connor, Davis (1994): *Managing the Environment with Rapid Industrialization: Lessons from the East Asian Experience,* Development Centres of the organization for Economic Co-operation and Development, Paris, pp. 28-34.
3. Kudesia, V.P. (1990): *Industrial Pollution,* Pragati Prakasan, Meerut, p. 8-9.
4. Kudesia, V.P. (1990): Ibid., pp. 9-16.
5. Rajalakshmi, N. and Birundha, Dhulasi (1994): *Environomics: Economy Analysis of Environment,* Allied Publishers, Madras, pp. 213.
6. Ross, R.D. (1972): *Air Pollution and Industry,* Van Nostrand Reinhold company, New York, pp. 2.
7. Ross, R.D. (1972): Ibid, pp. 15.
8. Ross, R.D. (1972): Ibid, pp. 16.
9. Singh, Indira P and Tiwari, S.C. (1980): Man and His Environment *Concept Publishing Company,* New Delhi, pp. 12.
10. Sarma, K.S. (1983): *Some Studies on Suspended Particulate Pollution and Trace Metals in the lower laysers of Visakhapatnam city Atmosphere,* a.U. Ph.D. Thesis (unpublished), pp. 65.
11. Rajalakshmi, N. and Birundha, Dhulasi (1994): Opit, pp. 225.
12. Kumar, H.D. (1977): *Modern Concept of Ecology,* Vikas Publishing House Pvt. Ltd. New Delhi, pp. 107.
13. Kumar, H.D. (1977): Ibid., pp. 117.
14. Goyal, K.C. (1994): *Industrial Management and Pollution Control,* RBSA Publishers, Jaipur, pp. 38-40.
15. Murthy, M.N., et. al., (1999): *Economics of Water Pollution: The Indian Experience,* Oxford University Press, Delhi, pp. 4.
16. Pitts, James N, et. al (1969): *Advances in Environmental Sciences,* Wiley-Interscience, USA, pp. 14.
17. Pitts, James N. et. al. (1969): Ibid, pp. 15.
18. Goyal, K.C. (1994): Opcit, pp. 46.

19. Agarwal, S.K. (1997): *Environmental Issues and Themes,* APH Publishing Corporation, New Delhi, pp. 80.

20. Ross, R.D. (1972): Opcit, pp. 2-3.

21. Agrawal, S.K. (1997): Opit, pp. 123-124.

22. Pordom, Walter P. and Anderson, Stanley H. (1983): *Environmental Science,* Charles E. Merill Publishing Company, Sydney, and pp. 325.

23. Goyal, K.C. (1994): Opcit, pp. 41.

24. Yasuo, Shun (1977): Impact of Water Pollution on Agriculture and Fisheries in Japan in *Environmental Pollution and Toxicology: Proceedings of International Symposium, November 28-30, 1977* ed by S.I. Rayachaudhuri and D.S. Gupta, Today and Tomorrow's Printers and Publishers, New Delhi, 1986, pp. 95.

25. Goyal, K.C. (1994): Opcit, pp. 47.

26. Varshney, C.K. and Sardesai, D.R. (1993): *Environmental Challenges,* Wiley Eastern Limited, New Delhi, pp. 3.

27. Agarwal, S.K. (1997): Opcit, pp. 124.

25

Levels of Living in Small and Big City Slums

Dr. G. Ramachandrudu
Dr. N. Appa Rao

Introduction

Throughout history, The poor usually had to build their own houses and neighbourhoods and they have almost always built them outside the official 'Legal' city of elite and contrary to their norms and regulations. These illegal settlements are normally situated within the vicinity of commercial centres, Industrial locations and centres of transit (railway and bus stations, sea and airports) around big residential colonies on the banks of big drains and culverts and other dangerous, hazardous locations. They utilise, wherever possible, techniques and settlement layouts which, specific to their region and to that period reveal to their own cultural values. These slum dwellers (men, women and children) work as casual, unskilled labour, domestic servants and other menial occupations. In this sense, slums are inseparable and integral part of urban life and may be termed as necessary evils in an urban environment.

As city grows, slums become the chief sources of crime and delinquency, of illness and death from disease. Slums vary from one type to another, but certain general patterns of slum life are universal. Although the slum is generally characterized by inadequate housing, deficient facilities, overcrowding and congestion, it involves much more than these elements. Sociologically it is a way of life, a sub culture with a set of norms and values, which is reflected in poor sanitation and health practices, deviant behaviour, characteristic attributes of apathy and social isolation.

To understand the overall condition of people living in slums, one needs to study the environmental situation i.e., housing conditions, sanitation, drainage, health and drinking water available to the people in these locations. The environmental situation in slums across different size class cities/towns is not the same. Hence there is a need to study the quality of life in slums with a holistic socio-economic and cultural approach. This study makes an attempt to examine the levels of living of slum people in different size cities and also make a comparative analysis of levels of living to identify the important variations that are prevalent in different size cities in Andhra Pradesh.

After independence, there has been a rapid growth of population in class-I cities (one lakh and above) in India resulting in the emergence of slums and squatter settlements. According to Task Force on Housing and Urban Development, it is estimated that by 2000 A.D., India's urban population would be 78 million, of which 36 millions would be living in the slums of metropolitan cities alone.

Visakhapatnam and Kakinada cities are the fast growing port cities on the east coast of the country. They are already established as industrial cities with all its evil consequences of pollution, slums, congestion and inadequate civic infrastructure. According to the survey conducted in Visakhapatnam in 1996, about 28 per cent of the city's population (10, 52, 000) live in slums and in Kakinada (1998), 36 per cent of the city's population (2, 79, 875) live in slums. The slum dwellers are obviously the worst victims of the rapid urban growth.

To mitigate the problems of the poor and to make provision for basic amenities to improve their quality of life, several policy inventions were made and several programmes were launched by the Government of India. Among all the programmes launched by the Government of India, Urban Community Development Programme (1958), Environmental Improvement of Urban Slums (1972), Integrated Development of Small and Medium Towns (IDSMT) and Integrated Child Development Service (ICDS) are important.

The study has been carried out in pursuance of the following objectives:

1. To compare the poverty, health status and levels of living of slum dwellers in a small city (Kakinada with a population of less than a million) and a big city (Visakhapatnam with a population of million plus).
2. To suggest policy measures to improve the levels of living of the slum dwellers.

Methodology

The study is based on the data collected from two slums each (one more developed and another less developed) of Visakhapatnam and Kakinada. A household survey was conducted in two selected slums of Visakhapatnam viz., Amar nagar and Bhupesh nagar by selecting 300 households out of more than 200 slums (subbarao,1996). To compare and draw conclusions for formulating the programmes to improve the levels of living of slum dwellers in different size class towns/ cities, we have conducted another independent survey by selecting 200 households in two selected slums of Kakinada viz., Yallavari doddi and J. Ramaraopeta out of 53 slums identified by the Kakinada municipality. The data are collected during september-november 1998.

Composite Index

The sampling procedure adopted for the study in the selection of slums and households:

With the intention of adopting a multidimensional and integrated approach for the study slums and keeping in view the known diversity of slum situation, the sampling design first adopted the social area of locality analysis, the 53 slums were accordingly grouped into 5 clusters, taking into account the spacial distribution and location pattern, age and history of development, physical proximity to core city area and industrial and service environment. The 5 clusters covered 11, 9, 15, 5 and 6 slums respectively. This was followed by stratification of the slums in each cluster on the basis of 11 indicators of development which articulates both the descriptive and normative dimensions of socio-economic development.

Demographic: (i) Density of population per acre, (ii) Average family size, (iii) Literacy rate,(iv) Percentage of SC and ST population in the total population, and (v) Percentage of thatched houses to the total housing stock (quality of housing stock).

Educational status: (vi) Percentage of children going to primary and high schools to total chidren.

Infrastructural facility: (vii) Road area per 1000 population, (viii) Drains per 1000 population, (ix) Water sources per 1000 population, (x) Number of latrines per 1000 population, and (xi) Number of street lights per acre.

Next, ranks are allotted to the slums cluster-wise. Indicator-wise ranks were assigned to slums in the ascending order with rank1 indicating developed status and the last rank indicating the least developed status. By combining all the 11 ranks, each slum gets in this process, a total (unweighted) index is arrived at for each cluster in each slum in each cluster. The total index of each slum was then divided by the number of indicators available for each slum for arriving at the average composite index for each slum. Because of the limited number of slums in each cluster, 2 slums from each one of the clusters, one least developed and one developed were selected.

Several statistical techniques are used for analysing the determinants of levels of living. These include Logit regression analysis, Chi-square test and different measures of poverty (Head Count Ratio, Poverty Gap Ratio and FGT index) and health status.

The following are the results of the primary data analysis.

1. Literacy Level

It can be observed that the overall literacy rate was more in Visakhapatnam (67.86 per cent) slums than in Kakinada (64.68 per cent) slums. The study clearly reveals that the inequalities in levels of education based on caste considerations have considerably come down. In the case of females, there is a higher growth in educational status at all levels in big cities even though it is comparatively less than that of males. Interestingly in the present survey, the female illiteracy rate is more in small cities (43 per cent in Kakinada) than in big cities (32 per cent in Visakhapatnam).

The study of educational levels shows that various literacy programmes launched by the Government succeeded satisfactorily with the primary and upper primary level, but secondary and higher education is still not brought within the reach of the slum dwellers.

2. Type of House

It can be observed that the percentage of the ownership of pucca houses will be more in both the slum surveys. It can also be observed that the percentage of the ownership of kutcha houses will be less in Visakhapatnam and Kakinada slums and there is a shift towards pucca houses. There is, thus, a substantial shift in the quality of housing from kutcha to semi-pucca and semi-pucca to pucca in both the slums. However, it is a mute point that the decline in the percentage of semi-pucca houses involving an excessive preference to the construction of pucca houses is a desirable change. It clearly indicates that the Government programmes are having a decisive influence on the housing status of the people.

3. Source of Water Supply

The analysis of the data on water supply reveals that more than half of the slum dwellers are depending on the tap water for drinking and other purposes in both Visakhapatnam and Kakinada slums. Safe drinking water is a critical input for improving the health status and it is, therefore, unfortunate that while there has been a substantial improvement in regard to housing, the provision of drinking water facility has not improved.

4. Poverty

An attempt is made to analyse the dynamics of urban poverty with reference to the sample slum surveys conducted in Visakhapatnam and Kakinada.

'Poverty' can be said to exist in a given society when one or more persons do not attain a level of material well being deemed to constitute a reasonable minimum by the standards of that society. Saying that poverty 'exists' is only the first step for many purposes, including policy analysis, one must also say 'how much' poverty exists.

Methodology

To calculate the poverty level of income (Z), we have taken all India consumer price index numbers (general) for industrial workers (Base 1982 = 100). The cut-off point for urban poverty is taken as monthly per capita expenditure of Rs. 224 for the year 1992 and it was inflated with all India consumer price index numbers for industrial workers (general) for the year 1998 for Kakinada. For Visakhapatnam, The monthly per capita expenditure of Rs. 224 for the year 1992 and it was deflated with all India consumer price Index numbers for industrial workers (general) for the year 1996.

Table 1 shows the estimated incomes (poverty line is Rs. 224 in 1992) and the results of alternative measures of poverty. An important conclusion of the analysis is that the percentage of households living below the poverty line is 47 in Visakhapatnam slums and it is 58 in Kakinada slums, the inequalities in incomes are less in Kakinada slums when compared to Visakhapatnam slums. Also the depth of poverty is more in Kakinada than in Visakhapatnam.

Table 1: Estimated Incomes (Poverty Line is Rs. 224 In 1992)

S.No.	Poverty Index	Visakhapatnam (N=300)	Kakinada (N = 200)
1.	Gini Co-efficient	19.1133	17.5970
2.	Head Count Ratio	47.7669	58.4081
3.	Poverty Gap Ratio	11.1301	12.9086
4.	FGT (a = 2)	3.5747	4.0417

The differential in poverty in Visakhapatnam slums compared to Kakinada slums can be ascribed to the socio-economic and environmental intervention programmes implemented by the Visakhaptnam Municipal Corporation (VMC) during 1988-1995 with the O.D.A. assistance. In addition, the trickle down effect of huge investments in large scale industries have caused the growth of the real incomes of the workers in the informal sector in Visakhapatnam.

Poverty in small city slums is far higher than that of big city slums. In Visakhapatnam, 47 per cent of the slum dwellers are below the poverty line, while in Kakinada 58 per cent of slum dwellers are living below the poverty line. The reason for such variation is mainly due to wage differentials and availability of employment opportunities, although to some extent education also plays an important role in earning capacity of the households. It was observed that poverty level in Visakhapatnam has been very high (72.00 per cent). It is only after the implementation of Visakhapatnam Slum Improvement Project (VSIP), Poverty levels have been brought down to the level of 47 per cent.

5. Health Status

The health status of slum dwellers is generally lower than that of their counterparts in the urban area. The slum dwellers are affected particularly by environmental factors such as (i) over crowding, poor quality of housing and sanitation and atmospheric and water pollution (ii) the specific types unhealthy occupations, dietary practices and low income and (iii) social and psychological problems relating to family structure and family disorganization.

A special approach is, therefore, generally adopted to understand and to solve the problems of health in urban slums. The VSIP's (Visakhapatnam Slum Improvement Programme) approach to tackle the health problems in Visakhapatnam has four components i.e., engineering, medicine, social and economic inputs. These components are aimed at improving the living conditions of the slum dwellers through their participation (community development approach). Environmental improvement scheme, low-cost sanitation scheme, Urban basic services programme, Cyclone emergency reconstruction project, Urban housing scheme, Nehru Rozgar yojana, Universal immunization programme, National slum development programme and family welfare programmes were launched in Kakinada municipality to improve the living conditions of the slum dwellers.

It is proposed to analyse the impact of the health inputs in small and big cities including the differences that may be seen in the attitudes of the people towards health, four major aspects of the health improvement are studied in the survey viz.,(a) Reproductive health (b) Immunisation programme (c) Morbidity patterns and (d) Family planning.

(a) Reproductive Health (Type of delivery)

The percentage of deliveries conducted at hospital is considerably increasing in both small and big city slums than the deliveries conducted at home.

The major reason for preferring delivery at home happens to be the 'expectation of easy delivery'. This is because of their economic status, which do not allow them to go to the hospital for delivery.

The observation of the data of big cities reveals that the achievement of greater percentage of pregnant women registered is not only due to the efforts of the health wing of UCD (Urban Community Development) but also reflects the increased awareness about the reproductive health care among the slum dwellers. But in small cities, still it needs greater awareness among the slum dwellers.

(b) *Immunisation Programme*

Universal immunisation programme and pulse polio are given top priority in the National Health Programme being implemented in India. Analysis of data reveals a remarkable improvement in the coverage of children under various immunisation programmes.

It appears that there is no gender discrimination with regard to immunisation coverage. The perfect implementation of immunisation programmes reflects rapid increase of awareness about the benefits of immunisation due to committed efforts of both Governmental and non-Governmental organisations. It appears that the slum dwellers have gained the awareness that preventive medicine is less expensive and more beneficial than curative health care.

(c) *Morbidity Patterns*

The analysis of morbidity data relating to general sickness provide evidence of the effectiveness of immunisation programmes but does not indicate any effective control over other types of sicknesses. The control over these diseases such as Malaria, T.B. and Diarrhoea depends on effective mitigation of atmospheric and water pollution in the area and improvement in the physical environment.

The chi-square test, on morbidity and poverty (Table 2) and also on morbidity and type of house (Table 3), shows significant association between them. The logit regression analysis (Table 4) shows that education, type of house and household income are consistently and significantly

Table 2: Morbidity and Poverty (For Chi Square Test)

Status	*Poor*	*Non-Poor*	*Total*
Healthy (Disease not reported)	69	30	99
Ill – Healthy (Disease reported)	47	54	101
Total	116	84	200

The chi square test on morbidity and poverty shows that there is a significant association between them.

Table 3: Morbidity and Type of House (For Chi Square Test)

Status	*Kutcha*	*Non-Kutcha*	*Total*
Healthy (Disease not reported)	14	45	59
Ill-healthy (Disease reported)	29	112	141
Total	43	157	200

The chi square test on morbidity and type of house shows that there is a significant association between them.

Table 4: Determinants of Morbidity: Results of Logit-Regression

		Visakhapatnam		*Kakinada*	
S.No.	*Variables*	*B*	*SE*	*B*	*SE*
1.	Literacy (Total)	0.301*	0.040	0.424**	0.036
2.	Literacy (Male)	0.315*	0.010	0.410**	0.009
3.	Literacy (Female)	0.345*	0.002	0.450**	0.005
4.	Caste	0.526**	0.125	0.226	0.102
5.	Occupation	0.141**	0.106	0.201	0.135
6.	House Type	0.767**	0.129	0.695**	0.019
7.	Household Income	0.707**	0.110	0.535**	0.123
8.	Number of Living Children	0.212	0.231	0.315	0.335
9.	Acceptance of Family Planning	0.201	0.302	0.101	0.325

* Significance at less than .001 Level.

** Significance at less than .01 Level.

explaining the variations in the incidence of morbidity both in Visakhapatnam as well as in Kakinada slums. However, caste and occupation also have significantly explained the morbidity in Visakhapatnam slums. Among the total male and female literacy rates, the female literacy rate is estimated to be significantly explaining the morbidity differentials in both Visakhapatnam as well as Kakinada slums.

(d) Family Planning

The predominant type of family planning is Tubectomy in both the household surveys. This shows that the burden of effective family planning is increasingly thrown on the women folk.

Though the differences in literacy rates are less in both Visakhapatnam and Kakinada slums, the family planning adopters are more especially vasectomy in Visakhapatnam slums. This is because of the implementation of VSIP (Visakhapatnam Slum Improvement Programme) in Visakhapatnam. To improve the family planning awareness among the slum dwellers, a special slum improvement programme is needed in Kakinada.

Policy Suggestions

1. The Visakhapatnam Slum Improvement Project (VSIP) has made a very significant impact on the living conditions of urban slum dwellers in Visakhapatnam. With the Urban Housing Scheme, Cyclone Shelter Programme, the impact is more significant in Kakinada slums. The new slums (like Amarnagar in Visakhapatnam and Yallavari doddi in Kakinada) have received greater share of the developmental activities when compared to old slums (like Bupeshnagar in Visakhapatnam and J.Ramarao peta in Kakinada). Hence more resources have to be spent on the less developed slums than the developed slums.

2. As the city grows, naturally new slums emerge. Hence the urban planners must prepare Master Plan for absorbing the poor migrant labourers by constructing low cost housing colonies.

3. The dichotomy of urban development, particularly the slum improvement programme is that the decline in poverty (as measured in terms of income) is not commensurate with the improvements in the

quality of life (sanitation, drinking water, fuel, reproductive health etc.). Hence more resources have to be spent on the social and physical environment of the slums.

4. The imposition of the partial prohibition and campaigning against smoking have reduced the proportion of household expenditure on drinks and tobacco (5 per cent in Visakhapatnam and 6 per cent in Kakinada). If the Government takes more stringent measures in this direction, the consumption may be reduced to zero.
5. Morbidity in slums is increasing owing to increase in industrial pollution, lack of basic amenities and increase in population density. The reproductive health status is improving because of effective functioning of primary and municipal health care centres. Therefore, it is recommended that the existing public health care centres in the slums have to be strengthened and more resources have to be provided towards medicine and other facilities.
6. Nearly 5 per cent of the total population in both the surveys are older women. 'State of World Population Report 1998' states that, as a result of reduced fertility and mortality, there will be a gradual demographic shift in all countries over the next few decades towards an older population. By 2050, 97 per cent of the growth of older population's will be in developing countries (more than one Quarter will be in India), compared to the present 77 per cent. Older populations in most parts of the world are predominantly female. The rapid growth of young and old 'new generations' is 'challenging societies' ability to provide education, health care for the young and social, medical and financial support for the elderly population. Special schemes have to be designed to help them, either through

payment of more old age pensions or undertaking old age homes.

7. The slum improvement largely depends on the availability of funds to the urban development. The Government is going to establish three or four financial institutions with an investment of Rs.1000 crores each. A 'Revolving Fund' would be created with all the investments for taking up slum development projects all over the country. The increase in funding for slum development was a part of two-pronged approach adopted by the centre for giving boost to housing sector in the country. A nation wide survey which was undertaken recently by the Ministry of Urban Affairs and Employment had revealed that 'close to half' of the urban populace in the country was living in slums under abysmal civic conditions. This was announced in the recent National Slum Development Policy. The fund should also be utilised to provide basic services like drinking water, sanitation, health care, pre-primary and primary education, basic nutrition and women development.

8. Development of small towns is needed to stop migration from small towns into over crowding big cities.

9. Environmental assessment has to be made for allocating funds for slum improvement programmes in different towns and cities.

10. The country is caught in the dichotomy of development and welfare policies. The globalisation process might lead to faster development particularly in the infrastructure sector, but it may be done at the cost of human development. Adequate social safety nets are needed for reducing inequalities especially in health care and education.

11. Enforcement of minimum wage policy is the urgent need of the day. Increasing privatisation leads to exploitation of labour particularly unskilled labour, who are the bulk of the poor.

12. There is a growing evidence that urban population growth is more due to natural increase (Birth rate minus Death rate) rather than migration. While death rate is falling, birth rate is not responsive so much to the improvement of levels of living. Hence efforts are to be stepped up to convince slum dwellers about contraception especially the spacing methods and Vasectomy, which are less popular than Tubectomy.

13. Small towns are disappearing into larger cities and into their surrounding rural areas. The small towns may be disappearing but Hyderabad grew up by 27 per cent, Visakhapatnam by 25 per cent and Vijayawada by 20 per cent in the last decade (1991-2001). Along with this, flow from villages to urban areas has drastically reduced. The rate of growth in the urban population has fallen from the above 43 per cent to less than 15 per cent in the past decade.*

Selvaraj and Rao (1993) have found glaring evidence to the growing trend of urban to urban migration. They observed "In urban areas, a large part of immigrants were from other urban areas (6.3 per thousand) than from other rural areas (0.9 per thousand)". There is an increasing trend of urban to urban migration in the two selected districts of Visakhapatnam and East Godavari district.**

---

* 'Every fourth urbanite lives in a slum', The Hindu, India's National News Paper, September,25, 2001, p. 5.

** Selveraj, K.G., and Rao, P.S.S., "Household migration -Urbanisation and Consequences", *Demography India*, Vol. 22, No. 2, 1993.

References

1. Alferd Demaris,(1992) *"Logit Modelling: Practical Applications"*, Sage Publications.

2. Battacharya Basabi, (1998) "Urbanisation and Human Development in West Bengal: A District Level Study and Comparison with Inter-State Variation", *Economic and Political Weekly*, Vol. XXXIII, Nos. 47&48, November 21- December 4.

3. Biswajit Chatterjee, (1998) "Poverty in West Bengal, What we have learnt?", *Economic and Political Weekly*, Vol. XXXIII, Nos. 47&48, November 21-December 4.

4. Brijesh, C., Purohit. et.al., (1994) "Utilisation of Health Services in India", *Economic and Political Weekly*, Vol. XXIX, No.18.

5. Chaubey, P.K., (1992) *"Poverty Measurement: Issues, Approaches and Indices"*, New age International Publishers, New Delhi.

6. Director of Town Planning, (1971), "Draft Outline Development Plan: General Town Planning Scheme for Kakinada", Government of Andhra Pradesh.

7. Donta Balaiah, et.al, (1995) "Contraceptive Use Differential in Two Slum Population of Greater Bombay", *The Journal of family welfare*, Vol.41, No.3.

8. Krishnaji N, (1997) "Human Poverty Index: A Critique", *Economic and Political Weekly.*

9. Martin Ravallion, (1992) "Poverty Comparisons: A guide to Concepts and Methods", *The World Bank*, Washington D.C.

10. Martin Ravallion, (1998) "Reform, Food Prices and Poverty in India", *Economic and Political Weekly,* XXXIII, November 1&2.

11. Municipal Commissioner, (1997) "Slum Improvement Project 1994-95 to 1996-97", Kakinada Municipality.

12. Ramachandrudu,G., (1996) *"Reproductive Health in Andhra Pradesh"*, Research notes, A Monthly bulletin from the research forum, Andhra University, Vol.2, No.3.

13. Ramachandrudu,G., (1997) *"First Referral Health Systems in Andhra Pradesh: An Evaluation"*, Study No. 68, Population Research Centre, Andhra University, Visakhapatnam.

14. Ram V. Baru, (1993) "Inter–Regional Variations in Health Services in Andhra Pradesh", *Economic and Political Weekly.*

15. Robert D. Retherford and Minja Kimchoe, (1993) "*Statistical Models for Causal Analysis*", John Wiley & sons Inc.

16. Vani, K. Borooah,(1991) "Problems in the Measurement of Inequality and Poverty: A Survey", *The Indian Economic Journal*, Vol. 38, No. 4.

26

House Environment and Health Status of Slum Dwellers in India

Dr. Subba Rao Pappala

Introduction

The World Health Organisation (WHO) warned India that if current life styles do not change, non-communicable diseases will account for 55 per cent of deaths in India by 2020, from the current level of 35 per cent Deaths due to heart diseases may be doubled. From the current 2.4 million in 1995 to 4.8 million by 2020: smoking related deaths from 0.8 million in 2000 to 4.0 million in 2020: and diabetes from 19.4 million in 1995 to a staggering 58 million in 2020.

Health cannot be achieved merely by taking a pill everyday, nor by observing a few restrictions. One can promote health by understanding what it is, on what it is dependent and then applying this knowledge meticulously in every day life. Health of the people is not only a desirable goal but is also an essential investment in human resource. An individual should be informed and educated regarding the maintenance of good health at all levels.

Even though urbanisation is not rapidly increasing in India, concentration of urban population in big cities is taking place which is leading to the growth of slums. The health status of urban slum dwellers is generally lower than that of their counter parts in the other urban area. The urban slum dwellers are effected particularly by environmental factors such as poor housing, low quality of sanitation, water pollution, unhealthy occupations and over crowding. Though there is a danger of increase in non-communicable diseases in future, the current situation is a higher incidence of communicable diseases as a result of poor physical environmental quality.

Health and Environment: A Review of Literature

The health in a slum is of a primary importance because of poor environmental and sanitary conditions prevailing in the slums. A majority of slum dwellers especially women and children are prone to several deadly disease like cholera, polio, tuberculosis, etc., and as a result, child mortality rate is very high in the slums. They also suffer from nutritional disorders and vitamin deficiencies.

In a study undertaken in Pune by Bapat, M(1991) brought out that the index of the environmental hygiene of the settlements and dampness at shanties is the significant determinant of reported sickness. It is noticed that even the relatively better off among the shanty dwellers can not protect themselves from polluted surroundings, and the socio-economic variables of income and literacy are not significant at the slum level in determining health status and poor environmental conditions also contribute to malnutrition among young children through diseases. In another study Bapat, M. and Crook, N(1993) found that the populations in all settlements suffered from heavy contamination of food and milk, and noted "A striking feature was that water pollution in the home was found even in those settlements where communal piped water existed".

J. Clark et al (1989) in their evaluation report of the Hyderabad slum improvement project analysing the environmental impact observed that a number of slums where sewerage systems have been installed lead to large septic tanks which are overflowing resulting insanitary conditions on the edge of slums which can promote the spread of disease.

Considering the environmental condition in Udaipur City, Ila Chakravarthi (1994) points out that due to bad sanitation, improper drainage system, absence of good habitat and cleanliness, led slum dwellers to various types of skin diseases and other related diseases among slum dwellers. Whatever income they have, half of the income is spent on food and 10 to 12 per cent is spent for doctors, mostly private and often unqualified and medicines. Many developing countries today, according to C. Gopalan (1994) said to be satisfied with the eradication of old diseases like Cholera, Small Pox etc. What surprises in many of the countries are facing severe problems from new disease like ARI, Pneumonia, HIV, V.D. etc., due to over population and unchecked industrialization.

According to the study conducted in Visakhpatnam slums during 1993-94 by B. Swarajyalakshmi, et al (1991), 40 per cent of the slum dwellers are using the health facilities by changing reasonably low fees. The study highlights the necessity of increasing public health facilities particularly at the secondary level to the slum population. Regarding the morbidity patterns, the study identified malaria, respiratory diseases, Gastro-intestinal disorders are on the increase in Visakhapatnam slums. The cost of treatment per patient for one illness is estimated at Rs. 246/- which comes to 20 to 25 per cent of the monthly income of the slum household.

The utilisation of health services has been discussed in their study by Brijesh. C. Purohit et al (1994), states that the majority of outpatients had utilized the services of private doctors. The in-patient care, however, has been availed more at the public hospitals. When we consider the health service from the patient point of view, several studies revealed illiteracy is the main cause for the improper use of these facilities. In another survey of Khandekar found that the slum dwellers are reluctant to utilise the health services provided by the Government because of the irregularities in the health centres.

According to Rajamani, A., the social change is the most important for proper utilization of the health services. Unless hygiene and cleanliness become a way of life, diseases are found to remain and rule. In another study Ravi Duggal point out on Central Government and State Government for their insufficient funds for the most needed area of health care. According to him the investment has not been effectively utilised.

Stressing on the importance of literacy among women, Vanita Nayak Mukherjee quotes, due to illiteracy, despite all achievements in India, millions are facing diseases arising out of malnutrition. Due to illiteracy the people in different states, specially in Bihar, Uttar Pradesh, Madhya Pradesh and Rajasthan are ignorant of the health problems and are not attending the medical experts.

Rajamani, A., found that due to the administrative negligence and insufficient funds, the relationships between the patients and doctors and the patients and nurses are not being properly defined or understood. C. Gopalan has also opined that due to the inefficiency in management of material and manpower the public health care is failed in serving the need of the country. Due to illiteracy, poverty and lack of involvement of the community are the factors in the improper administration of the system. According to Ramesh Batt, as Indian government is not able to cope-up with the ever growing population to that of health care, the private sector have expanded their health services.

Methodology and Analysis

The study is based on the primary data collected in the slums of Vizinagaram municipal town through a well structured scheduled administered to the respondents by interviewing in October, 2001 to study the socio-economic and environmental characteristics of the sample population. Vizinagaram is headquarter of Vizianagaram District. Which was formed on 1st June, 1979. As on October 2001, 65 slums are existed in Vizinagaram. Among these, three slums are selected (each slum have a neighbourhood committee with 200 households) and in each slum 50 per cent of the households were selected for the study. Accordingly, a total of 300 households were selected by adopting simple random sampling methodology. Questions were administered on the five main indicators viz., demographic, educational, monthly incomes, housing and environment and health status so as to bring out the salient features of the sample population.

The findings indicate that the average households size of the sample population is 4.90 and the sex ratio is 1148 which is higher than the sex ratio of Andhra Pradesh 978 and district sex ratio of 1004 females per 1000 males (2001 Census). The educational status show that 53.75 per cent of the sample population are literate and majority was attained primary education and higher education is still not within the reach of the slum dwellers. The distribution of the households according to monthly income groups, we find that nearly 60 per cent of the households have below the monthly income of Rs. 1200/-. As regarding the housing and environment, it is welcoming feature that 66 per cent of the household have pucca houses, 70 per cent of the households have separate latrines and 79 per cent of the households have ration card facility. The data shows only 30.67 per cent of the households have water facilities within their home and more than 87 per cent of the household have been using the water without boiling or filtering. As regarding the drainage system, 94.67 per cent of the households have covered with open drainage system where as a significantly higher proportion of households (70 per cent) reported regular garbage clearance. It is welcoming feature that 96.97 per cent of the children are fully immunised. The data also shows that the predominant method of family planning is tubectomy. It indicates that the burden of effective family planning is increasingly thrown on the women folk. The incidence of general sickness is as high as 8.3 per cent of the total population.

Summary

The above review and the analysis reflects the poor sanitary, water pollution and low income environment in the slum areas. To combat all these problems the Government to take appropriate steps to improve the income sources of the households through permanent income generating schemes rather than unworthy programmes. To improve the sanitary condition, it is necessary to take up the package of health education programmes with the involvement of the community. It is worthy to follow four pillars of primary health care with community participation, inter-sectoral co-ordination, equitable distribution and appropriate technology to improve the health status of the slum dwellers. There is also an urgent to improve the educational status of the slum dwellers. To achieve full literary among future generation, it is necessary to introduce compulsory education for children below 14 years. It is equally urgent to popularise modern family planning methods of spacing. Recently, the Government of Andhra Pradesh is introducing a project called Andhra Pradesh Urban Services for the Poor (APUSP) 32 towns with the financial assistance of Department for International Development (DFID) to assist the poor communities. We are looking forward at least the new project can improve the quality of life of the slum dwellers. Lastly, voluntary organisations should involve themselves to educate the slum dwellers for the proper utilisation of the services provided by the Central and State Government and also the peoples responsibility to react and cooperate.

References

Bapat, M. Developing Human Resources: Quality of Life: the Indian Journal of Social Science, Vol. 4, No. 4, 1991.

Bapat, M. and Crook, N., "Behind the Technical Approach to Slum Improvement", Waterlines, B(1), 1989, petitioner. 24-26, 1993.

Brijesh C. Purohit et al. "Utilisation of Health Services in India", Economic and Political Weekly, Vol. XVIX, No. 18, April 20, 1994.

Clarck, J., et al., "Evolution Study of Hyderabad slum Improvement Project" Overseas Development Administration, valuation Report, Eland House, Stage Place, London, 1989.

Gopalan. C, "Challenges to Public Health Systems", Economic and Political weekly, Vol. XXIX, No. 20, May 14, 1994.

Ila Chakravarti—"Health care services and Urban Slum Dwellers—A slum in Udiapur" Indian Journal of Economics, Vol. LXXIV, No. 294, petitioner. 284-291, January 1994.

Khandekar. J. et al. "Child Birth Practices among Women in slum areas" The Journal of Family Welfare, Vol. 39, Sept. 1993.

Muralidharan, V.R. "When is access to Health care equal? Some Public Policy Issues", Economic and Political Weekly, June 19, 1993.

27

Population, Employment and Human Poverty: Dimensions and Policy Issues

Prof. S. Mahendra Dev

I am grateful to the Department of Economic, Andhra University for inviting me to deliver the Inaugural address at the conference on India's Population Census 2001: Human Development in India. The subject chosen particularly human poverty for the seminar is timely and very important. Poverty alleviation has been on the national policy agenda for more than fifty years. As you know, the concept of poverty is multi-dimensional (viz., income poverty and non-income poverty). It covers not only levels of income and consumption, but also health and education, vulnerability and risk; and marginalisation and exclusion of the poor from the mainstream of society[1]. As early as 1938, the Indian National Congress constituted a National Planning Committee headed by Jawaharlal Nehru, which had declared that the social objective should be to ensure an adequate standard of living for the masses, in other words, to get rid of the appalling

1. "There has been much debate about how exactly poverty should be defined. In popular understanding, poverty is identified with lowness of income which prevents a family from obtaining and enjoying the basic necessities of life, including a minimum of food, clothing, shelter and water. This concept is defined as income poverty. For a comprehensive picture of poverty those other deprivations, such as in relation to health, education, sanitation and insurance against mishaps, much be taken into account" (Chellaiah and Sudarshan, 1999).

poverty of the people". The importance of reduction in poverty and provision of other basic needs has been emphasized in all the Five Year Plans since independence particularly since the 5th Five Year Plan.

The performance of India in terms of particularly non-income indicators (e.g. education and health) has not been satisfactory. This is not to deny that progress has certainly been made in reduction in both income and non-income poverty. The incidence of income poverty has declined from over 50 per cent in the 1950s to less than 30 per cent in the late 1990s.[2] The literacy rate has increased from less than 20 per cent in 1951 to 65 per cent in 2001. According to the recent Human Development Report of UNDP, India moved from the category of 'low' human development to that of 'medium' human development and its present rank is 115. Nevertheless, the performance of India in the social sector is far from satisfactory, and could have been much better (Dreze and Sen, 1995). The pace of reduction in poverty has been slow as compared to many other countries particularly those of South East and East Asia. The numbers on income and human development indicate that the social objective declared by the National Planning Committee headed by Jawaharlal Nehru in 1938 is largely unaccomplished even after 50 years of independence.

Turning to India's Population Census, it is a large scale exercise taken up in the country once in ten years in order to understand the socio-economic and demographic profile of the population. It collects vital information such as population, employment, literacy, migration, sex ratio, housing and other basic needs. The Census of India 2001 is the 14th decennial Census—the first Census starting from 1872. Unfortunately, the information from 2001 Census is available only on limited variables such as population, literacy, sex ratio and urbanisation. We do not have

---

2. There is a controversy on the estimates based on NSS data for 1999-2000.

information on employment and migration. Moreover, if one wants to examine the trends in poverty (income and human), one has to look at other sources such as National Sample Surveys (NSS) and National Family Health Surveys (NFHS). On employment, NSS is more reliable than Census. The NFHS provides valuable data base on demography, health and nutrition[3].

In this address, I will be dealing with dimensions and policy issues relating to population, employment and poverty with emphasis on human poverty. The issue of regional disparities is also considered wherever necessary. Regarding data base, I will be using Census, NSS and National Family Health Surveys.

Population and Other Demographic Aspects

Population Growth: India's population has increased from 683 million in 1981 to 846 million in 1991 and to 1027 million in 2001. The net addition during 1991-2001 was 181 million as compared to that of 163 million during 1981-91. The average annual growth rate for all India declined from 2.14 in the 80s to 1.93 in the 90s. On regional disparities, I have arranged the growth rates taken from a study on population (Balasubramanian, 2001) by regions. Table 1 shows that the biggest decline occurred in Southern states followed by Eastern states (except Bihar). In the case of northern states, the decline is only marginal while Western states showed a mixed picture. In terms of individual states, the highest decline (40 per cent) in the growth rate of population was noticed in Andhra Pradesh between 1980s and 1990s.

Fertility: The fertility rate has definitely declined over time in India. The NFHS data shows that the fertility rate in India in 1996-98 was 2.85[4]. However, there are significant regional disparities. Among the major states, the fertility rate

---

3. The NFHS-1 was conducted in 1992-93 while the second and more expanded one NFHS-2 was conducted in 1998-99.
4. SRS data gives higher levels of fertility levels.

Table 1: Growth Rates of Population across 15 major States

States	*Population 2001 (millions)*	*Av. Annual exponential growth rate (%)*		*Percentage decline in g.r. in 1990s*
		1981-91	*1991-2001*	
Southern States				
Andhra Pradesh	75.7	2.17	1.30	40
Karnataka	52.7	1.92	1.59	17
Kerala	31.8	1.34	0.90	33
Tamil Nadu	62.1	1.43	1.06	26
Northern States				
Haryana	21.1	2.42	2.47	+2
Punjab	24.3	1.89	1.80	5
Rajasthan	56.5	2.50	2.49	0
Uttar Pradesh	174.5	2.27	2.27	0
Western States				
Gujarat	50.6	1.92	2.03	+6
Madhya Pradesh	81.2	2.38	2.04	14
Maharashtra	96.8	2.29	2.04	11
Eastern Sates				
Assam	26.6	2.17	1.73	20
Bihar	109.8	2.11	2.40	+4
Orissa	36.7	1.83	1.48	19
West Bengal	80.2	2.21	1.64	26
All India	1027	2.14	1.93	

Source: Rearranged from Balasubramanian (2001).

varies from 1.96 in Kerala to 3.99 in Uttar Pradesh during the same period. In general, Southern and Western states show lower levels of fertility as compared to Northern and Eastern states.

There has been an interesting debate on the causes of fertility decline in countries like India and Bangladesh. The fertility decline observed in Bangladesh and many states in India still remains a paradox. The decline, in this region, had taken place in extremely difficult conditions, like, low standard of living, low literacy level, lack of modernisation etc. The so called Kerala Model can not explain the decline in fertility rates in some parts of India. For example, in Andhra Pradesh, fertility declined significantly in the 1990s. The decline occurred even among the poor people. One of the studies done at Centre for Economic and Social Studies (CESS) shows that community role is important in augmenting the pace of fertility transition[5]. In Andhra Pradesh, women's self help groups could have played significant role apart from Government's efficient family planning delivery systems in reducing fertility levels.

Sex Ratio: Gender discrimination is one of the all pervading forms of deprivation. A most telling demographic symptom of such deprivation is the presence of an adverse sex ratio which declined from 934 females per 1000 males in 1981 to 927 females per 1000 males in 1991. The sex ratio has increased to 933 per 1000 males in 2001 but was still below the level of 1981. Across states, the lowest sex ratio was in Haryana (861) and the highest was in Kerala (1058) in the year 2001. The causes for improvement in sex ratio between 1991 and 2001 needs some research. One of the factors could be that male mortality is higher than females. This proposition needs more investigation.

In the case of Andhra Pradesh, the overall sex ratio has increased from 972 in 1991 to 978 in 2001. However, one disturbing trend is the decline in sex ratio of population in the age group 0-6 from 975 in 1991 to 964 in 2001. It is not clear whether it is due to increasing incidence of female foeticide in the state through the use of modern technology.[6]

Urbanization: The share of urban population in total population increased from 25.7% in 1991 to 27.8% in 2001. The annual growth rate of urban population in India has declined from 3.1% during 1981-91 to 2.7% during 1991-2001.

---

5. See Mahendra Dev et al (2001).
6. See James (2001) for a discussion on sex ratio in Andhra Pradesh.

This goes against the popular perception of urban explosion. It was also shown that the pace of urbanisation is being skewed towards the developed states. Even here, the large cities have registered higher growth[7].

It may be noted that in the year 1991, all those Census towns included in 1981 were included as Census towns even if all the conditions for identifying urban areas were not satisfied. In 2001, all criteria were strictly applied without reference to the position in 1991. Thus, many towns were declassified. However, this alone may not explain the slow urban growth in India.

Migration

We are yet to get the migration tables from 2001 Census. However, some indirect estimates given in Table 2 shows that Maharashtra, Haryana and surprisingly Bihar have recorded highest growth in actual population. The difference between natural growth and actual growth is high in these states. It shows that indirectly more people are migrating to these states. On the other hand, Andhra Pradesh, Assam and Kerala are exporting population to other places.

Table 2: Migration Changes between 1991 and 2001

States	*Rise in population (91-01)*		*The difference*
	*Natural**	*Actual*	*Migration*
Maharashtra	17.5	22.6	5.1
Haryana	23.4	28.1	4.6
Bihar	23.9	27.1	3.2
Gujarat	20.0	22.5	2.5
Rajasthan	26.5	28.3	1.8
Punjab	17.9	19.8	1.8
Andhra Pradesh	15.8	13.9	–1.9
Assam	20.8	18.8	–1.9
Kerala	12.1	9.4	–2.7

*Estimated: birth rate minus death rates

Source: Economic Times, November 21, 2001.

7. More on this see Kundu (2001).

Labour Migration: The uneven development between urban and rural areas and between different regions has resulted in the movement of large mass of labour migrants from one area to another. Labour migration is characterised by different types of mobility which include permanent or semi-permanent migration, labour circulation and commuting (Srivastava, 1998). The Census and NSS capture the first stream more adequately. These national level data sources indicate that migration declined over time. On the other hand, micro-studies suggest an increase in labour mobility via seasonal migration and commuting. Both the censuses and NSS have limitations, the main being they ignore or severely underestimate short duration (circular) migrants and commuting labour. The National Commission on Rural Labour (NCRL) estimates more than 10 million circular migrants in the rural areas alone. These include an estimated 4.5 million inter-state migrants and 6 million intra-state migrants. The commission notes that there are large numbers of seasonally migrant workers in agriculture and plantations, brick-kilns, quarries, construction sites and fish processing. In addition, large numbers of seasonal migrants work in the urban informal manufacturing, construction, services or transport sectors—as casual labourers, head-loaders, coolies, rickshaw pullers, hawkers and so on. Information is not available on the trends in circulation of labour time but the few studies on migration over several decades that exist suggest a growth in labour circulation (e.g. Breman, 1996). Migration seem to have benefited the source areas in improving rural livelihoods while in the destination areas migrant labour are being exploited.

Issues on Employment

Expanding productive employment is central for sustained poverty reduction as labour is the main asset of the poor. Here we examine trends in some aspects of employment and discuss policies for raising employment and providing social security for the unorganised.

Worker-population ratios: The worker-population ratios provide an idea about the participation of population in economic activity. Both NSS and Census provide worker-population ratios and these are given in Table 3. The 1991 Census showed high work participation rates for males and females. The work force participation rates for males in census have been stable since 1971 between 52 and 53 per cent. On the other hand, for females it declined significantly in 1971 as compared to 1961 due to changes in the concepts of women work. Moreover, Census has not been :o capture women's work fully. However, there has been a continuous increase in work participation rates for women since 1971. On the other hand, NSS data shows stable work participation rates for females. In 1991-2000, the NSS data shows decline in work participation rates for males and females. The Census has not shown any decline in these participation rates in 2001.

Table 3: Worker-Population Ratios: Census and NSS data

Years	*Males*	*Females*
Census		
1961	57.1	28.0
1971	52.7	13.9
1981	52.6	19.8
1991	51.6	22.3
2001	51.9	25.7
NSS		
1972-73	53.5	28.2
1977-78	54.2	29.3
1983	53.8	29.6
1987-88	53.1	28.1
1993-94	54.5	28.6
1999-2000	52.7	25.4

Source: Visaria (1998) upto the early 1990s. The NSS data for 1999-2000. From NSS 55th Round while 2001 data is from Census of India

Some Characteristics of Employment

(*a*) More than 90 per cent of Indian workers are in the unorganised sector. Table 4 gives data on number of workers and the shares of unorganized workers by sectors in all India. Around 93 per cent of the workers were in unorganized sector in the year 1999-2000. It is clear that even in manufacturing sector, more than 80 per cent of the total workers were in the unorganised sector. Similarly, services also had high share of unorganised workers. The workers in the organized sector who have regular employment and assured source of income need only measures to protect their income when contingencies arise which tend to deprive them of the income or to reduce it. In the case of the workers in the unorganized sector who have no regular jobs or assured income their primary need is employment security and improvements in quality of employment.

Table 4: Organised and Unorganised workers and percentage share of Unorganised workers in the total: 1999-2000

Sector	*Organised Workers (millions)*	*Unorganised workers (millions)*	*Total workers (millions)*	*Share of Unorganised sector (per cent)*
Ag. Allied activities	1.39	236.11	237.61	99.42
Mining quarrying	1.01	1.25	2.26	55.31
Manufacturing incl. Repair services	6.79	37.27	44.02	84.67
Electricity, gas and water	1.00	0.05	1.05	4.76
Construction	1.18	16.41	17.59	93.29
Trade, hotel & restaurants	0.49	40.77	41.26	98.81
Transport, Storage & Communication	3.15	11.59	14.74	78.63
Financial Services	1.65	3.37	5.02	67.13
Community, social & personal services	11.49	21.95	33.44	65.64
All Sectors (Total)	28.11	368.89	397.00	92.92

Source: Computed from GOI (2001).

(*b*) *There has been diversification in rural areas over time* (Table 5). However, agriculture still accounts for 71 per cent for males and 85 per cent for females. Even if we take into account urban areas, agriculture still accounts for 60 per cent of the workers in 1999-2000. Thus, importance of agriculture can not be denied for provision of employment. Of course, the shares of manufacturing and services have increased substantially in the last two decades.

Table 5: Sectoral Distribution of workers at one digit level: Rural India, 1977-78 to 1999-00.

Persons				
0.4	0.5	0.6	0.6	0.5
6.2	6.8	7.2	7.0	7.4
0.1	0.1	0.2	0.2	0.2
1.3	1.6	3.3	2.4	3.3
3.3	3.4	4.0	4.3	5.1
0.8	1.1	1.3	1.4	2.1
4.5	4.9	5.1	5.7	5.2
100.0	100.0	100.0	100.0	100.0
Males				
0.5	0.6	0.7	0.7	0.6
6.4	7.0	7.4	7.0	7.3
0.2	0.2	0.3	0.3	0.2
1.7	2.2	3.7	3.2	4.5
4.0	4.4	5.1	5.5	6.8
1.2	1.7	2.0	2.2	3.2
5.3	6.1	6.2	7.1	6.1
100.0	100.0	100.0	100.0	100.0
Females				
0.2	0.3	0.4	0.4	0.7
5.9	6.4	6.9	7.1	7.6
-	-	-	-	-
0.6	0.7	2.7	0.8	1.1
2.0	1.9	2.1	2.1	2.0
0.1	0.1	0.1	0.1	0.1
3.0	2.8	3.0	3.4	3.7
100.0	100.0	100.0	100.0	100.0

(c) *Low Employment growth inspite of high growth in GDP:* There has been a concern that the acceleration of GDP growth in the post-reform period has not been accompanied by commensurate expansion in employment (GOI, 2001). The growth of employment has dropped from around 2 per cent per annum during 1983 to 1993-94 to less than one per cent per annum during 1993-94 to 1999-2000.

(d) *Casualisation of Workers:* The proportion of casual labourers for males and females in rural areas has increased from 22.0 to 36.2 per cent and 31.4 to 339.6 per cent respectively during 1972-73 to 1999-2000. The share of self employed workers declined for both males and females.

(e) *Self Employment is still high:* Inspite of decline in the share of self employed, the proportion is still high around 53 per cent in all India in 1999-2000. It was 58 per cent, 40 per cent, 48 per cent respectively in agriculture, secondary sector and tertiary sector.

(f) *The Problem of Working Poor and the quality of employment:* In India, unemployment *per se* is not the main problem. Many people are working in unorganized sector, which is characterized by low earnings, poor working conditions and lack of social security protection. Our estimates reveal and incidence of poverty is the highest for casual workers were below the poverty line with 49.4 per cent in rural areas and 57 per cent in urban areas. The incidence of poverty declined for all the categories of workers over the last decade. However, the rate of decline in poverty ratios was the lowest for casual workers while it was highest for regular workers. From these results, it can be interpreted that casualization may be associated with immiserisation in the sense of low incomes. Also our estimates show that the incidence of poverty for casual labourers and self employed was higher than that for the unemployed. Recent 2001 Census data also shows that the share of agricultural labourers is quite high in rural areas (Table 6).

Table 6: Total workers (main+marginal) by categories: Census 2001

Categories	*Rural*	*Total*
Cultivators	40.1	31.7
Agricultural Labourers	33.2	26.7
Household Industry workers	3.8	4.1
Others workers	22.90	37.5
Total	100.0	100.0

Source: Census of India, 2001.

(*g*) The future employment is likely to have more service orientation, more casual labour and self employed, multiple types of work, increase in demand for skilled work and educated labour. With increase in education levels the problems of educated will increase in India.

Employment and Education

Education is important for workers in order to get qualitative employment. Literacy alone is at best only one indicator. Literacy definition covers anyone who can write their name and this means many people may be classified as literate although they may not understand simple written instructions. Unless we have these abilities for workers, the efficiency of the labour force in many occupations is likely to remain low. Table 7 provides the educational standards of the workers in Rural India. It shows that the per cent of illiterates among male workers declined from 55 per cent to 40.3 per cent during 1977-78 to 1990-00. For females, the corresponding numbers declined from 88.1 per cent to 74.9 per cent. However, even in 1999-2000, 68 per cent of the rural males and 91 per cent of the rural females are either illiterate or have been educated only up to primary level. In other words, less than 10 per cent of the female workers have education of middle school or above. Table 8 shows that only 4 per cent of the casual labourers and 14 per cent of self employed are educated in rural areas.

A major effort to promote literacy and more importantly to bring about improvement in skill levels of those in working age group consistent with their level of education should therefore have high priority. One weakness of government supplied and directed education and training has been a divorce of the supply of skills from the demands of the market for skills.

Table 7: Percentage of Workers (age 5 years and above) by General education category: 1977-78 and 1999-00 (%)

Category	*Rural male*		*Rural female*	
	1977-78	*1999-2000*	*1977-78*	*1999-2000*
Not Literate	55.0	40.3	88.1	74.9
Literate & upto primary	30.8	27.7	9.1	15.7
Middle school	8.5	15.9	1.6	5.6
Secondary & Higher Sec.	4.7	13.0	1.0	3.0
Graduate & above	1.0	3.1	0.2	0.7
Total	**100.0**	**100.0**	**100.0**	**100.0**

Source: NSS Rounds on Employment and Unemployment.

Table 8: Distribution of Educated (Secondary & Above) Among employed/unemployed (5 years & above during 1999-2000

Status	*Rural*		
	Male	*Female*	*Persons*
Employed			
Self employed	17.5	3.3	13.5
Regular employed	46.9	39.3	45.7
Casual labour	6.2	1.1	4.4
Total	16.0	3.7	12.4
Unemployed	55.2	62.7	56.9

Source: NSSO, 2000.

Strategies for Employment Promotion and Security for the Unorganised Sector

In an earlier paper I have mentioned about growth mediated and support led security for promotion of employment and increase in quality of employment[8]. The Task Force on Employment Opportunities (GOI, 2001) identified the five broad areas of policy which together constitute a strategy for employment generation.

These are as follows:

(a) "Accelerating the rate of growth of GDP, with a particular emphasis on sectors likely to ensure the spread of income to the low income segments of the labour force.

(b) Pursuing appropriate sectoral policies in individual sectors, which are particularly important for employment generation. These sectional level policies must be broadly consistent with the overall objective of accelerating GDP growth.

(c) Implementing focused special programmes for creating additional employment of enhancing income generation from existing activities aimed at helping vulnerable groups that may not be sufficiently benefited by the general growth promoting policies.

(d) Pursuing suitable policies for education and skill development, which would upgrade the quality of the labour force and make it capable of supporting a growth process which generates high quality jobs.

(e) ensuring that the policy and legal environment governing the labour market encourage labour absorption, especially in the organised sector" (GOI 2001).

In the above list, a, b and d relate to growth promoting and skill improvement policies while c relates to support-led policies. On the other hand, area relates mainly to organised sector.

8. Mahendra Dev (2001).

In the growth-medicated security, the Government is supposed to act as facilitator for private investment and for skill improvements. Removing anti-poor laws, identifying growth engines, taking care of market failures (labour, credit, commodity/product) and infrastructure constraints, training and skill improvements etc. are parts of the growth-medicated strategy.

The approach of India regarding support-led social security has the following elements

(a) Land reforms to help the poor

(b) Promotional social security measures:

(i) Wage employment programmes such as EGS, JRY

(ii) Self Employment programmes such as IRDP and SGSY

(iii) Provision of basic needs: primary education, basic health services and so on.

(iv) Public Distribution System (PDS) and nutrition programmes such as Integrated Child Development Services (ICDS) and mid-day meal schemes.

(v) Reducing Social Exclusion: Reservations for certain classes is part of an attempt to reduce social exclusion.

It may be noted that some of the promotional measures listed above can also be protective.

(c) Protective social security measures: are national level and state level schemes to provide a financial cushion against contingent poverty that seriously affects the poor, such as sickness, accidents, old age and maturity.

Income and Human Poverty

Income Poverty

India's perhaps the only developing country which has the longest time series of national household surveys starting from the early 1950s. Till 1973-74, National Sample Survey (NSS) data were available annually. Between 1972-73 and 1999-00, six quinquennial surveys have been carried out with a large sample size of ten households per sample village. The official poverty ratios for all India and major states are given in Table 9. It shows that the rural poverty declined by about 10 percentage points in the 1990s while urban poverty declined by 9 percentage points during the same period. In almost all the states, poverty declined in the 1990s. However, rural poverty was above 40 per cent in three states viz., Orissa, Bihar, Assam and in three states (M.P., U.P., and West Bengal) it was above 30 per cent. In the case of urban poverty, states

Table 9: Incidence of Poverty Across States

States	*Rural*			*Urban*			*Total*		
	1973-74	*1993-94*	*1999-00*	*1973-74*	*1993-94*	*1999-00*	*1973-74*	*1993-94*	*1999-00*
A.P.	48.41	15.92	11.05	50.61	38.33	26.63	48.86	22.19	15.77
Assam	52.67	45.01	40.04	36.92	7.73	7.47	51.21	40.86	36.09
Bihar	62.99	58.21	44.30	52.96	34.50	32.91	61.91	54.96	42.60
Gujarat	46.35	22.18	13.17	52.57	27.89	15.59	48.15	24.21	14.07
Haryana	34.23	28.02	8.27	40.18	16.38	9.99	35.36	25.05	8.74
Karnataka	55.14	29.88	17.38	52.53	40.14	25.25	54.47	33.16	20.04
Kerala	59.19	25.76	9.38	62.74	24.55	20.27	59.79	25.43	12.72
M.P.	62.66	40.64	37.06	57.65	48.38	34.44	61.78	42.52	37.43
Maharashtra	57.71	37.93	23.72	43.87	35.15	26.81	53.24	36.86	25.02
Orissa	67.28	49.72	48.01	55.62	41.64	42.83	66.18	48.56	47.15
Punjab	28.21	11.95	6.35	27.96	11.35	5.75	28.15	11.77	6.16
Rajasthan	44.76	26.46	13.74	52.13	30.49	19.85	46.14	27.41	15.28
T.N.	57.43	32.48	20.55	49.40	39.77	22.11	54.94	35.03	21.12
U.P.	56.53	42.28	31.22	60.09	35.39	30.89	57.07	40.85	31.15
W.B.	73.16	40.80	31.85	34.67	22.41	14.86	63.43	35.66	27.03
India	**56.44**	**37.27**	**27.09**	**49.01**	**32.36**	**23.62**	**54.88**	**35.97**	**26.10**

Source: Economic Survey 2001-02, Government of India.

such as Orissa, M.P., Bihar, U.P. showed higher incidence in 1999-2000. Thus, although income poverty declined significantly at the all India level, regional disparities are quite high.

Alternative Estimates of Poverty: The official estimates of poverty are based on the Lakdawala Committee's methodology. If one notices the numbers in table 9, the urban poverty was higher than rural poverty in 9 states. This is unusual. Deaton (2001) estimates alternative poverty ratios based on the unit prices generated from NSS data. The alternative poverty estimates are given in Table 10. It shows that in all the states, urban poverty was lower than rural poverty. In the case of official estimates, the rural poverty in Andhra Pradesh was only 11 per cent while the alternative poverty estimate was 27.9 per cent in 1999-00. Similarly urban poverty in A.P. was much lower for alternative estimate as

Table 10: Alternative Estimates on Incidence of Poverty: 1999-2000

States	*Rural*		*Urban*	
	Official	*Alternative*	*Official*	*Alternative*
Andhra Pradesh	11.05	27.9	26.63	11.3
Assam	40.04	35.7	7.47	12.1
Bihar	44.30	39.3	32.91	23.5
Gujarat	13.17	20.4	15.59	6.6
Haryana	8.27	6.5	9.99	5.1
Karnataka	17.38	30.3	25.25	11.5
Kerala	9.38	11.6	20.27	10.5
Madhya Pradesh	37.06	31.2	38.44	14.1
Maharashtra	23.72	30.8	26.81	13.0
Orissa	48.01	41.3	42.83	15.6
Punjab	6.35	2.8	5.75	4.0
Rajasthan	13.74	16.2	19.85	10.6
Tamilnadu	20.55	25.6	22.11	11.1
Uttar Pradesh	31.22	20.8	30.89	16.5
West Bengal	31.85	22.7	14.86	11.4
India	**27.09**	**25.3**	**23.62**	**12.5**

Source: Economic Survey 2000-01 and Deaton (2001).

compared to official estimate. The alternative poverty estimates seem to be more reliable than the official estimates for Andhra Pradesh.

Human Development and Human Poverty

Human Development: The performance of India in terms of human development has not been satisfactory as compared to many of the developing countries. Although the human development index has improved for India, it is much lower than East and South east Asian countries like China, Indonesia, Republic of Korea, Malaysia, Philippines and Thailand. Selected human development indicators by states are given in Table 11. Literacy rates have improved for all the states over time. However, more than 50 per cent of the females are illiterates in Bihar, Rajasthan and Uttar Pradesh in 2001. Similarly infant and maternal mortality are high in Orissa, Rajasthan, U.P., Assam and Bihar.

Table 11: Selected Indicators of Human Development

	Literacy 2001			*Life Expectancy at birth (1993-97)*	*Infant mortality per 1000 live births 1999*	*Maternal Mortality per lakh live births 1998*
	Male	*Female*	*Total*			
A.P.	70.85	51.17	61.11	62.4	66	159
Assam	71.93	56.03	64.28	56.7	76	409
Bihar	60.32	33.57	47.53	59.6	63	452
Gujarat	80.50	58.60	69.97	61.9	63	28
Haryana	79.25	56.31	68.59	64.1	68	103
Karnataka	76.29	57.45	67.04	63.3	58	195
Kerala	94.20	87.86	90.92	73.3	14	198
M.P.	76.80	50.28	64.11	55.5	90	498
Maharashtra	86.27	67.51	77.27	65.5	48	135
Orissa	75.95	50.97	63.61	57.2	97	367
Punjab	75.63	63.55	69.95	67.7	53	199
Rajasthan	76.46	44.34	61.03	60.0	81	670
T.N.	82.33	61.46	69.68	64.1	52	79
U.P.	70.23	42.93	57.36	57.6	84	707
W.B.	77.58	60.22	69.22	62.8	52	266
India	75.85	54.16	65.38	61.1	70	407

Source: Census of India, 2001; Office of the Registrar General, India

Education: The approach paper to 10th Five Year Plan indicates that more than 60 million children are out of school. One of the highest failures of development policy in India is the neglect of primary education. Both supply and demand factors are important in putting these out of school children into school. Supply side factors like teachers, schools, infrastructure in schools, quality of school curriculum etc. have to be improved. Demand factors like opportunity cost of children attending school and poverty problem are also important. Quality higher education is equally important for the progress of a nation. I need not go into the details as the importance of primary, higher and technical education are well known.

Human Poverty: Human poverty is more than income poverty—it is the denial of choices and opportunities for living a tolerable life (UNDP, 1997). In one of its Human Development Reports, UNDP constructs Human Poverty Index (HPI). Three indicators are included in HPI: (a) survival deprivation represented by people not expected to survive to age 40 (b) deprivation in education and knowledge represented by the adult literacy rate and (c) deprivation in economic provisioning which is a combined index of the indicators of population without access to safe water, health services and of undernourished children below age 5. The estimates for the indicators of human poverty and HPI are given in: Table 12. The table indicates that human poverty for India was 41 per cent. At state level it ranges from 23 per cent (Kerala) to a high of 54 per cent (Bihar). It may be noted that among the three dimensions of human poverty, the highest deprivation at the all India level and for almost all states (except Punjab), is observed for provisioning followed by knowledge. Even in a state like Kerala, as high as 33 per cent of the population are deprived in terms of provisioning. There is also no strict correction between rankings based on HPI and rankings based on State Domestic Product (SDP).

Table 12: Human Poverty Index for Indian States in the Early 1990

States	*Health*	*Knowledge*	*Provisioning*	*Human Poverty Index*
Andhra Pradesh	14.88	49.51	42.88	40.78
Assam	21.81	41.37	61.62	47.18
Bihar	19.48	57.25	64.40	53.60
Gujarat	16.75	33.91	38.63	32.33
Haryana	15.37	35.67	36.43	31.90
Karnataka	15.68	39.14	41.12	35.42
Kerala	5.14	8.47	33.22	23.19
Madhya Pradesh	25.34	49.77	52.52	45.60
Maharashtra	12.27	29.59	36.65	29.49
Orissa	22.33	44.08	56.92	45.42
Punjab	13.87	33.86	32.32	29.27
Rajasthan	19.88	54.70	51.82	46.96
Tamil Nadu	13.45	30.69	32.98	28.19
Uttar Pradesh	22.24	51.83	57.32	48.32
West Bengal	14.82	38.97	47.78	38.52
India	**17.99**	**42.69**	**48.70**	**40.49**

Anaemia and Undernourished

Some related indicators on women and children based on NFHS data are given in Table 13. It shows that more than 50 per cent of women and more than 70 per cent of children have anaemia while nearly 50 per cent of the children are undernourished in the country. Considerable regional disparities can be noticed in these indicators.

Lack of correlation between income and human development: Income is not correlated with some of the human development indicators. For example, the infant mortality in Uttar Pradesh was five times higher than that of Kerala with both having the similar levels of poverty in the 1970s and 1980s. Kerala has higher human development but the economy (both agriculture and industry) has been stagnant and unemployment rates are high. Punjab and Haryana are having very high per capita incomes but gender inequalities are much higher than Southern states. The association

Table 13: Percentage of Women and Children with Anaemia and Percentage of Children Undernourished: 1998-99

States	*Percentage of Women with any anaemia*	*Percentage of children with anaemia*	*Percentage of children undernourished**
Andhra Pradesh	49.8	72.3	37.7
Assam	69.7	63.2	36.0
Bihar	63.4	81.3	54.5
Gujarat	46.3	74.5	45.1
Haryana	47.0	83.9	34.6
Karnataka	42.4	70.6	43.9
Kerala	22.7	43.9	26.9
Madhya Pradesh	54.3	75.0	55.1
Maharasthra	48.5	76.0	49.6
Orissa	63.0	72.3	54.4
Punjab	41.4	80.0	28.7
Rajasthan	48.5	82.3	50.6
Tamil Nadu	56.5	69.0	36.7
Uttar Pradesh	48.7	73.9	51.7
West Bengal	62.7	78.3	48.7
India	51.8	74.3	47.0

*weight for age

Source: National Family Health Survey (NFHS-2).

between poverty and child mortality is also weak. The basic point is that there is no "the problem' region in India. Each state has its own problems. In general, the northern (except Punjab and Haryana where gender bias is evident) and Eastern states like Bihar and Orissa have lower social development as compared to Southern states.

How to Reduce Income and Human Poverty?

Income poverty: Regarding rural poverty, since agriculture is the most important source of employment and income generation in rural areas, it is natural to expect that performance of agriculture will have impact on poverty. However, if the distribution of land and other assets are highly skewed, the benefits of agricultural growth may not be shared by the rural poor. In other words, incidence of poverty is determined by two major factors, namely, the average level of living in a region and the distribution parameters. Variables such as agricultural output, inflation rate/relative food prices, non-agricultural employment, Government's development expenditure, infrastructure and human development are important determinants of rural poverty. Most of these variables (with replacement of agricultural output with non-agricultural output) particularly inflation rate/relative food prices are important for explaining variations in urban poverty also. In the case of rural poverty, the role of rural non-farm sector is also increasing over time. I have already mentioned above the strategies for employment opportunities and quality of employment.

The government should have a twin-pronged strategy. Given the problem of unemployment for educated and unemployment for the masses, there is a need to have a twin strategies for improving the livelihoods. The first sub-strategy should aim at rural and urban masses who are illiterate/semi-literate, unskilled, semi-literate/skilled. The second sub-strategy is to address the problems of educated unemployed. Selected growth engines can be identified for both unskilled workers and educated unemployed.

Human Development and Human Poverty. Here public action plays much more important role than in the case of income poverty. Increase in social sector expenditures and efficient utilisation of these expenditures are important for raising human development and decline in human poverty.

A study on social sector expenditures for centre and states in the 1990s reveal the following:

1. Has social sector expenditure declined/increased in the 1990s?

(a) *Centre+States taken together*. As a proportion of GDP, the share of social sector expenditure has not increased during the reform period except in 1990-00. The shares in the 1990s were lower than those of 1980s. As a proportion of total public expenditure, the share for the social sector has definitely increased since the mid-1990s. The proportion was higher in the second half of the 1990s than it was in the late 1980s. The per capita real expenditure on the social sector has also increased since the mid-1990s. From the middle of the 1990s onwards, the per capita real expenditure was higher than what it was in the 1980s.

(b) *Central Government Expenditure:* Since 1993-94, the share of GDP devoted to the social sector was higher than that in the base year 1990-91, although not very much different from the shares in the late 1980s. As a proportion of public expenditure and as real per capita expenditure, there has been a significant increase in social sector spending since the mid-1990s. These figures were also higher than those of the late 1980s.

(c) *State Government Expenditure:* Taken as a proportion of GSDP or as a proportion of aggregate expenditure, social sector spending has come down in the States. In terms of per capita real expenditure, there has been some increase, but not in the first half of the 1990s, and not much for rural development.

One could be tempted to conclude, therefore, that the Centre has done better than the states in the post-reform period. This is, however, slightly misleading, since the two are not unrelated. One can also argue that the Centre has been able to perform better by withholding money from the States. Over the years the number of centrally sponsored schemes has continued to increase, at the expense of the allocation from the overall Plan outlay to the States.

2. Are there any improvements in education and health expenditures?

With regard to health, not much has happened. Neither the Centre nor the States increased its/their health expenditures considerably. The first half of the 1990s were especially bleak. In the second half of the 1990s, the per capital real expenditure on health by the States increased (but there was no increase in terms of proportion of GDP or GSDP). Intra-sectoral allocations shows that there has been a shift towards public health and maternal & child health.

With regard to education, the share of education expenditure from all the departments declined from around 4.1 per cent in 1990-91 to 3.8 per cent in 1998-99. This is mainly due to a decline at the State level. The Centre increased its expenditure after 1995-96. This increase is almost completely due to increases in spending on elementary education, and to a large extent (but not completely) related to the introduction and expansion of the midday meal programme.

In short, the shifts within education and health are in the right direction (towards social priority areas).

3. Are the social sector expenditures in India low/high compared to other countries and international norms?

Social sector expenditure in India in the 1990s is low. It is low as compared to what India spent in the 1980s; it is low as compared to other developing countries, and certainly as compared to east Asian countries, and it is low as compared to the UNDP recommended ratios.

Effectiveness of the Expenditures and Programmes

It may be noted, however, that importance should be given for effectiveness. In other words, we have to examine how efficiently funds are utilizaed and how much of it is reaching the poor. For reaching the government programmes effectively to the poor, decentralization access to information and social mobilization are important. These are elaborated below.

(a) **Decentralization:** There are many evaluations of the Government programmes in India. The effectiveness of these programmes, however, is limited because of 'top down' approach, lack of people's participation and poor delivery systems. However, one landmark that happened in the 1990s is the 73rd and 74th amendments to the Constitution. Nearly three decades later, interest in decentralization revived at the political level, for the first time, the Constitution provides a system of local Government based on mandatory elections. Panchayatis and Nagarpalikas should be involved in all the social security programmes including identification of the poor for targeted programmes like new revamped PDS, self and wage employment programmes, health and education and, protective social security schemes. There are reservations for women in panchayats for empowerment of women. However, as shown above, many women are illiterate and the power may still be in the hands of the elite. It is true that mere involvement of panchayats may not provide social security to the poor. The accountability of panchayats should be improved. Several conflicts involving the transfer of financial resources and powers to local authorities remain to be resolved. Kerala and West Bengal decided to devolve 40 per cent of the plan funds to panchayats.

(b) Access to Information: One way of increasing the accountability of panchayats and other local bodies is to have right to information on the panchayat funds in all the promotional and protective schemes in villages. The people of Rajasthan have pioneered the recent struggle on the right to information. The initiative for this struggle came out of a process begun by the Mazdoor Kisan Shakti Sangathan, a people's organization working in central Rajasthan. The struggle which began to gain focus in 1994 through the organisation of four public hearings in that region has now spread to other parts of

Rajasthan with the involvement of a cross section of citizens, organizations and the media. The public hearings articulated the need for transparency and social audit of development expenditure. The demand for transparency in development expenditure of the state, is a method by which the right may be realised.

(c) **Social Mobilization:** NGOs and CBOs can play an important role for creating an environment for social mobilisation and for sustainable human development. The main objective of social mobilization is to induce the poor to create participatory organizations based on the direct and full participation of all members of different varied socio-cultural backgrounds, irrespective of income, caste, gender or other discriminating characteristics. The eradication of poverty or reducing it to manageable limits in India would require a major political approach and strategic thrust in which social mobilization of the poor to contribute to growth plays a critical note. Even for the success of Government programmes for approach of social mobilization or empowerment of people is important.

Apart from this, there are anti-poor biases built into a host of existing policies, regulations and laws which cut across all sectors and vitiate any benefit that accrues to deprived communities.

Concluding Observations

I need not stress here the importance of reduction in population growth in India. As mentioned above, we need not wait for removal of poverty and high level of literacy in tackling population growth. Low sex ratio is a matter of concern in many states. There seems to be skewed growth of urbanisation in favour of rich states and big cities. Migration seems to have benefited the source areas while the migrants in the destination are being exploited. Although income poverty declined significantly at all India level many states are having high levels of poverty. Human poverty seems to be much higher than the income poverty. Based on human development and undernourished children, human poverty ranges from 40 to 50 per cent while income poverty is around 25 per cent.

I have given above briefly some strategies needed for reduction in income and human poverty. Some additional strategies are needed to take care of the vulnerable groups such as old age population, child labour, widows, SCs and STs categories.

It may be noted that economic growth and human development should go together in order to create opportunities for the population. As mentioned above, economic growth is not correlated with some of the human development indicators. Therefore direct public action is needed in some cases.

The economic reforms introduced in the country in 1991 would lead to greater economic opportunities for the population. However, in the context of marketisation, there is a substantial section of society which does not have the resource power to enter into market operations. The government and those who are already in the market have responsibility in providing social security for the large sections of unorganized workers and other vulnerable groups who are out of the market. It may be noted that Government alone can not provide social and economic security to population as there are limits to the capacity of the administration and finance. There is a need for public private partnership in tackling problems such as population growth, unemployment and underemployment, gender discrimination, income and human poverty.

References

Balasubramanian (2001), "India's Population: Second and Growing", paper presented at the workshop on "the implication of 2001 population Census results for Andhra Pradesh, organised by Centre for Economic and Social Studies, Hyderabad, 6th August, 2001.

Chellaiah, R.J. and R. Sudarshan (1999) "Income Poverty and Beyond: Human Development in India", Social Science Press, New Delhi.

Deaton, A. (2001), "Computing prices and Poverty rates in India, 1999-2000", Princeton, University, USA.

Dreze and Sen (1995) "India: Economic Development and Social Opportunity", Oxford, University Press, Delhi.

GOI (2001), Report of the Task Force on Employment Opportunities, Government of India, Planning Commission.

James, K.S. (2001) "Sex ratio and its implication", paper presented at the workshop on "the implication of 2001 population Census results for Andhra Pradesh, organised by Centre for Economic and Social studies, Hyderabad, 6th August, 2001.

Kundu, Amitabh (2001), "Brakes on Urban Sprawl", Business Standard, 28th August, 2001.

Mahendra Dev, S. (2001), "Growth-mediated and Support led social security in unorganised sector in India", key note paper presented at the annual conference of Indian Society of Labour Economics, Bangalore, 2001.

Mahendra Dev, S., James, K. and Binayak sen (2001), "Causes of Fertility Decline in India and Bangladesh", Centre for Economic and Social Studies, mimeo Srivastava, R (1998) "Migration of Labour in India", *The Indian Journal of Labour Economics,* Vol. 41, No. 4.

Visaria, P. (1998), "Unemployment among Youth in India: Level, Nature and Policy Implications", ILO, Employment and Training papers No. 36.

28

Poverty in India: Measurement and Trends

Prof. S. Subrahmanyam

Introduction

Poverty has been the major focus of planning in India. The National Planning Committee of the Indian National Congress proclaimed in 1938 that the aim of the planning was to ensure minimum standard of living to everybody through economic growth and equitable distribution of income and wealth. After independence, the Government of India Resolution of March 1950 stated that planning in India was intended to improve the standard of living of the people by efficient use of the resources and providing employment opportunities to all. Till the end of the Fourth plan the planners felt that economic growth and employment generation can tackle the problem of poverty in India. As there was no decline in the incidence till the end of sixties, it was realized that programmes for direct attack on poverty were needed, 'Garibi Hatao' became the main political slogan in the Fifth Five Year Plan period during which various anti-poverty programmes have been introduced. During the half century after independence a lot of research has been undertaken on various aspects of poverty. While the conceptual and measurement issues dominated the research for about two decades, policy issues for poverty alleviation were focused late seventies onwards. Interestingly, there was a controversy about the impact of planning on poverty during the sixties and seventies. The controversy subsided with continuous decline in the incidence of poverty between mid-seventies and eighties. With the introduction of economic reforms in 1991, policy debates on the appropriateness of reforms started and the official claims of decline in poverty in the nineties are being questioned. Thus the earlier debate on the trends in poverty is revived in the recent period. While the earlier debate was on the appropriateness of plan strategies, the present debate is on the appropriateness of the policy of liberalization, privatization and globalization. This paper focuses on the concepts and measurement of poverty and the long terms trends in the incidence of poverty. The various concepts of poverty are discussed in Section 2. Section 3 deals with measurement of poverty and the limitations of various measures. Section four deals with the estimates of poverty for different decades and also focuses on the reasons for controversy about the trends in poverty in the nineties. The major conclusions of the paper are brought together in section 5.

Concepts of Poverty

Poverty can be viewed from different angles. But it generally refers to the situation where an individual or a household is placed due to lack of resources. Poverty may be distinguished in four ways. Since each type of classification has significance in terms of understanding and policy needs, a brief discussion of them is useful.

Primary and Secondary Poverty

In the literature on poverty a distinction is made between 'primary' and 'secondary' poverty. Primary poverty is a situation in which total earnings of a family are inadequate to obtain the minimum necessaries needed for the maintenance of mere physical efficiency. On the other hand, families are said to be in secondary poverty if total earnings would be sufficient for the maintenance of physical efficiency provided the households change the pattern of allocation of expenditure. This concept indicates that living in a state of poverty is not necessarily a matter of income deficiency. Further, this concept throws light on the role of 'demonstration effect' as a cause of poverty and the leakages to household budgets by way of diversion of income for consumption of non-essential items even before the primary needs are met.

Absolute and Relative Poverty

Another distinction in poverty in between 'absolute' and 'relative' poverty. A household is considered to be poor in the absolute sense when it is unable to provide itself with the minimum subsistence defined usually in terms of nutritional norm. Relative poverty is defined in terms of income and wealth of a household in relation to that of the community. In relative poverty a household is treated as poor if its income falls below some standard fixed on the basis of the average income of the entire community. The absolute poverty concept is relevant for developing countries where minimum needs are not satisfied for a majority of the population since on the basis of relative poverty even persons with low food intake will be counted as non-poor. On the other hand, absolute poverty is not relevant for the developed countries since almost all the households satisfy the food intake norm. The Human Development Reports of the UNDP adopt 50 per cent of median disposable household income as the poverty line for developed countries.

Chronic and Temporary Poverty

When a household is unable to meet the minimum requirements due bad economic shocks like drought and gets adequate income in normal times, the household is temporarily poor. On the other hand, a household is chronically poor if its income is below the minimum level even during the normal times. This distinction is needed because policies needed to combat temporary poverty are different from those needed to combat chronic poverty. For instance, in a drought year, rural employment programmes are needed to tackle the problem of temporary poverty. This distinction is closely related to Friedman's classification of income into permanent and transitory.

Household and Individual Poverty

Data on expenditure is usually available at household level rather than individual level. But estimates of the poor are generated from this data assuming that the allocation of expenditure within the household is even and all members of the households are treated as non poor if the average per capita expenditure is more than that required for crossing poverty line. These estimates reflect household poverty rather than individual poverty. However, there are some evidences of intra-household inequalities the allocation of expenditure. It is argued that females and the elderly persons are the potential victims of poverty even in non-poor households. Some individuals in a non-poor household may be poor and some persons in a poor household may be non-poor. There is a need to supplement the macro estimates of poverty by micro level studies to identify the vulnerable sections in different categories of households. Further, these may be economies of scale in consumer expenditure because of the presence of fixed cost in setting up and running a household. In such a case the minimum income needed by a household depends on the household size also.

Measurement of Poverty

In order to measure poverty, the first requirement is the measuring rod known as poverty line and the second requirement is the method of measurement. Poverty line is the minimum level of income needed by a household for satisfying its minimum requirements. Once poverty is determined, a methods has to be evolved to estimate the incidence of poverty.

Determination of Poverty Line

Generally, the level of expenditure at which an average person will be able to derive his nutritional requirements is taken as the poverty line. Two methods are in vogue for determining the poverty line. The first method is to update the earlier poverty line for temporal and regional differences. An Expert Group constituted by the Government of India in 1962 determined that an expenditure of Rs. 20/- per capita per month as 1960-61 prices is needed for providing a reasonable standard of living. This norm is adopted in several studies and suitable adjustments are made for price variations. In the second method, the data on consumption of various food non-food items will be considered and the quantities of food consumed will be converted into calories. Then a relationship will be established between calorie intake and total income (or expenditure) and from this relationship the expenditure needed to attain the required calories is estimated. The data required for adopting this method is available from the consumer expenditure surveys carried out by the National Sample Survey Organisation. The method of determining the poverty line from the calorie expenditure relationship is shown in Figure 1. The horizontal axis shows per capita monthly expenditure and the vertical axis shows per capita calorie intake per day. If calorie requirement is 2400 per capita per day, the expenditure needed to attain this norm is read off from the horizontal axis corresponding to that requirement. If C is the calorie requirement the corresponding expenditure is X_p and this is the poverty line.

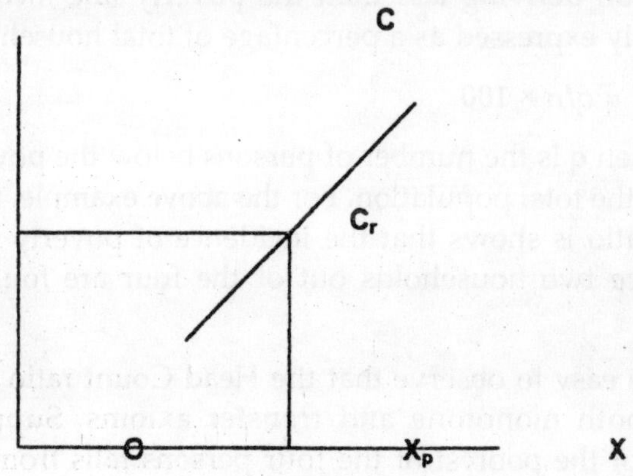

Measures of Poverty

Several measures of poverty have been evolved on be basis of the main focus in measurement. A measure of poverty is expected to satisfy certain important axioms. It is required that the measure should indicate increase in poverty when the income of any poor person declines, given the income of others. Similarly, the measure should indicate a decline in poverty when the income of any poor person increases, given the incomes of all others. This axiom is known as monotone axiom. If there is a transfer of income from a poor person to a relatively better off person, the measure should indicate increase poverty. Similarly, any transfer of income from a moderately poor person to a severely poor person must reduce poverty. This axiom is known as transfer axiom. Four measures of poverty viz., Head Count, Poverty Gap, Squared Poverty Gap and Sen's Poverty Index are frequently used in the studies of poverty. The distinctions between these measures can be understood clearly if each measure is applied for the same data set. Assume that there are four households with per capita monthly incomes of Rs. 100, 200, 300, 400. For simplicity we assume that poverty line is Rs. 300 per capital per month.

Head-Count Ratio (HC)

Head Court ratio is the proportion of households or population deriving less than the poverty line income. It is frequently expressed as a percentage of total households.

$$\mathbf{HC = q/n \times 100}$$

When q is the number of persons below the poverty line and n is the total population. For the above example, the Head Count ratio is shows that the incidence of poverty is 50 per cent since two households out of the four are found to be poor.

It is easy to observe that the Head Count ratio does not satisfy both monotone and transfer axioms. Suppose the income of the poorest of the four persons falls from Rs. 100

to Rs. 80. Still the Head Count ratio will be the same 50 per cent. Similarly, if the income of the poorest person increases Rs. 120, the Head Count ratio is again the same because the improvement is not adequate to lift him above the poverty line. Thus, the Head Count measure violates monotone axiom. The Head Count ratio does not fulfill the transfer axiom also. Suppose there is a transfer of income of Rs. 20 from the poorest person to the next person in the income order. The Head Count ratio is the same because both the poor persons continue to be poor even after this transfer. Even a transfer of Rs. 20 from the better off person to the poorest will keep the incidence of poverty at the same level. Thus, the Head Count ratio violates the transfer axiom of welfare. Sometimes the Head Count ratio gives a perverse result with transfer of income. For instance, if the entire income of the poorest person is transferred to the next person in the order, then the incomes of the four persons will be Rs. 0, 300, 300, 400. The Head Count ratio shows the perverse result of decline in poverty from 50 to 25 per cent.

The Head Count measure has also another drawback. A given increase in income will reduce poverty significantly if the improvement occurs to the persons whose incomes are close the poverty line. In the above example an increase in the income by Rs. 100 will reduce the Head Count ratio to 25 per cent if it accrues to the second poorest and there is no change in the Head Count ratio if it accrues to the poorest person. Because of this nature of the measure, targets on poverty removal based on HC can be easily achieved if the benefits are given to marginally poor rather than the poorest of the poor. In spite of the above limitations, the Head Court measure is popular because of its simplicity. It is easy to calculate and easy to understand. Its data requirements are less stringent.

Poverty Gap (PG)

The Poverty Gap represents the average distance between the poverty line and the actual income of the poor, using total population in calculating the average and expressing the average as a percentage of the poverty line.

$$PG = (1/n)\ \Sigma\ ((Z - Y_1)/Z) \times 100$$

where PG is the poverty gap, Z is the poverty line, Y_1 is the income of the poor person and n is the total population including non-poor. For the above example, the estimate of poverty gap comes to 25 per cent [(200 + 100)/(4 × 300) × 100]. The measure satisfied the monotone axiom but violates the transfer axiom. Suppose the income of the second poorest person declines from Rs. 200 to Rs. 100 with other incomes remaining constant. Then Poverty Gap increases to 33.3 per cent [400/(4 × 300) × 100].

The measure does not satisfy the transfer axiom. Suppose an amount of Rs. 20 is transferred from the next person. The Poverty Gap still remains at 25 per cent [(220 + 80)/(4 × 300) × 100]. Thus, the Poverty Gap measure is not sensitive to income transfers among the poor as long as they won't cross the poverty line. Another limitation of this measure is its inability to indicate the magnitude of the target population. It only gives the magnitude of income needed to remove poverty. However, this measure has the merit of revealing the depth of poverty, where as Head Count measure only gives the spread poverty. This measure can also be interpreted as a ratio of minimum cost of eliminating poverty with perfect targeting to the cost of when there no targeting.

Squared Poverty Gap (PG)

A given shortfall in income from the poverty line gives greater suffering for a person farther away from the poverty line than to a person who is closer to the poverty line. Hence, a rupee shortfall of a poorer person should receive a higher weight than that of a better off person. This measure achieves it by squaring the gap of each person's income from the poverty line and averaging these squared gaps:

$$SPG = (1/n)\ \Sigma\ ((Z - Y_t)/Z)^2 \times 100$$

where SPG is the poverty gap. Z is the poverty line, Y_t is the income of the poor person and n is the total population including the non-poor. For the above example, Squared Poverty Gap is estimated as follows:

Person	*Per capita monthly*	$(Z-Y_t)^2$
1	Income	40000
2	100	10000
3	200	—
4	300	—
	400	50000

SPG = 50000/4 × 90000 × 100 = 13.9%

Comparison of the three measures

Though the three measures appear to completely different, they are related in the sense that they are based on a common formula.

(1/n) Σ ((Z – Y_t)/Z)

where the value of differs for three measures. The values of zero, unity and two for give Head Count, Poverty Gap and Squared Poverty Gap respectively. The three measures of poverty serve different purposes. The Head Count measure gives the spread, the Poverty Gap measure gives the depth and the Squared Poverty Gap gives the severity. A sample numerical illustration makes the distinction very clear. Suppose we have two localities each with four individuals. Poverty line is 3 and the incomes are 1, 2, 3, 4 in locality A and 2, 2, 2, 4 in locality B. The Head Court ratio comes to 50 per cent (2/4 × 100) for locality A and 75 per cent (3/4 × 100) for locality B. The Poverty Gap ratio is 25 per cent [(2/3 + 1/3)/4 × 100] for locality A and 25 per cent [(1/3 + 1/3 + 1/3)/4 × 100] or for locality B, indicating that spread of poverty is more in locality B, but depth of poverty is same in both the localities. The Squared Poverty Gap is 14 per cent [4/9 + 1/9]/4 × 100] for locality A and 8 per cent [1/9 + 1/9 + 1/9]/4 × 100] for locality B, indicating that poverty is more severe in locality A than in locality B. The conclusion we can draw from this data is that though locality A has lower incidence than locality B, its poverty problem is more severe than in B. In terms of depth of poverty both localities are same. Thus the superiority of A in terms of lower incidence is lost when Poverty Gap is considered and its position became lower than that of B when Squared Poverty gap is considered.

Sen's Poverty Index

Sen's measure is also similar to that of squared poverty gap. Instead of squaring the gaps, Sen uses rank order weights. We arrange the poor households in the descending order of income, multiply each gap with the rank of the household and aggregate the weighted shortfalls. The formula of Sen's poverty index (P) is as follows:

$$P = 2/(q+1)NZ\ \Sigma\ (Z-Y_i)(q+1-1) \times 100$$

Where q is the number of households below the poverty line, Z is the poverty line, Y_i is the expenditure of the *i*th households arranged in descending order of magnitude and N is the total number of households. Sen's poverty index is computed for the data in the earlier example.

S.No.	Y_1	$Z-Y_1$	*Weights*	$(Z-Y_i)\ (q+1-i)$
(1)	(2)	(3)	(4)	(5)
1	100	200	2	400
2	200	100	1	100
Total				**500**

Sens's poverty index = 2/3 × 4 × 300 × 500 × 100 = 100000/36000 = 27.8%

Other Measures of Poverty

Since poverty is multi-dimensional phenomenon, it is reflected in other aspects of life. An improvement in nutritional poverty does not necessarily mean that poverty is removed. The earliest attempt of considering other aspects is reflected in the physical quality of life index (PQLI) suggested by Morris David Morris and Michelle B. Mc Alpin (1982) which takes into account life expectancy, infant mortality and literacy. The results on PQLI for the seventies for Indian states revealed that poor correlation (0.08) between calories intake and PQLI. Nor is there significant relation with infant mortality (0.20) or life expectancy at age on (0.27). The same concept is refined in the calculation of the human development index (HDI) and supplementary indices like human poverty index, gender-related development index (GDI) and gender empowerment measure (GEM).

The Human Development Index published by the UNDP measures the overall achievements in three basic dimensions of human development–longevity, knowledge and a decent standard of living. Longevity is measured by life expectancy, knowledge by adult literacy and school enrollment and standard of living is measured by GDP per capita adjusted for purchasing power parity (PPP) in US dollars. An index is calculated for each of these three dimensions and HDI is a simple average of the three dimension indices. To calculate these dimension indices, minimum and maximum values (goalposts) are chosen for each underlined indicator—the maximum and minimum values are 85 and 25 years for life expectancy, 100 and zero for adult literacy rate and gross enrolment ratio and 40,000 and 100 US dollars for GDP per capita. Performance in each dimension is expressed as a value lying between zero and unity by applying the following formula:

Dimension index = (actual value – minimum value)/ (maximum value–minimum value)

Human poverty index focuses on deprivation in three dimensions viz., longevity (probability at birth of not surviving to age 40), knowledge (adult illiteracy rate) and economic provisioning (percentage of people not using improved water sources and the percentage underweight children in the 0 to 5 age group). Since the above indicators are already normalized between 0 and 100, there is no need to create dimension indices in this case. Deprivation of a decent standard of living is measured as an unweighted average of the two indicators namely, the percentage of population not using improved water resources and the percentage of underweight children in the 0 to 5 age group. The formula for calculating in HPI-1 is as follows:

$$\text{HPI} = [1/3\,(p_1^{\alpha} + p_2^{\alpha} + p_3^{\alpha})]^{1/\alpha}$$

Where P_1 is probability at birth of not surviving to age 40 (times 100), P_2 is adult illiteracy rate and P_3 is the unweighted average of population not using improved water sources and underweight children under age five and α is 3.

The gender-related development index (GDI) measures achievements in the same dimensions and using the same indicators as the HDI, but captures inequalities in achievement between women and men. It is simply the HDI adjusted downward for gender inequality. The greater is the gender disparity in basic human development, the lower is a country's GDI compared with its HDI.

Estimates of Poverty in India

The five decades of planned development in India after independence can be classified into three periods. The first period covers two decades. There was not much change in the incidence of poverty and hence increase in the number of poor. The second period extending two decades witnessed significant decline in poverty. The third period covering one decade is a period for which no definite conclusions can be drawn regarding the trends in poverty.

Poverty in India during the Fifties and the Sixties

Dandekar and Rath (1971) adopted the nutritional norm of 2,250 calories per capita per day as the minimum requirement. On the basis of the distribution of NSS private consumer expenditure in 1960-61, they found that the calorie norm was satisfied at an annual per Capita expenditure or Rs. 180 in rural areas and Rs. 270 in the urban areas approximately. Using these poverty lines, they found that about 40 per cent of the rural population and about 50 per cent of the urban population fell below the poverty line in 1960-61.

Ojha (1970) also adopted a nutritional norm of 2,250 calories and estimated very high incidence of rural poverty in 1960-61 and a sharp increase in 1967-68. He measured poverty in terms of food grain intake alone. Assuming that 80 per cent of the calorie requirement in rural areas and 66 per cent in urban areas must be met from food grains, he worked out the minimum food grain intake as 518 gms. Per capita per day in rural areas and 432 grams. Per capita per day in urban areas. He estimated rural poverty at 52 per cent in 1960-61 and 70 per cent in 1967-68. His estimate of poverty for the urban areas is only 8 per cent in 1960-61.

Minhas (1970) used two norms of per capita consumer expenditure at 1960-61 prices viz., Rs. 240/- and Rs. 200/- per annum as poverty lines and estimated the proportion of the poor in rural areas. On the basis of Rs. 240/- norm, he arrived at the conclusion that the number of people below the poverty line had not changed much but the proportion below the poverty line declined from 65.0 to 50.6 per cent during the period 1956-57 to 1967-68. At the second norm (Rs. 200/-) it is not only the proportion of the poor that fell from 52.4 in 1956-57 to 37.1 per cent 1967-68, but the absolute number of the poor also declined from 173 millions to 154 millions. This decline was attributed to the growth rate of average per capita consumption at 1.24 per cent per annum achieved over this period rather than to the fall in the inequalities in the income distribution. It is to be noted that Minhas used official estimates of consumption rather than the estimates provided by the NSS. He used NSS data only for estimating the distribution of consumption across expenditure groups. Bardhan (1974) showed a sharp rise in the incidence of poverty from 38 per cent in 1960-61 to 54 per cent in 1968-69. He used the expenditure norm of Rs. 15 per cent per capita per month at 1960-61 prices as the poverty line for the rural India. He adopted the series of price indices pertaining to agricultural labourers and the weighing diagrams provided by the Second Agricultural Labour Enquiry. The estimates of Minhas and Bardhan are shown in table 1.

Table 1: Poverty in India Earlier Estimates

Year	Minhas B.S. (Rs. 200)	Bardhan P.K. (Rs. 180)
1956-57	52.4	-
1957-58	50.2	-
1960-61	46.0	38.0
1961-62	43.6	-
1963-64	44.2	-
1964-65	39.2	45.0
1967-68	37.1	53.0
1968-69	-	54.0

Source: Mihas, B.S. (1970) *"Rural Poverty, Land Redistribution and Development"*, Indian Economic Review (New Series) Vol. V, No. 1, June and December and, Bardhan, P.K. (1974), *"On the incidence of Poverty in Rural India in the Sixties"* Sankhyaa, series C. Vol. 36, Parts 2 & 4, June and December.

Vaidhyanadhan and Ahluwalia provided explanations for these contradictory results. Vaidhyanadhan estimated rural poverty adopting both the methods viz., using only NSS data and using official estimates for per capita consumption together with the NSS distribution. He adopted Rs. 240/- per capita per annum at 1960-61 prices as the poverty line. He adopted fractile group price indices worked out on the basis of the official wholesale price relatives for the commodity groups and the NSS weights. His estimates based on the NSS data revealed a rise in poverty from 59.5 per cent in 1960-61 to 67.8 per cent in 1967-68. On the other hand, his estimates based on the official estimates of per capita consumption showed a mild decline from 58.8 per cent in 1960-61 to 57.8 in 1967-69. These results are shown in Table 2.

Table 2: Incidence of Poverty: Based on NSS and Official Series

Year	NSS	Official Series
1960-61	59.5	58.8
1964-65	60.4	56.9
1967-68	67.8	57.8

Source: A. Vaidyanaathaan, (1974), *"Some Aspects of inequalities in living standards in rural India"* Sankhya, Series C, Vol. 36, Parts 2 & 4.

Ahluwalia (1978) estimated rural poverty for each year during 1957-58 to 1973-74 adopting Rs. 15/- per capita month at 1960-61 prices as the poverty line and consumer price indices of agricultural labourers prepared by the labour bureau. His results show that the time trend in the incidence of poverty cannot be judged by comparing the end points. Further, no significant trend was observed in the incidence of poverty during the period. The study also showed that the incidence of poverty is negatively associated with agricultural output. In other words, incidence of poverty will be lower during the years of higher agricultural output. These results are presented in Table 3.

Table 3: Estimates of Rural Poverty in India

Year	*Incidence of Poverty*		*Number of poor (Millions)*
	Estimate-I (Pov. India)	*Estimate II (States)*	
1956-57	54.1	-	-
1957-58	50.2	53.4	182
1958-59	46.5	-	-
1959-60	44.4	48.7	173
1960-61	38.9	42.0	152
1961-62	39.4	42.3	157
1963-64	44.5	49.1	189
1964-65	46.8	50.4	198
1965-66	53.9	51.1	205
1966-67	56.6	57.4	235
1967-68	56.5	57.9	241
1968-69	51.0	53.5	227
1970-71	47.5	49.1	217
1973-74	46.1	47.6	221

Source: M.S. Ahluwalia, (1978), "Rural Poverty and Agricultural Performance in India" Journal of Development Studies, Vol. 14, No. 3.

Poverty in India during the Seventies and the Eighties

The studies on poverty since 1970 have some distinct characteristics. Firstly, NSS data are not available for each year. Hence we have estimates only for six time points viz., 1972-73, 1977-78, 1983-84, 1987-88, 1993-94 and 1999-2000. For other years starting from 1988-89, estimates are available from thin sample surveys of NSS. Secondly, the Task Force on Projections of Minimum Needs and Effective Consumption Demand (1979) defined the poverty line as the per capita expenditure level at which per capita per day calorie intake was 2,400 in rural and 2100 in urban areas. Thirdly, official estimates of poverty are available for this period. These estimates were based on adjustments made for differences between the estimates provided by the National Sample Survey (NSS) and National Accounts Statistics (NAS). Usually the estimates of consumption based on the NAS have been found to be higher than those based on the NSS and the difference has been increasing over time. The practice is to raise the expenditure levels reported by the NSS across all classes by a factor equal to the ratio of private consumption as obtained from NAS and NSS. This procedure gives a lower estimate of poverty than the one derived without adjusting the NSS data. The Expert Group constituted by the Planning Commission in 1993 made two suggestions about the methodology of determining poverty line-to adopt state specific poverty lines instead of using the same all-India poverty line for all the States and to discontinue the adjustment of NSS data. The Planning Commission accepted the suggestions of the Expert Group in 1997. The estimates of poverty across States are shown in Table 4.

The incidence of rural poverty based on Head Count ratio declined from about 56 per cent in 1973-74 to 39 per cent in 1987-88. The decline is more than 1 percentage point per annum. Urban poverty declined from 49 per cent in 1973-74 to 38 per cent in 1987-88. The decline is less than 1 percentage point per annum. Thus, the decades of 70s and 80s witnessed greater decline in rural poverty than urban poverty (Table 5).

Poverty in India during the Nineties

The issue of poverty has become important in the nineties because of the policy debate on the effects of economic reforms introduced in 1991. There was no acceleration in the growth

Table 4: Estimates of Poverty by States

State	*1973-74*	*1977-78*	*1983*	*1987-88*	*1993-94*	*1999-00*
Andhra Pradesh	48.86	39.31	28.91	25.86	22.19	15.77
Assam	51.21	57.15	40.47	36.21	40.86	36.09
Bihar	61.91	61.55	62.22	52.13	54.96	42.60
Gujarat	48.15	41.23	32.79	31.54	24.21	14.07
Haryana	35.36	29.55	21.37	16.64	25.05	8.74
Himachal Pradesh	26.39	32.45	16.40	15.45	28.44	7.63
Jammu & Kashmir	40.83	38.97	24.24	23.82	25.17	3.48
Karnataka	54.47	48.78	38.24	37.53	33.16	20.04
Kerala	59.79	52.22	40.42	31.79	25.43	12.72
Madhya Pradesh	61.78	61.78	49.78	43.07	42.52	37.43
Maharashtra	83.24	55.88	43.44	40.41	36.86	25.02
Orissa	66.18	70.07	65.29	55.58	48.56	47.15
Punjab	28.15	19.27	16.18	13.20	11.77	6.16
Rajasthan	46.14	37.42	34.46	35.15	27.41	15.28
Tamil Nadu	54.94	54.79	51.66	43.39	35.03	21.12
Uttar Pradesh	57.07	49.05	47.07	41.46	40.85	31.15
West Bengal	63.43	60.52	54.85	44.72	35.66	27.02
All India	**54.88**	**51.32**	**44.48**	**38.86**	**35.97**	**26.10**

Table 5: Implicit Poverty Lines and Incidence of Poverty

Year	*Poverty lines (Rs. per capita per month)*		*Head Count Ratio (percentages)*	
	Rural	*Urban*	*Rural*	*Urban*
1973-74	49.63	56.96	56.4	49.0
1977-78	56.84	72.50	53.1	45.2
1983	89.45	117.64	45.7	40.18
1987-88	115.43	165.58	39.1	38.2
1993-94	205.84	286.72	37.3	32.4
1990-00	328.00	458.00	27.1	23.6

rate of gross domestic product in the nineties over the previous decade (Nagaraj, 2000). The growth rate remained more or less the same as in the eighties. The data on poverty are available from two large sample surveys conducted during 1993-94 and 1999-2000 (50th and 55th rounds of NSSO) and four small sample surveys conducted during the intervening years. The controversy about the trends in poverty during the nineties is mainly due to the change in methodology of data collection since 1994-95. NSSO has been using previous month has the reference period till 1993-94. But the reference period is changed to previous week from 1994-95 onwards. In all the four small sample surveys, this new reference period is adopted for one-half of the sample and the old reference period for the remaining half. The results based on week reference period showed significantly higher level of consumption and hence lower incidence of poverty than those based on month reference period. Further, there is no decline in the incidence of poverty between 1993-94 and 1998-99. The incidence fluctuated between 36 and 43 per cent as compared to 37 per cent in 1993-94 in rural areas. Similarly, the incidence in urban areas hovered around 32 and 35 per cent as compared to 33 per cent in 1993-94 (Table 6).

Table 6: Incidence of Poverty Based on week and Month Reference Periods

Year	*Rural*		*Urban*	
	Week	*Month*	*Week*	*Month*
1993-94	-	37.1	-	32.9
1994-95	22.8	41.2	18.3	35.5
1995-96	19.1	37.6	15.2	29.9
1997	20.7	35.9	17.8	32.3
1998 (Jan-June)	23.6	42.6	20.0	32.9

But in 55th round relating to 1999-2000 both reference periods are included in the same questionnaire and with this change the gap in per capita expenditure between the two estimate almost vanished and there was steep increase in the estimates based week reference period. It is felt that the consumption estimates from this round are not comparable to those from previous round (Abhijit Sen, 2000). The estimate of poverty for 1999-2000 is found to be 26.1 as against 36.0 per cent 1993-94. A lot of energy is being spent in adjusting the estimates of consumption and poverty for design changes. For instance, Deaton and Dreze (2002) adjust for design changes and show that the incidence rises slightly from 26.8 to 30.0 per cent in rural areas and 24.1 to 24.7 per cent in urban areas after adjustment. They conclude that the decline in the incidence of poverty in the nineties is real. However, these results have to be taken with a pinch of salt and no definite conclusions can be drawn till the results of the next NSS round are available.

The human development index (HDI) is calculated for 162 countries in the world in 1999. When the countries are ranked in the descending order of development, India obtained 115th position with a value of 0.571. The position of China is higher at 87 with a value of 0.718 and the Pakistan is lower at 127 with a value of 0.498. The human poverty index (HPI) places India at 555th position and China at 24th position. Pakistan is again at a lower position. The gender related development index (GDI) also the same order (Table 7).

Table 7: Trends in Human Development Index

Country	*Human Development Index*		*Human Poverty Index*		*Gender Related Development Index*	
	Rank	*Value*	*Rank*	*Value*	*Rank*	*Value*
India	115	0.571	55	34.3	105	0.553
China	87	0.718	24	15.1	76	0.715
Pakistan	127	0.498	65	39.2	117	0.466
USA	6	0.934	-	-	4	0.932
UK	14	0.923	-	-	12	0.920

Summary and Conclusions

Primary and absolute poverty concepts are more relevant than secondary and relative poverty concepts for a developing country like India. Chronic poverty is a more serious problem than temporary poverty. The former requires provision of assets which generate sustainable income and the latter needs employment and food distribution programmes. Even though a household is non-poor on the basis of the average level of income or consumption, some persons may still be deprived because of intra-household disparities in consumption. Along with anti-poverty programmes, welfare measures focusing on vulnerable sections like women and elderly persons have to be implemented.

Head Count measure of poverty became very popular despite its serious limitations. It violates both monotone and transfer axioms. Among the three related measures of poverty, head count measures spread of poverty, poverty gap measures depth of poverty and squared poverty gap measures severity of poverty. Sen's poverty index and squared poverty gap are based on the premise that a rupee shortfall gives a higher suffering to a poorer person than to a better off person. They differ only in the weighting pattern. Improvement in living conditions is reflected not merely in food consumption, but also on social indicators like health, education etc. In recent times, new measures like human development index, human poverty index and gender-related development index are evolved to compare the levels of development across countries.

The analysis of long period data reveals that incidence of poverty remained around 50 per cent till the end of sixties and then declined rapidly till the end of eighties. The performance is not clear due to changes made in the design of surveys of the National Sample Survey Organization. The results indicate that economic reforms have no positive impact on poverty. While gross domestic product grew at the same rate as in the eighties, there is no decline in the incidence of poverty in the nineties.

References

M. S. Ahluwalia, (1978), "Rural Poverty and Agricultural Performance in India" Journal of Development Studies, Vol. 14, No. 3.

Bardhan, P.K. (1974), "On the incidence of Poverty in Rural India in the Sixties" Sankhyaa, series C, Vol. 36, Parts 2 & 4, June and December.

I.Z. Bhatty (1974), "Inequality and Poverty in Rural India", Sankhya, Series C, Vol. 36, Parts 2 & 4.

V. M. Dandekar, and N. Rath (1971), "Poverty in India, Indian School of Political Economy.

Minhas, B.S. (1970) "Rural Poverty, Land Redistribution and Development", Indian Economic Review (New Series) Vol. V, No. 1. June and December

A. Vaidyanadhan (1974), "Some aspects of Inequalities in Living Standards in Rural India", Sankhya, Series C, Vol. 36, Parts 2 & 4.

Uma Datta Roychoudhury and Moni Mukherji (1984), "National Accounts System", Macmillan.

Morris, David Morris and Michelle, B. Mc Alpin (1982), "Measuring the Condition of India's Poor", New Delhi.

Deaton, Angus and Dreze, Jean (2002), "Poverty and Inequality in India: A Re-Examination", Economic and Political Weekly, September 7-13.

Sen, Abhijit (2000), "Estimates of Consumer Expenditure and its Distribution: Statistical Priorities after NSS 55th Round", Economic and Political Weekly, December 16-22.

NagaRaj, R (2002), "Indian Economy Since 1980: Virtuous Growth or Polarisation?", Economic and Political Weekly, August 5-11.

29

Components of Human Poverty Index: A Comparative Study of Indian States

K.C. Reddy
U.N. Moorthy
M. Sarojini

Introduction

The task of human development perspective obviously leads one to the most difficult but very obvious rediscovery that people are both the means and the end of economic development'. This idea coincides with the most beautiful expression of Telugu poet Gurajada that" Desamantae matti kadoi, desamantae manushuloi (Nation means not the clay but the people)". This simple but very important truth is very often forgotten because we tend to think in terms of numbers. The human development approach reminds us that human well being is the true end of development. "Human development is the process of enlarging people's choices by expanding human functionings and capabilities"[1]. There is a difference between the economic growth and human development schools. The first focuses attention exclusively on expansion of only one choice-income while the second (HDI) embraces the enlargement of all human choices-whether economic, social cultural or political[2].

Several approaches are used to measure human well being or its opposite human deprivation. One such distinction is based on outcomes and inputs. Outcomes consist of well being based on longevity, educational achievement, and ability to function in different dimensions, happiness and so on. Human Development Index is one among them. Measures supplementing Human Development Index such as Gender Development Index and Gender Empowerment Measure are vividly described in the UNDP's Human Development Report, 1995, Likewise the Human Development Report of 1997 presented the concept, measure and application of Human Poverty Index (HPI). The latter index tells us about the variation in incidence and intensity of poverty across different regional units such as Countries/States.

Poverty alleviation has been on the National policy agenda of Government of India since fifty years but more than a third of its population are still below poverty line. This may be due to failure to achieve rapid growth more in terms of quality and character of growth rather than its rate[3]. In the light of this an attempt is made in this paper to explain the components of Human Poverty Index and compare them across the 15 major States of Indian Union by using data for 1980s and 1990s. Alternative measures of educational attainment and health status available in the literature have been made use of. An attempt is also made to examine the relation between efficiency of the State in raising revenues as measured by Tax effort Index and attainment in education and health represented by their indices. After giving a descriptive picture of these two dimensions we also discuss the possible correlates of education and health status by calculating simple correlation. The paper is in three section. Section one introduces; section two defines the concepts and explains variables included in the analysis while section three presents the data analysis.

Concept and Variables in the Measure

Conceptually human poverty captures the multi-dimensional nature of poverty taking us much beyond the uni-dimensional income-poverty criterion. "HPI can help summarize the extent of poverty along several dimensions, the distances to go, the progress made"[4]. Being a composite index the human poverty Index has three basic dimensions i.e., deprivation in survival, in education and knowledge and in economic provisioning. The UNDP's Human Development Report of 1997 which developed this approach tried to assess the different routes to development in terms of improvement in the provision of three basic capabilities that go to determine quality of life that people lead in a state. The three capabilities chosen are health, knowledge and income. In human development approach longevity indicates health and is measured by life expectancy at birth. Similarly knowledge is represented by adult literacy and mean years of schooling (late modified to include gross enrolment ratio instead of mean years of schooling).

Professor N. Krishnaji criticised the aggregate measure and has given a strong critique of an index that "summarises information, but", he said that "it has no obvious merit as a summary measure"[5]. He asks a very basic question: Why do we need an index that combines different types of deprivation in a single measure as in every component of Human Poverty Index (survival, Knowledge) there are vast difference between various States of India. Thus a disaggregated approach seems to be more appropriate. The virtue of such an approach is that "it become clear precisely what the deficiencies in human capabilities and opportunities in various regions of the country are, and what specific area of human deprivation should concern policy makers in future regional plans"[6]. Therefore, by adopting the disaggregated approach, we compared the 15 major states of India along the two dimensions of Human Poverty Index i.e., survival (health) and education using data for 1980s and 1990s. Of these two, we give top priority to education as it is expected to determine to a great extent the achievement level of the State not only in educational but also health.

Education Expenditure

One of the biggest failures of development policy of India is the neglect of education. "Spreading education to everyone is an important means of spreading opportunities and incomes countering the tendency for inequality and social exclusion"[7] and this provides a strong base for development. Therefore it is aptly said that "there is in our time no well educated literate population that is poor, there is no illiterate population other than poor"[8]. This reveals that education or literacy is critical for economic and social development. Thus the achievement of social as well as economic objectives requires a higher level of average attainment in education by the people across the Countries/States/Regions. People with higher levels of schooling have higher levels of labour productivity. Differences in educational attainment across States are thus a major cause of variations in poverty as well as economic growth[9] though the returns to schooling are constrained until some minimum level of education coverage is reached across the population[10].

Therefore the immediate challenge is to increase the demand for schooling and to rapidly provide enough facilities to supply good quality universal primary schooling. This requires spending enough money through public intervention i.e., spending by the government (through construction of additional schools) of capital nature or (to meet expenditure on salaries of teachers) of revenue nature. However as a major portion of public expenditure on education is revenue expenditure for giving salaries to staff with the share of expenditure on materials and equipment being negligible the share of capital expenditure is much limited. Therefore, we have taken revenue expenditure on education as per cent of State Domestic Product as a variable accounting for differences in educational attainment. There are alternative ways of measuring the level of public expenditure on education such as proportion in Net State Domestic Product or as a proportion of total government budget or as expenditure per capita. We have chosen the first one; public expenditure as the proportion of State Domestic Product.

Index of Educational Achievement

Keeping in view problem arising out of availability of

data Bhaskar Datta et. al., have constructed such human development indices using alternative indicators for both education and health[11]. The education index they have used is based on gross school enrolment data at various stages of school education i.e., primary, middle and high school. They calculated gross enrolment as the ratio of total number of students enrolled at the relevant stage by the estimated population in a specified age group.

Primary level is defined as classes 1-5 and the corresponding age group being 6-11 years. Middle school is classes 6-8 with the associated age-group 11-14 years. High school is classes 9-12 with associated age-group 14-18 years. Despite many problems concerning the accuracy of the data especially regarding primary school enrolment they do not omit primary school data.

Non-linear achievement indices were constructed separately for primary, middle and high school levels of education as is done in the case of health explained below. In the second step these separate indices were converted into an overall index of educational achievement using weights of 0.4, 0.3 and 0.3 respectively.

Index of Health Achievement

Health is another important indicator of human development or well being. A country with healthy population will have efficient and skilled labour with their capacity to contribute to growth decidedly high. On the contrary the productivity of illiterate, unskilled, disease ridden, superstitious people is generally low and they do not provide any hope to development in a country/State.

The indicator variables for health are infant and child mortality rates provided by the Sample Registration System (SRS) reported by the Office of the Registrar General of India. These indicator variables are converted into achievement indices of health and education using the non-linear formula given below. The achievement index for health denoted by Infant Mortality Rate (X) is

$$AIMR(X) = 1 - \frac{[X - 10]^{0.5}}{[220]}$$

Specific values of 10 and 220 have been so chosen such that they are slightly lower than the minimum values and slightly than the maximum value achieved by the State during the reference period. The achievement index for health indicated by Child Mortality Rate (X) is

$$ACMR(X) = 1 - \frac{[X - 15]^{0.5}}{[118.5]}$$

The difference between achievement indices between the two period is seen as the improvement index between the two period.

Index of Tax Effort

The effectiveness of public expenditure on education or health is in turn determined by the efficiency of the state. In order to measure the efficiency of the State we have considered tax effort indices of the States calculated for the relevant periods[12]. Here the actual tax -SDP ratios are compared with the estimated taxable capable capacity ratios to find out whether a State is making adequate tax effort or not.

The actual tax-SDP ratio of a State depends upon (1) the ability of the people to pay tax (2) the ability of the administration to collect taxes and (3) the willingness to tax on the part of the government. Factors affecting the first two are tax capacity factors and those relating to the third represent tax effort factor[13]. Thus, the actual tax-SDP ratio depends upon the tax capacity factors and the tax effort factors. Therefore the taxable capacity is estimated by regressing the tax- SDP ratio on taxable capacity factors. After estimating the regression equation, the taxable capacity or estimated tax ratio for each State is calculated by plugging the actual values of taxable capacity of that State into the estimated equation. This ratio represents the relative taxable capacity of the States. Tax effort index is then calculated by taking the ratio of autual tax ratio to the estimated tax ratio.

In the present context tax-SDP ratio is regressed on three tax capacity factors: Per capita Net State Domestic Product, Urbanisation and Number Commercial Bank Branches per Lakh of Population. Multiple regression equation of the log-linear form is estimated by adopting ordinary least square method where

$$\text{Log } T/Y = b_0 + b_1 \log X_1 + b_2 \log X_2 + b_3 \log X_3 + e$$

T/Y = tax-SDP ratio,

X_1 = average per capita net State domestic product,

X_2 = per cent of urban population to total population

X_3 = number of commercial bank branches per lakh of population, b_0, b_1, b_2 b_3 are parameters to be estimated and

'e' = the error term

The tax effort is calculated for the 15 major States for two separate periods: 1982-85 and 1992-95 by taking three years averages of both dependent and independent variables to avoid any influence of fortuitous factors. The coefficient of Per Capita Net State Domestic Product, Urbanization and Number of Commercial Bank Branches per Lakh of Population is expected to be positive. These are the variables considered in this exercise and the next section presents the data analysis. Rank correlation coefficients between per capita income and tax effort index have been calculated to know the relationship between the level of development between the State and their tax performance. The rank correlation is 0.04 for 1982-85 and 0.21 for the period 1992-95. Though both are positive they are not significant. Thus we cannot say that rich States are making a relatively higher tax effort than poor States.

Analysis of Data

Bhaskar Datta et. al, have considered the period 1970 to 1990 but divided it into four sub periods. Like them we have choosen two periods: 1980s and 1990s covering two separate decades representing the pre-reform and the reform periods while making some adjustments as per the availability of data. States are arranged in descending order based on the tax effort index and the data are shown in Tables 1 and 2.

Table 1: Achievement in Education, Child Mortality and Infant Mortality Rates in the pre-reform period-1980s

State	*Educational Achievement (1980-81 to 84-85)*	*ACMR (1981 to 85)*	*AIMR 1981 to 85)*
Haryana	0.184	0.496	0.382
Andhra Pradesh	0.163	0.523	0.434
Tamilnadu	0.366	0.505	0.420
Assam	0.169	0.430	0.352
Kerala	0.475	0.721	0.684
Maharashtra	0.321	0.550	0.459
Madhya Pradesh	0.153	0.337	0.266
Rajasthan	0.121	0.382	0.330
Bihar	0.109	0.398	0.340
Gujarat	0.275	0.437	0.335
Karnataka	0.205	0.551	0.480
Uttar Pradesh	0.143	0.314	0.203
Orissa	0.174	0.401	0.258
West Bengal	0.274	0.498	0.423
Punjab	0.263	0.558	0.459

Source: Data on Achievement Index of Education at primary and high school level, ACMR, AIMR are taken from Bhaskar Datta et. al. "Human Development in India", in S.Subrahmanyam (ed.) Measurement of Inequality and Poverty, O.U.P, Mumbi, 1997, pp. 339-340 and 342.

From the Tables it is clear that the health indicators, child and infant mortality rates show similar results such that Kerala's achievement is far ahead of other States in both indices. Here Kerala as expected shows high levels of achievement in both health and education, which is not surprising. What is impressive is that Kerala also shows the highest rate of improvement in health as seen by the difference between the achievement indices of the two periods-pre-reform and the reform. At the other end we have the States of Madhya Pradesh, Orissa and Rajasthan not only with low levels of achievement but also with low levels of improvement. Another point of interest is that the disparity in health achievement levels across the States has not norrowed down over the two decades i.e. from the pre-reform to the reform period.

Table 2: Achievement in Education, Child Mortality and Infant Mortality Rates in the reform Period-1990s

State	*Educational Achievement 1985-86 to 88-89)*	*ACMR (1986 to 91)*	*AIMR (1986 to 91)*
Haryana	0.243	0.547	0.436
Tamilnadu	0.496	0.600	0.484
Kerala	0.501	0.799	0.764
Assam	0.234	0.477	0.387
Gujarat	0.342	0.511	0.411
Karnataka	0.285	0.564	0.457
Bihar	0.149	0.481	0.403
Andhra Pradesh	0.250	0.561	0.444
Rajasthan	0.166	0.439	0.379
Maharashtra	0.396	0.615	0.513
Madhya Pradesh	0.237	0.386	0.302
Orissa	0.225	0.427	0.283
Uttar Pradesh	0.169	0.400	0.307
West Bengal	0.264	0.580	0.477
Punjab	0.286	0.600	0.516

Source: Same as Table 1.

In the case of education once again Kerala tops, followed quickly by Tamilnadu. Andhra Pradesh is very much at its bottom in education though its achievement is slightly better. Andhra Pradesh has a plus point that though it has low achievement levels, it records high improvement between the two time periods, pre-reform to the reform periods.

The main focus of this exercise is to examine the relation between efficiency of the State in raising revenues as measured by tax effort index and attainment in health and education as represented by their indices. The simple correlations calculated for the purpose as shown in Table 3 have a correct sign i.e., positive for both periods but are not encouraginly high. One more significant feature is that the

Table 3: Correlation between Attainment in Education, Child and Infant Mortality Rates, Revenue Expenditure on Education and Tax Effort Index: 1980s and 1990s

Variable	*1980*	*1990*
EA-RECOND	0.382	0.154
EA-TEL	0.151	0.325
ACMR-RECOND	0.367	0.146
ACMR-TEL	0.268	0.261
AIMR-RECOND	0.437	0.239
AIMR-TEL	0.270	0.244
REOND-TEL	0.165	0.277

correlation coefficient is much higher during the later period i.e., 1990s compared to the earlier period 1980s. Liberalisation and economic reforms may be after all seem to be working! As regards the health indices, ACMR and AIMR show similar picture of positive sign but unfortunately the correlation seems to be reducing over time.

It is important not only to spend more money, but it is equally important that it is spent well[14]. Using time series data on public expenditure for individual States Bhaskar Datta et. al. have investigated that relationship between education and public expenditure separately for each State. The relationship between public expenditure on education and efficiency of a state on the one hand and the performance of the State in the field of education is of great interest to us. So we proceed to measure the strength of the inter-relationships using simple correlation with data presented in Table 4.

We also gave the scatter plot, relating the two variables, tax effort index and achievement index in education

Table 4: Tax Effort Index and Regression Coefficient of Real Per Capita Educational Expenditure in the States

States	*Tax Effort Index (1982-85)*	*RPCEX (1970-88)*
Haryana	122.11	0.79*
Andhra Pradesh	119.95	0.88*
Tamilnadu	115.90	2.16*
Assam	109.60	0.02*
Kerala	108.79	0.81*
Maharashtra	104.05	0.83*
Madhya Pradesh	100.46	1.42*
Rajasthan	98.69	0.83*
Bihar	95.91	0.08*
Gujarat	91.65	0.51*
Karnataka	91.19	0.69*
Uttar Pradesh	90.47	0.61*
Orissa	89.66	0.95*
West Bengal	88.14	0.74*
Punjab	84.66	-0.66*

Tel = Tax Effort Index.

RPCEX = Regression coefficient of achievement in primary and high school education represented by real per capital education expenditure.

represented by the regression coefficient of real per capita education expenditure denoted as (RPCEX). The same is presented in the figure below. The points denote that States with higher Tax effort index are having a higher real per capita educational expenditure too. This ultimately ensures that in the government policies, priority should be given to achievement in health and education.

Notes

1. UNDP: Human Development Report 1997, Oxford University Press, London, p.17
2. Mahabub Ul Haq: Reflections on Human Development 1996, Oxford University Press, New Delhi, p.14.
3. As seen in Srinivasan T.N: Eight Lectures in India's Economic Reform, Oxford University Press, New Delhi 2002, as seem in the review article by Vidya Pitre in RBI Occassional Papers, Vol. 21, No. 1, Summer 2002, p. 183.

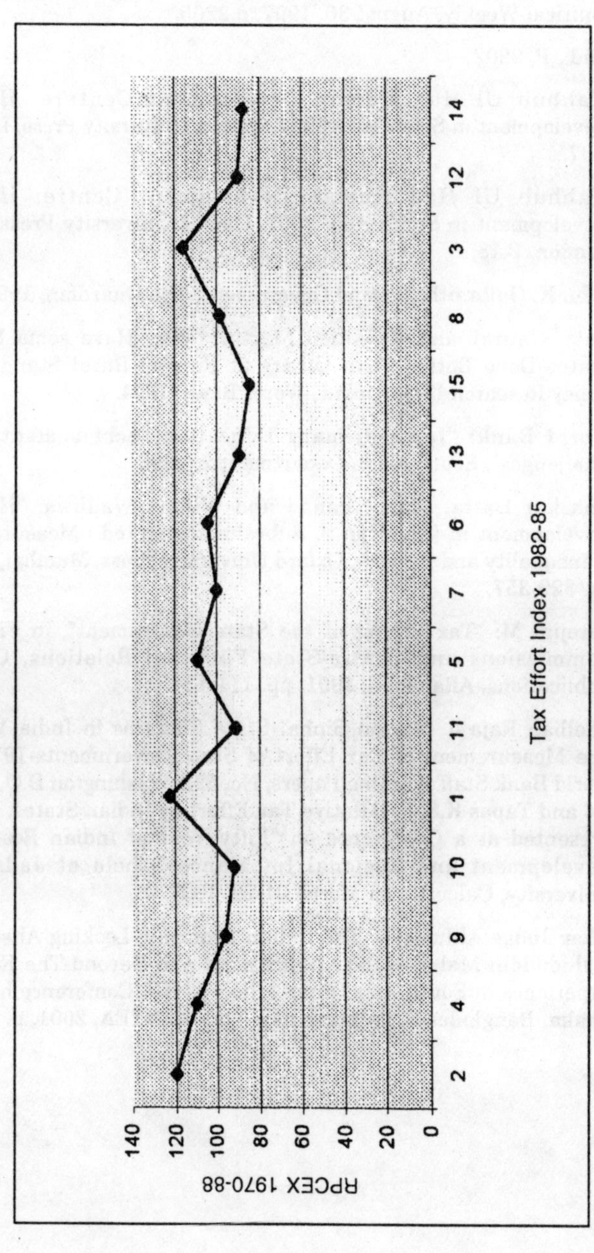

Relationship between Marginal Impact of Educational Expenditure and Efficiency of the States

4. Krishnaji N: "Human Poverty Index: A Critique", Economic and Political Weekly, August 30, 1997, p.2205.

5. Ibid., P. 2202.

6. Mahbub Ul Haq Human Development Centure: Human Development in South Asia 1997, Oxford University Press, London p.37.

7. Mahbub Ul Haq Human Development Centre: Human Development in South Asia 2001, Oxford University Press 2002, London, P.18.

8. John K. Galbraith: Beyond Government, The Guardian, 1994.

9. Datt, Gaurav and Ravallion Martin: "Why Have some Indian States Done Better Than Others at Raising Rural Standards?" Policy Research Department, World Bank, 1994.

10. World Bank: "India-Primary Education: Achievements and Challenges", South Asian Department 2, 1996.

11. Bhaskar Datta, Manoj Panda and Wilima Wadhwa: "Human Development in India", in S. Subrahmanyam (ed.) Measurement of Inequality and Poverty, Oxford University Press, Mumbai, 1997, pp. 329-357.

12. Sarojini M: "Tax Efforts of the State Government", in Finance Commissions and Centre-State Financial Relations, Chugh Publications, Allahabad, 1991, pp. 111-134.

13. Chelliah Raja J. Narain Sinha: State Finances in India Vol. 3, The Measurement of Tax Effort of State Governments-1973-76, World Bank Staff Working Papers, No. 523, Washington D.C. 1982, p.4 and Tapas K.Sen: Relative Tax Effort by Indian States, Paper Presented at a Conference on "Fifty Year of Indian Economic Development and Regional Imbalances", held at Jadavpur University, Calcutta, on March 21-22, 1997.

14. Ishar Judge Ahluwalia: The Indian Economy: Looking Ahead, in Wahiduddin Mahmud (ed.) Adjustment and Beyond-The Reform Experience in South Asia (Proceedings of IEA Conference held in Dhaka, Bangladesh), Palgrave new York with IEA, 2001, p. 18.

30

Livelihood Outcomes of Different Socio-Economic Groups in Andhra Pradesh

Prof. S. Galab
Dr. M. Gopinath Reddy

Introduction

In this paper, an attempt is made to assess and analyse the livelihood outcomes of different socio-economic groups across the districts. The livelihood outcomes considered for the analysis include income poverty, non-income poverty and gender empowerment. This paper addresses itself to the following issues, more specifically:

(i) What is income poverty status of different socio-economic groups in the district?

(ii) What is the non-income poverty status of different socio-economic groups in the district?

(iii) What is the status of gender empowerment?

Methodology

Asset Framework

Assets are stocks of different types of capital that can be used directly or indirectly to generate livelihoods. The Asset Framework (AF), one of the components of sustainable livelihood framework, basically assesses level and composition, clustering, sequencing and substitution of five capitals, viz., Human capital, Natural capital, Physical capital, Financial capital and Social capital, in relation to different socio-economic groups. The UNDP conceptual framework[1] has been adopted to analyse the AF of the households. This enables integration of different infrastructural facilities and common property resources, which are at the community level, with those capitals possessed by the household. Level and composition of capitals, given risk management and policy environment, determine livelihoods.

The income poverty has been examined in terms of extent, intensity, consumption inequalities, quality of consumption-composition of consumption basket and frequency of consumption, and food insecurity. The non-income poverty includes child labour, education and health status. Participation of women in decision-making at household level and supra-household level is considered to assess the status of gender empowerment. The indicators considered for assessing the status of livelihood outcomes are given below.

The status of poverty is examined in all its forms. The income poverty of the households is assessed on the basis of consumer expenditure data collected in the BLS from the households. The expenditure data are collected on 19 broad commodity groups. The reference period for the data collected is the last month for all the food items. However, the reference period is the last one year for some of the items like clothing and footwear, education, health, house rent, and consumer durables. It may be mentioned that the consumption data collected in the survey do not fully reflect the seasonal variations in consumption as the survey was carried out during the June-August 2001 months. The four dimensions of income poverty, viz., extent, intensity, inequality and quality of consumption are analysed. While the extent of

1. UNDP (1999)

Position of Livelihood Outcomes Sustainable Livelihood Framework

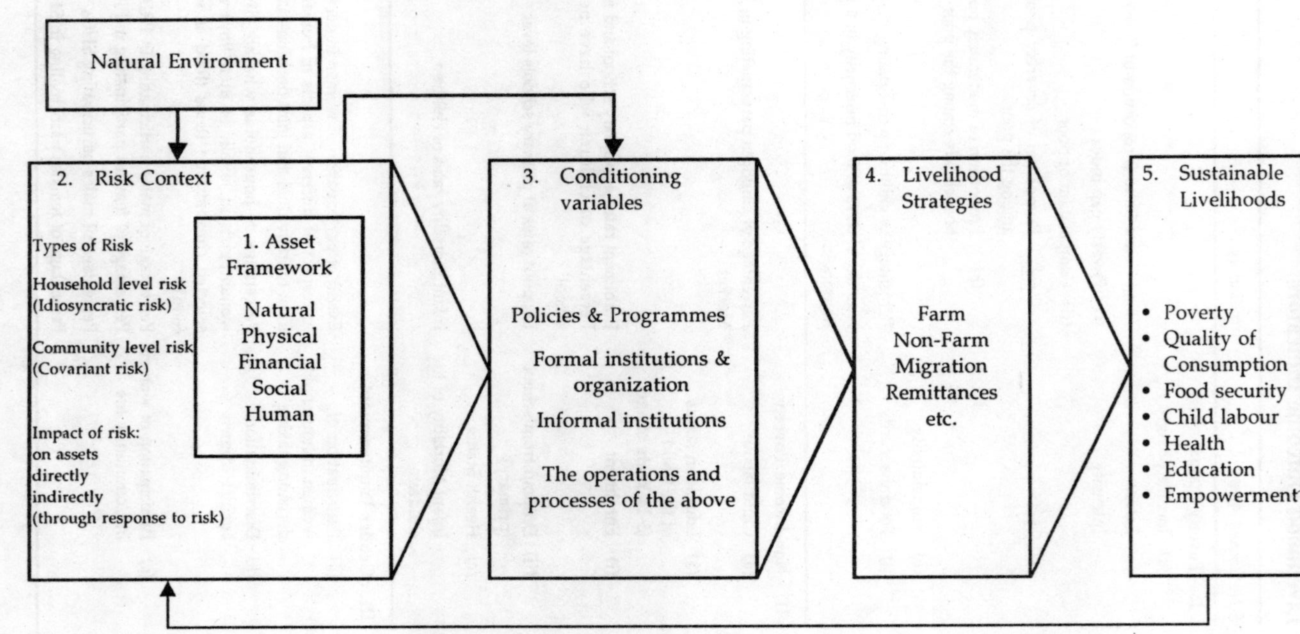

Livelihood Outcome Indicators

S.No	*Impact Area*	*Indicators*
I.	**Poverty Status**	
	(a) Income poverty	
	Extent	Head-Count Ratio (Proportion of Poor)
	Intensity	**(i)** Poverty gap index
		(ii) Composition of poor
		(a) Proportion of severely poor households among the poor.
		(b) Proportion of moderately poor households among the poor
	(b) Vulnerability	
	(i) Food insecurity	Percentage of children participating in labour Market
		Number of days of food insecurity in a year per household
II.	**Non-Income Poverty**	
	(a) Child labour	Percentage of Children participating in labour Market
	(b) Education status of the Child (5-14 Years of age)	
	(i) Enrolment	Enrolment rates at primary school and middle school Percentage of children who have never gone to school
	(ii) Dropout from school (primary)	Dropout rates at primary schools level
	(c) Health Status	
	Infant Mortality of the children	Infant mortality rates of children
III.	**Gender Empowerment**	
	(a) Participation of women in household decision-making	Extent of participation of women in decision-making in respect of different aspects of human life, in the form of individual and joint decision-making modes
	(b) Discrimination against women	Percentage of households who are discriminating women/girls in favour of men/boys according to selected consumption items (food as well as noon food)
	(c) Participation of women in Community life	Percentage of males participating in PRIs Percentage of females participating in PRIs
		Percentage of males participating SHGs
		Percentage of females participating in SHGs

poverty is measured through head-count ratio, the intensity of poverty is assessed through poverty gap index and composition of poor in terms proportion of very poor and moderately poor among the poor. The consumption inequality has been captured through usual inequality index, Gini Coefficient. The quality of consumption is assessed through two aspects of consumption, viz., composition of consumption basket and the frequency of consumption of some of the nutritionally important food items- milk/curd/butter milk, pulses, vegetables, fruits, eggs and chicken/meat/fish. The other dimension of poverty is vulnerability of the households. The vulnerability of the households is assessed through two aspects, viz., incidence and duration of food insecurity. Another dimension of poverty is non - income poverty. This is also called the deprivation dimension of poverty. We have considered two types of deprivations – deprivations in education and health. We have estimated the poverty indicators separately for programme and control mandals as well as for various caste groups and male/female headed households in the district.

For estimating the extent and intensity of poverty, we have used the poverty line of Rs. 300 per capita per month. This has been estimated by adjusting the official poverty line of Rs.263 for the year 1999-00 for the changes in the prices. As noted earlier, the composition of poor for measuring depth of poverty is also assessed. In this context, the poor are classified into two categories, viz., severely poor and moderately poor. Severely poor households are those whose consumption expenditure is less than 75 per cent of the poverty line and the moderately poor households are those whose consumption is above 75 per cent of poverty line but less than the poverty line. It may be mentioned here that the estimates of poverty based on the BLS are not strictly comparable to the official estimates available at the State level. This is because the BLS data do not capture the seasonality of consumption and also the consumption data is collected at aggregate commodity level unlike the National Sample

Surveys which collect the consumption data through a separate schedule at much disaggregated commodity levels.

Status of Income Poverty

Extent of Poverty

Poor constitute 42 per cent of households in the project districts. They are 48, 40 and 35 in Anantapur, Srikakulam and Adilabad, respectively. This indicates that the extent of poverty is relatively higher in the drought-prone district. Programme and control areas have 42 and 36 per cent poor respectively in the project districts. They have 46 and 56 in Anantapur; 40 and 23 in Adilabad; and 43 and 26 Srikakulam. This reveals that the extent of poverty is larger in programme areas over control in Adilabad and Srikakulam. Thus, it is evident that the poverty is specific to the areas of the project.

Across social groups, 44, 68, 38 and 30 per cent are poor among SCs, STs, BCs and OCs, respectively, in the project districts. They are 61,82,50 and 31 in Anantapur; 24,58,23 and 35 in Adilabad; and 51,74,31 and 18 in Srikakulam. This shows that the poverty is more pronounced among SC and STs in Anantapur, STs in Adilabad and Srikakulam. Between the male and female- headed households, female as well as male - headed households have more or less the same proportion of poor (42 per cent). The same is true in Anantapur and Srikakulam. But, male-headed households did have relatively larger proportion of poor in Adilabad. The proportion of poor is declining with the increase in landholding size of the households barring marginal farmers in the project area. Poor among medium and larger farmers is conspicuously absent. More or less, the same pattern is observed across the districts. It is striking to note that landless and marginal farmers have relatively larger proportion of poor in Anantapur, compared to their counterparts in the other districts. Thus, poverty is more concentrated, by and large among SCs and STs from landless, marginal farmers in the programmes areas of the districts. This account reveals that poverty can be alleviated by improving the asset base of households along with simultaneous improvement of the community assets and expanding opportunities to convert household assets into livelihoods, and possession of land, one of the components of natural capital, alone may not tackle the problem of poverty unless land productivity is enhanced through providing access to irrigation, another component of natural capital, for example.

Intensity of Poverty

Intensity of poverty has been examined in terms of poverty gap and compositions of poor, as noted earlier. Compared to the poor in the project area, the composition of poor reveals that the very poor constitute lesser proportion. The same is true across all the districts and also for the programme and control areas of each district. Strikingly, the proportion of very poor constitutes larger proportion among the STs, in contrast to other caste groups in the project area. Similarly, it is high among STs in Adilabad and Srikakulam and SCs in Anantapur. Female-headed households possess larger proportion of very poor compared to male-headed households in the project area. This is true only in Srikakulam. The proportion of very poor is negatively correlated with the landholding size of the households in the project area. It is the highest among the landless households in Anantapur; semi- medium farmers in Adilabad; and small and semi-medium farmers in Srikakulam. The patterns of intensity of poverty are further reinforced by the poverty gap index also. Thus, extent and intensity of poverty are correlated and concentrated among SCs and STs. This indicates that abject poverty (low-end poverty) is prevalent more among SCs and STs.

Consumption Inequalities

Consumption inequality, measured through Gini coefficient, is more or less the same across the districts. It is more pronounced in programme areas over the control in Anantapur and Srikakulam. Consumption inequality is pronounced among SCs over all the other castes in Anantapur;

more pronounced among SCs and STs compared to BCs and OCs in Adilabad; and among SCs and BCs over STs and OCs in Srikakulam. Between the male and female-headed households, the inequalities are less among female-headed households in Adilabad and Srikakulam. Thus, consumption inequality is highly correlated with poverty levels.

Quality of Consumption

The quality of consumption has been assessed in terms of composition of consumption basket and frequency of consumption of some important food items.

Composition of Consumption Basket

The composition of consumption basket reveals that the households are spending 65 percent and 35 per cent of consumption expenditure on food and non-food, respectively, in the project area. The same pattern is observed across the districts. This is also the same for the programme and the control areas in the project area as well as across all the districts. The proportion of expenditure on food is declining and non-food is increasing with the increase in the economic (MPCE) status of households. Similarly, proportion of expenditure on non-cereal food among the foods and health and education among the non-foods is increasing with the increase in the economic status in the project areas as well as across the districts. The same patterns of expenditure are observed across the different landholding classes in the districts.

Among the social groups, the proportion of expenditure between food and non-food, cereals and non-cereals among food, and health and education among non-food is, by and large, the same across all the social groups in the project area. However, the proportion of expenditure on health and education is relatively larger for OCs over all the other caste groups. The same pattern is observed across the social groups in all the districts. But, the proportion of expenditure on health and education is the lowest among all the social groups in

Adilabad. The above analysis reveals: the pattern of consumption is strongly correlated to the economic status rather than social status of the households; the higher expenditure of food among poor indicates that nutritional needs of the poor are not met; and the lower expenditure on health and education among poor leads to low level of human capital that leads to low labour productivity and thereby low income, which ultimately results in low access to food.

Frequency of Consumption

The pattern of frequency of consumption of food items in the project area reveals: milk/milk products are consumed either daily or never, dominantly; pulses and vegetables are consumed either daily or weekly, predominantly; and fruits, eggs and chicken/meat/fish are consumed either weekly or occasionally, dominantly. The same pattern is observed across all the districts. However, weekly once consumption of pulses, daily consumption of vegetables and occasional consumption of fruits predominantly in Srikakulam are the distinct features of pattern of consumption in relation to the other districts.

The same pattern of frequency of consumption is observed among all the socio-economic classes in the programme and control areas in the project areas as well as across all the districts, by and large. However, the deprivations in terms of never consuming across all the food items is more pronounced among SCs and STs vis-à-vis BCs and OCs; female vis-à-vis male headed; and the poorest of the poor and the poor vis-à-vis other economic (non-poor) classes. This leads to prevalence of "nutritional" and "non-nutritional" diseases among poor. This issue has to be resolved through two parallel initiatives. Measures should be initiated to increase the purchasing capacity of poor and building awareness on balanced dietary habits. This contributes to increase the demand for carotene-rich foods; and green leafy vegetables. Measures should be also initiated to increase supply of the carotene-rich foods, green leafy vegetables, and eggs. This can be done at household level through kitchen garden or on commercial basis through changing cropping pattern. In this context, there is also need to develop appropriate village-based techniques for the dehydration of carotene-rich foods and storage for the avoidance of wastage and for use in lean seasons, and for use in large-scale supplementary feeding programmes - such as those of the ICDS and school meal programme.

Food Insecurity

Incidence, and duration are the two dimensions considered to assess the status of food insecurity. A household is defined as the one, which didn't have two square meals[2] for all its members for at least one day. As per this definition, the data reveal that about ¼ of households reported that they have experienced food insecurity during the last year. The households who have reported food insecurity constitute 46, 11 and 10 per cent of households in Srikakulam, Adilabad and Anantapur, respectively. Thus, food insecurity varies across the districts. Relatively, more households in programme areas have experienced food insecurity compared to their counterparts in the control areas of all the districts. SCs and STs vis-à-vis BCs and OCs; and female-headed vis-à-vis male headed have experienced food insecurity in relatively larger proportions in the project as well across all the districts. The proportion of households reporting food insecurity is on the decline as the landholding size and economic status of the households' increases in the districts. The duration of food insecurity is estimated to be 11 days in the project area. It is the highest in Srikakulam (about 24 days) followed by Adilabad (About 9 days) and Anantapur (3days). The households in programme areas are experiencing food insecurity for a relatively longer period compared to their counterparts in the control areas of the project area. The same pattern is observed in Anantapur and Adilabad. STs and SCs

2. The definition of what is 'two square meals' is left to the surveyed households themselves.

are more food insecure over BCs in Anantapur, and Srikakulam; and STs in Adilabad are more food insecure. Female-headed households are more insecure over male headed in Anantapur and Adilabad. Higher MPCE and higher landholding can be equated with less food insecurity in the project areas and across the districts.

The food insecurity is relatively more pronounced during Rabi and summer in Anantapur, Kharif in Adilabad, and all seasons in Srikakulam across all socio-economic classes. The issue in question is why does the seasonal patterns of food insecurity vary across the districts. Groundnut under rain-fed conditions ensures food security in Kharif season in Anantapur. The crops grown in Rabi season, mostly confined to the irrigation wells, in limited area cannot ensure employment to many of the labouring households. In summer, the horticulture crops provide employment to limited labourers. Thus food insecurity during Rabi and summer is severe in Anantapur. In Adilabad, the crops grown in Kharif season, viz., cotton and jowar do not provide adequate employment, as the more labour intensive-operations - harvesting and post-harvesting - are undertaken in Rabi seasons, and in summer forest - based employment opportunities - beedi leaves collection and following activities ensures food security. This is the reason for more food insecurity during Kharif in Adilabad. Marginal and small farmers are large in number, while landless and medium and large farmers are small in number in Srikakulam. As and when the farmers receive rain, marginal and small farmers take care of the labour requirements through exchange labour. This leaves agricultural labourers with less employment. In addition to this, the crops grown in Rabi season are confined to limited area. This further aggravates the problem of food insecurity. The same is true in summer. Thus, food insecurity is spread across all the agriculture seasons. However, the duration of food insecurity among STs over all the other castes is low in summer, since they depend on forests for their livelihood during summer.

Non-Income Poverty

Non-income poverty includes child labour, education and health status.

Child Labour

Child labour is one of the forms of child poverty. Child labour is equated with child participation in wage labour. One of the goals of the DPIP is to reduce child labour. All the children out of school are considered as the child labour under DPIP. Identification of child labour, admitting them into bridge schools and mainstreaming them into regular schools subsequently is the plan of action under DPIP to reduce child labour. This means that reduction in child labour contributes to increase in enrolment in schools. School dropouts contribute to child labour. Then, the issues in question are listed below:

(i) What is the status of child labour?

(ii) What are the factors contributing to child labour?

(iii) Whether participation in SHGs (DWCRA and SHGs of SAPAP) has contributed to the decline of child labour?

The data reveal that 1/10 of children are child labour . The proportion of child labour is more or less the same among boys and girls in the project area. The incidence of child labour is varying between 6 percent in Adilabad and 12 percent in Anantapur. Child labour is more among girls than among boys in Srikakulam, while they are more or less the same among boys and girls in the other districts. There are variations in the incidence of child labour within the districts. This indicates that the child labour prevalence is specific to the local conditions. The incidence of child labour is closely associated with the economic stance rather than social status of the households. It is increasing from the poorest of the poor to poor and from there on declining drastically. The non-poor who has participated in groups is able to reduce child labour. The presence of child labour among non-poor households indicates that child labour has to be viewed beyond poverty. However, the incidence of child labour is on the increase from landless to marginal farmers and from marginal farmers it is on the decline drastically to zero among the large farmers.

Education

The education status of children who are in the age group of 5-14 years has been examined in terms of current enrolment for primary and middle school education, dropout rates at primary education, and children who have never gone to school.

As high as 90 percent of the children eligible for enrolment into primary school education have enrolled currently in the project area. Relatively larger proportion of boys compared to girls has enrolled for primary education. All the boys and girls who have enrolled have completed primary education. But, all who have completed primary education have not enrolled for middle school education. This is more pronounced among girls than among boys. Thus, enrolment inequalities between boys and girls are less recorded in case of primary education and highly imminent in case of middle education. Another dimension of education status is 'children who have never gone to school'. The data reveal that 9 percent of children have never gone to school in the project area. Relatively higher proportion of girls than boys have never gone to school (12 percent of girls vis-à-vis 6 percent of boys). The same patterns of educational status are in place in all the districts. However, there are variations across districts and between areas with in each district. This is due to region-specific variations in terms of availability of adequate infrastructure and quality of education. These are supply side factors of education. Economic status rather than social status is closely associated with educational status of children across the districts. The close correlation between holding status of the households and educational status of children reinforces this. Lack of Upper primary schools in the villages is contributing to enrolment inequalities in middle school education among economic classes and between boys and girls. Absence of complete enrolment of eligible children even among non-poor classes is a pointer to the lack of quality of education in the schools.

Health Status

Infant Mortality has been chosen among the indicators available from the data to measure health status of the people in the project area. It has been considered as surrogate indicator to assess the health status of people.

The data on infant mortality indicates that 30 children from among 1000 live births are dying before attaining three years of age in the project area. The figure is 33 for the programme areas and 20 for the control areas of the project. It is 36, 32 and 25 for Srikakulam, Adilabad and Anantapur, respectively. Programme areas compared to control possess higher incidence of infant mortality in all the districts. This indicates that incidence of infant mortality is specific to the areas. The location specific factors are determining the incidence of infant mortality. Poor quality of water is one of the dominant reasons for the variations in the incidence of infant mortality across different areas of the project.

The incidence of infant mortality is higher among SCs and STs compared to BCs and OCs in Anantapur and Adilabad, in contrast to Srikakulam. But, the association of incidence of infant mortality is stronger with regional factors than with socio-economic stance of the households. The infant mortality is lower among girls over boys in all the areas. The participation in groups has not made any difference in infant mortality rates. The SHGs have not directly focused on child health care.

Empowerment of Women

Empowerment of women is concerned with the participation of women in different dimensions of human life.

It differs from gender development, which is primarily concerned with basic capabilities and living standards. In order to assess the gender empowerment, the following dimensions are considered:

(i) Participation in household decision- making

(ii) Discrimination against women

(iii) Participation in community life

(a) Participation in formal political institutions, viz., Panchayat Raj Institutions (PRIs)

(b) Participation in Self Help Groups (SHGs) promoted by the State, community based organizations (CBOs) and NGOs

The details on these issues are in order.

Participation in Household Decision-Making

Socio-cultural activities/marriages, purchase of durable goods, what to cook, debt, saving, income generating activities, children's education, health care, number of children, spacing of children, and family planning are the activities for which the participation of women in decision-making has been assessed.

The data reveal that joint decision-making is invariably the dominant method of household decision-making in all the aspects of human life in the project area, except the decisions relating to cooking and health. However, as far as individual decision-making is concerned the decision-making by men alone is dominant over the women alone. The same pattern of decision-making is prevalent in programme as well as control areas of the project. A comparison across the district reveals that joint decision - making is the dominant method across all the areas of decision-making in Adilabad. The same is true, except decisions relating to debt in Anantapur and except decisions relating to debt, saving and income generating activities in Srikakulam. This indicates that 'males alone' in Srikakulam take all the decisions relating to economic aspects. Moreover, the decisions taken by 'male alone' are more dominant in Srikakulam compared to the other districts. The pattern of decision-making is more or less similar between programme and control areas in each district. This indicates that the decision-making patterns are district specific.

A comparison across caste groups indicates that the patterns of decision-making observed at the district levels are reflected across all social groups in all the districts. The same is true across all economic classes. This indicates that the decision-making patterns are not related to socio-economic status of the households. Thus, the patterns of decision-making are a manifestation of patriarchal social values of the society.

By and large, males take all the decisions relating to economic issues in male-headed households and females in female-headed households dominantly in all the districts. As far as the individual decision-making is concerned, the decisions by 'male alone' are dominant among male-headed households and the decisions taken by 'female alone' are predominant among female-headed households. This further reinforces our earlier observation.

Discrimination Against Women

Qualitative information has been obtained from the households regarding discrimination against women in household consumption. This type of discrimination is examined among adults as well as children of families.

Foot wear, clothing, health and entertainment are the four non-food items considered to assess the pattern of preferential spending between male and female adult family members. Besides all these items, education is considered to assess gender discrimination among the children.

The data reveal that there is no discrimination between male and female in regard to clothing and health. As a matter of fact there is positive discrimination in favour of adults female. This is true across poor and non-poor among female as well as male-headed households in all the districts. However, there is lot of discrimination between males and females in regard to footwear and entertainment. As a matter of fact adult males are favoured against adult females among poor and non-poor, and among female headed as well as male-headed households in all the districts.

There is no discrimination in regard to clothing and health between the boys and girls. This is true across poor and non-poor among female and male–headed households. But the girl children are discriminated in favour of male children in case of footwear, entertainment and education. These discriminations are more pronounced among poor over non-poor, and among male-headed over female- headed.

Participation of Women in Self Help Groups Promoted by the State

State has promoted broadly three types of Self Help Groups, viz., natural resource management, social sector development and poverty alleviation. Then the issue in question is: what is the level of participation of women in these groups?

The data reveal that women constitute 12 percent of the participants in all these groups in the district. The participation of women is the highest in poverty alleviation groups (16 percent), followed by social sector development groups (57 percent) and natural resource management groups (16 percent) in the project area. The same pattern of participation is observed between the programme and control areas of he project. The same pattern is also observed across the districts and between the programme and control areas of each district. However, there are variations in participation in respect of natural resource management groups and social development groups across the districts. The extent of participation of women is almost negligible in Srikakulam and Adilabad, while women constitute 47 percent of the members in Anantapur in case of natural resource management. The participation in social sector development groups is less in Srikakulam. Thus, the participation of women in natural resource management and social sector development groups is less in Srikakulam. The same patterns are in place across socio-economic groups in all the districts.

Participation of Women in Panchayat Raj Institutions (PRIs)

The participation of women in all PRIs, which include Gram Panchayats (G.P), Mandal Praja Parishads (MPPs) and Zilla Praja Parishads (ZPPs), is considered for the analysis. The data unfold that the women constitute around 20 percent of members of PRIs in Anantapur and Adilabad. But they are only 15 percent in Srikakulam. The participation levels are higher in control over programme areas in Anantapur and Srikakulam. This indicates that the level of development influences the level of participation of women in PRIs. The participation of women is higher among non-poor over poor in all the districts. It is not related to social status of households. This indicates that the participation of women is highly correlated with economic stance rather than social status of the households. Interestingly, the participation of women from female headed is higher than from male-headed households. This indicates that the patriarchal values of the society are hindering the participation of women in PRIs.

Implications for DPIP

- Poverty can be alleviated by improving the asset base of households along with simultaneous improvement of the community assets and expanding opportunities to convert household assets into livelihoods.
- Possession of land, one of the components of natural capital, alone may not tackle the problem of poverty unless land productivity is enhanced through

providing access to irrigation, another component of natural capital, for example.

- Deprivations in terms of never consuming many of the non-cereal food items among poor may lead to prevalence of "nutritional" and "non-nutritional"" diseases. This has to be solved through two parallel initiatives. Measures should be initiated to increase the purchasing capacity of poor and building awareness on balanced dietary habits. This contributes to increase the demand for carotene-rich foods, green lefty vegetables, and eggs. Measures should also be initiated to increase supply of the carotene-rich foods, green leafy vegetables, eggs and milk and milk products. This can be done at household level through kitchen garden or on commercial basis through changing cropping pattern. In this context, there is also need to develop appropriate village-based techniques for the dehydration of carotene-rich foods and storage for the avoidance of wastage and for use in lean seasons, and for use in large-scale supplementary feeding programmes such as those of the ICDS and school meal programme.
- PDS system at the habitation level has to be strengthened. All the provisions should be distributed through PDS at reasonable rates for the poor as well as the non-poor. The consumption need of cereal over and above PDS supplies can be arranged through SHGs on credit line.
- Incidence of child labour can be reduced by initiating the following steps: sensitising parents of child labour; child labour and concerned officials on the negative affects of child labour; establishing bridge schools and residential schools; improving infrastructure facilities and quality of education for mainstreaming the child labour; establishing

supplementary school on RDT line; and vitalizing of village education committees to monitor the functioning of schools.

- Provisions of health related community infrastructure such as safe drinking water facilities, drainage and sanitation facilities, and solid waste management should be accorded high priority to improve health status of poor.

Sensitising men and women on the need to empower women through improving their participation in household and supra-household level institutions for the democratic functioning of the society at large in all the spheres of human life

Summary of Findings

- Poverty is more concentrated among SCs and STs from landless and marginal farmers, by and large in the programme areas of the districts. Abject poverty (low- end poverty) is more prevalent among SCs and STs. Consumption inequalities are more pronounced among SCs and STs.
- Higher expenditure on food among poor indicates that nutritional needs of the poor are not met.
- Lower private expenditure on health and education among food leads to low level of human capital formation that lead to low labour productivity and thereby low income, which ultimately results in low access to food.
- Deprivations in terms of never consuming many of the non-cereal food items is more pronounced among SCs and STs vis-à-vis BCs and OCs; female-headed vis-à-vis male-headed; and the poorest of the poor and the poor vis-à-vis other economic classes. This leads to prevalence of "nutritional" and "non-nutritional" diseases among the poor.

- Incidence and duration of food insecurity is high among poor over non-poor. Thus poverty and food insecurity are strongly correlated in all the districts.
- Nearly 1/10 of children are child labour in project area. Incidence of child labour is ranging from 6 percent in Adilabad to 12 percent in Anantapur. Child labour is more among girls than among boys in Srikakulam, while they are more or less the same among boys and girls in other districts. It is increasing from the poorest of the poor to poor and from there on declining drastically.
- Lack of infrastructural facilities and quality of education is contributing negatively to the enrolment rates at primary and middle school; enrolment inequalities between boys and girls; and between poor and non-poor households.
- Health status of households is more determined by the health related infrastructure like safe drinking water, drainage and sanitation facilities.
- The pattern of decision-making across different socio-economic groups in the districts reveals that the pattern of decision-making is more related to patriarchal social values of the society.
- Females are discriminated in favour of males in regard to footwear, entertainment and education (with regard to children). This is more pronounced among poor over non-poor.

Participation of women in natural resources management and social sector development is relatively lower compared to men across all socio-economic groups in the districts. Participations of women in PRIs is lower compared to men among the poor households. Patriarchal values of the society are hindering the participation of women in PRIs.

(This article heavily draws from report 'Andhra Pradesh District Poverty Initiatives Project (APDPIP): *Baseline Survey Report in Sustainable Livelihood Framework*', **Prepared for the Society for Elimination of Rural Poverty (SERP), May 2002).**

31

Gender Inequalities and Human Poverty

Prof. P. Leela

Introduction

"The real wealth of a nation is its people. And the purpose of development is to create an enabling environment for people to enjoy long, healthy and creative lives" [U.N.D.P. 1990]. Even though the 20th century has witnessed substantial progress in these areas, the World of the 21st century still faces huge backlogs of deprivation, poverty, inequality and gender disparities. In the case of the Indian economy, while there has been a steady decline in poverty over the last two decades, the total number of poor people has perhaps remained constant because of the growth in population [G.O.I., 2000-2001, p.194]. "While international comparisons of poverty are fraught with errors available estimates indicate that India has the highest poverty rate amongst the major countries" [K.S. Parikh, 1999-2000, p.5]. Poverty may be defined as a human condition resulting from inability to participate in economic activity and exchange sector [Machiraju, 2000,p.178]. Socially, economically, culturally and legally, all over the World, women have faced gender-linked handicaps resulting in females accounting for a large proportion of the poverty-ridden population [S. Narasimhan, 2000, p.221] In this context, the object of the present paper is to examine the gender dimension of the problem of poverty in India, as the nation gets poised towards emerging as the most populous country in the World.

Women and Poverty

Unemployment and poverty are closely interlinked and unemployment is considered to be one of the important factors contributing to poverty. In early times it was generally believed that a woman's place is at home. But since the early 20th century, women are being slowly drawn into the economic activities outside their homes. This is mainly due to two important reasons viz (i) economic necessity and (ii) emancipation. There is a sizeable increase in female labour force participation. Consequently, new Theories of Employment like New Household Economics one dealing with the interconnection between the role of women and the characteristic features of women employment.

Employment of women is generally characterised by discontinuities associated with marriage, child-birth, post-natal care, care of the sick and elderly people. Apart from these factors, women are usually pushed into low paid and dead-end jobs due to minimum work preferences, low time allocation for labour market, low literacy levels, lower skills and low productivity vis-a-vis men. Hence, men but not women are paid more and men but not women are employed more, leading to the dual market theory. [Y. Shanmugasundaram 1933, pp. 6-7]. The situation is still worse in respect of women in the rural areas, where poverty and unemployment are rampant. The problem of poverty of women can be mitigated by employment and income for which literacy and training become important. This is particularly true in respect of rural women, who when properly trained could bring about substantial improvement in the lives of themselves, their families and the community around them.

Progress Achieved and Shortfalls

Women and children represent 76.7 per cent of the country's total population and constitute the most important target groups in the context of developmental planning. The role of women in economic development is being gradually realised as reflected in the many steps being taken by the Government to move from the 20th century concept of emancipation of women to the 21st century concept of empowerment of women.

In terms of the conventional indicators, much progress has been achieved in the areas of health and education. Life expectancy of women increased from about 23 years at the beginning of the 20th century to about 62 years today. Female literacy rate has increased from about 7 per cent to about 9 per cent in the Nineties and to 54.16 per cent as per Census 2001. There has been an increase in the female work participation rate also. These represent quantifiable economic gains achieved by women. Important Laws have been enacted to strengthen the claims of females as individuals. They include: the Hindu Succession Act, the Maternity Benefits Act and the Equal Remuneration Act. They represent the legal gains achieved by women indicating the Government's commitment to Gender Equity, as enshrined in the Constitution.

The Human Development Report of the U.N. has developed a new criterion called the Gender Empowerment Measure or G.E.M. It includes three indicators:

(i) access to economic opportunities

(ii) access to professional opportunities and

(iii) access to decision-making process.

In this context, it is noteworthy that the 73rd Amendment to the Constitution of India introduced 1/3 rd reservation for women at the local administration level. It represents a very important exercise by the Government in the empowerment of women.

Both the Central and the State Governments are implementing a number of programmes for the development of women and children. In the last five years (1995-2000) the Andhra Pradesh Government has allotted Rs. 440.61 crores for the following schemes:

- Integrated Child Development Services
- Child Welfare Institutions
- Women Welfare Institutions
- Nutrition
- Women Education

Under the Vision 2020 programme, Women Empowerment Policy has been formulated. The main thrust of the policy is convergence of all activities pertaining to women in order to improve education, health and nutrition for women and children. The policy also calls for the setting up of a Women Development Agency at the district level to focus on women and child development activities and for gender sensitization.

In spite of the substantial progress made by women, they continue to live in an unequal environment. Taking into account one of the most important indicators viz., literacy rate, the progress achieved is found to be very uneven.

Table 1: Literacy Rates and Ranks for Southern States (2001)

State/ Country	*Rate*	*Female*	*Total*	*Rank (in India)*
Andhra Pradesh	55.13	32.72	44.09	26
Karnataka	67.26	44.34	56.04	20
Kerala	93.62	86.17	89.81	1
Tamil Nadu	73.75	51.33	62.66	12
India	**64.13**	**39.29**	**52.21**	

The table indicates that female literacy rate in A.P. is below the all India level. The State continues to show lowest literacy among the Southern States falling behind Kerala, Tamil Nadu and Karnataka. A.P. is still one of the least literate States in the country [Census 2001, p.34]. With in the State of

A.P., there are wide inter-district variations and disparities regarding female literacy rate, as can be seen from Table 2. Female illiteracy rate is as high as 67.17 per cent in Mahbubnagar district.

Conclusion

Women have come a long way from emancipation to empowerment. But they still have miles to go for achieving equality. Their work continues to be undervalued. They are still denied opportunities and recognition. Poverty is a major problem faced in particular by the rural women, due to lack of education, employment opportunities and access to resources. Employment of women today depends on giving them information, providing them awareness and bureaucratic help, eliminating gender bias in development policies and above all bringing about changes in social-cultural and psychological attitudes of people towards the role of women and their contribution to the economy.

References

Census of India 2001

Government of India, Economic Survey 2000-2001.

Machiraju, H. R (2000). "Poverty: Concept and Alleviation, in R.V.R. Chandrasekhar Rao, A. Prasanna Kumar and K. C. Reddy (ed.), Perspectives on Indian Development, Sterling Publishers Pvt. Ltd., Delhi.

Narasimhan, S (2000): " Reflection of Indian Economic Development and Poverty Eradication-development as if people Mattered", in R.V.R. Chandrasekhara Rao et al (ed.), Perspective on Indian Development.

Parikh, K.S (1999-2000): India Development Report.

32

Micro Credit through Self Help Groups: A Strategy in Poverty Alleviation

Dr. B. Devi Prasad
Dr. S. Haranath

Overview

It has been increasingly realized world over that the best way to tackle poverty and improve quality of life in the community is through social mobilization of the poor, especially women, into self-help groups. The Micro Credit Summit in Washington in the year 1997 and the attempts made thereafter, have focused to address the poverty issues through forming women into micro groups to promote micro credit, micro enterprise, and market support for their products.

The State of Andhra Pradesh having more than 10 million rural families (about 50 million individuals) has been making efforts in a similar direction. During the last few years the Government has placed on its development agenda, the theme of women's empowerment as one of the main strategies to tackle socio-economic poverty. Under this initiative, the Government, the NGOs, the Community Based Organizations and the civil society have come together to enable the poor to organize themselves into Self Help Groups with thrift as the entry point activity. In the last few years, there was a massive scaling up in SHG activities. At present, Andhra Pradesh alone has about half of the SHGs existing in the country. Thus there are about 3.3 lakhs women SHGs in Andhra Pradesh, covering nearly 45.8 lakhs of rural poor women (please see table 1).

Table 1: District wise position of SHGs

S. No.	*District*	*Groups*	*Total Members*
1.	East Godavari	42000	546000
2.	Karimnagar	21829	305606
3.	Ananthapur	18486	277290
4.	Nellore	13850	240615
5.	Guntur	16323	235000
6.	Krishna	20000	234572
7.	Nalgonda	15550	232816
8.	Srikakulam	15409	232485
9.	Medak	15500	221055
10.	Chittor	13927	208860
11.	Warangal	14397	207678
12.	Mahboobnagar	14737	194415
13.	Kurnool	12826	192390
14.	Prakasam	17000	180015
15.	Visakhapatnam	11069	170428
16.	West Godavari	13842	166116
17.	Ranga Reddy	10586	159180
18.	Vizianagaram	10075	129016
19.	Adilabad	9082	118066
20.	Nizamabad	9417	117712
21.	Khammam	9750	115880
22.	Cuddapah		95203
	Total	333774	4580398

Source: www.andhrapradesh.com.

Thrift and internal loan lending are the two major activities of the SHGs. They are to take small loans out of the corpus available with the group. The groups' corpus consists of their savings, and government assistance and bank loan, if made available. Initially, members use the loan out of the groups' corpus for their personal needs. However in the long run, such loans are utilized for income generation activities. Both Government and the NGOs are working in close coordination with DRDA in the capacity building, and skill development training of the SHGs to help them learn group management skills. In addition to these activities, the SHGs have become focal points for women to participate in such programmes as family welfare, nutritional and educational schemes, environmental awareness, and public health through sanitation and clean drinking water. Due to this massive Self—Help movement, there is a perceptible improvement in the socio-economic status of the rural women. Women have become very active, assertive and became sensitive to the issue relating to them and their surroundings.

Introduction

Self-Help groups are defined as small groups, which are formed voluntarily with members who want to solve their common problems through mutual aid. Micro credit means quantum of amount given for self-employment activities to members belonging to lower income groups. Where as the SHG is an institutional means to provide access to credit to poor people.

The analysis of poverty situation reveals that lack of access to capital; whether monetary, educational, health is one of the major reasons for continued poverty especially in rural sector. The following phases briefly show how the response to rural poverty underwent changes in India context.

1960s—Lack of access to credit, one form of capital, is seen as one of the important reasons for poverty. A look at the credit sources reveals that the lower income groups depended more on non-institutional credit sources as compared to the well to do sections.

1970s—Therefore, it was thought that one of the significant strategies for poverty alleviation would be provision of credit to the poor.

Events

Nationalization of commercial Banks	1969
Establishment of Cooperative Banking (committee on rural credit)	1964
Establishment of Regional Rural Banks	1975
No. of rural credit outlets opened up	1,34,000

1980s—But the situation did not improve. In spite of the provision of the credit through the formal credit mechanisms, the rural poor's access to institutional credit did not improve much.

Situation of the rural credit sector.

- Most of the RRBs are in losses.
- By and large the cooperative credit system has become collateral.
- Both cooperatives and RRBs fail to recover 60% of their advances.
- Even commercial banks, the non-payment of dues stood at 40-45%.

Similarly, the informal credit systems continued their stronghold (Table 2).

Table 2: Comparison of formal and informal rural credit system

Official Rural Credit	*Informal Rural Credit*
Subsidized credit	Flexible forms & conditions
Concessionary rate of interest	Highly varied interest rate
Need for collateral	No. collaterals needed
Inaccessible for majority rural poor	Highly exploitative
Poor quality of lending	Repeated loans
Delayed credit	Timely credit
Leakages	
Low recovery	
Absence of healthy banker-customer relationships	Personal involvement in utilization & monitoring of loan.
Gender-bias	Gender-bias

Source: Kapoor, S., 1999.

Thus, in spite of the huge banking network, 36% of rural households were still dependent on informal credit agencies for meeting their credit needs. Further, the percentage share of the amount of debt contracted from institutional and non-institutional credit agencies by each asset holding classes at all India level reveals that the households in the lower asset groups are more dependent on non-institutional credit agencies. The share of debt from the non institutional credit agencies is as high as 58% in the case of lowest asset group of less than Rs. 5000, as against a low of 19% in the highest asset group of Rs. 2.5 lakh and above (Debt and Investment survey, GOI).

There was again a soul searching about how to deal with rural poverty. An analysis of the credit needs of rural poor reveals the following characteristics. They are:

- Small
- Frequent
- Urgent
- Unpredicatable

Therefore, there was a rethinking about how to evolve a programme, which can effectively meet the needs of rural poor women? Thus, SHGs emerged as an important poverty alleviation strategy.

One important milestone in SHG movement is the micro credit summit held at Washington on 1997 which aimed at providing micro-credit to 100 million rural families in the world by 2005.

The AP Scenario

We have about 10 million rural families in AP. There are 3.3 lakh SHGs in AP comprising of 45.8 lakh women. They are also popularly called as DWCRA groups. Broadly two kinds of linkages are available for SHGs in the state. They are:

(a) SHG-NABARD linkage scheme and

(b) Provision of revolving fund.

The government released Rs. 44 crores during 2000-01 to assist 44,000 groups covering 6.6 lakh women @ Rs. 10,000 as revolving fund to each group. This is in addition to the grant of Rs. 4.5 crore from the Government of India. NABARD, Commercial Banks and Regional Rural Banks are providing direct assistance to the SHGs under the "Self-Help Linking Scheme" of NABARD.

While the performance of SHGs has been encouraging, the legal and organizational form such SHGs should take is another important issue. In Andhra Pradesh, the Mutually Aided Cooperative Societies Act of 1995 provides for individual groups to become members of a society. It is expected that these societies will be federated at mandal and district levels and later at the state level, this will particularly help in tapping finance from several sources. Further, these groups will have to develop strong marketing channels as the number of such groups and, consequently, the output increase (Rangarajan, 2000:285).

Some examples of project related to promotion of SHGs in AP:

- Small Economic Activity Development (SEAD) by CARE.
- Women's Thrift Cooperatives in Warangal and Karimnagar Districts promoted by Cooperative Development Foundation (CDF).

What SHGs can do?

- Poor can access small credit.
- Timely and adequate credit.
- No. collateral is needed, group acts as one.
- Loan procedures simple and flexible.
- Linkage with formal banking.
- Best judge of members credit needs.

- Negligible defaulters.
- Less paper work/more informal.
- Credit as entry point.
- Can open up SHGs to other areas of social issue and concerns.

What is Good SHG?

Characteristics of a Good SHG

- Group formation through consensus
- Meetings: periodicity and time.
- Participation of members & transparency of operations.
- Homogeneity of members.
- Savings: periodicity & amount.
- Credit: prioritization and rates of interest.
- Threshold limit.
- Fine system.
- Leadership; Competencies and skills
- Maintenance of books & records.
- No dependence on external agency.
- Going beyond credit activity towards empowerment.
- SHGs seen as → Viable Institutions to provide access to small credit; → Vehicles to take women towards empowerment.

Role of NGOs

NGOs working with micro credit or SHGs can be classified under 3 broad categories:

1. Those organizations that promoted chit fund groups and formalized these into the thrift programme. This was the phenomenon mostly found during 1970s and 1980s.
2. Innovative efforts by NGOs in mobilizing people in small groups, promoting their entrepreneurial skills, leadership development, awareness about social issues etc. Prominent among them are MYRADA etc. The emphasis on the mix between empowerment and credit may vary.
3. NGOs coming from a professional group. Management graduates and specialists with little or no exposure to empowerment strategies promoted SHGs. Their major focus is on selection of economic activity of the group, its market potential, viability of the operation and so on. For example, BASIX in Hyderabad, however, they lacked awareness of social factors.

As regards the specific role played by NGOs in Andhra Pradesh, for the beginning they have been working for the cause of women and more than 200 NGOs have been involved in facilitating the formation of SHGs and in efforts for their sustenance. The NGOs are working in close coordination with DRDAs in training and capacity building, skill development training programmes, building SHG organizations etc. The information in Table 3 gives us a glimpse into the scenario of SHGs in AP.

Table 3: Status of SHGs in Andhra Pradesh

Status	
Total Groups (NGOs.)	4,00,731
Women Covered (Members)	53,63,899
Women savings (Rs. in crores)	551.40
Government Assistance (Rs. in crores)	492.38
Total Corpus (Rs. in crores)	1043.78
SHGs up to year 1994 (Nos.)	10,000
SHGs Initiated in 1999-2000 (Nos.) 95,000	95,000
SHGs initiated in 2000-01 (Nos.) 60,441	60,441

Impact of the SHG strategy

Now, practitioners are increasingly realizing that micro-credit/SHGs without addressing the livelihood or empowerment issues will not sustainable as a mere credit activity. In this light, we need to ask certain relevant questions:

- Has it resulted in the reduction of exploitation in the immediate environment? For example, exploitation of intermediaries.
- Has it resulted in the control over assets by women gained through the micro credit?
- Has it built networks of trust and confidence among the members and in the community?

Some Issues and Concerns about SHGs

- Tangible reduction of exploitation in the immediate environment. For example, role of middlemen.
- Deciding about appropriate legal structure for the SHG or for their federation. The APMACS is one way out.
- Transfer of economic power into gender justice at the household level.
- Control over productive resources gained by the primary constituency i.e., women.
- Dependency syndrome on external agencies, be they NGOs or the local leader.
- Maintenance of internal democratic functioning.
- keeping political interference under check.
- Skill development through SHGs participation.
- Marketing.
- Political empowerment.

References

Biswas, A and Mahajan, V. (1997), "Sustainable Banking with Poor: A case study on Women's Thrift Cooperative System in Warangal and Karimnagar Districts of Andhra Pradesh, Hyderbad: Cooperative Development Foundation (CDF).

Kapoor, S. (1999), "Need and Concept of Self-Help groups, SEARCH Bulletin, XIV, (Jan. March): 14-17.

Kapoor, S. (1999), "Need and Concept of Self-Help Groups, SEARCH Bulletin, XIV, (Jan.-March), 9-13.

Mohan Rao, R.M., and Appa Rao, Ch. (1999), "A study of Women Self Help Groups in Andhra Pradesh (A comparative study of bank-linked SHGs, DWCRA and IRDP beneficiaries), NABARD Unit, Dept. of Cooperation & Applied Economics, Andhra University, Visakhapatnam.

Pardhasaradhi, G. & Kalyani, (1995), "Economic Impact of Women's Thrift and Credit Societies in Cuddapah District, Visakhaptnam, IDPS.

Rangarajan, C. (2000), "Rural Credit-some Concerns and Answers (pp. 227-286), in C. Rangasrajan, Perspectives on Indian Economy, New Delhi, UBSD.

Stephen, F. (1999), "Micro Credit: Trends and Pitfalls Empowerment Revisited, SEARCH Bulletin, XIV (Jan.-March), 1-8.

33

Employment, Income and Poverty Among Labour Households (A Study of Visakhapatnam District, A.P.)

Dr. Ramakrishna Rayavarapu

India is primarily a rural economy where agriculture is the mainstay of its population. More than three/fourths of total population of the country lives in rural areas and majority among them are small and marginal farmers and agricultural labourers. The National Commission on Rural Labour states, "During the seventies and the eighties, the rural population registered an annual growth rate of 2 per cent and 1.5 per cent respectively. However, for the corresponding decades, the growth in the number of agricultural labourers has been at higher levels of 4.1 per cent and 3 per cent per annum respectively" (Government of India, Ministry of Labour, 1991).

Many empirical studies have brought out the fact that there is high incidence of unemployment, under-employment among the rural poor may be due to slow growth of employment, growing causalisation of rural labour and our inability to generate non agricultural employment. The income of the household generally indicates the economic status of the household. Most of the agricultural labourers having no land or less than one acre of land, depend mostly on wage employment. Due to absence of gainful employment, their income is very low. Lower income of the household, leads to economic crisis, which escalates poverty (Bardhan, P.K. 1974; Gaurav Datta, 1996; Gupta, S.P. 1995; John W. Mellar and Gunvant M. Desai, 1986; Kakwani, N. and Subba Rao, K; 1992; Minhas, B.S.; 1974; Montek, S. Ahluwalia, 1978).

The concept of poverty has been developed mainly as a concept of nutritional deficiency and lack of minimum subsistence. Many empirical studies have revealed that, among different occupational groups, the magnitude of poverty is comparatively high among agricultural labourers, marginal farmers, rural artisans etc. In a majority of cases, there is a deficit of income over expenditure, which largely reflects the need to borrow by the labour households. These borrowings lead to interlinked transactions (Bardhan, P.K. and Ashok Rudra, 1978; Bhaumik, S. and Abdur Rahim, 1978; Bhaumik Shankar, 1999; Sarap, K. 1991; Swain Mamata, 1999) and result in poverty.

Studies on employment pattern, levels of income and incidence of poverty among agricultural labour households are limited. Further, certain issues like mode of repayment, the loan repayment performance of this class to formal credit agencies and particularly to informal agencies have not received enough attention. Information on these aspects is vital in evolving appropriate procedures for channelling formal credit to agricultural labour households. Therefore, there is a need to examine the role of formal credit agencies in improving the employment prospects and income levels and in mitigating poverty among the agricultural labourers.

The specific objectives are: (a) to estimate the employment and unemployment among the agricultural labourers; (b) to study the levels of income and determinants of income of the labourers and (c) to study the incidence, magnitude and dimensions of poverty among the labourers.

Data Base

To examine the pattern of employment, income levels and incidence of poverty of agricultural labourers, 375 agricultural labour households in five mandals of Visakhapatnam district of north coastal Andhra Pradesh were selected for the study. While 250 of those households had access to formal credit agencies (IB), 125 households had no access to formal agencies (NIB). The primary data were collected for the year 1999-2000.

Employment Pattern

The study on employment revealed that the proportion of persons employed according to usual status was slightly higher among IB (498 per 1000 persons) than NIB (465 per 1000 persons). The worker-population ratio was also higher among IB (70 per cent) than NIB (67.50 per cent) (Table 1). The difference may be due to the coverage of IB households under poverty alleviation programmes of the Government.

Table 1: Worker-Population Ratio (Usual Status)

Category	*No. of persons*	*No. of persons employed for a greater part of the year*	*No. of persons employed per 1000 persons*	*Worker-Population Ratio*
IB	1052	524	498	70.00
NIB	510	237	465	67.50

Levels of Income

The average annual household income and the average per capita income are estimated separately. The study on income revealed that nearly 30 per cent of IB are in the income range of above Rs. 30,000/- per year as against only less than 10 per cent in the case of NIB (Table 2). Source-wise, income from wage employment is the major one, accounting for more than 50 per cent of the income for both groups, followed by income from agricultural activities, accounting for nearly one-fourth of an annual income of households (Table 3). Estimation of per capita income of the households indicates that distribution of per capita income of IB is relatively higher (Rs. 5,078/-) than the per capita income of NIB households as a whole (Rs. 4,446/-). This may be due to the advantage of the programmes/assets provided by the Government.

Table 2: Distribution of Households by Annual Income Groups

Category	Income (Rupees)					Total
	Below 10000	10000-20000	20000-30000	30000-40000	40000 & above	
IB	41 (16.40)	80 (32.00)	60 (24.00)	46 (18.40)	23 (9.20)	250 (100.00)
NIB	20 (16.00)	58 (46.40)	36 (28.80)	10 (8.00)	1 (0.80)	125 (100.00)

Table 3: Distribution of Average Annual Household Income by Source

Category	Wage income	Agricultural income	Livestock income	Other than wage income	Total
IB	59167 (53.09)	30338 (26.71)	3588 (2.16)	20493 (18.04)	113586 (100.00)
NIB	46892 (51.61)	21770 (23.96)	2400 (2.64)	19797 (21.79)	90859 (100.00)

Incidence of Poverty

The incidence, short-fall and severity of poverty among agricultural labour households in the study area are measured by Head Count Ratio, Poverty Gap Ratio and Modified Sen's Index of Poverty.

Head Count Ratio: For the IB as a whole, about 47 per cent of total sample households are found below the poverty line, while this picture accounted for above 50 per cent in the case of NIB as a whole. Based on the above fact, it can be concluded that the incidence of poverty among NIB households is comparatively higher than IB households.

Poverty Gap Ratio: As said earlier, it has an extremely attractive interpretation from policy point of view. It indicates the poverty, as a fraction of total income needed to support everyone in the population at the poverty line. Therefore, the largest the estimate, the larger is the requirement of resources to guarantee the entire population an income equivalent to the poverty line. Moreover, its smaller estimated value denotes lesser resources requirement to do the needful.

The empirical results, when analyzed, helped us in deriving the following inferences. The results of this poverty measure shows that, the poverty gap ratio was found higher in NIB households where head count ratio is also high (07.28). Accordingly the largest effort to bring the population near the poverty line was required in NIB households. The lowest poverty gap ratio, on the other hand, was found in IB (06.49).

Modified Sen's Index of Poverty: Sen's modified poverty measure overcomes the limitation of the earlier measure, viz., poverty gap ratio. The latter measure suffers from the limitation of being insensitive to redistribution of income among poor. The Modified Sen's Index of Poverty overcomes this drawback by the use of a specific rank order weighting scale. Empirical values of modified measure of poverty lie between zero and unity. It assumes zero value when every one's income is above the poverty line and becomes unity when every one has zero income. Thereby we may infer that the lower the vale of this measure the closer is the distribution of the poor to be poverty line and vice versa. The measure of modified Sen's Index of Poverty assumed values close to zero in IB (0.060). This indicates that the distribution of poor in IB households is closer to the poverty line. On the other hand, the highest value of 0.067 of the Sen's index of poverty is observed in NIB households. This indicates that there was sizeable deviation of the poor households from the poverty line (Table 4).

Table 4: Estimates of Three Poverty Measures

Category	*Head Court Ratio*	*Poverty Gap Ratio*	*Modified Sean's Index of Poverty*
IB	47.00	06.49	0.060
NIB	50.00	07.28	0.067

Finally it can be concluded that, in all the three measures of poverty, the highest severity of poverty is observed in NIB households while the lowest intensity of poverty is registered in IB households.

Conclusions and Suggestions

To sum up, it is evident from the study that the IB has an edge over the NIB, regarding employment, income and extent of poverty. Yet, we found that there are many labour households which are forced to go to informal lenders for credit. It is also evident from the study that even those households, having access to formal agencies are also approaching informal agencies for productive credit. Therefore, there is a need, to pump in more credit to these sections of population, by liberalizing the credit limits on one hand and by expanding the network of formal credit structure throughout rural India on the other.

References

Bardan, P.K., (1974), "On the Incidence of Poverty in Rural India in the Sixties", Sankshya Series. C; parts 2 and 4, Vol. 36, pp. 264-80.

Bardhan, P.K., and Ashok Rudra (1978): "Interlinkage of Land, Labour and Credit Relations: An Analysis of Village Survey Data in East India", EPW, Vol. 13, Nos. 6 and 7, February.

Bhaumik Shankar (1999), (Interlinked Credit Transactions in Rural West Bengal", Indian Journal of Agricultural Economics, Vol. 54.

Bhaumik Shankar and Abdur Rahim (1998), "Structure and operation of Rural Credit Markets: Some Results Based on Field Surveys in West Bengal, Paper Presented at the International Conference on Decentralization, Revolution and Participation, Organised by the State Planning Board, Govt. of West Bengal, Dec. 28-30, Calcutta.

Gaurav Datt (1996), "Poverty in India: 1951-52: Trends and Decompositions", Mimeo, World Bank.

Government of India, Ministry of Labour (1991): "Report of the National Commission on Rural Labour", Vol. 1, P. 59.

Gupta, S.P., (1995), "Recent Economic Reform and its Impact on Poor", paper presented at the national conference on poverty and employment, New Delhi, pp. 8-9, March, 27-29.

John W., Mello and Gunvant M. Desai (1986), "Agricultural Change and Rural Poverty", Oxford University Press, Delhi.

Kakwani N. and Subba Rao, K. (1992), "Rural Poverty in India: 1973-86", in Kadekodi, G.K. and Murthy, G.V.S.N. (ed.), Poverty in India: Data base issues (Vikas Publishing House, New Delhi, pp. 273-345).

Minhas, B.S., (1974), "Rural Poverty and Land Distribution and Development," Sankhya series C; Vol. 36, pp. 255-63.

Montek, S. Ahluwalia (1978), "Rural Poverty and Agricultural Performance in India," Journal of Development Studies, Vol. 14, No. 3, pp. 298-324, April.

Sarap, K. (1991), "Interlinked Agrarian Markets in Rural India", Sage Publications, New Delhi.

Swain Mamata (1999), "Agricultural Tenancy and Interlinked Transactions: Neo Classical and Marxist Approaches I & II", EPW, Vol. 34, Nos. 37&38, Sep.

34

The Current Scenario of Human Poverty in India

Dr. (Mrs.) P. Usha Devi

Prologue

The number crunching is still on, but the first set of results is out. At last count, India had more people, a higher literacy rate and a better sex ratio than in 1991. The total population of India as at 0.00 on 1st March 2001 stood at 1,027,015,247 persons. These provisional results of census 2001 indicate that India has become the second country in the world after China to cross the one billion mark.

India's share in world population has gone up to 16.7 per cent even while the country registered a fall in its decadal growth rate by 2.52 per cent and an improvement in its sex ratio and literacy rate. The sex—ratio (i.e., number of females per thousand males) of population was 933, rising from 927 as at the 1991 census. Total literacy rate was returned as 65.38 per cent.

The Concept of Human Poverty

Although it is observed from the statistical evidences that income poverty is declining in India, human poverty still remains a challenge to the millions of people living in remote rural and tribal areas. The latest poverty survey in 2001 by the National Sample Survey Organization (NSSO) indicates that the poverty has come down from 36.19 per cent in 1991-92 to 26.10 per cent in 1999-2000. While these figures tend to give a rosy picture about the 'growth', the ground reality points to the increasing inequality between the rich and the poor, urban and rural areas, and the creamy layer of the middle class and the historically marginalized sections like Dalits and tribal. The serious question of balancing the economic growth and free market ethic in delivering distributive justice and promoting equitable social change is still in deep.

Poverty remains an enormous problem world wide, despite major reductions over the past 50 years. Within the developing countries, about one third of the population lives on less than US $ 1 a day. (The World Bank defines poverty as an income of less than US$1 per day, using purchasing power parity-in other words, exchange rates adjusted to the local currency). By this measure, although the percentage of the world's population living in poverty declined slightly between 1987 and 1993 (from 30.1 per cent to 29.4 per cent), the absolute number of people living in poverty increased from 1.2 billion to 1.3 billion people.

Poverty can also be defined more broadly than by income alone. The human poverty index developed recently by the United Nations Development Programme (UNDP), is an aggregate index that measures other forms of deprivation, including low life expectancy, illiteracy, and measures of access to health services, safe water, and adequate nutrition. More than one quarter of the world's population lives in this condition of "human poverty", according to UNDP. Both types of poverty-income and human-usually coincide, but not always.

Perhaps the most glaring economic trend to emerge in the past 30 years is the growing gap between rich and poor. Disparities have widened at the international level, despite a boom in much of the developing world.

The Current Scenario of Social Development of India

One needs to understand the human poverty and social development of India not merely in terms of the macro-economic indicators and like economic growth, poverty alleviation, per capita expenditure, employment opportunities and the social indicators like inequality, gender bias & community bias, urban-rural divide, caste deprivation and the increasing instances of cumulative marginalisation of the poorest sections of the Indian society are helpful in providing guidance in analyzing the current status.

Economic Growth

The GDP has gone down from 6.6 per cent in 1998-99 to 6.4 per cent in 1999-2000 and to 6 per cent in 2000-2001. The agricultural productions index has further declined from –0.7 per cent in 1999-2000 to –3.5 per cent in 2000-2001 and the industrial production index has sunk from 6.5 per cent to 5.7 per cent. There has been a continuous deterioration of fiscal balances of central and state governments. The combined fiscal deficit reached nearly 10 per cent of the GDP in 1999. The total debt of all states without taking the debt of the central government is around US $ 88.97 billions in 1999-2000. These trends show the path of 'economic growth' promised by liberalization and structural adjustments.

Poverty Alleviation

According to the latest poverty survey (NSSO-1999-2000), the percentage of people below the poverty line is 26.10. The instances of poverty is maximum in the rural areas. The emerging global regime controlled by WTO and Bretenwood institutions has begun to create a deepening economic insecurity and social paranoia among the majority of the rural poor and vulnerable middle class. As agriculture is the course of livelihood for the majority of the rural people, it is important to understand the trend in agriculture sector. The skewed agricultural policies and the lack of comprehensive price structuring, import liberalization and the predominance of WTO have contributed for the crisis of agriculture sector in India.

Poverty alleviation remains a pronounced challenge before the government. There is an observable decline in the poverty over the two decades but the total number of poor people remains unchanged due to the population explosion. The rural-urban poverty lines, which almost intercepted in 1987-88, have widened during the reform period, the inter regional disparities in poverty levels are quite alarming. Poverty alleviation programmes still remain ineffective because they are not completely succeeded in their task.

Table 1: Percentage of people below poverty line.

Years	*Rural*	*Urban*	*All India*
1973-74	56.4	49.0	54.9
1977-79	53.1	45.2	51.3
1983	45.7	40.8	44.5
1987-88	39.1	38.2	38.9
1993-94	37.3	32.4	36.0
1999-2000	27.1	23.6	26.1

Soruce: Economic Survey 2000-2001.

Per Capita Expenditure

The per capita expenditure of the country on social sector has decreased substantially. The total expenditure of both the governments on health as a percentage of GDP has considerably decreased from 1.25 per cent to 1.11 per cent from 1993-1994 to 1988 to 1999. Total expenditure on education as a percentage to GDP has decreased from 2.74 to 2.49 over the same period mentioned earlier.

Employment Opportunities

The employment opportunities provided in India are mostly from informal/unorganised sectors. They constitute 91 per cent of the total employment opportunities. The overall growth of the organised employment owes to the private sector. The liberalisation of market and the restructuring of the economy seem to provide benefits to the middle class in providing employment opportunities in the global market. At the same time large sections of urban middle class without adequate technological leverages are kept so casualisations. The following table gives a clear picture of employment opportunities in organised sectors.

Table 2: Percentage of growth of employment in the organised sector

Years	Public sector	Private sector	Total
1991	1.52	1.24	1.44
1992	0.8	2.21	1.21
1993	0.6	0.06	0.44
1994	0.62	0.01	0.73
1995	0.11	1.63	0.55
1996	-0.19	5.62	1.51
1997	0.67	2.04	1.09
1998	-0.09	1.72	0.46
1999	0.00	0.11	0.04

Source: Report Planning Commission

Gender Inequality

The literacy rate among women has gone up to 54.16 per cent in 2001, but the per cent of women in parliament is mere 8.9 per cent in 1999. Though about a million women are getting elected to the local bodies at the village and district levels, a majority of them are prevented from active participation in decision-making. The male-female ratio has also no substantial improvement (from 927 to 933 per 1000 males). This indicates the persistent and systematic patriarchal bias against women. According to 1991 census only 4 per cent of women are employed in organised sector and 94 per cent in informal sector. The majority of women are employed in unorganised sector for low wages resulting in feminisation of work force. Violence against women is increasing year after year and there is still a long way to cross the barriers of gender equity in India.

Health

"Health for all by 2002" is the goal of a global conference in 1978, but unfulfilled. Though poverty is proved to be one of the chief causes of health problems, some other reasons like facilities in the vicinity, lack of skilled doctors, lack of medicines and lack of awareness also play a vital role in health aspects which can not be undermined. Access to basic health care, especially in the rural areas, remains unavailable to a dangerous diseases like leprosy, AIDs, Polio, Measles etc. The rural urban divide is clearly visible in public health services too. 70 per cent of the hospitals are located in urban areas while 70 per cent of the population living in rural areas. Two fifths of the children in India are malnourished, over half of the women are anaemic and almost 265 million live below the poverty line with no medical facilities at all. Good health facility is still a dream for the vast majority Indians living in congested urban slums and extremely backward rural areas.

Literacy and Education

According to the provisional figures of the census-2001, the literacy has gone up to 65.38 per cent, but at the same time 25 per cent of men and 45 per cent of women are illiterates (men literacy per cent is 75.58 and women literacy per cent is 54.16) though there has been a considerable increase in the enrollment ratio of boys and girls in schools, the ratio is still unsatisfactory stressing gender bias. Though there has been better school enrolment, there are significant inequalities based on sex, region, caste, creed etc. in education. Almost 70 per cent of the tribal population is illiterates. Greater attention is needed to cope this problem up. There is no considerable increase on expenditure of central and state governments on education from 1993-94 to 1998-99 i.e., 2.74 per cent to 2.75 per cent of the GDP.

Epilogue

Market driven and technology dominated economy has adverse effects on the poor and rural. The reform processes has facilitated the middle class in all aspects through liberalisation, globalisation and privatisation. We need to stress policies facilitating poor. Free and compulsory elementary education, access to health facilities, ensure human rights to all in spite of sex, case, creed, religion etc., ensure gender equity, employment opportunities, livelihood (food) security etc., pave the way for sustainable social development.

References

National Reports: India 2001 English version Whithering of Welfare state. Liberalised market and development Delusion by John Samuel and Gnana Prakasam.

http://www.censusindia.net/results/provindia3.html

http://www.soicalwatch.org/2001/eng/.national%Oreports/india2001 eng.html

Occasional Paper 30.

35

Socio-Economic Impact of Public Expenditure on Local and Non-Local Farmers in Backward Regions–A Micro Analysis on Vizianagram District

N. Bhaskara Reddy

Soon after independence the regions which are agriculturally backward have given much importance in providing infrastructure facilities like Irrigation, Roads, Education and Health both by the central and state Governments. At the time of Independence, the North coastal districts were not well developed agriculturally for several reasons like lack of Irrigation facilities, less fertile soils, frequent droughts and lack of capital. Vizianagaram district is one in lacking these facilities. Though the state and central Governments have made serious efforts in providing Irrigation, land development, Education, Health and Roads in this district but the benefits from some of these facilities were initially enjoyed by the Migrated Non-local farmers from the neighboring districts. But migration of these farmers had positive impact for the development of agriculture in this district in changing cropping pattern, development of irrigation through private investment and moderate effect in changing living habits of local farmers.

These are the objectives of the study

(a) To examine the impact of Migrated Non-local farmers on Local farmers in developing Agriculture.

(b) To analyse the progress of Health and Education facilities to meet the growing population in the district.

To enquire about the above mentioned objectives the district of Vizianagaram was chosen. In this district the area under the Vengalaraya and Andhra Irrigation projects are sample area for this study. A sample of 75 non-local farmers and 100 local farmers were chosen for the study spread over 5 selected Mandals under these Irrigation projects. The aim of the selection of newly irrigated project areas is that irrigation has multidimentional impact on the people and their economy. The study is based on both primary as well as secondary data from the district.

The primary data collected from the selected local and non-local farmers to know the impact of non-local farmers on local farmers in agricultural development for the reference period of 2000-2001 agricultural year. The secondary data for the two points of time i.e., 1987-88 and 1997-98 mainly based on 1981 and 1991 census used to know the growth of population, levels of literacy, progress in medical and health facilities in the district. Thus, it is aimed to know the benefits of public expenditure on irrigation through primary data from the sample of local and non-local farmers. And to know the levels of literacy, progress of medical and health facilities and village road communications, a two-point of time series data from secondary sources was used.

Population

The increase in population during the decennium ending 1981 census over 1971 was 13.50 per cent for the district. The increase in population during the decennium ending 1991 census over 1981 was 17 per cent in the district which is less than the rate of growth of A.P. State population. But there is an increase of population between 1981 and 1991 compared to 1971 to 1981. But the growth of population between 1991 and 2001 is 0.6 which is less than decennial growth between 1981 and 1991. But the infant mortality rate between 1991 and 2001 is 99 for the district. In the selected mandals the decennial growth of population between 1981 and 1991 ranges between 8.32 per cent and 17.11 per cent.

Literacy

In the district as per 1981 census literacy rate is only 21.74 per cent and as per 1991 census the literacy rate is 34.28 per cent this is increased to 51.82 per cent in 2001. In selected mandals the literacy rate has been increased when compared to 1981 census. Female literates also increased between 1981 and 1991. In the district the female literacy rate between 1971 and 1981 was 12.5 per cent and this was increased to 40.73 per cent between 1991 and 2001. (Table 1)

Table 1: Levels of Literacy between 1981 and 1991

S. No.	*Mandal*	*1981*			*1991*		
		Male	*Female*	*Total*	*Male*	*Female*	*Total*
1.	Makkuva	31.6	9.9	20.7	41.7	17.2	29.5
2.	Saluru	33.7	16.7	25.1	45.5	27.1	36.2
3.	Seethanagaram	28.6	8.0	18.2	49.9	20.6	35.2
4.	Mentada	19.0	5.1	12.0	29.9	10.9	20.4
5.	G. Nagaram	26.3	9.9	18.0	37.2	16.4	26.7
6.	District	31.0	12.5	21.7	46.0	22.5	34.2

Source: Hand Book of Statistics Vizianagaram District 1987-88 and 97-98.

Medical and Health Facilities

The details about the medical and health facilities are presented in Table 2. The data reveal that there is a marginal progress in providing medical and health facilities (allopathic) in the district. In the district during 1987-88 there are about 3743 people per bed and 19399 people per doctor. In the year 1997-98 the per bed, 3164 people and per doctor, 17445 people are in the district. In the selected mandals in the year 1987-88 the strength of population per doctor was more than twenty

Table 2: Progress in Medical and Health Facilities (Allopathic) in Vizianagaram District between 1987-88—1997-98

Mandal	*1987-88*					*1997-98*				
	No. of Hospitals	*No. of Doctors*	*No. of Beds*	*Strength of Population Per Doctor*	*Strength of Population Per Bed*	*No. of Hospitals*	*No. of Doctors*	*No. of beds*	*Strength of Per Doctor*	*Strength of Per Bed*
Makkuva	2	1	6	38707	6451	2	3	12	14393	3593
Saluru	2	3	22	24868	3391	4	7	36	12867	2502
Seetanagaram	2	1	12	51513	4292	2	2	12	28280	4713
Mentada	2	1	12	44999	3749	2	3	12	16380	4095
Gajapatinagaram	1	1	6	44504	7417	1	5	30	10324	1720
District	69	93	482	19399	3743	74	121	667	17445	3164

Source: Hand Book of Statistics 1987-88 and 1997-98.

24,000 and per bed it was more than 3,500 people. In the year 1997-98 though the doctors and beds increased, but per doctor and per bed people ratio has not substantially changed.

Village Road Communications

The village road communications in the district was presented in the Table 3. The length of rural and other district roads increased from 1927.19 K.M to 2651 K.M. between 1987-88 and 1997-98 an increase of 37.56 per cent. The length of other roads under Z.P. control as substantially increased recording 63.83 per cent in the district. But out of total length of these roads, about 57.71 per cent was non-metalled roads which are not useful in all conditions. This percentage was more in the case of rural roads. In the year 1997-98 the proportion of non metalled roads is 48.83 per cent and in the case of rural roads this was 58.15 per cent.

Cropping Pattern of Local Farmers

A detailed enquiry was made about the cropping pattern observed by local farmers and it is presented in Table 4. The cropping pattern of local farmers was analysed under two situations. The situation–I refers to before migration of non-local farmers and the Irrigation development in this region. The situation–II is after migration of non-local farmers and irrigation development under private and public investments. The above table shows that there is a substantial change in cropping pattern between situation I and situation–II. Before irrigation development by constructing Vengala Raya and Andra Projects and also due to the adoption of bore well technology through private investment in this region. The local farmers have much depended upon traditional sources of tanks and dug wells, which are not assured irrigation sources and also not sufficient for adequate irrigation. However, the local farmers allocated more land for light irrigated food crops like millets, pulses and rainfed paddy. More than 50 per cent of gross cropped area (GCA) was allocated for food crops in both the situations. But in the later situation more land is allocated for paddy than millets. About 36.62 per cent of GCA

Table 3: Progress of Road Communication in Vizianagaram District between 1987-88 and 1997-98

	Category/Road Length	*1987-88*		*1997-98*		*Progress (%)*
		Total Length in Km	*Non Metalled Roads in KM*	*Total Length in KM*	*Non Metalled Roads in KM*	
1.	Other Roads Under Z.P.	538.84	68.00 (12.62)	882.50	245.10 (27.77)	63.83
2.	Rural Roads	1388.35	1044.30 (75.22)	1768.55	1024.40 (58.15)	32.14
3.	**Total**	**1927.19**	**1112.30 (57.71)**	**2651.05**	**1273.50 (48.03)**	**37.56**

Source: Hand Book of Statistics 1987-88 and 1997-98

Figures in backets percentage to total length.

Table 4: Change in Cropping Pattern of Selected Local Farmers Before and After Migration of Non Local Farmers (Figures in Percentage)

S. No.	*Crop*	*Before Non Locals Migration and Irrigation Development*	*After Migration and Irrigation Development*
1.	Paddy	21.00	36.62
2.	Millets	19.00	12.68
3.	Pulses	16.00	4.37
4.	Vegetables	-	8.87
5.	Chillies	3.00	4.22
6.	Banana	2.00	17.60
7.	Sugarcane	0.25	1.40
8.	Mesta	28.0	1.54
9.	Tobacco	0.75	0.56
10.	Fruit Crops	-	2.82
11.	Oil Seeds	10.00	5.07
12.	Cotton	-	4.22
		100.00 (598 acres)	**100.00 (710 acres)**

allotted for paddy cultivation. Among the non food crops the area under Mesta is 28 per cent under situation–I. The area under Banana, fruit crops and tobacco together is 3 per cent under the situation–I. In the situation–II the area under Banana and sugar cane has increased. The crops like vegetables, fruit crops and cotton are cultivated under situation–II which are not represented in the situation–I. The area under oil seeds, pulses, tobacco and mesta substantially decreased in the situation–II which are less remunerative when compared to other crops grown in these mandals.

Cropping Pattern of local and non-local farmers: Most of the land purchased by the non-local farmers was dry land which has no assured irrigation facilities. A small extent of wet land with surface irrigation facilities is purchased from local farmers. The non-local farmers have good knowledge about modern agricultural practices in cultivating wet and dry lands by adopting suitable and remunerative cropping pattern at their native district. After migration the non-local farmers have developed ground water irrigation with assured and quality of irrigation to cultivate highly remunerative cropping pattern. By observing the non-local farmers cultivating practices in growing more remunerative crops the local farmers have also attempted to grow those crops. The details about the present cropping pattern observed by both local and non-local farmers is presented in Table 5. It is observed from the table that both local and non-local farmers followed the more diversified cropping pattern. But there is large difference in area cultivated under each crop by local and non-local farmers. Out of the GCA an extent of 36.62 per cent was under paddy by local farmers and in the case of non-locals it was only 21.06 to respective farmers' GCA. Non-local farmers did not grow the millets but local farmers allotted 12.68 per cent of GCA. The non-local farmers have concentrated in raising crops like banana, sugarcane, fruit crops (mango, guava, orange etc.) palm oil and cotton by allotting an extent

Table 5: Cropping Pattern of Selected Local and Non Local

(Areas in Acres)

Crop	*Non-Locals*			*Locals*		
	Kharif	*Rabi*	*Total*	*Kharif*	*Rabi*	*Total*
Paddy	268	200	468(21.06)	200	60	260(36.62)
Millets	—	—	—	70	20	90(12.68)
Pulses	50	20	70 (3.15)	15	16	31 (4.37)
Vegetables	150	150	300 (31.51)	63	—	63 (8.87)
Chillies	—	—	—	30	—	30 (4.22)
Banana	580	—	580 (26.11)	125	—	125 (17.60)
Sugar cane	101	—	101 (4.54)	10	—	10 (1.40)
Mesta	—	—	—	11	—	11 (1.54)
Tobacco	—	—	—	4	—	4 (0.56)
Fruit Crops	290	—	290 (13.05)	20	—	20 (2.82)
Oil Seeds	70	40	110 (4.95)	26	10	36 (5.07)
Palm Oil	210	—	210 (9.45)	—	—	—
Cotton	93	—	93 (4.18)	30	—	30 (4.22)
Total	**1812**	**410**	**2222 (100.00)**	**604**	**106**	**710 (100.00)**

Figures in brackets percentage to total area.

of 57.33 per cent of the total GCA. On the other side, the local farmers have allotted only 26.04 per cent to grow these crops. The crops like mesta, and tobacco are cultivated by local farmers. But non-locals do not show any interest in growing these crops. The local farmers are accustomed to grow these crops which require less moisture and survive under any erratic and irregular monsoon conditions and semi-drought situations. Thus, the fore going analysis has clearly revealed that local farmers are slowly shifting to highly remunerative cropping pattern and at the same time they are following their traditional cropping pattern by growing millets, pulses, mesta, tobacco etc. The non-local farmers are following highly remunerative cropping pattern which yields them more remuneration. They are getting Government subsidy, loans and other benefits if they desire to get them. Thus, the non-locals have more scope to get every benefit from both the state or central Government policies.

Intensify of Cropping and Irrigation: The intensity of cropping and irrigation is presented in Table 6. The intensity of cropping and irrigation is more in the case of non-local farmers than for local farmers. The intensity of cropping for non-local farmers was 122.62 per cent and it was 117.54 for local farmers. Non-local farmers's cropping intensity on season acre basis was 171.80 per cent and for local farmers it was 139.90 per cent. The intensity of irrigation for the non-local farmers was 190.81 per cent and for local farmers it was 148.00 per cent. Thus, the above analysis reveals that there is a substantial gap between local and non-local farmers in intensity of cropping and irrigation.

Crop Return

Table 6: Intensity of Cropping and Irrigation of Non-Local and Local Farmers

	Farmers Category	*Intensity of Cropping*	*Intensity of Cropping (season Acre)*	*Intensity of Irrigation*
1.	Non Locals	122.62	171.80	190.81
2.	Locals	117.54	139.90	148.00

In the study area most of the local farmers have been cultivating their land by participation of their family labour and also their bullock labour. But the non-local farmers are cultivating their land with hired labour. The per acre returns for non-local farmers are found to be higher than those for the local farmers. The per acre crop return for non-locals is 84.80 per cent higher than that for the local farmers. In absolute terms the per acre crop return (for all crops) for locals is Rs. 6507 and for non-locals it is Rs. 12,025. After migration of non-local farmers to these regions the local farmers attempted to cultivate some of the crops like paddy (H.Y.V.), sugarcane, cotton, vegetables and oil seeds on commercial lines. The local farmers adopted the cultivation practices of the non-local farmers and to some extent have improved their crop returns. But, there is a lot of difference between local and non-local farmers in crop returns.

The impact of non-local farmers in intensive use of land clearly showed by increasing cropping intensity and irrigation intensity. The per farm agricultural incomes were increased. The local farmers followed the cultivation practices of non-local farmers and succeeded in intensive use of land and increased their agricultural incomes. Moreover, these families slowly are interacting with the life styles of non-local farmers. Previously the local agricultural labour were habituated to migrate to other districts for work opportunities. But, at present the migrating families are very less in number. Thus the study reveals the expenditure on agriculture and education had given positive result. But, expenditure on medical, health and family welfare programs did not give expected results in the district taking the figure of 99 infant mortality in the district.

Index